AF411646

Urban Sustainability in the US

Melissa Keeley • Lisa Benton-Short

Urban Sustainability in the US

Cities Take Action

Melissa Keeley
George Washington University
Washington, DC, USA

Lisa Benton-Short
George Washington University
Washington, DC, USA

ISBN 978-3-319-93295-8   ISBN 978-3-319-93296-5   (eBook)
https://doi.org/10.1007/978-3-319-93296-5

Library of Congress Control Number: 2018948757

This Palgrave Macmillan imprint is published by the registered company Springer Nature Switzerland AG
The registered company address is: Gewerbestrasse 11, 6330 Cham, Switzerland

Acknowledgments

Our experiences consulting with cities and community groups on sustainability-related projects and urban planning have deeply informed this book project and were, in many ways, its impetus. Similarly, our approach to the topic was shaped by over ten years of teaching courses on urban sustainability. This effort brought together those experiences and is a collaboration that we have enjoyed tremendously.

We were encouraged by colleagues in the Department of Geography at the George Washington University. The institution where we have made our intellectual home has supported us in other ways as well: the Columbian College of Arts and Sciences supplied a "nick in time" grant during manuscript preparation and the university's Sustainability Collaborative provided money to hire student research assistants. Finally, funding for this project also came in part from the National Science Foundation's Arctic PIRE (Award #1545913).

We included ideas for the book and initial findings in the courses we each teach on urban sustainability. We challenged our students to help us find best practices among US cities, and integrated these in our classroom discussions and class projects. There are hundreds of students who have offered keen insight, good comments, and astute observations. Many students have actively helped us with research, and we are very thankful for all their efforts. Thank you to Samantha Buchalter, Catherine Choate, Jason Davidson, Sujung Lee, Sophia Lin, Hannah Moskowitz, Shannon Patty-Stoddard, Jennifer Rowland, Kriselle Sanchez, Virginia Streeter, Emily Schamberger, Kelsey Taylor, Julia Wagner, Sophie Wascow, and Jiajing Zhang. Four students helped with citation management and progress updates during manuscript preparation: Wyn Dobbs, Thomas Lane, Megan Rohrer, and Anna Zhu. Also, a big shout out to Sam Guilford for his expert talent in making many of the graphs and tables for this book.

Finally, we thank our families for their support and patience throughout this project, particularly: John, Chris, Bram, and Madeleine. And we of course appreciate our muses: Pepper, Columbus, and MacKinders.

Melissa Keeley and Lisa Benton-Short

CONTENTS

LIST OF FIGURES

LIST OF TABLES

LIST OF BOXES

CHAPTER 1

Conceptualizing, Planning, and Implementing Sustainability in US Cities

INTRODUCTION

In recent years and for a variety of reasons, cities have taken the lead in sustainability efforts in the United States.[1] As federal leadership in the creation of environmental policies has faltered, there has been growing support for local initiatives, often referred to as a "new localism" in environmental policies.[2] The city scale can be a beneficial starting point for local activism and community involvement around sustainability.[3] Local policy is important for many reasons, including that cities have tremendous control over significant tools for change such as land use, public education, and economic development.[4]

Cities also already undertake a myriad of planning exercises. It is not uncommon for a city to have 20 or more separate plans, often very detailed and focused on specific key areas such as open space and recreation, land use, climate action, resilience, hazard mitigation, urban forestry, water, historic preservation, or for specific neighborhood projects. Figure 1.1 captures the numerous plans for the city of Arlington, Virginia. Notably, these plans are generally undertaken and managed by just one or two city agencies.

However, we argue that sustainability plans serve a different purpose and are unique in several key ways. Municipal sustainability plans are comprehensive visions, goals, and priorities for sustainability set forth by a government or other civic organizations. They typically are created with community input and the involvement of multiple departments. Such

© The Author(s) 2019

M. Keeley, L. Benton-Short, *Urban Sustainability in the US*,
https://doi.org/10.1007/978-3-319-93296-5_1

Fig. 1.1 Many cities create separate plans for topics such as health, transportation, water, and waste. These plans are often siloed in specific departments, and as such are different from comprehensive sustainability plans which attempt to integrate across departments and agencies. (Source: Adapted from the City of Alexandria, Virginia, "Environmental Action Plan" (Alexandria, Virginia, 2009), at https://www.alexandriava.gov/uploadedFiles/tes/eco-city/EAP_FINAL_06_18_09.pdf)

plans cover a diverse range of issues: climate, energy, transportation, green jobs, housing, human health, recreation and parks, and so on. These plans often inventory current problems and standings, identify solutions and priorities, and set indicators for measuring progress.[5] Sustainability plans are more holistic than most other planning documents and consider multiple goals relating to improving environmental, economic, and social equity conditions simultaneously. For this reason, sustainability plans often serve as an "umbrella" or connector between initiatives, and they both prioritize and highlight ways in which projects and programs can provide multiple benefits to the city.

Urban sustainability planning is a growing and important trend. The United Nations' newly launched 2030 Sustainable Development Goals call for a substantial increase in the number of cities and human settlements adopting and implementing integrated policies and plans towards inclusion, resource efficiency, mitigation and adaptation to climate change, and resilience to disasters. We know that many cities will undertake sustainability planning in the next five to ten years. In addition, many US cities that created plans in the early 2000s will certainly update their plans over the next decade.

European cities have led in sustainability planning, having embraced the United Nations' Local Agenda 21 in the 1990s (which called for local government-led sustainability efforts to affect global change) with European Union support of these efforts. Paris, Freiburg, Helsinki, Oslo, and London are pioneers in the area of sustainability planning and have spearheaded many urban innovations such as bikeable cities, car sharing, and climate action plans. Malmo and Copenhagen often rank among the top of many "green cities" lists; however, sustainability planning has not been limited to Europe. Many cities including Singapore, Seoul, Bangkok, Rio, and Mexico City have all recently developed sustainability plans.[6]

Despite increasing environmental concerns and growing citizen support, the United States has lagged behind many European countries, and even some developing countries, in crafting progressive sustainability policies.[7] US cities began to rapidly develop sustainability plans in the mid 2000s. However, a 2015 survey of 2000 local governments in the United States (of all sizes, and including small towns and rural planning divisions) indicated that, while about 47 percent see environmental protection as a priority, only 31 percent report adoption of a sustainability plan.[8] While large cities like New York City and Chicago have led the way in plan creation, medium-sized cities like Cincinnati, Chattanooga, Portland, and Salt Lake City and small cities like Topeka and Burlington have thoughtfully and innovatively engaged in sustainability planning as well.

There is a great diversity in the sustainability plans of US cities. This novelty clearly challenges assessment and benchmarking and the efforts of cities to learn from the experiences of others. Yet we argue that there is also great potential here. We choose to see this variation as part of a normal learning curve for a new undertaking and a reflection of the diversity that exists among US cities. We see this variety as a rich learning opportunity, given the diversity of plans that already exist. Below are some of the reasons that we currently see such great variety in sustainability plans in US cities, and why there is such a need for more study in this area.

First, there is no national standard for sustainability plans in the United States. Some countries have national mandates requiring sustainability planning; in the United States, this is largely a bottom-up process (although some states, like California, set state-level requirements for some elements of sustainability, like green building codes or creating state-wide goals for recycling, and therefore help raise the bar for cities).

Second, although there are a number of other actors stepping in to assist cities in planning sustainability efforts, there is no "one" lead agency, no single website or publication where plans or best practices are shared, nor where emerging trends are discussed. Recently, a profusion of organizations has begun to address what Devashree Saha described as insufficient coordination of sustainability management among local governments.[9] For example, Local Governments for Sustainability (ICLEI) is an international network of some 1500 cities and regions which provides capacity building and collective learning for sustainability.[10] A number of non-profit organizations, including ICLEI, the U.S. Green Building Council, the Center for American Progress, and the National League of Cities, sought to address the void in sustainability planning by developing the STAR Community Rating System (STAR), released in 2012.[11] This rating system is a framework and certification program for local sustainability and, additionally, the organization provides education and training programs around best practices. In 2005, the C40 Cities Climate Leadership Group was formed. The network provides access to tools, resources, and shares data-driven information that enables cities to take action to address climate change and to band together to use their collective power to access resources. In 2013, the Rockefeller Foundation began a global effort to increase urban resilience through its global "100 Resilient Cities Network" which provides funding for cities to hire a Chief Resilience Officer and offers technical support, access to planning services, and networking with other member cities.[12] Other actors include the United States Conference of Mayors, the Urban Sustainability Directors Network, and a variety of organizations focusing on climate change mitigation. It will be interesting to see how the prominence and effective reach of these organizations and initiatives evolves. Box 1.1 highlights the numerous sustainability networks available for cities, and we encourage more cities to investigate how these networks can support their sustainability planning efforts.

Third, the kind of holistic, interdepartmental, and interdisciplinary planning which is central to sustainability planning is a novel, conceptual, and logistical challenge for many cities, particularly smaller ones. Municipal sustainability plans are a relatively new phenomenon—especially in the United States where sustainability planning first began in the early 2000s.[13] Many cities begin the process of sustainability planning with shorter, more

Box 1.1 Sustainability Networks and Measurement

As cities plan for sustainability, companies and organizations have created a wide variety of networks and benchmarking systems that collect data, measure and rank sustainability; help cities develop and apply practical strategies, tools and methodologies; or provide a venue to share best practices and lessons learned around sustainability. Below, we highlight some of these:

Organization	Ranking tool name	Other information
Arcadis	Sustainable Cities Index	This global design and consultancy firm ranks 100 global cities on 3 dimensions of sustainability: people, planet, and profit
C40 Cities on Climate	n/a	Facilitates networking and provides technical support
The Carbon Disclosure Project	The Carbon Disclosure Project	This non-profit organization operates a global disclosure system for companies, cities, and regions to report and track greenhouse gas (GHG) emissions
The Economist Intelligence Unit and Siemens	The US and Canada Green City Index	Assesses the environmental performance of 27 major US and Canadian cities
European Foundation for the Living and Working Conditions	Urban Sustainability Indicators	Their indicators document describes a broad range of sustainability indicator measures; developed to aid indexing of urban sustainability performance
Global Cities Institute at the University of Toronto	Global Cities Indicators Facility	Free online platform with standardized indicators that allows for global comparison of city performance and knowledge sharing
ICLEI—Local Governments for Sustainability	n/a	Global network of over 1500 cities, towns, and regions providing networking and technical assistance

(*continued*)

Box 1.1   (continued)

Organization	Ranking tool name	Other information
The National League of Cities	n/a	A forum for mayors and city officials to share best practices
The Rockefeller Foundation	n/a	"100 Resilient Cities Network" supports planning and action to increase resilience from shocks and challenges for cities within global network
STAR Communities	STAR (Sustainability Tools for Assessing and Rating) Community Rating System	Transparent and data-driven tool for cities to measure performance and track progress in social, economic, and environmental areas
SustainLane	SustainLane US City Rankings	Benchmarks the largest US cities performance in 16 areas of urban sustainability
University of Pennsylvania, commissioned by the Office of Policy Development and Research, US Department of Housing and Urban Development	n/a	Assessed hundreds of available indicators to develop recommended "urban sustainable development indicators"
The United States Conference of Mayors	n/a	Official, non-partisan organization of cities with populations of over 30,000; a forum for mayors to share ideas and information
The U.S. Green Building Council	LEED for Cities and Communities	Features an online platform that helps cities set goals, implement strategies, track progress, and share performance data; recognizes city achievements with certification
The Urban Sustainability Directors Network	n/a	Peer-to-peer network of civil servants from cities across the United States and Canada sharing best practices

conceptual "visioning" documents, and then, several years later, follow up with more action-oriented plans that include concrete goals, propose specific programs to reach these, and establish a timeline for completion. This is a common trend: later plan iterations are, often, more holistic than earlier efforts, more likely to embrace what seem to be more challenging issues of equity, or more thoughtfully integrate the work of different municipal departments. Nearly 60 percent of local governments report that a lack of staff capacity hinders their sustainability efforts, while 50 percent indicate that a lack of information on how to proceed with sustainability is a problem.[14] Clearly, under conditions of resource constraint, most cities are likely to utilize an incremental approach to sustainability, gradually incorporating this agenda into municipal operations and policies.

Fourth, as priorities can be so varied across different cities and geographies, sustainability plans may differ in the way they are created and organized, the topic areas they contain or omit, and the regional and local problems they prioritize. The different sizes and geographies of US cities make for an interesting study that covers a wide range of both human and environmental conditions. In Phoenix, for example, a major issue is how to prepare for increased droughts and heat waves, while Philadelphia is focused on improving stormwater systems to meet federal regulations and deal with increased flooding as climate shifts. Detroit seeks to re-envision itself as a location for innovation and design in an effort to stabilize population, land use, and economy following losses from deindustrialization. Another unique perspective is offered by the joint Honolulu/State of Hawaii sustainability plan, which prioritizes efforts to "preserve and perpetuate the 'Kanaka Maoli' and island cultural values."[15] Their distance from the mainland also means they are more interested in how to increase production and consumption of local foods and energy. The diversity of cities and their geographies complicates and enriches a broader analysis of the state of sustainability in US cities.

For all of these reasons, a systematic analysis of sustainability plans in US cities is needed and can contribute to our growing understanding of urban sustainability practices. Most of the literature related to urban sustainability planning has been either theoretical in nature, considered one area of sustainability (like climate change), examined just one city's plan, or focused on non-US cities.[16] Deficits are particularly prominent when considering US sustainability planning, as sustainability planning in the United States has lagged behind Europe.

The purpose of this book is to examine how US cities are planning for sustainability and to highlight, when possible, best practices in sustainability planning and action. We hope this book will contribute to an understanding of how sustainability has been both conceptualized and operationalized by US cities.

DEFINING SUSTAINABILITY

The idea of sustainability coalesces around the three issues of environmental protection, economic development, and the advancement of social equity. Importantly, sustainability is not focused only on the environment: at its root it is concerned with the quality of human life over the long term. The concept emerges from a long and rich intellectual evolution of ideas that redefined nature-society relationships.

In 1987 the United Nations World Commission on Environment and Development issued a report called *Our Common Future*. The report was the product of a commission of foreign ministers, finance and planning officials, economists, and policymakers in agriculture, science, and technology. The report is often referred to as the *Brundtland Report*, after Gro Harlem Brundtland, Chair of the Commission. The report defined sustainable development as "development that meets the needs of the present without compromising the ability of future generations to meet their own needs."[17] As the concept has evolved, sustainability has come to consist of three pillars: economic development, social development, and environmental protection. These are often referred to as the "three Es"— economy, equity, and environment/ecology (Fig. 1.2). Sustainability is now the guiding agenda for the protection of both the local and global commons—the biosphere and the atmosphere. Although the Brundtland definition has become the most widely accepted definition of sustainability, ideas about what is sustainability and how to achieve it differ.

The focus on cities and the recognition of their integral role in sustainability has been slowly growing. The 1992 United Nations Rio Earth Summit was a key turning point. There, the importance of local planning and efforts to increase the sustainability of development was highlighted. Cities and other local governments were each called upon to create a "Local Agenda 21" strategy for sustainability through a community participatory process which would prioritize action. These plans included vision statements, in which main sustainability issues were identified, an action plan that included goals and actions, timelines to achieve those goals, and a discussion of how success would be measured.[18] Certainly, this initiative was the progenitor of modern sustainability plans.

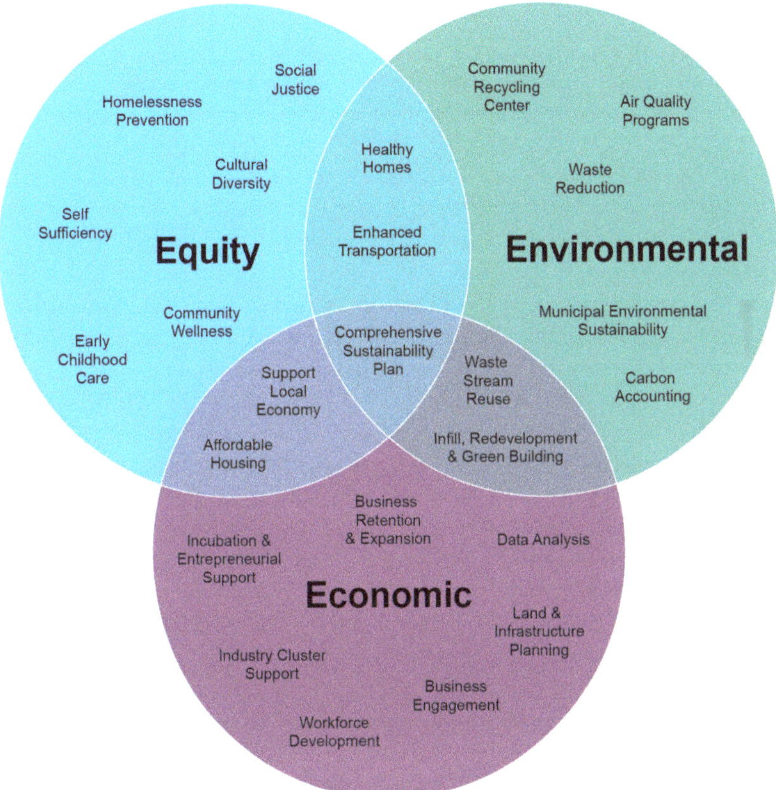

Fig. 1.2 The three Es of sustainability are equity, environment, and economics. This figure highlights that a comprehensive sustainability plan will incorporate a wide range of topics associated with each of the three Es. Some efforts, represented in the overlapping regions, promote multiple sustainability goals. (Source: By authors.)

In 2015, after three years of negotiations and debate, 193 countries agreed to adopt the United Nations' Sustainable Development Goals. These 17 Sustainable Development Goals confront the causes of poverty and environmental degradation in an integrated fashion and tackle a range of issues including ending hunger, improving health, combating climate change, and protecting ocean and forest resources. Sustainable cities and communities are among these interconnected goal areas.

Urban Sustainability

The cities of the twenty-first century are where human destiny will be played out, and where the future of the biosphere will be determined. There will be no sustainable world without sustainable cities. — Herbert Girardet[19]

In the United States, a majority of the population has been urban throughout most of the twentieth century. Today, about 85 percent of the US population lives in urban areas. North American cities vary in size, form, and fortune. The New York metropolitan region has 22 million people, Los Angeles has 18 million, and Chicago has 10 million. Atlanta, Houston, Miami, Philadelphia, and Washington, D.C. have 5 million or more, while Baltimore, Denver, and Portland have about 2 million people each. There are some 40 cities that have at least 1 million people, and many that have 500,000 or more. It is an undeniable fact that the United States is an urban nation—and this means that what cities are doing to plan for sustainability will be absolutely critical in the coming decades. Can cities change the ways in which they negatively impact the environment? Can cities effectively deal with growth and urban sprawl? Can cities achieve sustainability that ensures economic prosperity and social justice? These are among the most dramatic, and for the time being, unanswered questions facing us in the twenty-first century.

Moving towards urban sustainability is critical because cities have tremendous impacts on the environment. The city can be modeled as an ecosystem with inputs of energy and water and outputs of noise, sewerage, garbage, and air pollutants.[20] The notion of the ecological footprint of the city is one way to think about these relationships.[21] It is defined as the amount of land required to meet the resource needs of a city and absorb its waste. US cities, which outpace most of the world in energy usage and waste production, have a much larger footprint than cities of the developing world. At the same time, many dense urban areas in the United States have lower ecological footprints per capita than surrounding suburban areas because of urbanites' reliance on public transportation (resulting in fewer vehicle miles traveled per person) and other factors.

Cities also modify the environment. The most obvious example of this is the urban heat island. Cities tend to be warmer than surrounding areas because of the amount of extra heat produced in the city, the lower amounts of evapotranspiration, and the heat absorption of man-made materials such as tarmac, asphalt, and concrete. Heat is absorbed by these surfaces during the day and released at night. Human activity in the city also produces pollutants. Industrial processes and auto engines emit substances that include carbon oxides, sulfur oxides, hydrocarbons, dust, soot, and lead.

However, moving towards sustainability is not simply "greening" the city. A genuinely sustainable city is a place where the environment is protected, where the economy is sufficient to provide its residents with basic needs such as food and shelter, and where the residents who live there have opportunities to live good lives. A sustainable city is also a just city.

Box 1.2   Concepts and Terms: Resilience and Sustainability

Community resilience, like sustainability, is another term with multiple definitions. It generally deals with a community's capacity to respond to, withstand, and recover from adverse situations. Resilience efforts are varied but include increasing local capacity to cope effectively with and learn from adversity. Planning for resilience is another growing trend within city planning, as cities are seeking to prepare for a variety of threats ranging from terrorism to climate-driven disasters like flooding and hurricanes. In 2013, The Rockefeller Foundation ramped up their "100 Resilient Cities" initiative to help more cities build resilience. Cities across the globe applied to join the network. Benefits of participation include technical assistance, networking opportunities, and funds to establish a Chief Resilience Officer in each city to lead resilience efforts.

The less politicized nature of the term resilience (in contrast with "climate change" and "sustainability") and its direct connection to hazard management—a traditional role of cities—are some of the reasons that the term resilience is gaining popularity. Many cities in traditional "red" states find that residents are more willing to accept the need for resilience planning. Another reason, perhaps, is the reticence of many scientists to fully embrace the term "sustainability" or their role in it. Historical understandings of ecology envisioned a climatically determined, predicable assortment of plants and animals (a climax community) that would be "sustained" in a steady state or

(*continued*)

> **Box 1.2   (continued)**
>
> equilibrium over time. Ecologists have rejected this theory, and now understand that much more variation in the process of succession exists, as individual species respond to environmental change and opportunities in unique ways. Today, few ecologists would expect that a specific city, or our current way of living could "sustain or remain the same over time." And while we agree that this vision or version of sustainability is disconnected from reality, a reluctance to use the term sustainability is mostly about semantics.
>
> This book views sustainability quite differently from resilience. Considerations of resilience—planning for and learning from adversity—should be a part of sustainability planning. We argue that resilience planning, on the other hand, may or may not holistically balance considerations of environment, economy, and equity, which we see as the essential value of a "sustainability" approach.
>
> Source:
>
> "100 Resilient Cities Network," Rockefeller Foundation, 2018, https://www.rockefellerfoundation.org/our-work/initiatives/100-resilient-cities/

There is good news. One of the biggest developments in the last ten years is the profusion of cities finding meaningful ways to address environmental, economic, and social equity within their cities and developing sustainability plans. Many of these plans are comprehensive in that they address a range and diversity of issues that include the "three Es." Among the most common issues in sustainability plans are:

- Food
- Air quality
- Climate change
- Water quality
- Water supply
- Parks and recreation
- Social justice and equity
- Green economy/green jobs
- Transportation

- Energy use
- Housing
- Garbage and recycling
- Risk and resilience to hazards.

Creating sustainable cities will require changing processes and mind-sets that have dominated the developed world for the past several hundred years. We must overcome siloing which has separated departments, sectors, and disciplines. It will challenge us to overcome a long-standing dichotomy between those who want to save trees for aesthetics and to protect habitat and those who see trees as jobs and resources alone. Instead, a sustainable mind-set acknowledges that saving the environment can generate jobs. While the modern age worked on an economic, profit-based model, the age of sustainability recognizes the limits and external costs of environmental degradation and social inequity, such as waste, pollution, and social injustice.[22] Indeed, in this light, equity enhances the economy as members across society have the education, tools, and support they need to contribute productively. We are optimistic that since cities are the ultimate social creation, they can become important sites of positive transformation and pivotal places of social progress.

ORGANIZATION AND STRUCTURE OF THE BOOK

Throughout the book, we refer to the plans for sustainability that US cities have developed over the last decade or so. Of course, we cannot examine the plans and practices of every US city in depth. Instead, we highlight cities that represent a cross-section of the United States in terms of size and geography. The book is not just a collection of "best practices" but a rigorous examination of trends, omissions, connections, and approaches in sustainability planning. The chapters explore how cities are applying sustainability concepts—warts and all. We highlight trends and deficiencies, where these exist, and analyze best practices.

While our book's analysis and the organization will follow topical themes such as water, climate change adaptation, green space, and environmental justice, underlying themes and trends thread through the entire project. Specifically, this book is concerned with how cities **conceptualize** sustainability, how they **plan** for sustainability, and how they **implement** these plans and take action. Below, we discuss these three overarching themes.

Conceptualizing Sustainability

Municipal sustainability plans are holistic and multi-departmental documents and outline a city's goals, visions, and priorities for a sustainable future. However, we see great variety in the aspects of sustainability that cities prioritize or address first, and great differences in the roles that cities take in furthering the sustainability agenda that they outline.

Sustainability plans are frequently introduced by a letter from the mayor, which often clearly lays out guiding principles and the importance of sustainability planning in their city. These letters can be an important way for mayors to signal their priorities to residents and city departments and agencies alike. While many introductory letters generally discuss "three E" goals, or cite the Brundtland definition of sustainability, these letters often emphasize different priorities, focus on local or regional problems, or discuss specific ways that global issues, like climate change, will have local impacts.

A sustainability plan is meant to provide both short-term and long-term guidance for current and future decision-makers, city employees, city leaders, city residents, and other community groups and entities. They are a starting point for change. And visions, even general ones, can be powerful. Consider the vision statement in Washington, D.C.'s sustainability plan:

> In just one generation – 20 years – the District of Columbia will be the healthiest, greenest, and most livable city in the United States. An international destination for people and investment, the District will be a model of innovative policies and practices that improve quality of life and economic opportunity. We will demonstrate how enhancing our natural and built environments, investing in a diverse clean economy, and reducing disparities among residents can create an educated, equitable, and prosperous society.[23]

Previously we discussed the great variety in topical priorities emphasized in sustainability plans across US cities. Other variation exists as well. While many plans prioritize data collection, the joint plan created by Memphis and Shelby County stood out in its call for action. In 2008 then Mayor A C Wharton Jr., claimed that they would "emphasize action over analysis" in the sustainability plan titled "A Future of Choice, Not Chance." He noted that "because of our strong sense of urgency, the goal of our process was to create immediacy and action-oriented strategies, recognizing that most of us are familiar with the data, and that there is time for ongoing research and continued benchmarking."[24]

A significant way in which sustainability efforts vary from city to city is the "modes of governance" that cities will use to enact change. This is one way that we see cities taking different "roles" in sustainability. For instance, for some cities—particularly those in the earliest stages of their sustainability efforts—the focus is on the actions that the city can take to improve sustainability of their own, internal practices. Other cities are much more focused on encouraging the public to take action. New York City describes the importance of this approach in this way: "changes by individuals and households…have the potential to be quicker and more cost-effective than policy initiatives. While it could take years to implement a new capital project or pass and implement a law, it only takes months to develop and execute a marketing campaign and seconds for a person to decide to switch off a light or choose to bike to work."[25] Palm Springs makes a similar acknowledgment: "The city's role is important in addressing policy, planning and service issues related to climate change, water and energy use, waste generation and other sustainability factors. But ultimately, public involvement and community wide behavior change will be the key to the long-term success of the Palm Springs Path to a Sustainable Community."[26]

Planning for Sustainability

In addition to the plans themselves, we also pay attention to the planning creation process and, particularly, the ways in which the community and other stakeholders were involved in the planning process. A good example is Chattanooga. A former manufacturing town, its transformation began in 1984 when the city created a long-term plan, *Vision 2000* (although it was not a sustainability plan per se). Thousands of residents participated and collectively set goals and established priorities for improving their city. The plan was successful in meeting many of the goals, so in 1993, the city updated that plan to create *Revision 2000*. More than 2600 residents participated, including 30 percent of those under the age of 25 and 23 percent over the age of 55. Twenty-seven goals were identified and 122 recommendations emerged for further improving the community.[27] Today, Chattanooga sees itself as a "living laboratory" for sustainable projects and is implementing its new "take charge" attitude in the areas of education, business development, and community action.[28]

Cities have many decisions to make as they create their plans for sustainability. First, they must decide who the main audience of their plan will be. For some cities, this will be a primarily internal document and, in these cases, it could be appropriate to use more technical language or acronyms. More cities write plans with the general public as their main audience. The best plans of this type provide some background on the importance of action in each topic area using local examples. They feature units of measurement that are meaningful to the average public. They might use boxes to add interesting case studies or use and graphics to simplify and illustrate key points. These "tools" add context and communicate information to multiple audiences simultaneously.

Second, they must decide what type of plan they will create. Although many US cities have developed comprehensive sustainability plans that are a single document, other cities plan for sustainability without a single comprehensive sustainability plan. Some have compiled a set of resources that integrate sustainability in many facets of government. These might be groupings of online resources or a website devoted to sustainability. One advantage of this option is that some cities then hyperlink various programs and supporting city plans, such as an energy plan or a climate plan. For some cities, many individual plans aid in promoting and enacting sustainability in various city departments, while the city's sustainability plan is more of an overarching framework which connects and enables cooperation between departments and agencies. In this book, we examine both types of sustainability plans, although we believe that cities that have a single holistic sustainability plan are in a better position to make coordinated, substantial, and unified changes across departments and best identify opportunities for projects with multiple benefits.

Third, a clear best practice that we see in planning for sustainability is for cities to clearly articulate ambitious goals, and to pair these with specific actions that will be taken to achieve them. The strongest goals are often those that are quantitative and measurable and include benchmarking data so that progress can be easily tracked. Other best practices include listing an agency responsible for each action and providing a timeline for completion of each goal. Los Angeles, for example, strove to set transparent metrics to measure progress in their city. Within each of their 14 topic chapters, the city's sustainability plan—called "pLAn"—defines measurable goals for 2017, 2025, and 2035, as well as specific strategies to reach these.[29]

Another best practice is to designate an office, agency, or group who will be responsible for leading interdepartmental sustainability efforts and collecting and reporting progress towards goals. While this is sometimes an office of sustainability, what is crucial is that this office exist over the long-term and that it is well-funded. This imperative was highlighted by

Tulsa. They noted that a working group's past sustainability efforts had faltered. It had "ceased to function as a group and (it was) not able to follow through with many of its recommendations…because the Team was not established as a permanent entity within the City's organizational structure."[30] Tulsa learned from this experience and noted that, in the future, such groups must be provided "with necessary personnel, resources, authority, and budget" to lead identified sustainability efforts.[31]

Sustainability planning and action is complex and challenging, and every person and every organization has limited bandwidth. For that reason, we suggest that cities can maximize impacts by creating and prioritizing projects and approaches with multiple benefits. For instance, cities should consider ways to incorporate equity into every goal within their plans. Concretely, instead of simply setting a goal to increase the tree canopy citywide to 35 percent, a city could instead increase the tree canopy to 35 percent in each neighborhood, more evenly providing urban forest benefits across the city. Or, they could target tree planting efforts specifically in neighborhoods experiencing the most heat stress or air quality challenges.

Implementing Sustainability

We are also interested in how cities have used their plans for sustainability to take action. Perhaps the first and most important step many cities take in the implementation of sustainability is to create an office of sustainability. These are sometimes located in the mayor's office, which gives them a measure of political power over other departments. However, as we explore below, it can also make them more vulnerable to political change. Some cities opt, instead, to create offices focused on sustainability within existing departments of planning, the environment, or facilities management. While in many cases, such offices have less clout among peer departments, they do have more political cover when mayoral administrations change. Such institutionalization may also protect sustainability initiatives in times of recession, a time when some offices of sustainability see significant staff reductions.

We see efforts to institutionalize sustainability practices throughout all city operations as an important and common best practice. Madison, Wisconsin, for example, prioritizes improved collaboration between city agencies, departments, and committees, and seeks to enhance this by co-locating departments that should be working more closely together, mandating quarterly meetings for department heads on related topic areas, and considering creating positions for communication liaisons between key departments.[32] These steps are important, given the time and continual work needed to coordinate multi-benefit projects and to keep channels of communication open.[33]

Similarly, Spokane, Washington's sustainability plan is particularly process-focused. Primary plan goals include "building stewardship into local government" and "foster(ing) strong connections among people and their communities."[34] They further note that "this Action Plan does not contain all the answers or solutions. It is not a bundle of regulations and mandates," rather, it should be "considered groundwork for the development of internal policy by decision makers."[35]

While we have focused on local-level planning in this book, the environmental, economic, and social equity challenges that cities face do not obey political boundaries. In order to undertake meaningful action, sustainability must be coordinated regionally. Washington, D.C. struggles with this issue and, to address this, participates in a regional non-profit association, the Metropolitan Washington Council of Governments, a membership of 300 elected officials from 24 local governments, the Maryland and Virginia state legislatures, and the US Congress. Together, this group attempts to address regional issues such as transportation, environment, public safety, and national security.[36]

Measuring and reporting progress is another crucial step in sustainability plan implementation. Several cities, citing the importance of measuring progress towards established goals, quipped the old adage: "What gets measured gets done." Many cities publish annual progress reports. We see the creation of online and sometimes real-time dashboards, which transparently display progress as an important best practice. As a result of the socioeconomic profile of different neighborhoods or the disproportionate risk or impacts across a region, many issues addressed and programs implemented are fundamentally spatial. For this reason, we encourage cities to make more frequent use of maps as they report progress.

Finally, planning is an iterative process. Plans are implemented and outcomes are assessed so that this information can be used to reassess strategies, goals, and actions for the future. Figure 1.3 shows planning as a process, not an end result. The pace of innovation in the realm of sustainability is rapid, and cities will do well to reassess and integrate emerging best practices in the process of re-evaluation. For example, private partnerships play an increasingly important role in sustainability planning, but the long-term impacts of these arrangements should be monitored. Another emerging trend is the "smart city" movement, which uses sensors and data to inform the management of systems and services. Cities must embrace

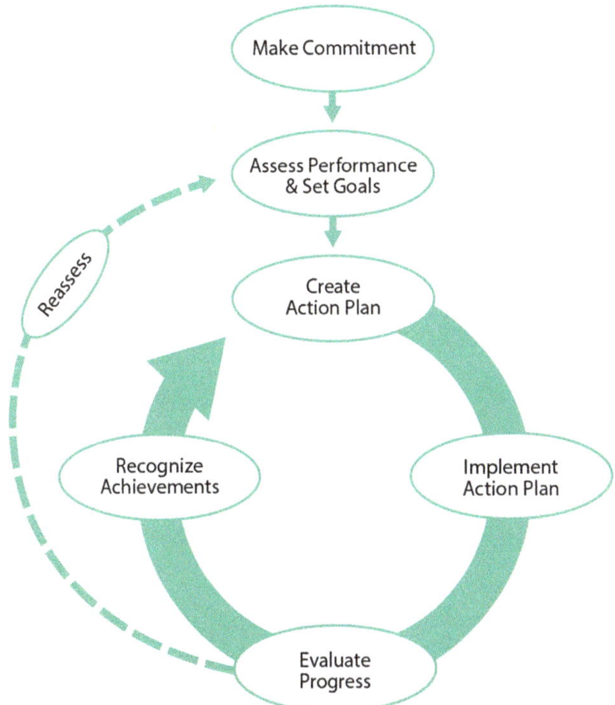

Fig. 1.3 The planning process is one that is continually dynamic. Once a plan is created, a city must implement the plan, evaluate progress, reassess the strategies and results, recognize what it has achieved, and then set new goals. (Source: Adapted from the U.S. EPA "Energy Star Guide to Energy Efficiency Competitions for Buildings & Plants" (September, 2014), accessed April 11, 2018, https://www. energystar.gov/sites/default/files/tools/Building%20Competition%20 Guide_092514.PDF)

the potential of new technology while monitoring and managing associated challenges and risks as they seek to address complex challenges.

Our research has identified a range of best practices in implementing sustainability. We highlight these in each of the subsequent chapters.

Cross-Cutting Strategies

In addition to the three overarching themes explored, a goal of this book is to share strategies that have been sucessful in some cities. This is particularly important given that sustainability planning in the United States is relatively diffuse, uncoordinated, and still in its early stages. We hope that this book helps to better highlight some of the best practices of US cities.

We have identified cross-cutting strategies in eight categories that we highlight with boxed case studies throughout the book. These include:

- **Governance**: how cities organize, coordinate, and integrate within city government and with key community stakeholders
- **Planning Process**: how cities identify solutions, and articulate and set goals
- **Education and Communication**: how effectively cities talk to the community, disseminate information, and motivate behavior change
- **Equity**: to what degree a city incorporates equity within their sustainability plan in a clear and compelling way, and identifies vulnerable communities
- **Implementation and Results**: how effectively cities achieve goals report and report progress
- **Multiple Benefits**: how cities recognize, articulate, and prioritize projects or programs that produce multiple benefits, effectively coordinating across departments
- **Innovation**: unique efforts and using technology in new and novel ways
- **Emerging Trends**: are trends, projects, or programs of increasing importance but which are recent enough that best practices are not yet well established

Finally, each chapter will highlight what is missing from the majority of US sustainability initiatives.

Structure of the Book

We organize this book around eight critical topics in sustainability. We recognize the irony of a book that stresses the importance of holistic planning yet features topical chapters. We therefore implore readers to approach this organization in the same way that St. Louis asks of its sustainability plan readers. That is: subject area categories are used to organize the document but are not "intended to limit or separate information."[37] To that end, we note interconnections between chapters, utilize boxes to highlight cross-cutting themes throughout the book, and feature actions with multiple benefits in every chapter. We begin by focusing on equity and economics;

the remainder of the book then examines critical issues that include climate change, transportation, energy, water, urban greening, and waste.

Chapter 2 explores equity and environmental justice. Despite the fact that sustainability is defined as the "three Es," equity remains the most underemphasized component of sustainability, particularly within sustainability plans themselves. The term "equity" is frequently replaced with more generalized discussions of "community" or "society." These discussions largely lack specificity in populations or areas in need of special attention. This chapter also explores participatory and distributional equity in relation to education, health, food, and housing.

Chapter 3 considers how cities are moving towards a more sustainable economy. We explore how cities are investing in people (i.e. green jobs and training programs) and how they are investing in places (redevelopment of brownfields and waterfronts) as a way to create jobs and stimulate economic growth. We also look at the ways cities are attracting green businesses, and particularly the clean tech and energy sectors.

Chapter 4 examines climate change. We have discovered that in the United States, climate change has motivated many cities to create climate action plans, which have then led to crafting broader and more comprehensive sustainability plans. We consider how cities view the importance of climate change generally. While our discussion of climate change mitigation extends to Chap. 5 (Transportation) and Chap. 6 (Energy), this chapter examines climate change adaptation more specifically. We consider how climate change is a motivator for adaptation initiatives in three areas: (1) the built environment and infrastructure, (2) natural systems, and (3) human systems.

Chapter 5 discusses sustainable transportation. We begin by noting that US cities face a significant challenge in overcoming automobile dependence as they seek to create more sustainable transportation options. We explore the challenges of deteriorating transportation infrastructure in the face of reduced government support and funding. We then examine how cities are beginning to rethink urban design and to support efforts to create more diverse, sustainable transportation, such as car and bikeshares. Transit-oriented development is a major trend in planning that holds the promise to reduce the need for automobiles in cities. We also examine ways that cities link transportation to climate change and economics. Cities are taking action to reduce emissions that contribute to both climate change and localized air pollution through programs designed to increase fuel-efficient transportation.

Chapter 6 covers energy issues in cities. We find that most cities are addressing energy in some capacity, although we found that despite climate change being a prime motivator for sustainability plans, few cities focused their discussion on alternative energy sources as a means of reducing greenhouse gasses. Rather, energy tends to be discussed in terms of the economy—such as providing cleaner jobs and reducing energy costs. We also discovered that many cities have lackluster energy conservation and weatherproofing initiatives. An exception exists surrounding new green building initiatives and regulations.

Chapter 7 examines the ways cities are dealing with water issues, both in terms of water supply and quality. Geography plays a critical role in this regard, as some challenges relate to weather and climate. For example, most cities in the US Southwest are challenged by water supply and drought, but other, less obvious, areas, like Atlanta and southern Florida, face water supply challenges as well. Many Northeastern cities, however, pay more attention to aging infrastructure and issues around stormwater management. We discovered that few cities explore both challenges. This chapter also considers the trend of green infrastructure as an approach for stormwater management.

Chapter 8 examines the role of urban green space in cities and how this connects to climate, water, and energy. We explore the varied characteristics, benefits, and programs associated with three categories of urban green space: (1) parks, green space, and open space, (2) the urban forest, and (3) community gardens and urban agriculture. An overarching trend is that vegetation can contribute multiple benefits in urban areas but has often been dismissed or taken for granted. More attention and work are necessary to include these amenities actively in planning and regulatory practice, as well as provide sufficient and ongoing maintenance.

Chapter 9 discusses waste and recycling efforts. We begin by exploring the scope of the issue around waste and recycling. A few cities are setting ambitious targets, such as zero waste goals. However, we found that waste and recycling is not prioritized within most plans. In particular, insufficient attention is placed on reducing the consumption of goods and developing a market for recycled materials and the products made from these materials.

Finally, Chap. 10 reviews the cross-cutting strategies and provides a set of recommendations for best implementing sustainability in the United States.

About the Research for This Book

We both have taught courses on urban sustainability for more than ten years. Early in our teaching, we focused our readings and class discussions on European cities, which had been at the forefront of sustainability efforts. Literature and case studies on US cities was less available. In 2010, we developed an idea for a class research project that would allow us to shift our focus to growing sustainability efforts in the United States. This project also paralleled our own research for this book project.

To engage students in the research project, we began by assigning each student a specific US city to research and discuss throughout the semester. Initially, we selected 20 US cities as case studies based on three criteria. First, to be included in the study, a city must have had a holistic sustainability plan that was formally approved by city council, included a publication date, and existed in a downloadable format. Second, plans also had to have a primary focus on sustainability. Preference was given to plans that used the term sustainability in their title or description (as opposed to climate action plans). Third, we selected cities that represent a range of diverse population sizes and geographic regions around the United States.

After a few years of research focused on these 20 cities, we realized many other cities had begun planning for sustainability, some of which were doing so without formal plans. We thus expanded our research to include more cities and those using other planning approaches in order to capture the full diversity and range of how US cities are approaching sustainability.

The research for this book is now based on what we have learned from more than 60 US cities. Figure 1.4 is a map of cities that we reference in this book (Appendix A lists all of the cities we examined). We don't claim to have read every plan in every US city—but we have covered a broad range of geographies, city sizes, and approaches to sustainability planning.

Our research utilized mixed methods to determine how sustainability is defined, used, measured, and conceptualized. Content analysis provided us with a systematic and objective means of describing and quantifying specific elements in these plans to determine the importance of certain features or characteristics. We analyzed both quantitative and qualitative data for themes across cities, and for unique and innovative applications. We also examined city sustainability websites and progress reports to compliment information from the initial plans. We spoke with numerous city offices that house sustainability plans to further understand the planning process. Finally, we have attempted to explain these efforts in the context of other sustainability literature.

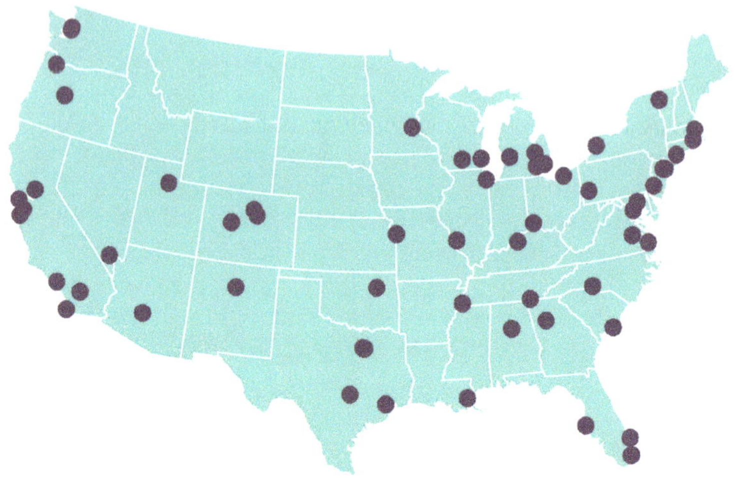

Fig. 1.4 Map of cities researched for this book. (Source: By Authors.)

NOTES

1. Kent Portney, *Taking Sustainable Cities Seriously: Economic Development, the Environment and Quality of Life in American Cities* (Cambridge MA: The MIT Press, 2003); Zhenghong Tang et al., "Moving from Agenda to Action: Evaluating Local Climate Change Action Plans," *Journal of Environmental Planning and Management* 53, no. 1 (2011): 41–62.
2. Paul Parker and Ian Rowlands, "City Partners Maintain Climate Change Action Despite National Cuts: Residential Energy Efficiency Programme Valued at Local Level," *Local Environment* 12, no. 5 (2007): 505–17; Portney, *Taking Sustainable Cities Seriously: Economic Development, the Environment and Quality of Life in American Cities.*
3. Christopher Boone and Ali Moddares, *City and Environment* (Philadelphia: Temple University Press, 2006); Matthew Gandy, *Concrete and Clay: Reworking Nature in New York City* (Cambridge MA: MIT Press, 2002); John Rennie Short, *The Humane City* (Oxford: Blackwell Publishing, 1989); Paul Robbins, *Political Ecology: A Critical Introduction*, 2nd ed. (Chichester, West Sussex: Wiley-Blackwell, 2012).
4. Stephen Wheeler, *Planning for Sustainability: Creating Liveable, Equitable, and Ecological Communities*, 2nd ed. (New York: Routledge Press, 2013).
5. Kelly Evenson et al., "Involvement of Parks and Recreation Professionals in Pedestrian Plans," *Journal of Park and Recreation Administration* 27, no. 3 (2009): 132–42.

6. Lisa Benton-Short and John Rennie Short, *Cities and Nature*, 2nd ed. (New York: Routledge, 2013).
7. Timothy Beatley, "Planning for Sustainability in European Cities: A Review of Practice in Leading Cities," in *The Sustainable Urban Development Reader*, ed. Stephen Wheeler and Timothy Beatley, Second, 2003; Jonas Rabinovitch, *Cities Fit for People: A Success Story of Urban Planning: Curitiba* (New York: United Nations Press, 1997).
8. ICMA, "Local Government Sustainability Practices, 2015," 2016, 1, https://icma.org/sites/default/files/308135_2015%20Sustainability%20 Survey%20Report%20Final.pdf.
9. Devashree Saha, "Empirical Research on Local Government Sustainability Efforts in the USA: Gaps in the Current Literature," *Local Environment* 14, no. 1 (2009): 17–30.
10. ICLEI Global, "Who Is ICLEI," accessed February 13, 2018, http://www.iclei.org/about/who-is-iclei.html.
11. STAR Communities, "Get Started," accessed February 13, 2018, http://www.starcommunities.org/get-started/.
12. 100 Resilient Cities, "Frequently Asked Questions (FAQ) About 100 Resilient Cites," accessed February 13, 2018, http://www.100 resilientcities.org/100rc-faq/.
13. Stephen M. Wheeler, "Planning for Metropolitan Sustainability," *Journal of Planning Education and Research* 20, no. 2 (December 1, 2000): 133–45, https://doi.org/10.1177/0739456X0002000201.
14. ICMA, "Local Government Sustainability Practices, 2015," 8.
15. State of Hawaii, "Hawai'i 2050 Sustainability Plan: Charting a Course for Hawai'i's Sustainable Future," 2008, 2, http://www.oahumpo.org/wp-content/uploads/2013/02/Hawaii2050_Plan_FINAL.pdf.
16. Samuel Brody et al., "A Spatial Analysis of Local Climate Change Policy in the United States: Risk, Stress, and Opportunity," *Landscape and Urban Planning* 87, no. 1 (2008): 33–41; Maria Conroy and Philip Berke, "What Makes a Good Sustainable Development Plan? An Analysis of Factors That Influence Principles of Sustainable Development," *Environment and Planning* 36, no. 8 (2004): 1381–96; ICLEI Global, *Resilient Cities: Cities and Adaptation to Climate Change – Proceedings of the Global Forum 2010*, ed. Konrad Otto-Zimmermann, Local Sustainability (Springer Netherlands, 2011), https://www.springer.com/us/book/9789400707849; Leith Sharp, Geoff Scott, and Daniella Tilbury, "Executive Leadership Programme for Sustainability in Higher Education: The Sustainable Futures Academy Salzburg," 2010; Tang et al., "Moving from Agenda to Action: Evaluating Local Climate Change Action Plans."
17. World Commission on Environment and Development United Nations, "Our Common Future," 1987.

18. United Nations Sustainable Development, "United Nations Conference on Environment & Development: Rio de Janerio Brazil, 3 to 14 June 1992," 1992.

19. Herbert Girardet, *Cities, People, Planet: Livable Cities for a Sustainable World* (Chichester: Wiley, 2004).

20. Ian Douglas, "The City as an Ecosystem," *Progress in Physical Geography*5 (1981): 315–67.

21. Mathis Wackernage et al., "The Ecological Footprint of Cities and Regions: Comparing Resource Availability with Resource Demand," *Environment and Urbanization* 18 (2006): 103–12.

22. Lester Brown, *Eco-Economy: Building an Economy for the Earth* (New York: Norton, 2001).

23. Sustainable DC, "Sustainability DC," 2012, 5, https://sustainable.dc.gov/sites/default/files/dc/sites/sustainable/page_content/attachments/DCS-008%20Report%20508.3j.pdf.

24. Memphis-Shelby County, "Sustainability Shelby Implementation Plan," 2008, 2, https://www.sustainableshelby.com/sites/default/files/Implementation%20Plan/01_SustainableShelbyImplementationPlan.pdf.

25. The City of New York, "Small Steps, Big Strides, Insights from GreeNYC: The City of New York's Behavior Change Program," n.d., 18, http://www1.nyc.gov/assets/sustainability/downloads/pdf/publications/greenyc_lessons_2017_online_final.pdf.

26. City of Palm Springs, "The Palm Springs Path to a Sustainable Community Draft," March 25, 2009, 15, http://www.palmspringsca.gov/home/showdocument?id=5610.

27. Green Policy 360, "Chattanooga, TN Sustainability Plan," n.d., accessed January 19, 2018.

28. Green Policy 360, "Chattanooga, TN Sustainability Plan," n.d., accessed January 19, 2018.

29. The City of Los Angeles, "Sustainable City PLAn: Transforming Los Angeles" (Office of the Mayor, 2017), http://plan.lamayor.org/wp-content/uploads/2017/03/the-plan.pdf.

30. City of Tulsa, "City of Tulsa Sustainability Plan: Resource Efficiency, Clean Energy, and Leading Growth in the New Economy," October 27, 2011, 13, http://cdn.cityoftulsa.org/parks/COT%20Sustainability%20Plan_FINAL.pdf.

31. City of Tulsa, 13.

32. The City of Madison, "The Madison Sustainability Plan: Fostering Environmental, Economic, and Social Resistance," 2011, 31, https://www.cityofmadison.com/sustainability/documents/SustainPlan2011.pdf.

33. Melissa Keeley et al., "Perspectives on the Use of Green Infrastructure for Stormwater Management in Cleveland and Milwaukee," *Environmental*

Management 51, no. 6 (June 2013): 1093–1108, https://doi.org/10.1007/s00267-013-0032-x.

34. City of Spokane, "Sustainability Action Plan: Addressing Climate Mitigation, Climate Adaptation, and Energy Security," 2009, 11, https://static.spokanecity.org/documents/publicworks/environmental/sustainability-action-plan.pdf.

35. City of Spokane, 8.

36. Metropolitan Washington Council of Governments, "COG & Our Region," accessed February 13, 2018, https://www.mwcog.org/about-us/cog-and-our-region/.

37. City of St. Louis Planning Commission, "City of St. Louis Sustainability Plan," February 6, 2013, 13, https://www.stlouis-mo.gov/government/departments/mayor/documents/upload/STL-Sustainability-Plan.pdf.

CHAPTER 2

Equity

An Introduction: Equity and Social Sustainability

There is more to sustainability than simply minimizing our environmental impact, developing policies that promote recycling, or passing legislation to prevent environmental degradation. Increasingly, cities will also have to pay equal attention to the third "E" of sustainability—equity.

Income inequality has been sharply increasing in the United States since the 1970s, and the country currently has one of the most inequitable distributions of wealth in the developed world. In the United States, the top 0.1 percent held 7 percent of wealth in 1979, and 22 percent of wealth in 2012. This concentration of wealth is contrasted with the experience of the bottom 90 percent, whose share of wealth fell from a high of 35 percent in the mid-1980s to about 23 percent in 2012. Drivers of these changes are contested, but likely include the slow growth of middle-class income, financial deregulation, predatory lending, and tax policy, among other factors.

Inequities extend beyond just income, and the patterns that we see in the US today—in affluence, education, occupation, and health—are the result of trends that have intersected and reinforced each other over generations. We will leave a treatment of the many historical racial and gender inequities (slavery, disenfranchisement, and forms of discrimination woven into public policies and everyday attitudes) to other authors. However, we note that new drivers of inequality have arisen in many modern economies while disparate impacts from the past have been compounded.

M. Keeley, L. Benton-Short, *Urban Sustainability in the US*,
https://doi.org/10.1007/978-3-319-93296-5_2

Socioeconomic and racial segregation remains an intractable problem, particularly in large cities in the Northeast and Midwest. This spatial distribution reinforces existing patterns of inequity in that amenities like high-quality schools, full-service grocery stores, banks, doctors and hospitals, and well-maintained parks are more available to privileged communities.[1] Below, we examine the ways that socioeconomic and racial segregation impact peoples' lives and city sustainability efforts.

Environmental Justice

The US Environmental Protection Agency (EPA) defines environmental justice as the "fair treatment and meaningful involvement of all people regardless of race, color, national origin, or income with respect to the development, implementation, and enforcement of environmental laws, regulations, and policies."[2] "Fair treatment" implies that no single group should bear a disproportionate share of negative environmental consequences (disamenities) or a disproportionate lack of positive environment consequences (amenities). "Meaningful involvement" implies that people should be treated with dignity and have the opportunity to participate in decision-making and exercise choice in deliberations that affect their lives.

The impact of the distribution of disamenities in cities and disproportionate impacts on poorer communities and communities of color has been the subject of intensive study. For instance, race continues to be the most significant variable associated with the location of hazardous waste sites. One study showed that three out of every five Black and Hispanic Americans lived in communities with one or more toxic waste sites. In the United States, among counties that have three or more pollutants that exceed EPA levels, 12 percent are majority white, 20 percent are majority African American, and 31 percent are majority Hispanic. Although socioeconomic status was also an important variable in the location of these sites, race was the most significant.[3]

Environmental inequities occur not only through the presence of environmental disamenities, but they are also found in absences of environmental amenities. For example, geographers mapped trees in Milwaukee and found an inequitable distribution of trees in the city. The more affluent white areas had more extensive urban tree canopy than the poorer and blacker areas of the city. Trees can positively affect the quality of neighborhoods, because of their aesthetic qualities and ability to absorb and filter pollution, so uneven distribution of trees reinforces uneven social spaces.[4]

As a result, there is a direct correlation between socioeconomic status and the quality of one's environment.[5] The causal web is sometimes complex but often simple. In some cases, low-income communities have formed in areas that are more affordable because of existing disamenities—like proximity to polluting factories or potential for flooding. Particularly during deindustrialization, low-income neighborhoods may also have been places where cities could find affordable vacant land to construct needed, but polluting facilities like trash transfer stations. These communities may lack the political power and bargaining strength to affectively protest and block the siting of such facilities in their neighborhoods in the way that more affluent neighborhoods can and do.

In 2015 the EPA released EJSCREEN, an environmental justice mapping and screening tool that allows Americans to identify sources of pollution and contamination near their homes (Fig. 2.1). EJSCREEN users choose a geographic area, and the tool then provides demographic and environmental information for that area. EJSCREEN lets you compare a community to the rest of the state, EPA region, and nation by using national percentiles. Users can identify areas with more and less potential for exposure, risk, and proximity to certain facilities and understand how this relates to the minority populations.

The Challenge of Equity

Despite equity's prominence in definitions of sustainability, equity is often the least defined and operationalized of the three "E's" and frequently takes a back seat in sustainability planning.[6] In many cases, if equity is on the agenda at all, it seems to be an implied afterthought.[7] We found that many US cities have failed to meaningfully include equity goals and actions in their sustainability efforts.[8] Indeed, the ways equity is raised indicates that it may be primarily symbolic or a low-priority concern. [9] For this reason, we have deliberately placed this chapter at the beginning of the book to keep equity at the forefront of the remaining chapters we cover. It is too important to be an afterthought.

One possible reason for the absence of equity in many sustainability plans is that information and data about equity can be difficult to assess. For instance, many studies show that information on the access, provision, and quality of green space is very limited.[10] Community members most in need of special inclusion in the planning process are often difficult to reach through traditional means. They may feel disconnected from official

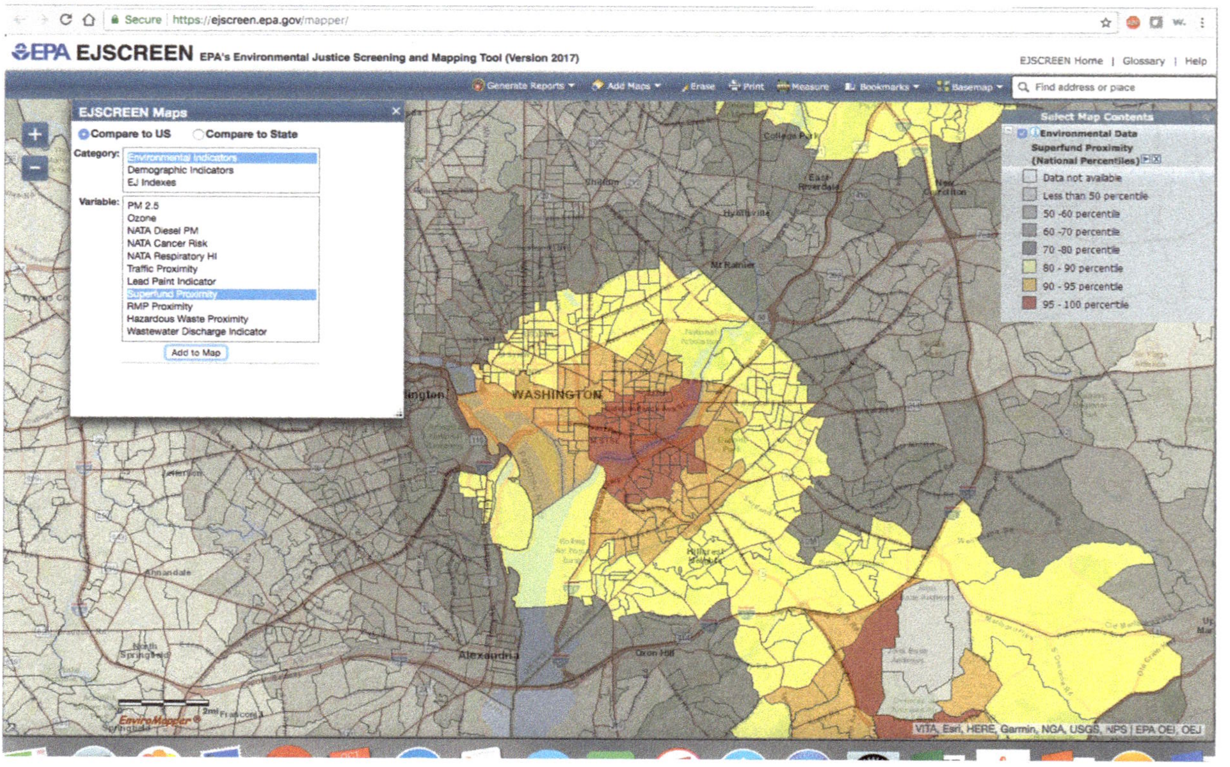

Fig. 2.1   This example of EJSCREEN shows the proximity of superfund sites to neighborhoods in Washington, D.C. The neighborhoods most at risk are the poorest and predominately African American. (Source: The US "EPA EJSCREEN: EPA's Environmental Justice Screening and Mapping Tool" (Version 2017), accessed April 10, 2018, at https://ejscreen. epa.gov/mapper/)

processes by a language barrier, or their immigration status or that of a family member. Individuals struggling with housing affordability may move frequently, living temporarily with friends and family and do not show up in official records. Issues surrounding the collection and assessment of qualitative information further exacerbates equity-related knowledge gaps. Collecting, assessing, and understanding the cleanliness, safety, and other qualities of infrastructure and services from the perspective of those living and working in near proximity cannot be adequately completed without on-the-ground discussions with those residents and workers.

It is important to distinguish between equality and equity. As Fig. 2.2 shows, equality is treating everyone the same. Equity, however, is about giving everyone what they need to be successful. An example is school funding. Advocating for equality would mean ensuring that all schools had the same amount of resources per pupil, which could be an improvement for some schools. On the other hand, advocating for equity would mean recognizing that some schools—like those serving students in low-income or minority communities—may actually need more resources (funding, experienced teachers, relevant curriculum, etc.) to reduce existing educational disparities.

This understanding of equity highlights its importance within considerations of sustainability. A society is stronger when more members have the education, health, and other support they need to reach their full potential and contribute fully to society. Such a community would be more stable, require fewer support goods and services, and potentially generate more

Fig. 2.2 Visualizing equality vs equity. (Source: By Authors.)

revenue to pay for sustainability initiatives. But what is clear is that inequities are a barrier to sustainability.

As the city of Portland notes, "equity is achieved when identity—such as race, ethnicity, gender, age, disability or sexual orientation — has no detrimental effect on the distribution of resources, opportunities and outcomes for group members in a society."[11] Yet, we can see that the role of equity within sustainability is one that our society still grapples with. Connecting equity to discussions of climate change is of increasing importance given the disproportionate impacts that will be experienced by more vulnerable communities.[12] Genuine sustainability requires us to consider our actions in relation to others, and to pursue a more democratic civic politics. It involves ensuring environmental and economic benefits are distributed more equitably among all citizens. Thus, there are no easy "fixes." Addressing underlying problems of economic and social inequity could be one of the biggest challenges to a more sustainable future.

Cities' Role in Promoting Equity and Social Sustainability

In order to adequately address inequities, cities should thoroughly integrate equity initiatives throughout all aspects of sustainability planning and action. If equity is not taken into account while developing other goals and actions for sustainability, it can easily get pushed aside or even worse result unintendedly in increasing inequity in a city.

We have found that many cities lack measurable goals or fail to describe programs to address equity issues. In her essay, "Social Equity: The Forgotten Leg of Sustainability," Jessica Chapman argues that social issues are too frequently neglected in the creation of sustainability plans. She notes that many sustainability plans "often address narrow, technical problems, but often ignore (perhaps inadvertently) the needs of the entire community."[13] While we have identified some cities which have woven equity more thoughtfully throughout their plans for sustainability, our research largely agrees with this assessment.

Many sustainability plans specifically cite the "three Es" of sustainability but do not specifically use the term "equity" in their discussions of sustainability, substituting the terms "community" or "social." Some might argue that this is a matter of semantics and that the substitution of community for equity was chosen to make it clearer to a lay audience or to help residents broadly connect and identify with the benefits of sustainability planning. Others, however, criticize this as sidestepping a critical issue.

Some cities do have plans that better integrate equity. For example, Washington, D.C., St. Louis, Los Angeles, and Fayetteville, Arkansas, effectively integrate equity into their plans. Portland, Oregon, refers to its Portland Plan 2012 as "a Framework for Equity."[14] Yet, we also found that many cities avoided the topic of equity, focusing more on environmental issues.

Other cities such as Memphis, Seattle, Portland, and Boston have distinct and separate equity plans, which shape their city's approach to the subject. However, we consider weaving issues of equity throughout a comprehensive sustainability plan as a best practice. This is a first step towards integrated planning, in which goals are set and projects implemented in a manner that aligns decisions and projects with equity.

For example, while a general goal of increasing tree canopy citywide might be laudable, it would be more effective to set a goal that each neighborhood reaches some minimum tree canopy percentage, or to prioritize tree planning efforts in neighborhoods with the worst air quality or urban heat island problems, or where childhood asthma rates are highest. Without such priority, a tree planting program could reinforce existing inequities instead of ameliorating them.

When equity is a part of sustainability planning, it is incorporated for different reasons. The sustainability plan of Newark, New Jersey, notably includes a discussion on environmental justice, and developing "policies that will support the right of all members of the community to enjoy the benefits of a healthy environment, regardless of income, race, class, or location."[15] Their discussion is shaped by a legacy of industrial environmental pollution that continues to impact low-income groups and communities of color.[16]

San Francisco addresses issues of equity as a way to support areas experiencing gentrification. Gentrification—an important issue in many US cities—is reinvestment and renovation in deteriorated urban neighborhoods, which can have the intended or unintended effect of displacing poorer, historic communities with more affluent, and often whiter residents. San Francisco wants to support neighborhood improvements yet keep cultural heritage, populations, and businesses in place. Their prototype project addresses gentrification in the Mission Neighborhood, a historically Latino community.[17]

Some US cities have elevated diversity as a community value and vital part of community identity, such as Grand Rapids, Michigan, which states that "we know the differences in cultures and experiences of all of our citizens make us a strong and enriched community. All citizens matter and deserve to be treated with dignity and respect, have access to services, and have opportunities to succeed. We will practice fairness, listening with an open mind, and mutual understanding."[18]

Public declarations of the importance of diversity in our communities and the value of all people, coupled with actions that put these values into practice are much needed. Our current political and civic culture has given a voice to intolerance. Patterns of discriminatory policing, planning from the top down, and public policy that prioritizes economic gain over equity have left some people of color, immigrants, and low-income groups feeling that city officials do not represent them and are not working in their best interest.

Part of facing this reality and working to unravel this complex challenge of discrimination, mistreatment, and disempowerment is to take action on equity, and to elevate goals of equity alongside those of economics and environmental protection in city planning and policy efforts. Sustainability plans that prioritize and integrate equity could be a step in the right direction. We see that equity is included in sustainability plans in different ways and for different reasons according to the existing and historical dynamics unique to individual cities. However, our research leads us to agree with other scholars who found that there is a gulf between the frequency with which equity is mentioned and the depth with which it is explored.[19]

Taking Action on Equity and Social Sustainability

It is clear that equity is a challenge for many cities. The good news is that some cities are addressing equity through creative and important strategies that include:

1. Procedural equity: decision-making and participation
2. Distribution and access to services, amenities and disamenities, for example:

   a. Education
   b. Health
   c. Housing

Procedural Equity: Involving the Community in Decision-Making and Participation

Geographers Hamil Pearsall and Joseph Pierce identify procedural equity as the right of all people to have "meaningful involvement" in decision-making—for example, in the planning process, or in prioritization of sustainability projects.[20]

Procedural equity includes systems to ensure that all people are treated openly, fairly, and inclusively. Engaging residents in the process of planning for and implementing a sustainability agenda for their city and neighborhood is important and can also help to develop cohesion and connectedness in a community and build social capital, a vital "end product" in and of itself. As explained by the City of Grand Rapids:

> In order for a community to flourish, social capital is essential and requires a willingness to engage in collective civic activities. This is accomplished through trust, mutual understanding, and shared values. Thus, developing social capital and working cooperatively in a community go hand in hand.[21]

In order to make choices about how to use limited resources, communities need decision-making processes based on understandings of the important linkages and trade-offs that exist between their community's quality of life, social, economic, and environmental assets and the potential for various stakeholders to benefit differently from the choices made.[22] Participatory planning is a set of processes through which diverse groups and interests engage together in reaching for a consensus on a plan and its implementation. People want effective and accessible ways to participate in shaping their future but often feel disaffected, disconnected, and discouraged. Wise planners recognize that engagement is not just *listening to* the community but *learning from* the community. Many planners say public participation is now outmoded. Instead, cities need to strive for participatory planning.

Inclusion of a diversity of voices in the planning process is a crucial first step in creating a plan that identifies the most pressing concerns of the community. This is because sustainable outcomes cannot be expected without the input and buy-in of all residents. While some goals are universal, communities with different age, gender, or socioeconomic compositions are likely to have unique needs and wishes.[23] Thus, deliberative and inclusionary processes and procedures which actively engage the public and ensure that community needs are met and that new or improved amenities and services are not perceived as inferior, unwanted, or even unsafe.[24]

Participatory equity begins with planning but is also a crucial throughout plan implementation. This is because many sustainability efforts will require informed, responsible, individual choice and action.

Community involvement and engagement are commonly invoked in municipal sustainability plans, especially with respect to the creation of the overall plan.

Boston is piloting neighborhood-level sustainability planning to "establish personalized and realistic goals for communities."[25] These community planning exercises involve residents and local stakeholders working to create a vision for their community while "respecting each neighborhood's past and present."[26] Dallas is bolstering the ability of neighborhoods and neighborhood associations to engage in planning by providing materials on "how to organize" to interested groups.[27]

Many cities have conducted lengthy public engagement exercises in developing their sustainability plans, often over the course of two or more years. Burlington, Vermont, utilized several creative approaches to obtain feedback from individuals who might not otherwise participate in a planning process. They held informal conversations at food pantries, homeless shelters, and senior citizen centers around the city. Burlington leaders conscientiously included youth in the creation of its plan by holding conversations at student council meetings and conducting essay and art contests through which students could express their desires for the future of Burlington.

Other cities have also reached out to populations that may otherwise have not participated in planning by including childcare provision, meetings in languages other than English, and partnerships with local institutions like places of worship. Such efforts to include otherwise unaccounted for segments of the population will extend sustainability plans and more effectively address the needs of these populations.

For example, one strategy in Minneapolis to elicit views of female residents was to bring toys to a local park and use the time that children were playing to talk with their mothers.[28] Terminology barriers must also be overcome in effectively advertising and drawing crowds to targeted sustainability planning meetings. One sustainability director found that discussions of "sustainability and the future of the city" were too vague to attract community members, but advertising discussions centered on pressing neighborhood problems, like childhood asthma or the fate and status of the local recreation center or playground, drew more participants and could be leveraged into broader discussions of community needs and priorities.

Language barriers can also be an impediment to community involvement. Many cities have large numbers of immigrants who speak languages other than English and already publish important materials such as voting information and campaign materials in languages other than English. This practice should be extended to sustainability planning as well.

Leveraging community partnerships is another important best practice. Non-profit organizations, community groups, and religious congregations can help cities connect with and understand the needs of different constituents, mobilize volunteers, and identify key community leaders. Such groups can provide local-scale information about many issues including safety, traffic, or walkability and may be in a position to help implement programs given their established networks of participants and on-the-ground experience.

Box 2.1   Best Practices in Planning: Participatory Planning and GIS

The use of Geographic Information Systems (GIS) data and maps can inform participatory planning, empower neighborhood organizations, and be a tool to convey needs to funders and governmental agencies. GIS uses spatial location to map, organize, and analyze information. Beyond just mapping, GIS reveals relationships between data. For instance, it might be used to understand the distribution of asthma in a neighborhood in relationship major roads, parks, and sources of air pollution or to examine heat maps of the city and the current distribution of street trees to prioritize areas for planning more trees.

Use of this powerful tool is on the rise due to new technologies and innovations. While specialized equipment had been required to collect location information, this function is now available in the smart phones many of us use. While the licenses to operate GIS have been prohibitively expensive for many non-profits, "Open source" GIS platforms are available free of charge.

Participatory planning is a term that describes a variety of planning techniques designed to meaningfully involve the entire community in the planning process. GIS is one of these tools, however, incorporation of GIS into neighborhood-based participatory planning brings a unique set of considerations:

(*continued*)

Box 2.1 (continued)

1. Using GIS in a community planning can raise the level of expertise or education that a resident needs to understand and contribute to the planning process. This technology can inadvertently marginalize elderly residents, those with a limited education, or literacy or English language challenges.
2. Participatory planning that utilizes GIS carries an additional layer of resource requirements, including costs, time, and training resources. To make use of GIS applications, community groups need hardware and software but also support services over the long term.
3. The GIS must be constructed to be sufficiently flexible to include diverse and unexpected forms of community information, such as narratives, citizen reports, digital photographs, and to model scenarios that may diverge from local government priorities in a planning process.

Source:

Cliff Hague et al. "Participatory Planning for Sustainable Communities: International experience in mediation, negotiation and engagement in making plans," (2004, page 34), http://www.chs.ubc.ca/archives/files/Participatory%20planning%20for%20sustainable%20development.pdf, accessed January 2018.

Distribution and Access to Services, Amenities, and Disamenities

Urban sustainability requires an examination of the distributive consequences of urbanization.[29] Distributional equality is concerned with the access to amenities like quality, affordable goods, clean water, and health services, as well as protection from disamenities like flooding, pollution, and crime. There are two main approaches to addressing these disparities. One is to use policy mechanisms to create more integrated communities such as inclusionary zoning; another is to more equitably distribute amenities and disamenities throughout cities and regions.

The clustering of environmental hazards in communities of color and the uneven impacts on these communities continue to challenge many cities. This is not a new problem. As the city of Los Angeles admits "underserved, low-income individuals and communities often bear the burden of environmental pollution, health impacts and economic health challenges, and therefore need and deserve specific improvements and investments."[30]

One of the most powerful tools cities use to identify and understand inequity in distribution and access is GIS and mapping (See Box 2.2). Maps are tools for priority setting; they serve as starting points in understanding community assets or problems. Mapping amenities or disamenities can start a community conversation and discussion, with the hope that more people are drawn into the conversation to continually strengthen data and identify place-specific solutions. While many cities have established GIS offices, our research showed that few sustainability plans included maps that identified the distribution of services, amenities, and environmental problems. (We do recognize that it is quite possible that geospatial techniques were used in the planning process and were not included in the plan itself.)

Box 2.2   Best Practices in Innovation: Using Geospatial Technologies to Map Environmental Justice in Phoenix

The US National Science Foundation funds long-term ecological research projects at 24 sites in a Long-Term Ecological Research Network (LTER). Only two of them specifically study the ecology of urban areas. The two sites, one in Baltimore, Maryland, and the other in Phoenix, Arizona, provide information on urban ecological process and trends. The goal of the Central Arizona-Phoenix LTER based at Arizona State University is to foster social-ecological urban research aimed at understanding complex urban systems using a holistic, ecology of cities perspective. There are numerous ongoing research projects.

One project examined soils for lead, a toxin that affects cognitive abilities in children. Children can be exposed to lead through contaminated soil. Using 200 soil samples from around the area, researchers mapped lead levels with GIS and found elevated lead concentrations in central and southeastern parts of the Phoenix metropolitan area. They then compared lead concentrations with the construction years of the housing stock and found that areas with housing built before the 1940s had the highest lead concentrations, and areas with housing from before 1978 were also elevated (1978 is the year that lead paint was banned in the United States).

(*continued*)

Box 2.2   (continued)

Their next challenge was to understand who in the Phoenix metropolitan area was most likely to be exposed to lead-contaminated soil. Using US Census data, they focused on wealth, race, and vulnerability to lead exposure (children under the age of five). Statistical techniques of regression analysis and spatial autocorrelation revealed that areas with relatively high soil lead concentrations are more likely to be Hispanic neighborhoods with a large percentage of renters.

These results reveal an environmental justice issue in the Phoenix area where there is an inequitable distribution of risk associated with lead exposure. The Hispanic population at risk includes many immigrants, some of whom have limited English skills and may be undocumented in the United States. Landlords do not always maintain properties in low-income neighborhoods, allowing paint (which, before 1978, generally contained lead) to peel on properties, and low-income renters seldom have much leverage over their housing conditions. In Phoenix, Hispanic renter households—those with perhaps the most limited ability to mitigate lead exposure and the least social and political power—are the most exposed to this toxin. GIS and other spatial tools are increasingly used to identify areas of environmental injustice, helping the city to more concentrate resources for those most in need of intervention.

Source:

Xiaoding Zhuo, Chris Boone, and Everett Shock, "Soil lead distribution and environmental justice in the Phoenix metropolitan region," Environmental Justice, 5 no. 4 (2012): 206–213.

To learn more about the CAP-LTER, go to https://sustainability.asu.edu/caplter/research/

Education

Although the United States has long thought of itself as a land of opportunity, where those "willing to work hard can get ahead," historic and ongoing inequities in educational quality and access (from pre-kindergarten through higher education) contribute to growing disparities in wealth and opportunity. Despite efforts to address the "achievement gaps" within student populations, educational inequity in the United States appears to be more entrenched than in other industrialized countries. While one might expect schools in low-income communities to receive extra resources, the reverse is often true; a Department of Education study found that 45 percent of high-poverty schools received less state and local funding than was typical for other schools in their district.[31] The inequitable funding system and other structural disparities contribute to challenges faced by underserved students, including minority and low-income students who are suspended, expelled, and dropped out at higher rates and who attend and complete college at far lower rates than their peers.[32]

National politicians on both sides of the isle call education the "civil rights issue of our time" (although they disagree on strategies to redress this issue). While education is a topic often raised in sustainability plans, many of these discussions are superficial and insufficiently connected to other key sustainability efforts and priorities. Goals pertaining to education are poorly defined and lack specific strategies for goal achievement in sustainability plans.

Salt Lake City addressed issues of educational equity in more detail than other cities have. The city wants to expand access to early childhood education to reach 25 percent of its underserved residents, promote STEM (science, technology, engineering, mathematics) programs in the hopes of career development in these fields in the future, and pledge to support community learning centers, in an effort to "cultivate a community of lifelong learners."[33]

Another best practice for equitable education is developing culturally responsive (or relevant) curriculum and classrooms. This approach to education recognizes, respects, and values cultural differences within a classroom with inclusive practices and "using knowledge of ethnically diverse cultures, families, and communities to guide curriculum development, classroom climates, instructional strategies, and relationships with students."[34] Advocates say this approach will help address the achievement gap between minority and majority students and ensure equitable educational opportunities.[35] However, such efforts have generated a backlash. Opponents say these approaches promote resentment towards a race or class of people and advocate ethnic solidarity instead of the treatment of pupils as individuals. Such opposition led to a 2010 Arizona law ending a Mexican-American studies program that offered elective classes in Tucson public schools since the 1990s and restricts public school districts from offering ethnic studies classes. Supporters of this program countered that it was a way to reach marginalized students and highlight the fact that students who took these classes scored higher on state tests and had a higher rate of graduating high school.[36]

Sustainability Education and Environmental Literacy
Educating the public on issues of sustainability is crucial to the success of these initiatives because implementing sustainability requires the buy-in and support of individuals to enact measures. As we will discuss in Chap. 3, many cities are seeking to grow or rebuild their economies by attracting new, sustainable industries to their communities. This requires a workforce with advanced technical skills and a basic understanding of sustainability concepts. Yet with a few exceptions, sustainability education is rarely addressed in the overall vision for sustainability among many cities.

Washington, D.C. is one exception. The District passed the Healthy Schools Act of 2010 that directed the development of a citywide Environmental Literacy Plan. Environmental literacy is the development of knowledge, attitudes, and skills necessary to make informed decisions concerning the relationships among natural and urban systems.[37] The program defines an environmentally literate person as someone who can:

- Discuss and describe ecological and environmental systems and human impacts on these systems;
- Engage in hands-on, outdoor learning experiences that involve discovery, inquiry, and problem solving;
- Formulate questions and analyze information pertaining to his or her surrounding environment; and
- Understand how to take actions that respect, restore, protect, and sustain the health and well-being of human communities and environmental systems.[38]

Another best practice related to sustainability education—particularly for children—is providing for outdoor learning opportunities. Richard Louv's 2008 book *Last Child in the Woods: Saving Our Children from Nature-Deficit Disorder* generated an increased interest in children's environmental awareness.[39] The "No Child Left Inside" movement has grown since the book was published, and numerous studies show that children who spend time outdoors and in green environments have increased attention, higher test scores, and better behavior. Many states and cities have established programs in local parks and schools that increase children's connections with nature.

Health

Health inequality—differences in health that are avoidable, unfair and unjust—have long persisted. Issues such as poverty, insurance status, and individual-level factors such as diet and physical activity, are related to negative health outcomes including obesity, heart disease, diabetes, and cancer. Deficits in bike paths, local parks, grocery stores, safe housing, primary care facilities, and fitness centers play an important role in health outcomes. Poverty at a neighborhood level can also negatively influence health experiences.[40] Planners and health policymakers, with the help of GIS and other spatial tools, can and should identify and target communities most in need of intervention.

Incidents of chronic disease are rising, healthcare costs are spiraling up, and governments have inadequate funds to address these interwoven problems.[41] Even when funds are allocated, change may be difficult or slow. For instance, Louisville, KY, faces high rates of obesity which are nearly 62 percent and 73 percent for white and African American adults, respectively.[42] While the city has implemented several programs to address this through exercise, such as public campaigns advocating more walking and biking and providing low-cost fitness classes, the rates of obesity continue to rise, and the percentage of the population reporting any physical activity outside of work has remained nearly the same.[43] While the implementation of these programs targeting obesity is commendable, the results indicate that the programs did not adequately overcome the complex set of issues that underlay unhealthy behaviors.

Louisville's challenges highlight the fact that solutions to complex health problems are often well beyond the mandated reach of public health agencies. This has led to the development of a new approach called "Health in All Policies" which seeks to improve the health of all people by incorporating health considerations into decision-making across sectors and policy areas.[44] These include non-traditional health partners such as those involved in education, parks and recreation, transportation, and housing.

Two leaders have been the city of Richmond, California and Boston. In 2012 the city of Richmond embarked on a process to research, develop and implement Health in All Policies at the city level. The first step was to begin speaking the language of health equity and to understand the range of city services and programs that could be coordinated to promote health equity. It also set out to systematize data collection. In 2015, the city issued its first progress report. Its website also features a toolkit for other cities to use.[45] Boston has also been a leader in the adopting Health in All Policies. In 2013, they created a set of priorities for incorporating health equity into street design, housing developments, building projects, and park planning throughout the city. One outcome was their Complete Streets program that ensures that all street redesigned projects support walking, cycling, and public transit uses that are equally safe and accessible as car transit, allowing residents to incorporate more physical activity into their daily travel.[46]

Many cities are now considering adopting "Health in All" policies (see Box 2.3). However, our research shows that most cities failed to include this discussion in their sustainability plans, thus missing the opportunity to more fully integrate concerns of public health into the decision-making of agencies across our cities.

Box 2.3   Best Practices in Multiple Benefits: Health in All Policies

Health in All Policies, or "healthy public policy," is based on the idea that health starts where people live, work, learn, and play and that community health is influenced by more than individual choices. One's physical and social environments, along with local government decisions and actions that shape these environments, have an impact on health outcomes.

Health in All Policies is a response to a variety of complex and often inextricably linked problems such as the chronic illness epidemic, growing inequality and health inequities, rising healthcare costs, an aging population, climate change causing more frequent disasters, and the lack of efficient strategies for achieving governmental goals with shrinking resources. Such "wicked" problems are extremely challenging. Addressing them requires innovative solutions, a new policy paradigm, and structures that break down the silos of government to advance multidisciplinary and inter-sectoral thinking.

Health in All Policies is a collaborative approach to improving the health of all people by incorporating health considerations into decision-making across sectors and policy areas.

(*continued*)

Box 2.3   (continued)

Health is influenced by the combination of social, physical, and economic environments, collectively referred to as the "social determinants of health." Health in All Policies support improved health outcomes and health equity through collaboration between public health practitioners and those nontraditional partners who have influence over the social determinants of health. Health in All Policies approaches include five key elements:

1. Promoting health and equity
2. Supporting inter-sectoral collaboration
3. Creating multiple benefits to attract many partners
4. Engaging stakeholders and
5. Creating structural or process change

Health in All Policies encompasses a wide spectrum of activities and can be implemented in many different ways. It is increasingly emerging as a best practice in health that promises to have multiple benefits to a community.

Sources:

"Health in All Policies," American Public Health Association, accessed September 16, 2017, https://www.apha.org/topics-and-issues/health-in-all-policies

Linda Rudolph, Julia Caplan, Karen Ben-Moshe & Lianne Dillon. "Health in All Policies: A Guide for State and Local Governments," (Washington, DC and Oakland, CA: American Public Health Association and Public Health Institute, 2013), https://www.apha.org/~/media/files/pdf/factsheets/health_inall_policies_guide_169pages.ashx September 16, 2017.

Food Deserts

Increasingly, cities are recognizing that some neighborhoods are food deserts. Food desserts occur where residents do not have access to affordable and healthy food close to their homes. Some communities, particularly those of low income, lack ready access to full-service supermarkets, especially when one considers that low-income residents may lack access to a car. Instead, residents in these areas frequently rely on small neighborhood convenience stores. These businesses, however, often have limited offerings of fresh foods needed for a healthy diet including fresh fruits and vegetables, whole grains, fresh dairy, and lean meat products. Table 2.1 highlights some of the effective ways cities are addressing food desserts.

Salt Lake City has focused on this issue in their sustainability plan, with an entire section on this topic—"Food Production & Nutrition." A first goal was to complete a Community Food Assessment to better understand the challenges and needs of their communities, which they published in 2013. The city assessed "challenges and opportunities for a more sustainable local food system" holistically, examining food production, processing, and distribution and food consumption, nutrition, and health and managing food waste.[47]

Another city addressing food deserts is Baltimore, Maryland. A recent study found 30 percent of residents do not have easy access to a car, and one in four needs to travel more than a quarter-mile to find a supermarket. One in three school-aged children in Baltimore lives in a food desert, and African Americans are disproportionately affected: 34 percent live in food deserts as compared to only 8 percent of white residents. The city has implemented a program to provide residents in senior, disabled, and public housing the opportunity to purchase groceries online through the Virtual Supermarket Program. By 2017, 200 households in neighborhoods classified as food deserts no longer had to invest a disproportionate

Table 2.1 Best practices in addressing food deserts

The following strategies have been effective at addressing food deserts:

- Host stakeholder-driven food policy councils to develop relevant priorities, programs, and food-related policy recommendations
- Provide incentives to encourage full-service grocery stores to open in food deserts
- Create and support partnerships with banks and community development financial institutions to create loan funds for businesses that increase healthy food access in low-income communities
- Encourage grocery stores to stock food that is culturally appropriate for customers and addresses dietary restrictions, such as lactose intolerance, or halal meats
- Improve offerings at existing convenience stores by coordinating produce deliveries or providing refrigeration units
- Establish and support farmers markets or mobile food stores in underserved areas
- Provide the resources (such as technical infrastructure) necessary to facilitate the use of services such as the Supplemental Nutrition Assistance Program (SNAP), Women, Infants and Children (WIC), and other food-benefit programs at farmers markets
- Coordinate and provide technical assistance for community gardens in food deserts

amount of time and resources in traveling to a supermarket, because the Virtual Supermarket brings groceries directly to their housing complexes.[48]

Cities have found that large, high-quality grocery stores are unwilling to locate in some underserved areas. Supporting or facilitating the development of new grocery stores is one technique to combat food deserts. New York City launched their Food Retail Expansion to Support Health (FRESH) program in 2009, which provided zoning incentives (like bonus floor area ratio and lower parking requirements) and financial incentives via tax credits incentives to develop or renovate grocery stores in underserved areas. Another example is the increase in community gardens that provide job training as well as fresh food in local areas (Fig. 2.3).

Fig. 2.3 Common Good City Farm in Washington, D.C. This community garden does more than grow food in a gentrifying neighborhood; it is committed to issues of equity. During summer months it runs a youth program for disadvantaged teens to teach them how to grow food on the farm, run their own farm stand, prepare lunches, and learn about sustainable agriculture, food access, cooking and nutrition, and workplace readiness. (Source: Lisa Benton-Short.)

Box 2.4   Best Practices in Innovation: Cleveland's City Fresh Program

In the Cleveland metro area there are an estimated 400,000 people living in food deserts. The non-profit City Fresh is addressing the issue through its "Fresh Stops" program which connects urban residents and local farmers, thus bridging the social justice and local food movements. The program is similar to a CSA (community-supported agriculture), with customers buying "shares" of crops from local farmers, and features a centralized pickup location for goods. Customer costs are kept down as local growers avoid marketing costs and minimize transportation expenditures.

The program has been deliberate about involving low-income communities who have not been historically included in CSA initiatives. "Fresh Stop" venues are hosted by community-based organizations, such as neighborhood churches and community associations. A community group can register as a "Fresh Stop" if they have at least 25 shareholders. Volunteers both operate the "stop" and recruit participant shareholders. The program offers produce 20–40 percent cheaper than the grocery store. Shares are available at both a market price and a subsidized price for qualifying families. For those below the poverty level, a family share of produce for the season will cost only $18 a week. The program also accepts federal food-benefit program vouchers such as SNAP. Shares are flexible and can be purchased weekly or for the entire season. "Fresh Stops" are organized like farmer's markets, and individuals can choose their own food based on availability for that week. Finally, educational material including recipes, food samples, and nutritional information is also available.

The results have been impressive. In 2016, more than 100,000 pounds of fresh produce was delivered to residents in 14 food deserts, and the program employed more than 60 small farmers. Even more impressive, the entire program operates using 102 volunteers and only two full-time and three part-time staff, showing that innovative solutions do not necessarily require tremendous investment.

Sources:

"How City Fresh Works," City Fresh 2018, https://cityfresh.org/?page_id=2782

Punam Ohri-Vachaspati, Brad Masi, Morgan Taggart, Joe Konen and Jack Kerrigan, "City Fresh: A Local Collaboration for Food Equity," *Journal of Extension*, 47, no. 6 (December 2009), https://joe.org/joe/2009december/a1.php. January, 2018.

Housing

Housing affordability is a serious concern for many Americans. Harvard's Joint Center for Housing Studies has reported that 33 percent of American households pay more than 30 percent of their income on housing, a significant financial burden.[49] The cost burden poses a strain on families who struggle with tight budgets and can lead to long commute times, as workers seek lower-cost housing further from employment. Today, gentrification is accelerating as educated millennials—20 to 30 somethings—are increasingly choosing to live in the central city.[50] The result is rapidly increasing housing prices, which can displace long-term residents unable to afford increasing rents or rising property taxes.

Improving the amount and quality of low-income and workforce housing and assuring that such housing is integrated into inclusive neighborhoods should be of utmost concern. Our research shows that while cities often mention affordable housing in plans or on websites, they rarely provide concrete details about how such goals will be achieved.

One possible solution is inclusionary zoning. Inclusionary zoning is a tool that is used to help provide a wider range of housing options than a free market provides on its own. In the United States, the term inclusionary zoning refers to municipal and county planning ordinances that require a given share of new construction to be affordable by people with low or moderate incomes.

Generally inclusionary zoning policies require some percentage of the new construction (often between 10 percent and 25 percent) be affordable housing. Inclusionary zoning can be mandatory (such as requiring inclusionary housing) or voluntary (such as offering incentives such as zoning bonuses, expedited permits, reduced fees, cash subsidies for developers who voluntarily build affordable housing). Today, more than 200 communities in the United States have inclusionary zoning policies.

Another emerging trend is inclusionary upzoning, a variation on inclusionary zoning. When cities adopt new land use plans that allow taller height limits, greater development density, or new land uses such as housing in formerly industrial or commercial areas, they can require or give incentives for lower-priced, income-targeted housing. Inclusionary upzoning can provide a helpful workaround in communities where inclusionary housing has run into legal barriers, such as Oregon, Washington, Texas, Colorado, and more recently California.[51] Inclusionary upzoning has been most common in mixed-use and transit-oriented development (which we explore in detail in Chap. 5). We do caution that cities ensure they require developers to provide a specific percentage of below-market-rate housing options and to include other community amenities aimed for all income levels (particularly in mixed-use developments).

Another best practice to improve housing equity is to regularly review, revise, and streamline the development review process for affordable housing to be sure that zoning and other requirements do not pose unnecessary barriers to construction.[52] In some areas affordable housing can be integrated into existing neighborhoods by creating accessory dwelling unit (ADU) ordinances, which allow single-family homeowners to legally rent a basement apartment, apartment over a detached garage, or a "tiny house" in their backyard. Portland, Oregon, for instance, has passed such an ADU ordinance viewed as successful at integrating smaller, more affordable apartments throughout the city. San Francisco is similarly seeking to change zoning regulations to allow alternative housing models, such as co-housing and other shared housing options.

Both inclusionary zoning and ADU ordinances are important elements in providing affordable housing but importantly are also effective tools for reducing socioeconomic segregation. This stands in stark contrast to housing projects of the past, which often had the effect of concentrating, segregating, and stigmatizing poverty.

Box 2.5   Best Practices in Multiple Benefits: Housing in St. Louis

St. Louis stands out for its thoughtfully organized and clearly articulated sustainability plan. The plan has concrete objectives listed for each of its major topic areas, an indication of the time horizon in which each objective will be completed, and prioritization of equity throughout the document.

One objective in their plan is to "develop affordable housing in concert with long-range transit and economic development planning." Significantly, the city clearly identifies the many benefits that can be achieved when developing more sustainable affordable housing

(continued)

Box 2.5   (continued)

options (Fig. 2.4). For example, the city considers the development of housing that has embedded supportive services as positively impacting health and educational goals. Similarly, experimenting with new ways to raise money and create partnerships to build sustainable and affordable housing will improve urban infrastructure, the economy, and public health.

The linking of housing with other benefits is a vital step and makes these explicit to all readers of the plan. Further, without actively making these connections, opportunities for collaboration and multiple benefits may be missed. The city additionally calls out specific departments and other stakeholders that will be involved in each goal area.

Source:

City of St. Louis Planning Commission, "City of St. Louis Sustainability Plan," February 6, 2013, https://www.stlouis-mo.gov/government/departments/mayor/documents/upload/STL- Sustainability-Plan.pdf

The Multiple Benefits of Affordable Housing	Urban	Empowerment	Arts	Health	Infrastructure	Education	Prosperity
Goal: Increase access to affordable housing in neighborhoods with access to transit and amenities							
• Develop affordable housing in concert with long range transit and economic development planning	•						•
• Encourage mixed income/use affordable housing in high amenity neighborhoods	•	•					•
• Expand inclusionary policies in order to create economically-integrated communities	•	•					
• Integrate low income housing into market-rate and mixed use developments	•	•					•
• Promote neighborhood stabilization efforts	•	•					
• Experiment with new ways to raise funds and build partnerships to build sustainable and affordable housing	•	•		•	•		•
• Support the development of housing with embedded supportive services	•	•		•		•	
• Offer housing that is energy efficient and environmentally sustainable	•			•			

Fig. 2.4   The multiple benefits of affordable housing policy

WHAT'S MISSING: HOMELESSNESS AND ADDICTION

We found few discussions of two significant community challenges within sustainability plans: homelessness and addiction (Fig. 2.5). Yet, we argue populations experiencing homelessness or addiction are among the most vulnerable in a city. Partnerships between agencies and non-profit organizations which could provide wrap-around services at centralized locations would provide efficiencies and improve outcomes for individuals and their families. Such efforts require ready communication and coordination across agencies and with non-profit actors. Some new developments are

Fig. 2.5 Homeless in San Diego. There are an estimated 10,000 homeless in the metro region, making the city home to the fourth largest number of homeless in the US. Some critics say the city has neglected and ignored its increasing homeless population. (Source: Lisa Benton-Short.)

on the horizon. For instance, Austin is planning to offer individuals who are homeless blockchain technology (or unique digital identifiers) which would help then organize and access records necessary to receive health and housing services and validate job applications.[53] Along similar lines, some are hoping that the nation's opioid crisis might be addressed in part through improvements in electronic medical records infrastructure that "nudge" prescribers away from exposing people to opioids, suggest appropriate short-use prescriptions, and help identify and track overuse and over-prescription patterns.

These examples show promise in addressing the two large and intractable problems of homelessness and addiction which impact individuals, families and communities. These are precisely the kinds of far-reaching challenges may be more effectively addressed with more treatment and space holistic sustainability planning efforts.

Summary

For many cities, equity is an underrepresented facet of sustainability, with some cities substituting the term "equity" for a discussion of more general "social" goals. In addition, we were disappointed to find that few cities appeared to be taking advantage of GIS and other geospatial techniques to explicitly identify communities which require special considerations or assistance. The general conclusion is that cities need to do much better in deliberately addressing equity if they aspire to achieve genuine sustainability.

On the other hand, some cities have thoughtful and specific efforts to increase equity, and some have begun to develop stand-alone equity plans. We argue that equity should be integrated throughout sustainability plans. This is one reason we have selected equity as a cross-cutting theme throughout other sections of this book. Below Table 2.2 summarizes best practices in equity.

Table 2.2 Best practices in equity

Procedural equity

- Name, identify, and locate communities that might require particular outreach and attention
- Remove barriers to participation: hold meetings in languages other than English, at houses of worship and other community facilities, and provide childcare
- Develop a municipal government staff that reflects the demographics of the city's residents

Distribution and access

- Use GIS and other spatial technologies to identify problems of distribution and access of services, amenities, and disamenities
- Prioritize investment and programs in underserved neighborhoods

Education

- Cultivate a community of lifelong learners
- Invest in STEM curriculum that prepares students for high-tech jobs and clean energy
- Develop culturally relevant curriculum and classrooms
- Develop environmental education and outdoor education curriculum

Health

- Develop Health in all Policies
- Recognize the co-benefits of health in other areas of sustainability
- Provide subsidies for full-service grocery stores to locate in food deserts
- Work with corner grocery stores to provide more fresh food options
- Provide financial incentives for Electronic Benefits Transfer (EBT) users to buy produce at farmers markets

Housing

- Create mixed income neighborhoods
- Locate affordable housing near public transportation amenities
- Remove regulatory barriers to affordable housing construction
- Promote inclusionary zoning
- Confront the challenge of homelessness

Notes

1. John Logan, "The Persistence of Segregation in the 21st Century Metropolis," *City Community* 12, no. 2 (2013), https://www.ncbi.nlm.nih.gov/pmc/articles/PMC3859616/.
2. US EPA, "Environmental Justice," Collections and Lists, November 3, 2014, https://www.epa.gov/environmentaljustice.
3. United Church of Christ Commission for Racial Justice, *Toxic Wastes and Race in the United States: A National Report on The Racial and Socio-Economic Characteristics of Communities With Hazardous Waste Sites* (New York: Public Data Access: Inquiries to The Commission, 1987).

4. Nik Heynen, Harold A. Perkins, and Parama Roy, "The Political Ecology of Uneven Urban Green Space: The Impact of Political Economy on Race and Ethnicity in Producing Environmental Inequality in Milwaukee," *Urban Affairs Review* 42, no. 1 (September 1, 2006): 3–25, https://doi.org/10.1177/1078087406290729.

5. Robert J. Brulle and David N. Pellow, "Environmental Justice: Human Health and Environmental Inequalities," *Annual Review of Public Health* 27 (2006): 103–24, https://doi.org/10.1146/annurev.publhealth.27.021405.102124.

6. Stephen Wheeler, *Planning for Sustainability: Creating Liveable, Equitable, and Ecological Communities*, 2nd ed. (New York: Routledge Press, 2013).

7. Rob Krueger and Susan Buckingham, "Towards a 'Consensual' Urban Politics? Creative Planning, Urban Sustainability and Regional Development," *International Journal of Urban and Regional Research* 36, no. 3 (2012): 486–503.

8. Devashree Saha, "Empirical Research on Local Government Sustainability Efforts in the USA: Gaps in the Current Literature," *Local Environment* 14, no. 1 (2009): 17–30; Kent Portney, *Taking Sustainable Cities Seriously: Economic Development, the Environment and Quality of Life in American Cities* (Cambridge MA: The MIT Press, 2003); Lisa Benton-Short, *The National Mall: No Ordinary Public Space* (Toronto: University of Toronto Press, 2016).

9. Hamil Pearsall and Joseph Pierce, "Urban Sustainability and Environmental Justice: Evaluating the Linkages in Public Planning/Policy Discourse," *Local Environment* 15, no. 6 (2010): 571.

10. Stephan Pauleit, "Perspectives on Urban Greenspace in Europe," *Built Environment* 29, no. 2 (2003): 89–93; Barbara Szulczewska and Ewa Kaliszuk, "Challenges in the Planning and Management of 'Greenstructure' in Warsaw, Poland," *Built Environment* 29, no. 2 (2003): 144–56.

11. City of Portland, "The Portland Plan Progress Report," February 2017, 9, http://www.portlandonline.com/portlandplan/index.cfm?c=45722&a=632343.

12. Geraldine Gardner and Emily Yates, "Equity Can Help Cities Win the Sustainability Race," Citiscope, accessed March 20, 2018, http://citiscope.org/habitatIII/commentary/2016/03/equity-can-help-cities-win-sustainability-race.

13. Jessica Chapman, "Social Equity: The Forgotten Leg of Sustainability" (Sustainable City Network, May 12, 2014).

14. City of Portland, "The Portland Plan April 2012," 2012, 17, http://www.portlandonline.com/portlandplan/index.cfm?c=58776.

15. The City of Newark, "The City of Newark Sustainability Action Plan," 2013, 1, https://rucore.libraries.rutgers.edu/rutgers-lib/42923/PDF/1/play/.

16. The City of Newark, 3.
17. MAP 2020, "Mission Action Plan 2020," MEDA, accessed January 16, 2018, http://medasf.org/programs/community-real-estate/mission-action-plan-2020/.
18. City of Grand Rapids, Office of Energy and Sustainability, "FY 2011 Through FY 2015 Sustainability Plan," 2011, 4.
19. Wendy Steele et al., "Planning the Climate-Just City," *International Planning Studies* 17, no. 1 (February 1, 2012): 77, https://doi.org/10.1080/13563475.2011.638188.
20. Pearsall and Pierce, "Urban Sustainability and Environmental Justice: Evaluating the Linkages in Public Planning/Policy Discourse."
21. City of Grand Rapids, Office of Energy and Sustainability, "FY 2011-FY 2015 Sustainability Plan, As Amended April, 2013," April 2013, 17.
22. Virginia Seitz, "A New Model: Participatory Planning for Sustainable Community Development," Reimagine, accessed February 14, 2018, http://www.reimaginerpe.org/node/920.
23. Laura L. Payne, Andrew J. Mowen, and Elizabeth Orsega-Smith, "An Examination of Park Preferences and Behaviors Among Urban Residents: The Role of Residential Location, Race, and Age," *Leisure Sciences* 24, no. 2 (April 1, 2002): 181–98, https://doi.org/10.1080/01490400252900149.
24. Heather Wright Wendell, Joni A. Downs, and James R. Mihelcic, "Assessing Equitable Access to Urban Green Space: The Role of Engineered Water Infrastructure," *Environmental Science & Technology* 45, no. 16 (August 15, 2011): 6731, https://doi.org/10.1021/es103949f.
25. City of Boston, "Greenovate Boston: 2014 Climate Action Plan Update," 2014, 30, https://www.cityofboston.gov/eeos/pdfs/Greenovate%20Boston%202014%20CAP%20Update_Full.pdf.
26. City of Boston, "Greenovate Boston: 2014 Climate Action Plan Update."
27. The City of Dallas, "Sustainability Plan Revisions 2015" (Office of Environmental Quality, May 26, 2015), 23, http://greendallas.net/wp-content/uploads/2016/01/QOL_4_sustainabilityplanrevisions2015_combined_052615.pdf.
28. Office of the Deputy Prime Minister, "Participatory Planning for Sustainable Communities," 2003, http://www.chs.ubc.ca/archives/files/Participatory%20planning%20for%20sustainable%20development.pdf.
29. Engineering National Academies of Sciences, *Pathways to Urban Sustainability: Challenges and Opportunities for the United States* (Washington, DC: The National Academies Press, 2016), 11, https://doi.org/10.17226/23551.
30. The City of Los Angeles, "Sustainable City PLAn: Transforming Los Angeles" (Office of the Mayor, 2017), http://plan.lamayor.org/wp-content/uploads/2017/03/the-plan.pdf.

31. U.S. Department of Education, "Equity of Opportunity," accessed January 16, 2018, https://www.ed.gov/equity.
32. U.S. Department of Education.
33. Salt Lake City Division of Sustainability, "Sustainable Salt Lake: Plan 2015," 2015, 24, http://www.slcdocs.com/slcgreen/sustainablesaltlake_plan2015.pdf.
34. Bob Schroeder, "LibGuides: Culturally Responsive & Inclusive Curriculum Resources: What Is Culturally Responsive Curriculum?," accessed January 16, 2018, https://guides.library.pdx.edu/c.php?g=527355&p=3623937.
35. Salt Lake City Division of Sustainability, "Sustainable Salt Lake: Plan 2015."
36. NPR, "Arizona's Ethnic Studies Ban In Public Schools Goes To Trial," accessed January 16, 2018, https://www.npr.org/2017/07/14/537291234/arizonas-ethnic-studies-ban-in-public-schools-goes-to-trial.
37. DDOE, "DC Environmental Literacy Plan," accessed January 16, 2018, https://doee.dc.gov/service/dc-environmental-literacy-plan.
38. DDOE.
39. Richard Louv, *Last Child in the Woods: Saving Our Children From Nature-Deficit* (Chapel Hill, NC: Algonquin Books, 2008).
40. Jens Ludwig et al., "Neighborhoods, Obesity, and Diabetes — A Randomized Social Experiment," *New England Journal of Medicine* 365, no. 16 (October 20, 2011): 1509–19, https://doi.org/10.1056/NEJMsa1103216.
41. Linda Rudolph et al., "Health in All Policies: A Guide for State and Local Government" (American Public Health Association and Public Health Institute, 2013), https://www.apha.org/~/media/files/pdf/factsheets/health_inall_policies_guide_169pages.ashx.
42. CDC, "CDC - Community Profile - Louisville, KY - Communities Putting Prevention to Work," accessed January 16, 2018, https://www.cdc.gov/nccdphp/dch/programs/communitiesputtingpreventiontowork/communities/profiles/obesity-ky_louisville.htm.
43. City of Louisville, "Sustain Louisville: Louisville Metro Sustainability Plan," March 2013, 28, https://louisvilleky.gov/sites/default/files/planning_design/general/sustain_louisville.pdf.
44. Rudolph et al., "Health in All Policies: A Guide for State and Local Government."
45. City of Richmond, California, "Health in All Policies Report," 2015, http://www.ci.richmond.ca.us/DocumentCenter/View/36978.
46. Boston Public Health Commission, "Health In All Policies," accessed February 14, 2018, http://www.bphc.org/whatwedo/healthy-eating-active-living/health-in-all-policies/Pages/default.aspx.

47. Salt Lake City, "Salt Lake City 2013 Community Food Assessment," 2013, http://www.slcdocs.com/slcgreen/slc_food_assessment_report_complete.pdf.
48. Amanda Behrens Buczynski, Holly Freishtat, and Sarah Buzogany, "Mapping Baltimore City's Food Environment," 2015, http://mdfood-systemmap.org/wp-content/uploads/2015/06/Baltimore-Food-Environment-Report-2015-11.pdf.
49. Joint Center for Housing Studies of Harvard University, "The State of the Nation's Housing," 2017, http://www.jchs.harvard.edu/sites/jchs.harvard.edu/files/harvard_jchs_state_of_the_nations_housing_2017.pdf.
50. Derek Hyra, "Commentary: Causes and Consequences of Gentrification and the Future of Equitable Development Policy," *Cityscape* 18, no. 3 (2016): 169.
51. Robert Hickey, "'Inclusionary Upzoning' Is Gaining Ground. Here's Why.," *Shelterforce* (blog), October 11, 2014, https://shelterforce.org/2014/10/11/inclusionary-upzoning-is-gaining-ground-heres-why/.
52. Urban Land Institute, "Bending the Cost Curve: Solutions to Expand the Supply of Affordable Rentals" (Terwilliger Center for Housing, 2014), http://uli.org/wp-content/uploads/ULI-Documents/BendingCostCurve-Solutions_2014_web.pdf.
53. Karen Hao, "Austin Wants to Use Blockchain Technology to Help the Homeless," Quartz, February 22, 2018, https://qz.com/1212566/bloomberg-philanthropies-selected-35-us-cities-to-test-ideas-for-solving-their-most-pressing-challenges/.

CHAPTER 3

Economic Sustainability

ECONOMIC SUSTAINABILITY: AN INTRODUCTION

A strong economy is the single most pressing priority for nearly every US city.[1] North America's cities, in all their complexity, are elaborate economic engines, which means sustainability is both a challenge and an opportunity. From an economic perspective, the goal of urban sustainability is to create decent jobs, boost incomes, and build the tax base of the city—all with a commitment to secure long-term stability. Sustainability is about taking advantage of new economic opportunities and, equally important, ensuring that environmental and economic benefits are distributed equitably among all citizens. However, at the same time the economy grows, cities must safeguard those aspects of urban living that attract people to the city in the first place. This includes protecting the city's natural environment, preserving historically significant buildings and neighborhoods, reducing or eliminating pollution sources, and improving quality of life. Although economic growth is a major priority, many cities have struggled to figure out how to effectively and genuinely integrate economic strategies with sustainability.

Moving Past the Misconception of Jobs Versus Sustainability

Sustainability challenges us to move past the conceptual framework that prioritizes growth and progress while discounting negative environmental or social impacts. Instead, the economy is seen as dependent on the

© The Author(s) 2019

M. Keeley, L. Benton-Short, *Urban Sustainability in the US*,

https://doi.org/10.1007/978-3-319-93296-5_3

environment for all production inputs and as a sink for all waste outputs. We must also challenge a common misconception that economic development and sustainability are mutually exclusive activities. Critics argue that regulations limiting carbon emissions curb innovation and limit employment opportunities in the private sector. On contrary, a sustainable economy can create jobs. First, green businesses—those that use environmentally benign processes or that manufacture goods that are environmentally benign—employ workers directly, often locally. Second, sustainable practices reduce material and energy consumption, which results in cost savings that can be reinvested in new job creating activities or to make companies more financially secure. Third, sustainable practices improve worker health, productivity, and security, as workplaces become healthier and less toxic. Finally, all of these practices increase competitiveness, which leads to sustained job growth.

Although some cities have embraced the challenge of integrating sustainability and economic development, many cities have not. Moving towards economic sustainability means cities must rethink their economy, what defines progress and success, and how to address the enduring problem of poverty and inequity. This is particularly pressing, since many sustainability experts question the idea of constant steady growth.

Developing a strong green industry sector is also a smart business strategy. A recent Brookings Institute report noted that jobs in the "clean tech" sector experienced growth rates of 8–16 percent from 2003 to 2010. The highest job growth was in wave/ocean power, solar thermal, and wind. A recent study of some 90 percent of the world's leading CEOs suggests that sustainability will become a market and business driver over the next decade. Being seen as sustainable is not only an economic advantage, it is increasingly the new normal for businesses and cities alike. Table 3.1 lists a diversity of green jobs.

Cities' Role in Economic Sustainability

Cities increasingly see the potential in sustainability to generate economic growth. As Memphis acknowledges, "In truth, all of the sustainability strategies are economic development strategies. It is in creating the kind of community that values and invests in parks, bike lanes, walkable neighborhoods, green jobs, recycling, and green buildings that we develop the competitive advantages that lead to our success in growing our economy."[2]

Table 3.1   Examples of the fastest growing green jobs

- Clean car engineers
- Water quality technicians
- Urban growers for sustainable food and restaurant industry
- Recyclers
- Green builders and green design professionals
- Wave energy producers
- Biofuels jobs
- Ecotourism
- Socially responsible investing
- Developing clean technology
- Developing the next generation of electric vehicles
- Constructing energy efficient buildings
- Energy efficiency and building retrofit industry (weatherization, energy auditing and retrofits, building operations, etc.)
- Landscaping and forestry
- Cleaning up brownfields
- Installing solar and wind energy systems,
- Deconstructing, salvaging and reselling building materials
- Electricians building wind turbines
- Pollution control technicians and analysts

Source: Compiled from a variety of green job sites

Some cities have made the economy a major component of their sustainability plan. Portland, St. Louis, Chicago, Detroit, and Grand Rapids have emphasized economic development, job creation, and supporting vital business districts within their visions of a sustainable city.

Other cities including New York City, Chattanooga, and Charleston have integrated economic issues throughout their sustainability agenda, often by framing sustainability projects and policies as opportunities for savings. For example, Chattanooga highlights that it can engage in energy savings and purchase solar energy to offset 2000 metric tons GHG emissions at no additional cost. Palm Springs notes that it will benefit by playing to its strengths in tourism, renewable energy, and clean tech.[3] Similarly, Madison set a goal to build the economy in areas such as renewable and clean energy, eco-tourism, and alternative transportation.[4]

Cities also see the potential to link economic development in addressing critical issues such as climate change. Portland believes that achieving climate protection goals creates local jobs and local wealth (see Box 3.1).[5] By supporting projects such as home winterization and installing solar panels, the city says it will realize energy savings and create new jobs at the same time.

Few cities fully consider connections between equity and economic development. Burlington, however, argues that "providing economic security and meeting the basic needs of all the people of Burlington is fundamental to achieving a sustainable city."[6] The city recognizes that their residents need "superior training, education, and social supports" in a multi-pronged effort to increase access to livable-wage jobs.[7] They specify that "earning a livable wage means having enough income to provide a family with the basic needs of decent housing, sufficient food and clothing, and quality health and child care."[8] Finally, Burlington also proposes the creation of an economic "safety net" for those unable to earn enough to cover their basic needs.[9]

As cities implement plans for economic sustainability, they must turn to creative solutions.

Box 3.1   Best Practices in Implementation and Results: Green Jobs in Portland

If there is a poster child for urban sustainability, Portland, Oregon, is it. Well-known for its progressive planning and "outdoors" lifestyle, the city consistently receives top honors in green city rankings. According to Sustainlane.com, which used a variety of metrics to rank the 50 most populous cities in the United States, Portland's high marks can be explained by the fact it has had a "30-year jump" on the competition. City planners in Portland have been thinking green since the 1970s, when the rest of the country was still embracing the strip mall. The city enacted strict land use policies, implementing an urban growth boundary, encouraging density, and setting a strong precedent for sustainable development.

As successful as Portland has been in implementing a variety of sustainability measures, its economy has remained its Achilles heel. Hampered by a high unemployment rate relative to the rest of the nation, creating jobs has long been a challenge. A new economic development strategy released in 2009 identifies several niche sectors

(continued)

Box 3.1   (continued)

where Portland could take advantage of its strengths. These include streetcar production and the bicycle sector.

The city's streetcar—first built in 2001—has proven very popular with residents and tourists alike, carrying 12,000 riders per day and reducing annual vehicle miles traveled by 70 million. Although the transit system itself provides jobs, Portlanders hope that United Streetcar, a subsidiary of local manufacturer Oregon Iron Works, will manufacture streetcars locally. Currently, dozens of cities are considering adding new streetcar systems. If they do, there may be new business opportunities—and jobs—in Portland.

Another potential growth area for Portland is also related to transportation—bicycles. The city has created more than 300 miles of bike lanes and trails. In Portland, bikes are well-integrated in the "transportation mix"; more workers commute to the office by bike than any other city in the United States. All these bikers have opened the door to dozens of new businesses, from basic maintenance and repair shops to manufacturers of precision components and custom frames to helmet makers like Nutcase, a homegrown company which also caters to the needs of skateboard, inline skating, and scooter enthusiasts. Portland hopes that its early commitment to sustainability will allow it to capitalize on this reputation to meet local and national demands for a changing transportation sector.

Source:

Mikkel Ibsen and Tyler Bump, "The Economic Impact of the Bicycle Industry in Portland," (Portland, Oregon: Bureau of Planning and Sustainability, November 2015), https://www.portlandoregon.gov/bps/article/555482

Financing Sustainable Economic Development: The Rise of Public-Private Partnerships

There is a new fiscal reality: cities are more cash-strapped than ever. The federal government no longer makes the same level of investment in public housing, infrastructure, or social welfare programs. This makes it more difficult for cities to invest in large-scale economic development.

Any new project or program requires capital investment, at least initially. We discovered that some cities lament that a "lack of funding is a significant or very significant factor hindering local sustainability efforts."[10] Even those cities that developed sustainability plans years ago have found it difficult to implement many of their plans because of insufficient funds.

In the face of these constraints, public-private partnerships have become an important way for cities to undertake larger-scale economic development projects such as expanding public transportation networks, providing parks, and constructing convention centers. Public-private partnerships are when a government agency (such as a municipality) and private sector company collaborate to finance, build, and operate projects. The city (public) usually develops the project scope, ensures that it provides public benefits, and controls the land on which the project will be built. The private company typically funds a large part of the project's construction in exchange for receiving the operating profits once the project is complete. Many of the strategies for economic sustainability we discuss in this chapter—brownfield redevelopment, waterfront redevelopment, and mixed-use development projects—are achieved through public-private partnerships.

Taking Action for a Sustainable Economy

In this section, we examine ways in which US cities are advancing a more sustainable economy. We borrow a framework from Boulder, Colorado, which identified three broad strategies that can strengthen a city's economic sustainability:

1. People
2. Place
3. Process[11]

The People-Place-Process framework is a set of interconnected strategies cities are using to attract new businesses, a key to economic growth.[12] We first examine efforts to develop *people* (the workforce). Second, we discuss efforts to create vibrant, connected, mixed-use urban *places* in an effort to attract business and retain highly skilled workers. Third, we focus on *process* and examine ways cities are attracting and growing new businesses generally, and sustainable or "green" business specifically. These efforts often include incentives or a change in city processes and procedures to streamline business activities. Within each of these broad strategies are a diverse range of policies, projects, and other actions cities can take to advance sustainability.

Investing in People

Sustainability experts note that human capital, even more than physical infrastructure, explains which cities succeed and which languish. Many studies suggest that skilled people are better at adapting to changing circumstances and that "skilled cities" are better at attracting innovative businesses and equipped to weather economic crises. Investing in people is critical to long-term economic growth. We note that most US cities focus on educating and/or retraining a workforce as their major investment in people. In contrast, there is less focus on other poverty reduction, health, or support strategies.

Some municipalities want to strengthen their economy and promote equity by providing employment opportunities to the underemployed. Others are more focused on developing a workforce with the skills demanded by high-tech or green industries. Many cities realize the advantages of green jobs in one of two ways; first, as higher-paying jobs that require specialized skills, and second, as inherently local jobs—such as installing and maintaining green infrastructure or solar panels, managing zero waste measures like recycling and composting, or conducting home weatherization audits and improvements. These jobs must be undertaken locally and, thus, cannot be shipped overseas.

Especially as cities try to attract high-tech and green-tech businesses to their communities, they must improve coordination between economic development and workforce development. A best practice is to develop public-private boards and advisory committees, comprised of industry leaders, local educational establishments, city officials, and other stakeholders, to determine the "training gap"—that is, skills and credentials that are needed in important industry sectors—and build training programs.

Another workforce associated best practice is to fund job-readiness training centers for specific higher-skills jobs. Charlotte, NC, partnered with the North Carolina Community College System to provide free training support for employees of companies that created new full-time production and service positions.[13] Madison is developing training pathways in green industries that lead to qualifications and credentials for those from low-income backgrounds which will "train workers in high demand, quasi-technical skills that can be utilized by area businesses and industries, including energy, construction, advanced manufacturing, biotechnology, health, agriculture and IT."[14]

While many programs focus on retooling the skills of adults, including sometimes specifically people of color, women, low-income residents, or those with disabilities, a growing trend is to focus interventions earlier and develop programs for youth. Washington, D.C. stands out for its focus on young, elementary-aged students through improvements in environmental education curriculum and community youth programs.[15] Similarly, St. Louis suggests developing a youth conservation corps to build "skills, confidence, … interest in sustainability, green jobs, healthy eating, … active lifestyles, and…an appreciation for equity and social justice."[16] A sustainable, high-quality green-collar jobs program depends on connecting workers to good, permanent jobs with opportunities for career advancement (minimum-wage jobs do not always offer such opportunities).

An established and successful program along these lines is that run by Greencorps Chicago, a public-private partnership between the Chicago Department of Transportation and WRD Environmental (a locally based sustainable development firm).[17] The Greencorps program has a youth initiative which has provided 2000 high school students experience in bicycle maintenance, horticulture, and urban forestry over the course of its 21-year history. Their adult program has provided over 600 Chicago residents with barriers to employment (including a history of incarceration or other challenges) with "practical experience, academic enhancement, professional development and training in a variety of environmentally-related jobs with skills that are easily transferable to other industries." Program participants are provided wrap-around social services, assistance identifying employment options post-program, and further support as they begin their careers. Between 2012 and 2015, about 70 percent of those who completed the program were employed in fields relevant to their training.[18]

Cities have also taken advantage of either federal or state support for green jobs training. Examples of federal support include grants and other incentives that were available through the 2007 US Green Jobs Act and the 2009 American Recovery and Reinvestment Act. Through the Recovery and Reinvestment Act, the US Department of Labor made $500 million in green jobs training available for states and municipalities.

Box 3.2   Best Practices in Innovation: Doing Economic Development Differently in Detroit

Deindustrialization—the loss of manufacturing employment starting in the 1980s—marked a critical shift in the economies of many US cities. Pittsburg, Syracuse, Buffalo, Cleveland, and Detroit watched as companies fired or relocated workers, closed factories, or left the region or country entirely. These cities were transformed from "industrial" to "rust belt." Many of these cities, once vibrant manufacturing centers, have struggled to reinvent themselves and these impacts reverberate even today.

Federal and state dollars have been used to rebuild these economies. Hundreds of millions of public sector dollars have been invested in Detroit—in housing, transportation infrastructure, and so on—with little input or direct benefit to local community residents. In response, a broad community and labor coalition formed to ensure that investments in public infrastructure and housing in the Detroit area create economic opportunities for residents and local businesses in communities impacted by public project investments. This coalition—Doing Development Differently in Metro Detroit (D4)—is working to create community benefit agreements in several key areas, including residential housing development projects. For example, they worked with Better Buildings for Michigan, a state-sponsored and federally-funded effort to promote mainstream adoption of home energy upgrades, to incorporate language in their neighborhood competitive bid process that encourages bidding building contractors to indicate whether and how they plan to hire local residents. D4 consistently connects infrastructure projects and local community economic development opportunity. This is an example of how integrating sustainability invites a rethinking of economic development.

Source:

Michael DiRamio and Tammy Coxen, "Working toward a Sustainable Detroit: Investing in Sustainable Industry and "Green Collar" Careers for Residents in Detroit," (Detroit Michigan: Detroit Regional Workforce Fund and United Way for Southeastern Michigan, 2012), http://skilledwork. org/wp-content/uploads/2014/01/Working_Towards_a_Sustainable_ Detroit.pdf

A good example is Detroit (also see Box 3.2). The Detroit Regional Workforce Fund secured $8 million from the Recovery Act for green jobs training and programs.[19] In addition, the Detroit Talent Hub is a local business and career development portal that coordinates and brokers employer workforce solutions and services. The hub will pre screen and find qualified job seekers, including graduates of the many green jobs training programs around the Detroit area, and maintain a database of workers with green certification. This database is used to match qualified, ready-to-work candidates with employer job requisitions for both permanent jobs and temp-to-permanent contract staffing. In the Detroit metropolitan area, green jobs grew by 4.7 percent annually during most of the past decade even as the overall number of jobs declined. A glance at the January 2018 website listing green jobs for Detroit lists 272 current postings, including LEED architectural designers, landscaping jobs, and master growers in community gardens.

Investing in Place

Increasingly, cities realize that investment in their natural and built environment is an effective way to enhance the environment, generate jobs, and spur economic growth. We have identified three types of investment that have become a signature element of the best sustainability plans and planning efforts: brownfield redevelopment, waterfront redevelopment, and mixed-use development.

Former Chicago Mayor Richard Daley bemoaned that, "as a nation, we recycle aluminum, glass, and paper, but we don't recycle our most valuable commodity, our land."[20] But what each strategy has in common is precisely this—reusing and redeveloping land, one of the most valuable commodities in a city. Greenfields (undeveloped land) tends to be located on the urban periphery. In contrast, most of the developable land in a city center is on abandoned, neglected, or often contaminated land. Abandoned land is not adding to the tax base and, in many cases, is a burden on city coffers. By redeveloping land, cities create jobs, revitalize neighborhoods, increase the tax base, clean up a legacy of pollution, and often create more dense urban development (which brings a host of environmental benefits, such as less reliance on cars).

Brownfield Redevelopment

A brownfield is property—often a former industrial or commercial site—in which redevelopment is complicated by the presence of actual hazardous substances or by potential contamination. This problem is a complex one. Industry—even quite polluting operations—had traditionally been located in urban areas and were relatively unregulated until late in the twentieth century. As these businesses left for less expensive operating locations, the properties became difficult to sell because of the uncertainty surrounding liability and cleanup of environmental contamination. These often vacant sites decrease a city's tax base, are a blight, and pose potential health and environmental hazards. Although brownfields can be found anywhere, many are concentrated in cities in the Northeast and Midwest that were home to manufacturing activities (and then deindustrialization). Some brownfields are large abandoned industrial sites; others are smaller, including abandoned gas stations or other vacant commercial properties. The EPA estimates there are more than 450,000 brownfields in the United States.

Large brownfields can require extensive rehabilitation and decontamination work, and the costs are considerable. Prospective buyers and developers of contaminated properties may be leery of becoming responsible for cleanup and many of the parties who caused the original contamination (and thus could be liable for cleanup) may be long gone. Yet brownfield redevelopment is a form of land recycling that can restore and regenerate formerly derelict and toxic urban spaces. Remediating brownfields improves health and safety issues and can counter suburban sprawl. In formerly industrial cities, reintegrating brownfields into urban space can promote sustainable development.

In order to encourage the cleanup and redevelopment of these urban sites, the EPA developed the Brownfields Initiative, a successor of sorts to the Superfund. It has encouraged many states and local governments to establish programs that provide tax credits and other financial incentives such as low-interest loans to attract private investment. There are grants to provide funding for brownfield inventories, environmental assessments, remediation job training, cleanup, and community outreach. Many programs prioritize brownfields in low-income areas or economically depressed areas. To date the program has created over 123,000 jobs and leveraged over $23.6 billion dollars towards brownfield cleanup. In fact, a study found every EPA dollar spent leverages approximately $16 in other

Fig. 3.1 Seattle's Gas Works Park was one of the first brownfield redevelopments. One of the distinctive features is that the old gas works industrial buildings were incorporated into the park. (Source: Wikipedia Commons, https://upload.wikimedia.org/wikipedia/commons/e/ea/Seattle_Gas_Works_Park_old_gas_plant2013.jpg)

investments.[21] The study also noted 85 percent of cities said that they had successfully redeveloped a brownfield site.

Brownfields are redeveloped in a variety of ways: for industrial reuse, commercial or residential uses, or as green spaces such as parks, playgrounds, trails, and greenways. Some brownfield sites, such as Seattle's Gas Works Park, which retains old industrial infrastructure, are not just a local amenity but also a tourist attraction (Fig. 3.1). The projects can be modest—the reuse of a single isolated property—or more ambitious such as the revitalization of an entire distressed neighborhood. However, since brownfield policy can be dominated by short-term commercial interests, there is concern that the redevelopment process can be regressive, in that low-income communities, affected worst by the pollution, do not necessarily benefit the most.[22] Further, remediation can sometimes produce new environmental problems.[23]

However, cities have identified the economic, social, and environmental advantages of brownfield redevelopment. For example, St. Louis established priorities for remediation of contaminated sites in strategic locations.[24] In an innovative step, St. Louis discusses using "gap financing" as a way to leverage private funds and facilitate the development of key projects.[25] Gap financing may provide a shorter-term loan, which allows the project to move forward and gives the borrower more time to make full payment, or secure a long-term loan—either of which might be easier to accomplish as the development gets closer to completion. The St. Louis Brownfields Cleanup Fund provides these low-interest loans to encourage brownfield redevelopment within identified empowerment zones and in places that help meet other goals, such as providing long-term jobs, engaging the community, and providing environmental amenities like stormwater management.

One example of effective brownfield redevelopment is Burlington, Vermont. The state of Vermont and the City of Burlington have incentivized brownfield redevelopments through a statewide Brownfields Revitalization Fund, tax credits for Downtowns and Village Centers, and Community Development Block Grants. This has led to the successful redevelopment of numerous brownfields in the Burlington area, including:

- Architectural Salvage Warehouse: abandoned warehouse into fully redeveloped Architectural Salvage operation
- River View Apartments: former gas station into affordable housing and office space
- Multigenerational Center: former dry-cleaning facility into senior center/daycare/community center facility
- Thelma Maple Housing Coop: former roofing company site into affordable housing

Box 3.3   Best Practices in Multiple Benefits: Brownfields in New York City

New York City's sustainability plan confronts the challenge of brownfield remediation and reuse in some depth, with 11 goals relating to this issue. Their initiatives were notable, because, in addition to brownfields reuse, their programs are constructed to provide other benefits as well, such as encouraging small and medium-sized businesses and providing job training program in the growing "green-collar" brownfield remediation field.

Brownfield remediation is a process with much uncertainty, since the types and extent of contamination is often unclear. A number of efforts are targeted at reducing risk and increasing the number of

(*continued*)

Box 3.3 (continued)

developers willing to work on brownfields. Actions to this end include expanding the Brownfield Cleanup Program and working with financial lending institutions to limit the financial risks associated with brownfield redevelopment. The city also hopes to provide free consulting to small and medium-sized developers to expand the number of firms undertaking brownfield redevelopment projects. Finally, the city is partnering with area non-profits to provide environmental training programs including brownfield remediation job training. The city's *BrownfieldWORKS!* program subsidizes the wages of program graduates for up to six months.

Source:

The City of New York, "PlaNYC A Greener, Greater New York," 2011, p. 56. http://www.nyc.gov/html/planyc/downloads/pdf/publications/planyc_2011_planyc_full_report.pdf

Waterfront Redevelopment

At the height of the industrial era, waterfront locations were the site of warehouses, factories, or docks. Water quality was abysmal, and rivers often stank from a mix of untreated sewage and dumped chemicals. Considered dangerous and polluted, these areas were frequently cut off from the rest of city by rail yards and highways. Deindustrialization and new shipping technologies left many cities with abandoned warehouses, buildings, and unused port facilities on their waterfronts. Progress was made in implementing the Clean Water Act, and water quality improved. Beginning in the 1980s, waterfront redevelopment became a widespread strategy in urban planning and is now among the most prominent urban efforts to simultaneously revitalize both the economy and the environment.[26]

Waterfronts, once the city's "back door," have become focal points and are regaining "their rightful role as prized public treasures."[27] Cities in the United States, and around the world, have transformed their waterfronts into vibrant, public spaces that offer a wide range of activities for people to enjoy, attracting both locals and tourists. Waterfront redevelopment takes a number of forms, some focused on increasing parkland and recreational trials, others on mixed-use retail and housing, and still others on creating tourist destinations or revitalized commercial space.

Fig. 3.2 A view of Boston's Waterfront. The city has developed several areas of its waterfront starting in 1984. The revitalization has been successful in creating a highly active district where visitors stroll freely around the wharves, the old buildings, and boats. (Source: Lisa Benton-Short.)

The waterfronts of Boston and Pittsburgh have become the new festival spaces filled with sports stadiums, restaurants, and hotels (Fig. 3.2). Even smaller cities such as Austin, Buffalo, Charleston, Cleveland, Savannah, and Syracuse have transformed their harbors, lakes, or riverfronts. San Antonio's Riverwalk is a vibrant waterfront, despite several characteristics that make its success unlikely: it was an early waterfront redevelopment project, includes much flood prevention hardscape and infrastructure, and is a grade below street level. Yet, many downtown businesses feature their proximity to this amenity and have created separate river entrances to their properties.

Baltimore's Inner Harbor is often cited as a model US waterfront redevelopment project. It has become the city's gathering place: home to the national aquarium, two sports stadiums, hotels, restaurants, museums, high-rise condominiums, and hotels (Fig. 3.3). A 2012 study of Baltimore's Inner Harbor has estimated the development that year created over $2.3 billion in tourism and business activity, created 21,000 jobs in the city and state, and increased tax revenue by $102 million.[28]

Fig. 3.3 The success of Baltimore's Inner Harbor, one of the earliest waterfront redevelopment projects in the United States, has influenced many cities to redevelop their waterfronts. (Source: Lisa Benton-Short.)

Such large-scale development as in Baltimore is not without its costs. The reconstruction of Baltimore's Inner Harbor cost $2.9 billion, and, while it does generate tourism revenue, there are hidden social costs. The diversion of funds to Baltimore's Inner Harbor contrasts with the city's poor public school system and the perceived decline in many public services. In some cases, waterfront development is part of a valorization of selected parts of the urban landscape that allow for the further enrichment of real estate interests, sometimes at the expense of social welfare programs. While Baltimore's Inner Harbor flourishes, many inner city neighborhoods continue to experience high crime rates, population loss, and housing abandonment.

Despite the substantial costs, waterfront transformations represent a dramatic story of economic and environmental recovery. However, cities must work within public-private partnerships to ensure that waterfront development integrates equity—affordable housing, for example—and that other areas of the city are not neglected.

Mixed-Use Development

Mixed-use development has been a strategy for economic redevelopment since the 1990s and is frequently a central part of any large-scale urban redevelopment project. Mixed-use developments blend two or more uses, such as residential, commercial, cultural, institutional, or industrial uses. This marks a significant change from traditional zoning practices that separated use types.

Planners now know that "mixed-development that promotes a walkable built environment can help revitalize a downtown, increase private investment, lead to higher property values, promote tourism, and support the development of a good business climate."[29] This myriad of economic benefits exists largely because walkability is desirable. One survey indicated that 80 percent of 10–24-year-olds and 60 percent of those over 50 want to live in walkable neighborhoods. Many cities see that mixed-use developments can help them attract young, educated residents (the "creative class"). They feature walkable neighborhoods, the arts and design, and cultural opportunities in an effort to attract innovative businesses and their future employees.[30] Walkable areas also attract pedestrians and consumers. These areas feature higher office, residential, and retail rents and higher retail revenue.[31] Given all these trends, it is not surprising that a majority of venture capital is going to walkable urban areas and that the creation of vibrant, mixed-use urban centers and transit-oriented development strategies (a related idea discussed in Chap. 5) are seen as critical to economic redevelopment.[32]

Washington, D.C. stresses that supporting the development of vibrant urban centers could provide new economic opportunity for neighborhoods, a high quality of life for residents, and help accommodate a growing population.[33] There are numerous mixed-use developments in the District and more under construction. Even smaller cities, such as Burlington, see advantages in allowing development to "build up, not out" because it creates an environment that is safe, accessible, and attractive while also allowing for scenic viewscapes.[34]

Since 2010, there has been a surge of mixed-use developments around the country—it is the "new paradigm" of urban planning. Many of the redeveloped brownfields or waterfronts discussed previously have been built as mixed-use. The success of mixed-use development has influenced other cities to prioritize the creation of mixed-use urban centers and to include mixed-use development in sustainability plans. In 2017, Salt Lake City unveiled its plans for a new nine-acre downtown mixed-use redevelopment project to "revive" a challenged neighborhood, bringing "mixed-use…with retail, commercial and residential developments in an area that's already well served by all major public transit modes." The planned development was touted as "the most transit-connected neighborhood in Utah."[35] The design includes start-up micro-unit apartments, business incubator space, creative office space, affordable and market-rate apartments, and ground-level retail and restaurant space. St. Louis plans to reinforce the City's Central Corridor as the dynamic "heart" of the region and "encourage a diversity of office, convention, hospitality, tourism, shopping, cultural, institutional, arts, entertainment, production, and dense residential uses."[36]

In New York City, the Time Warner Center consists of two 750 feet towers bridged by a multi-story atrium containing upscale retail shops (Fig. 3.4). Construction began in November 2000 and was largely

Fig. 3.4 New York's Time Warner Center is an example of mixed-use development. (Source: "Time Warner Center", Wikipedia/Wikimedia commons, (created May 13, 2010), accessed April 10, 2018, https://upload.wikimedia.org/wikipedia/commons/7/72/Time_Warner_Center_May_2010.JPG)

completed by 2003. The development encircles the western side of Columbus Circle and straddles the border between Midtown and the Upper West Side. The total floor area of 2.8 million square feet is occupied by office space, residential condominiums, and the Mandarin Oriental hotel. The Shops at Columbus Circle, an upscale shopping mall, is located in a curving arcade at the base of the building, with a full-service Whole Foods grocery store on the lower level. Other notable mixed-use development includes The Streets of Buckhead in Atlanta, the River City building in Chicago, and the Gateway in Salt Lake City.

Mix-use developments and the redevelopment and/or remediation of brownfields and waterfronts are now key strategies in economic sustainability. We point out that the use of these types of development encourages economic diversification in neighborhoods and the creation of economically integrated communities via the inclusion of affordable housing along with other development projects.

Process: Attracting and Nurturing (Green) Businesses

Cities like Detroit have taken a pragmatic approach to sustainability, recognizing and prioritizing one of the most pressing, immediate needs of the city and its populace: steady, living-wage jobs. In 2013,

---

Box 3.4   Best Practices in Implementation and Results: Historic Preservation in Charleston and Savannah

Even as cities are reinventing themselves to attract new businesses and tourism and reconfiguring their economies for a new and hopefully more sustainable future, preservation is more important than ever. Historic preservation is an important part of urban sustainability because it contributes to creating a community's sense of place. Those things that make an area special and unique draw investment and can be used to rally a community together to participate in sustainability efforts. Heritage and place can have an "anchoring" effect, especially at a time "characterized by high mobility and virtualization."[a] Further, "individuals whose identities are based, at least in part, on the place where they reside" are more likely to "engage in environmentally responsible behaviors."[b]

(*continued*)

Box 3.4   (continued)

The most important piece of historic preservation legislation in the United States is the National Historic Preservation Act of 1966. It established new laws, authorized funds for preservation activities, and encouraged locally regulated historic districts. It went beyond merely protecting landmarks to recognizing a variety of historically and architecturally significant buildings, sites, structures, districts and objects.

Charleston and Savannah are "belles" of the South. About 100 miles apart, they have long been regional rivals. But these cities have something in common: a strong legacy of preservation. Charleston has the oldest historic district in the country (dating back to the 1930s). It has carefully preserved the city's grand public buildings, as well as the mansions along the Battery, and the famous Rainbow Row. While not as old as Charleston, Savannah's historic district is much larger, stretching from the waterfront to neighborhoods where homes with gas lanterns and intricate iron work sit beneath the Spanish moss.

Both Charleston and Savannah have achieved international reputations for historic preservation and have been able to turn that into a multi-billion-dollar tourist industry.

Charleston does an exemplary job of developing a motivation for its sustainability initiatives and reminding citizens of the value of the city's physical history:

Before the Civil War, wealth from rice, lumber, and trade transformed Charleston into a prosperous community. Today, the abandoned rice fields attract wildlife, and Charleston's wealth is preserved in its historic buildings and landscape… Charleston's history is intertwined with the lushness of the Low country environment, and this historical reliance on the environment has led to a culture of preservation and a respect for nature.[c]

Charlestown further connects historic preservation and environmental conservation to tourism, and pronounces these efforts as a cultural

(continued)

Box 3.4   (continued)

tradition. "Sustainability is a Charleston tradition. We may not have been using the word 'sustainable' for long, but Charleston has been at the forefront of this movement since 1931, when the City passed the nation's first historic preservation ordinance."[d]

Sources:

[a]Claudia Manenti, "Sustainability and place identity" Procedia Engineering 21, (2011): 1104–1109, https://doi.org/10.1016/j.proeng.2011.11.2117

[b]Donelson R. Forsyth, Mark van Vugt, Garrett Schlein, Paul A. Story, "Identity and Sustainability: Localized Sense of Community Increases Environmental Engagement" Analyses of Social Issues and Public Policy 15, no. 1 (June 2015): 233–252, https://doi.org/10.1111/asap.12076

[c]Charleston Green Committee, "Charleston Green Plan," April 2007, 2, http://www.charlestongreencommittee.com/charlestongreenplan2010.pdf

[d]Charleston Green Committee, 3.

Detroit became the largest US city in history to enter "Chapter 9 bankruptcy" and had an unemployment rate that peaked at 18 percent. Detroit recognized that "we must re-energize Detroit's economy to increase job opportunities for Detroiters within the city and strengthen the tax base."[37] An incubator that the city created to start new businesses is featured in the next section. Similarly, for Grand Rapids, a major concern was "increasing the number of permanent jobs, and those that pay higher than the Cost of Living Index."[38] To achieve this goal, Grand Rapids planned to "increase the number of new businesses locating in the city, particularly in the fields of green or applied clean technology."[39]

Indeed, other cities have focused their efforts specifically on attracting "sustainable" or "green" businesses to their jurisdictions. The kinds of businesses that fall into these categories are varied. The term may refer to businesses overtly contributing to an environmental agenda—such as constructing or installing solar panels or producing plastic paneling from post-consumer plastic waste. Others use the term loosely to mean any business that balances social, economic, and environmental concerns in their business practices. There is great potential for economic growth and vitality by attracting green business (Table 3.2).

One example of a new green business is the "green" factory operated by Method in Chicago—the first new factory to be built on the South Side in nearly 30 years.[40] The company was attracted to Chicago in part by state and city tax incentives totaling $9.6 million. The new factory was designed by William McDonough + Partners (McDonough co-authored the book *Cradle to Cradle: Remaking the Way We Make Things*, an early manifesto on how to design products and systems so that materials can be reused). The factory was sited near a rail line and designed to carefully minimize its water and energy usage (part of its energy comes from a wind turbine), and its roof hosts a 75,000 sq ft rooftop farm which distributes fresh food locally. Despite the new factory's many green features, we note that the factory received large state and city incentives yet only has 66 direct employees and creates another 20 jobs through a subcontractor.[41]

Another major trend we have identified is that many municipalities are trying to attract clean technology or alternative energy companies. The clean energy sector is now creating new jobs 12 times faster than almost

Table 3.2 Policy options to drive demand for green-collar jobs and businesses

Public sector investment:

- Energy efficiency retrofits of public buildings
- Solar or other renewable energy systems on public buildings financed with capital budgets, bonds, or performance contracting
- New public buildings constructed to green standards
- Public transit infrastructure
- Green products and services from local providers

Incentives or requirements to drive private sector investment:

- Tax incentives, rebates, reduced fees, or streamlined permitting for private building owners that invest in energy efficiency, renewable energy, or green building
- Technical assistance or innovative financing for private investment in renewal energy, efficiency, green building, alternative vehicles, or green space
- Green building codes, energy conservation ordinances, or other requirements for new green buildings or retrofits of existing buildings
- Land use and infrastructure policies to support green manufacturing companies

Source: Apollo Alliance and Green For All, 2008. *Green-Collar Jobs in America's Cities.* At, https://www. cows.org/_data/documents/1165.pdf, January 2018

any other sector in the American economy (Fig. 3.5). Employment in the renewable energy and energy efficiency sectors in both the United States and abroad continued to experience growth and today accounts for some 3.3 million jobs directly (by comparison, 2.9 million work directly in the fossil fuel industry).[42]

Cities increasingly recognize these opportunities. Miami Beach states that its first economic stability indicator is the number of green economy businesses located within its city limits.[43] The rationale behind this indicator is that: "community resilience depends on a diverse economic base that is supportive of emerging technologies."[44] Chicago wants to establish itself "as a hub for the growing sustainable economy" and sets a goal of "recruit[ing] companies and individuals with the most innovative clean energy and sustainability solutions to Chicago."[45] Palm Springs is trying to incubate, grow, and attract new sustainable industries by focusing on innovation, renewable energy production, clean technology, green products and services, and climate change.[46] Renewable energy promotes local businesses, because the fossil fuels are not locally sourced, while jobs working with renewable energy are.[47]

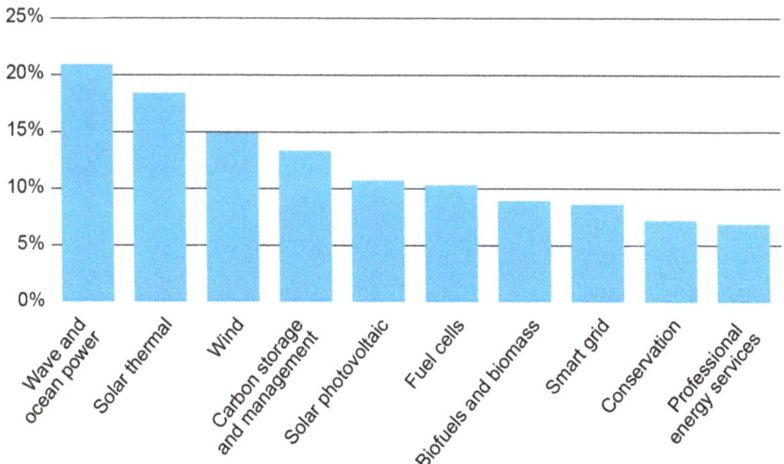

Fig. 3.5 Percentage increase in jobs in the clean energy sector since 2010. (Source: Adapted from "5 of the Fastest Growing Jobs in Clean Energy" US Department of Energy, Office of Energy Efficiency & Renewable Energy, accessed February 2, 2018, https://www.energy.gov/eere/articles/5-fastest-growing-jobs-clean-energy)

Municipalities propose a variety of strategies for attracting high-tech, sustainable businesses to their communities. Figure 3.6 summarizes one best practice in stimulating green-collar jobs in the energy sector. Financial incentive such as offering tax credits is a common practice but is increasingly under scrutiny. As cities compete for firms looking to relocate, incentive packages become more generous for business and potentially more costly for cities. A recent study found that counties and cities nationwide were providing over $80 billion each year to companies.[48] We suggest that, as cities use incentives, they should ensure the appropriate use of funds and the quality and sustained nature of jobs provided. One way to do this is to include a provision that city funding must be repaid if job creation and quality standards are not met.[49]

Another trend is for cities to brand themselves as hubs for innovation. For example, Chicago proposed hosting a major clean energy conference every year. To date the city has hosted dozens of conferences and trade shows on energy, including the annual Illinois Renewable Energy Conference. Others aspire to facilitate partnerships with local universities and synergies via environmental business clusters.[50] Washington, D.C. believes one way to stimulate a green economy is to leverage anchor institutions as partners. Anchor institutions are place-based institutions that are firmly rooted in a community (and so will not relocate). They typically include "eds and meds" (universities and hospitals), but in the capital city this also include many cultural institutions

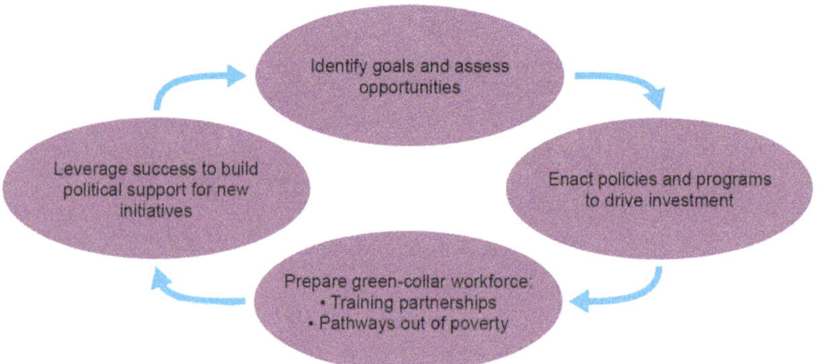

Fig. 3.6 Ways to stimulate green-collar jobs in the energy sector. (Source: By Authors.)

(the Smithsonian Museums) and government institutions. D.C. was the first US city to form a compact with the entirety of the city's higher education sector—eight colleges and universities—and its local government to advance sustainability.[51]

Another key element in attracting green businesses is increasing the demand for sustainable products. Boston seeks to increase demand for green services by raising city standards.[52] Similarly, San Jose wants to provide opportunities for locally produced sustainable products. Madison intends to "map and develop supply chains for sustainable businesses," which will also support local businesses and provide well-paying jobs.[53]

Incubating (Green) Start-Ups

An important best practice is nurturing the entrepreneurial spirit of residents. Incubators, accelerators, and co-working spaces provide a variety of services start-ups need such as professional or collaborative workspace, networking opportunities, business support services, and education, training, and mentorship. Some specialize in a specific industry and provide required, specialized infrastructure, such as industrial kitchens or a digital device-bar, where software developers can work on multiple platforms. One workshare company is Cove which operates in Boston and Washington, D.C. and has several locations in each city. Cove advertises itself to companies as a way to cut operating costs, increase employee happiness, and enable flexibility. Cove offers Wi-Fi, printing, beverages, and a range of spaces—meeting rooms, quiet spaces, and social spaces included with monthly memberships starting as low as $80 a month.

Grand Rapids and Madison were two cities that stood out for their creative attention to nurturing small, local businesses. Madison identified an opportunity to diversify its economy by promoting and supporting entrepreneurs using what they call "the informal economy"—transactions through websites like Craigslist, eBay, and Etsy. They also suggested a need to research the kinds of resources and activities that could help move these entrepreneurs towards a more "standard business formation."[54] Grand Rapids launched neighborhood micro-local business enterprises to create a nurturing environment for such businesses.[55] Together, Grand Rapids and Neighborhood Ventures, a local NGO, provide access to start-up and expansion capital. One particularly innovative strategy, shared by Grand Rapids Mayor Rosalynn Bliss, "is to accelerate five African American-owned businesses that are up and running and could be growing faster" as a way to identify and remove the systematic barriers that prevent such businesses from thriving.[56] This strategy is important from an equity perspective, to ensure that all residents are afforded opportunities to contribute to the economic life of the city. This kind of close study is essential to determine municipal processes that need to be changed or developed to support the growth of small business generally.

This strategy has been used in other innovative ways as well. In Chicago, the city supported University of Chicago's development of a start-up incubator by providing $20 million of seed money directed to entrepreneurial development of the city's South Side, an area of the city identified as in need of economic development assistance.[57] Detroit helped support the creation of the Green Garage, which opened in 2016. Currently, the Green Garage hosts more than 50 small businesses as they develop their ideas and business plans for $50 a month. Detroit took advantage of a $2.1 million grant from the Southeast Michigan Advanced Energy Storage Systems Initiative to support small business development strategies in the rapidly emerging advanced energy storage systems industry cluster. This cluster has strong ties to the automotive industry but also to defense, alternative energy, and other strengths the city is interested in developing.

Box 3.5   Best Practices in Multiple Benefits: Green Incubation in New York City

New York City has a strong record of supporting start-up opportunities within the city. One of these is La Marqueta, which supports many of the city's sustainability goals. The city modernized an underutilized historic market space in East Harlem (the home of one of the city's largest Latino populations) and included fully equipped kitchen facilities. The city leases this space at significant subsidy to small neighborhood ventures, by providing maintenance staff, and even subsidizes utilities costs.

The main tenant of the facility is HBK Incubates, a kitchen incubator with "two production kitchens, two prep kitchens, a chocolate kitchen, a specialty production space and dough room, ...dry and cold storage facilities...(and) a demonstration kitchen available for classes and other events." HBK has specialized in helping people with "small, artisanal, and ethnic food businesses make the transition

(*continued*)

Box 3.5   (continued)

from working in their home kitchens to using fully-equipped, professional facilities," providing classes in professional baking, food safety, and business skills.

In addition to developing new small business ventures, the market has become an important resource in a neighborhood with a paucity of healthy food options, but also a destination for ethnic foods and related dry goods not available elsewhere in the city.

Sources:

"HBK Incubates," New York City Economic Development Corporation, accessed December 2, 2017, https://www.nycedc.com/program/hbk-incubates

"La Marqueta," New York City Economic Development Corporation, accessed December 2, 2017, https://www.nycedc.com/project/la-marqueta

Green Tourism Industry

Tourism is an important part of the service sector of many cities yet brings both pros and cons for cities. On the one hand, tourists spend money. On the other hand, visitors and their transportation choices have significant environmental impacts. For these reasons, some cities are examining strategies to increase tourism generally, and green tourism specifically, as well as to make the stays of these visitors more environmentally sustainable. Green tourism itself has many definitions and implications, ranging from reduced environmental footprints, to investing in local residents and community, or encouraging guests to participate in local cultural and natural experiences. Most of the efforts at including tourism within municipal plans for sustainability that we have observed are in the early stages of development.

The most common and straightforward efforts in this area include marketing environmental and cultural attractions to visitors and distributing information about green businesses in the area. However, even cities like Palm Springs and Miami Beach—resort towns famous for their unique environments—have made surprisingly little progress in promoting green tourism and capitalizing on ecotourism opportunities.

Some small-scale efforts deserve note. Chattanooga launched a Green Lodging Certification Program, which has certified 19 hotels and 10 restaurants in the hopes of attracting "savvy tourist groups."[58] Bend, Oregon, is hoping to capitalize on sustainability tourism. The city is home to a large-scale photovoltaic solar panel manufacturer, Advanced Energy, and a locally owned coffee roaster, Strictly Organic. Downtown, the Oxford Hotel made national headlines as an "Eco-Chic" boutique, boosting tourism. Bend is also one of the fastest growing cities in Oregon, demonstrating that being an "eco" destination can boost a city's reputation.

Charleston is another city that established goals to make tourism—a vital economic sector in that city—more sustainable by limiting vehicle use in congested tourist areas.[59] The city outlines the clear economic benefits this action would have on tourism, such as making the city more convenient for visitors, becoming attractive to tourists seeking "green" options, improving walkability, and increasing property values. They plan to increase public transit, place vehicle restrictions on some streets, and provide rental bikes and green (or low-emission) taxis.

Help Businesses Adopt Greener Practices and Save Money
We see a need to engage existing businesses in the adoption of greener practices so that they can enjoy cost savings and better contribute to sustainability objectives. Common efforts include speakers series or developing a "green handbook" for business owners. Other cities go farther and offer sustainability certification programs, as Portland does. Chicago hosts competitive challenges like the "Green Office Challenge" and "Chicago Sustainable Industries," and the city hopes to double the number of offices and business participating in those initiatives.[60]

Finally, Madison is helping existing businesses transition to the green or clean tech economy by identifying ways to help them "overcome market barriers" to adopting green practices.[61] For instance, the city suggests targeting businesses in industries that have the potential to retool to produce sustainable products, or that are high energy users that could benefit from energy efficiency efforts or transitioning to renewable energy sources. Madison has also organized the Madison Green Economic Symposium as a venue for sharing best practices.[62]

Box 3.6   Best Practices in Education and Communication: Portland's Sustainability Work Certification

The city of Portland, Oregon offers a "Sustainability at Work" certification to incentivize businesses to adopt sustainability practices. They match Portland businesses and non-profits with a sustainability

(*continued*)

Box 3.6   (continued)

advisor—at no cost. Advisors learn about the business and workplace culture and help create strategies that conserve resources, improve efficiency, save money, and provide a healthy and quality workspace for employees.

The Sustainability at Work program offers three levels of certification (Certified, Silver, and Gold) that recognize a business's positive impact on the environment and the community.

The program cites the following certification benefits:

- Use of the award logo in marketing materials
- Social media announcement by Sustainability at Work
- Listing in local newspaper advertisements
- Listing in the business directory
- Spotlight at sustainability events
- Award plaques

To date several hundred companies have certified their businesses.

Source:

"Sustainability at Work," The City of Portland, accessed November 11, 2018, https://www.portlandoregon.gov/sustainabilityatwork/62171

What's Missing: The Sharing Economy

The sharing economy is a recent enough innovation that it is absent in most plans for sustainability. In fact, it appears that many cities are just starting to consider the opportunities and challenges that these "disruptive technologies" may present their cities.[63] Although sharing a ride or having a guest in your spare room is not new, the shared economy is a new proposition in which "citizens have gained the power to call and track a ride, rent out their homes, and share goods instead of purchasing more than they need or can afford."[64] It is made possible by a widespread use of social media, constant (although inequitable) online access, and a changing social predisposition to goods and services. Examples of the sharing economy are all around us and include Airbnb, Lyft, Uber, Etsy, and TaskRabbit. Websites like Airbnb or SnapGoods match up owners and renters. Smartphones and GPS systems allow consumers to request rides from Uber or Lyft on demand, while PayPal and Venmo are online payment systems that handle the billing.

While elements of a sharing economy dovetail with ideas of sustainability and the use of fewer resources (i.e. everyone need not own a car), they also pose many new challenges to cities.[65] While some point to increased ride services in neighborhoods that taxis rarely ventured, others are concerned that residents without cell phones (including the elderly) or credit cards will not have access to ride-share services. Other potential challenges exist, particularly with regard to regulation and fairness. For example, New York City's yellow cabs pay a 50-cent surcharge per ride that helps to subsidize the subway system. Ride-sharing companies like Lyft and Uber do not yet pay that tax. Dockless bikes (discussed in Chap. 5) have streamlined bikesharing, yet have cluttered sidewalks in some areas.

Very early research indicates that there may be unintended consequences of sharing economies, which have quickly and dramatically impacted the urban experience. For instance, one study of the impacts of Airbnb in New York City suggests that this has removed between 7000 and 13,500 housing units from the city's long-term rental market, resulting in a 1.4 percent ($380) median rent increase in one year.[66] Results from the first studies of the impacts of ride-sharing on public transportation ridership are mixed, but there is concern that ride-sharing might be contributing to public transportation ridership declines in some cities.[67] More research is clearly needed.

How can cities embrace these platforms and their benefits while also regulating them for safety, making sure service provision is equitable, and capturing revenue from this new kind of economic activity? One best practice that we can suggest is that cities negotiate with sharing economy providers for at least partial access to data that companies collect on use patterns (which companies naturally view as proprietary), which can help cities respond to and regulate the sharing economy. Several cities, including Cincinnati and Washington, D.C., have successfully done so. According to the US-based National League for Cities, the sharing economy presents an oft-changing regulatory environment that requires cities to be nimble and re-evaluate regulations on a regular basis.[68]

Summary

Not surprisingly, economic development is the single most pressing priority for nearly every US city.[69] While most cities include "economics" in their definition of sustainability, we discovered some cities have no substantive discussion of the economy within their sustainability plans. We believe this is a missed opportunity. In addition, cities that claim to have developed a "sustainability" plan but mostly focus on environmental issues reinforce a false notion that one "E" is more important than the others and fail to create a holistic, integrated vision for their city that addresses economic concerns together with concerns about environment and equity.

The challenge is how best to advance economic growth and development while simultaneously promoting other aspects of sustainability. Cities must recognize that sustainable economy requires investment in people, place, and process and that the best practices integrate economic development strategies with equity and environment. Table 3.3 identifies the important trends and best practices.

Table 3.3 Best practices in economic sustainability

Equity and (green) jobs programs
- Create public-private steering committee to identify in-demand skill sets
- Enhance environmental education and skills training at elementary school level

Land development and redevelopment
- Create dense, mixed-use, vibrant downtown, or neighborhood centers
- Incentivize infill and brownfield redevelopment through information about availability and reducing development risks
- Redevelop waterfronts
- Leverage public-private partnerships

Attracting (green) business
- Attract and retain young professionals and the creative class through place-based approaches
- Support emerging technologies
- Work with anchor institutions to create environmental business clusters
- Map and develop supply chains to increase the demand for sustainable products

Incubating (green) start-ups
- Support "neighborhood micro-local business enterprises"
- Remove the systematic barriers to small business success

Greening existing businesses
- Target energy efficiency outreach efforts to high energy users

Notes

1. ICMA, "Nearly a Third of Local Governments Have Adopted Sustainability Plans," icma.org, March 21, 2016, https://icma.org/articles/nearly-third-local-governments-have-adopted-sustainability-plans.
2. Memphis-Shelby County, "Sustainability Shelby Implementation Plan," 2008, 119, https://www.sustainableshelby.com/sites/default/files/Implementation%20Plan/01_SustainableShelbyImplementationPlan.pdf.
3. City of Palm Springs, "The Palm Springs Path to a Sustainable Community Draft," March 25, 2009, 18, http://www.palmspringsca.gov/home/showdocument?id=5610.
4. The City of Madison, "The Madison Sustainability Plan: Fostering Environmental, Economic, and Social Resistance," 2011, https://www.cityofmadison.com/sustainability/documents/SustainPlan2011.pdf. 44.
5. City of Portland, "The Portland Plan April 2012," 2012, 17, http://www.portlandonline.com/portlandplan/index.cfm?c=58776.
6. City of Burlington, "The Burlington Legacy Project," October 2000, 14, https://www.burlingtonvt.gov/sites/default/files/CEDO/Legacy_Project/Legacy%20Action%20Plan.pdf.
7. City of Burlington, 14.
8. City of Burlington, 13.
9. Wanda Heines, "Legacy Action Plan- 2013 Amendment" (Burlington Legacy Project, 2013), 5, https://www.burlingtonvt.gov/uploadedFiles/BurlingtonVTgov/Departments/Legacy/The_Legacy_Plan/Legacy%20Action%20Plan%20Update-all%206%20sectors%201-31-13.pdf.
10. ICMA, "Nearly a Third."
11. The City of Boulder, "Economic Sustainability Strategy," October 29, 2013, 9, https://www-static.bouldercolorado.gov/docs/Final_ESS_Adopted_by_Council_-_reduced_file_size-1-201312121401.pdf.
12. Christiana McFarland et al., "Local Economic Conditions 2017: The Untold Story of the Varied Middle" (The National League of Cities, 2017), http://nlc.org/sites/default/files/2017-08/local-economic-conditions-2017_6.pdf. 3.
13. Charlotte Regional Partnership, "Charlotte USA - Workforce," accessed December 2, 2017, http://charlotteusa.com/business-info/workforce/.
14. The City of Madison, "The Madison Sustainability Plan: Fostering Environmental, Economic, and Social Resistance," 2011, 53, https://www.cityofmadison.com/sustainability/documents/SustainPlan2011.pdf.
15. Sustainable DC, "Sustainability DC," 2012, 36, https://sustainable.dc.gov/sites/default/files/dc/sites/sustainable/page_content/attachments/DCS-008%20Report%20508.3j.pdf.

16. City of St. Louis Planning Commission, "City of St. Louis Sustainability Plan," February 6, 2013, 65, https://www.stlouis-mo.gov/government/departments/mayor/documents/upload/STL-Sustainability-Plan.pdf.

17. Greencorps Chicago, "Greencorps Chicago," accessed December 2, 2017, https://greencorpschicago.org/.

18. City of Chicago, "2015 Sustainable Chicago Action Agenda: 2012–2015 Highlights and Look Ahead.," December 2015, 5, https://www.cityofchicago.org/content/dam/city/progs/env/Sustainable_Chicago_2012-2015_Highlights.pdf.

19. Michael DiRamio and Tammy Coxen, "Working toward a Sustainable Detroit: Investing in Sustainable Industry and 'Green Collar' Careers for Residents in Detroit" (Detroit Regional Workforce Fund, May 2012), http://skilledwork.org/wp-content/uploads/2014/01/Working_Towards_a_Sustainable_Detroit.pdf.

20. The United States Conference of Mayors, "Written Testimony of Elizabeth Mayor J. Christian Bollwage For The U.S. Conference of Mayors Before the House Transportation and Infrastructure Subcommittee on Water Resources and Environment on 'Building a 21st Century Infrastructure for America: Revitalizing American Communities through the Brownfields Program,'" 2017, 2, https://transportation.house.gov/uploaded-files/2017-03-28_-_bollwage_testimony.pdf.

21. Chris Bollwage, "'Building a 21st Century Infrastructure for America: Revitalizing American Communities through the Brownfields Program,'" United States Conference of Mayors, March 27, 2017, https://www.usmayors.org/2017/03/27/building-a-21st-century-infrastructure-for-america-revitalizing-american-communities-through-the-brownfields-program/.

22. Sangyun Lee and Paul Mohal, "Environmental Justice Implications of Brownfield Redevelopment in the United States," *Society and Natural Resources* 25 (2012): 602–9.

23. Alexander Lee, Oliver Baldock, and John Lamble, "Remediation or Problem Translocation: An Ethical Discussion as to the Sustainability of the Remediation Market and Carbon Calculating," *Environmental Claims Journal* 21 (2009): 232–46.

24. City of St. Louis Planning Commission, "City of St. Louis Sustainability Plan," 67.

25. City of St. Louis Planning Commission, 67.

26. David Gordon, "Managing the Changing Political Environment in Urban Waterfront Development," *Urban Studies* 34, no. 1 (1997): 61–83.

27. Project for Public Spaces, "The Global Waterfront Renaissance," The Global Waterfront Renaissance, August 1, 2008, https://www.pps.org/reference/theglobalwaterfrontrenaissance/.

28. HR&A Advisors, Inc., "Baltimore's Inner Harbor: Economic Impact, Importance, and Opportunities for Investment," October 31, 2013, http://baltimorewaterfront.com/wp-content/uploads/2015/06/Economic-Impact-Study.pdf.

29. University of Delaware Institute of Public Administration, "Benefits of Mixed-Use Development | Planning for Complete Communities in Delaware," accessed December 2, 2017, http://www.completecommunitiesde.org/planning/landuse/mixed-use-benefits/.

30. City of St. Louis Planning Commission, "City of St. Louis Sustainability Plan," 82.

31. Christopher Leinberger and Mariela Alfonzo, "Walk This Way: The Economic Promises of Walkable Places in Metropolitan Washington, D.C." (Brookings Institution Metropolitan Policy Program, May 2012), https://www.brookings.edu/wp-content/uploads/2016/06/25-walkable-places-leinberger.pdf.

32. University of Delaware Institute of Public Administration, "Benefits of Mixed-Use Development | Planning for Complete Communities in Delaware."

33. Sustainable DC, "Sustainability DC," 49–50.

34. City of Burlington, "The Burlington Legacy Project," 23.

35. Clayton Scrivner, "Mayor, City Redevelopment Agency to Launch Expansive Downtown Development Project," accessed December 2, 2017, /mayor-city-redevelopment-agency-launch-expansive-downtown-development-project.

36. City of St. Louis Planning Commission, 36.

37. Detroit Future City, "2012 Detroit Strategic Framework Plan," 2013, 8, https://detroitfuturecity.com/wp-content/uploads/2014/02/DFC_ExecutiveSummary_2ndEd.pdf.

38. City of Grand Rapids, Office of Energy and Sustainability, "FY 2011 Through FY 2015 Sustainability Plan," 2011, 8.

39. City of Grand Rapids, Office of Energy and Sustainability, 8.

40. AJ Latrace, "Inside Method's Colorful New Soap Making Factory in Pullman," *Curbed Chicago*, April 29, 2015, https://chicago.curbed.com/2015/4/29/9966136/method-factory-tour.

41. Melissa Harris, "Chicago Gets New Method Soap Factory, Glimpse of Future with Fewer Workers," The Chicago Tribune, April 28, 2015, http://www.chicagotribune.com/business/ct-confidential-method-soap-0429-biz-20150428-column.html.

42. Environmental and Energy Study Institute, "Fact Sheet - Jobs in Renewable Energy and Energy Efficiency (2017)," February 15, 2017, http://www.eesi.org/papers/view/fact-sheet-jobs-in-renewable-energy-and-energy-efficiency-2017.

43. The City of Miami Beach, "Sustainability Plan Energy Economic Zone Work Plan," November 12, 2009, 18, http://www.miamibeachfl.gov/green/scroll.aspx?id=63975.

44. The City of Miami Beach, 18.

45. City of Chicago, "2015 Sustainable Chicago Action Agenda," September 2012, 9, https://www.cityofchicago.org/content/dam/city/progs/env/SustainableChicago2015.pdf.

46. City of Palm Springs, "The Palm Springs Path to a Sustainable Community Draft," March 25, 2009, 20, http://www.palmspringsca.gov/home/showdocument?id=5610.

47. City of Portland, "The Portland Plan April 2012," 17.

48. Louise Story, "As Companies Seek Tax Deals, Governments Pay High Price," *The New York Times*, December 1, 2012, http://www.nytimes.com/2012/12/02/us/how-local-taxpayers-bankroll-corporations.html?pagewanted=all.

49. The City of Madison, "The Madison Sustainability Plan," 2011, 44.

50. City of Chicago, "2015 Sustainable Chicago Action Agenda," 9; The City of San Jose, "San Jose's Green Vision," 2007, 11, http://www.globalurban.org/San_Jose_Green_Vision.pdf; City of Chicago, "2015 Sustainable Chicago Action Agenda."

51. Sustainable DC, "District of Columbia Mayor's College and University Sustainability Pledge," accessed February 2, 2018, https://sustainable.dc.gov/page/district-columbia-mayor%E2%80%99s-college-and-university-sustainability-pledge.

52. City of Boston, "Greenovate Boston: 2014 Climate Action Plan Update," 2014, 33, https://www.cityofboston.gov/eeos/pdfs/Greenovate%20Boston%202014%20CAP%20Update_Full.pdf.

53. The City of Madison, "The Madison Sustainability Plan," 2011, 52.

54. The City of Madison, "The Madison Sustainability Plan," 2011, 47.

55. City of Grand Rapids, "FY 2011 Through FY 2015 Sustainability Plan," June 21, 2011, 16.

56. Emily Robbins and Dana D'Orazio, "Economic Priorities at City Hall: Employment, Entrepreneurship, and Equity," National League of Cities, June 15, 2017, http://www.nlc.org/article/economic-priorities-at-city-hall-employment-entrepreneurship-and-equity.

57. Harris, "Chicago Gets New Method Soap Factory, Glimpse of Future with Fewer Workers"; City of Chicago, "2015 Sustainable Chicago Action Agenda: Year Two Progress Report Fall 2014," 2014, 7, https://www.cityofchicago.org/content/dam/city/progs/env/SCYear2Report.pdf.

58. Chattanooga Green Committee, "The Chattanooga Climate Action Plan," February 24, 2009, 67; Glenn Hasek, "Chattanooga Launches Green Lodging Certification Program," Green Lodging News, July 31, 2009,

http://www.greenlodgingnews.com/chattanooga-launches-green-lodging-certification-program/.

59. Charleston Green Committee, "Charleston Green Plan," 2007, 95, http://www.charlestongreencommittee.com/charlestongreenplan2010.pdf.

60. City of Chicago, "2015 Sustainable Chicago Action Agenda," 9.

61. The City of Madison, "The Madison Sustainability Plan," 2011, 44.

62. The City of Madison, 44.

63. Lauren Hirshon et al., "Report: Cities, the Sharing Economy and What's Next" (National League of Cities Center for City Solutions and Applied Research, 2015), http://www.nlc.org/sites/default/files/2017-01/Report%20-%20%20Cities%20the%20Sharing%20Economy%20and%20Whats%20Next%20final.pdf.

64. Hirshon et al., 6.

65. Arun Sundararajan, *The Sharing Economy: The End of Employment and the Rise of Crowd-Based Capitalism* (Boston: MIT Press, 2016), http://www.jstor.org/stable/j.ctt1c2cqh3.

66. David Wachsmuth et al., "The High Cost of Short-Term Rentals in New York City" (Urban Politics and Governance Research Group, 2018), https://mcgill.ca/newsroom/files/newsroom/channels/attach/airbnb-report.pdf.

67. National Academies of Sciences, Engineering, and Medicine, *Broadening Understanding of the Interplay Between Public Transit, Shared Mobility, and Personal Automobiles* (Washington, DC: The National Academies Press, 2018), https://doi.org/10.17226/24996; Regina Clewlow and Gouri Shankar Mishra, "Disruptive Transportation: The Adoption, Utilization, and Impacts of Ride-Hailing in the United States" (UC Davis Institute of Transportation Studies, 2017), http://www.reginaclewlow.com/pubs/2017_UCD-ITS-RR-17-07.pdf.

68. National Academies of Sciences, Engineering, and Medicine, *Broadening Understanding of the Interplay Between Public Transit, Shared Mobility, and Personal Automobiles*.

69. ICMA, "Nearly a Third."

CHAPTER 4

Climate

CLIMATE: AN INTRODUCTION

"Warming of the climate system is unequivocal" stated the leading international organization on the subject, the Intergovernmental Panel on Climate Change (IPCC) in its 2014 report.[1] This group has provided balanced information for policymakers by rigorously assessing published scientific studies on climate change for over 20 years. Their updated report includes stronger evidence of the many ways the planet is already experiencing the effects of climate change such as rising average land and ocean temperatures, sea level rise, shrinking glaciers, decreasing snow and ice cover, hydrologic system changes such as droughts and floods, and increased frequency of extreme weather events.

Impacts of climate change are visible in numerous US cities. 2017 was dominated by one of the most destructive hurricane seasons on record, with three separate category 4 hurricanes making landfall in the United States. Hurricane Harvey dumped 52 inches of water on Houston's low-lying metro area and rebuilding efforts are ongoing.[2] A hailstorm in Denver caused $1 billion in damage.[3] California experienced a range of disasters: early in the year severe weather, flooding, and a strange winter storm made headlines; in the fall, wildfires devastated the northern San Francisco Bay Area and coastal cities in Southern California. The National Oceanic and Atmospheric Administration estimated that weather and climate disasters cost the United States a record $306 billion in 2017.[4] While

M. Keeley, L. Benton-Short, *Urban Sustainability in the US*,
https://doi.org/10.1007/978-3-319-93296-5_4

the year 2017 was a record, it was not an outlier. Over the last decade, cities have repeatedly experienced record-breaking floods, tornadoes, droughts, heat waves, and wildfires—sometimes in the same month.

Climate Basics

The changes we are seeing in the climate are linked to greenhouse gas (GHG) emissions. In report after report, the IPCC has expressed increasing certainty over the connections between climate change and anthropogenic (human-caused) GHG emissions, and now states that these "are extremely likely to have been the dominant cause of the observed warming since the mid-20th century."[5]

GHGs absorb some of the energy that is radiated from the surface of the earth and trap it in the atmosphere, essentially acting like a blanket that makes the earth's surface warmer than it would be otherwise. This is called the greenhouse effect (Fig. 4.1). Most GHGs are naturally occurring, and are necessary for life as we know it, because without them the planet's surface would be about 60° Fahrenheit cooler than present

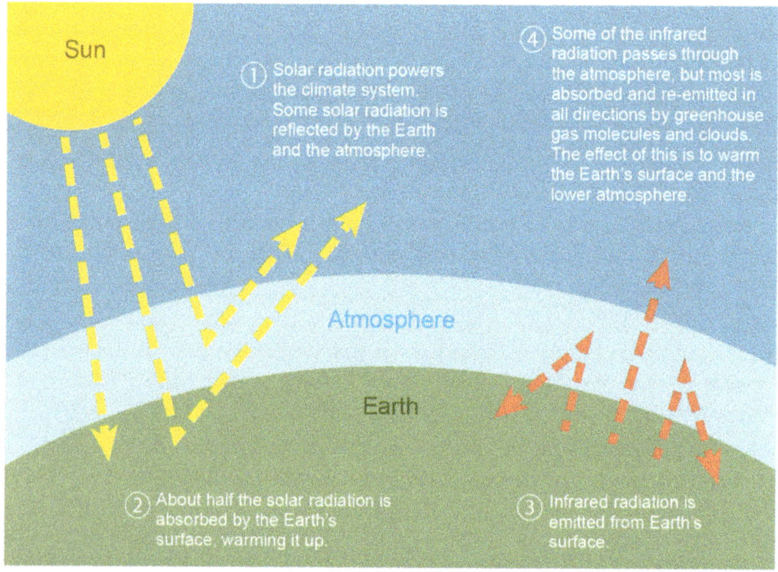

Fig. 4.1 The greenhouse effect. (Source: Adapted from a diagram from the U.S. EPA "The Greenhouse Effect", last updated March 3, 2016, accessed March 27, 2018, https://www3.epa.gov/climatechange//kids/basics/today/greenhouse-effect.html)

temperatures. But, as humans increase the concentrations of these gases, the earth's temperature is climbing above past levels. According to data from both the National Oceanic and Atmospheric Administration (NOAA) and National Aeronautics and Space Administration (NASA), the earth's average surface temperature has increased by about 1.3 to 1.9 °F since 1900.[6] While this number may at first seem small, it is important to remember that climate change is not just about warming temperatures but the instability that these changes cause in the systems that humans depend on, such as our hydrologic system.

There are four principle greenhouse gases: carbon dioxide, methane, nitrous oxide, and fluorinated gases. Three of the four gases are naturally occurring, while fluorinated gases are man-made. Carbon dioxide, methane, and nitrous oxides are continuously emitted into and removed from the atmosphere by natural processes on earth. Anthropogenic (man-made) activities, however, can cause additional quantities of these and other greenhouse gases to be emitted or sequestered, thereby changing their global average atmospheric concentrations. Most anthropogenic emissions come from the combustion of carbon-based fuels, principally wood, coal, oil, and natural gas. According to the EPA, the primary sources of these gases are:

- Carbon dioxide (CO_2): Carbon dioxide enters the atmosphere through burning fossil fuels (coal, natural gas, and oil), solid waste, trees, and wood products, and also as a result of certain chemical reactions (e.g. manufacturing of cement). Carbon dioxide is removed from the atmosphere (or "sequestered") when it is absorbed by plants and oceans as part of the biological carbon cycle. Currently CO_2 accounts for about 82 percent of all US greenhouse gas emissions from human activities.
- Methane (CH4): Methane is emitted during the production and transport of coal, natural gas, and oil. Methane emissions also result from livestock and other agricultural practices and by the decay of organic waste in solid waste landfills.
- Nitrous oxide (N2O): Nitrous oxide is emitted during agricultural and industrial activities, as well as during combustion of fossil fuels and solid waste.
- Fluorinated gases: Hydrofluorocarbons, perfluorocarbons, and sulfur hexafluoride are three synthetic, powerful greenhouse gases that are emitted from a variety of industrial processes.

So, is there a genuine "climate debate?" Yes and no. Scientists are increasingly certain that human activities are changing the composition of the atmosphere and thus changing the planet's climate. But they are not sure by how much it will change, at what rate it will change, or what (and where) the exact effects will be. This uncertainty is what many climate change deniers use in their efforts to prevent regulation of energy use or derail international treaties to limit emissions. Extreme climate change deniers also question whether anthropogenic emissions are significant and point to the earth's history of fluctuating climate patterns. In truth, the cause of climate change is impossible to prove definitively, since it can't be physically tested. However, climate scientists have used computer models to demonstrate that anthropogenic GHG emissions explain the climate changes we are measuring, while other possible causes do not.

CITIES' ROLE IN CLIMATE CHANGE

Because of geography, US cities have different vulnerabilities to climate change. For example, western cities such as Las Vegas and Denver may see an increased frequency of drought. Cities in the Midwest and Northeast may experience more frequent large storm events, wetter winters, and heavier snowfall. Some cities located on rivers such as Kansas City, Cincinnati, Memphis, and Sacramento may see rivers flood in the spring as more snowpack melts sooner, but reduced flows in the summer. Coastal cities such as Miami, San Diego, and New York City may experience sea level rise that results in increased flooding and storm surges. Figure 4.2 summarizes some of the major expected impacts, which vary by region.

Climate change is already impacting cities and is a major motivator and unifying theme behind many cities' plans for sustainability. Our research confirms that within the United States, cities are at the forefront of taking action on climate change. For example, Denver expressed sentiments that are echoed across many of the city planning documents we have read, affirming that climate change "is a defining issue of the 21st century" and that "facing the challenges of a changing climate through preparedness, forward thinking, and cost-effective strategies" will allow the city "not only be one of the greenest cities in the nation, but also one of the most innovative and climate resilient cities in the face of rapid climate change."[7]

Cities are responding to climate change in two main ways: mitigation and adaptation.[8] While mitigation addresses the causes of climate change, adaption concerns preparing society, our infrastructure, and ecological

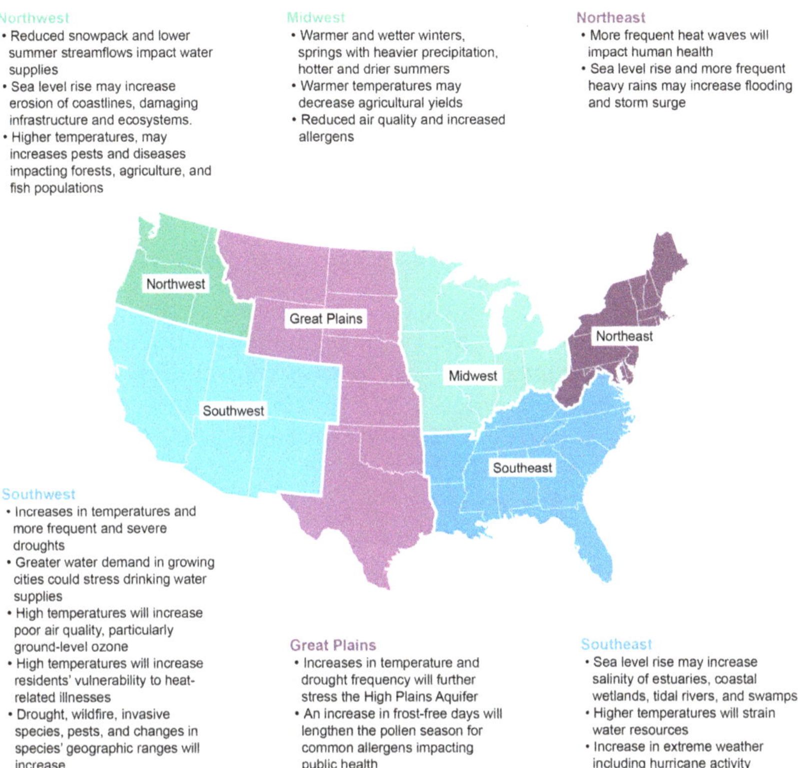

Fig. 4.2 Impact of climate change by region. (Source: Adapted from data in "Climate Change Impacts by Region," the U.S. EPA, accessed April 1, 2018, https://archive.epa.gov/epa/climate-impacts/climate-change-impacts-region.html)

systems for the effects. One of the most pressing questions today is: "Can cities manage unavoidable changes and avoid unmanageable changes?"[9]

Briefly, mitigation focuses on reducing the concentrations of GHGs in the atmosphere either by reducing their sources or increasing their sinks. Strategies can include reducing fossil fuel use (by using renewables), energy efficiency and conservation (encouraging weatherproofing and green buildings) and the promotion of carbon sinks (carbon sinks—such as trees—sequester carbon).

Adaptation, on the other hand, is the process of adjusting to our changing climate. In human systems, adaptation seeks to moderate or avoid harm. Examples could include: relocating critical infrastructure such as electrical substations to higher ground, enacting water conservation plans, or preparing disaster response and evacuation plans. Currently, climate adaptation is still a very evolving field.

Below, we explore city's changing roles first in climate change mitigation and then adaptation.

Cities' Role in Climate Change Mitigation

Climate change has been the subject of numerous international efforts. Many countries agree on the need to stabilize GHG emissions; however, the US federal government has been lax in its commitment to accepting and arresting global climate change. Fortunately, the federal government's lack of political will to reduce emissions has been countered at the local level. In 2005, several hundred US mayors met in Seattle to sign the Mayors Agreement on Climate Change, pledging to achieve the Kyoto protocol's climate protection goals (Box 4.1). To date, more than 1100 mayors have accepted the protocol's goals. This is important because it shows that despite the lack of progress on the national level, cities throughout the United States are taking action on climate change.

Box 4.1   Best Practices in Governance: Seattle's Leadership in Climate Change

In March 2005, Seattle Mayor Greg Nickles and nine other US mayors joined together to invite cities from across the United States to significantly reduce global warming pollution. Three months later in June, the Mayors Climate Protection Agreement was passed unanimously by the US Conference of Mayors. This Climate Agreement is remarkable in that it occurred primarily because the Bush Administration refused to ratify the Kyoto Protocol. In the absence of national leadership, cities committed themselves to the agreement. Participating cities were tasked with three actions:

1. Strive to meet or exceed the Kyoto Protocol targets in their own communities,

(continued)

Box 4.1   (continued)

2. Encourage their state governments, and the federal government, to enact policies and programs to meet or exceed Kyoto Protocol targets, and to
3. Urge the US Congress to pass greenhouse gas reduction legislation, which would establish a national emission trading system.

This group of mayors has had sustained impacts. They pushed for the federal Energy Efficiency and Conservation Block Grant program, which has provided funding for energy efficiency projects. By 2018 some 1060 mayors—from all 50 states, the District of Columbia and Puerto Rico, representing a total population of over 88 million citizens—have signed. Signatory mayors are encouraged to develop a Climate Action Plan, and this process has encouraged many cities to develop more comprehensive sustainability plans. The fact that many US cities now have sustainability offices and sustainability plans can be traced back to the 2005 meeting in Seattle.

Source:

"Mayors Climate Protection Center" The United States Conference of Mayors, 2018, https://www.usmayors.org/mayors-climate-protection-center/

The most recent international effort to address climate is the 2015 Paris Agreement. The Paris Agreement will work towards making sure the earth's temperature does not rise more than 2 °C (or 3.6 °F) above pre-industrial levels. This temperature marks the upper limit that scientists and policymakers view as reasonable and acceptable risk; there is concern that higher temperatures increase risks of irreversible change and even more dramatic effects of climate change. The Paris Agreement requires that ratifying nations "peak" their greenhouse gas emissions as soon as possible and pursue the highest possible ambition that each country can achieve. One hundred ninety-five nations—including the United States—signed the Paris Agreement, the first time that the world has agreed on a path forward. However, in spring of 2017, the Trump Administration announced it was withdrawing the United States from the Paris Agreement, turning its back on the fight against climate change. Currently, the United States is the only country to have rejected or withdrawn from the Paris Agreement.

Following Trump's announcement, over 50 US mayors pledged to uphold the Paris Agreement. Governors from California and New York said they will keep pursuing their own programs to reduce emissions, and the private sector is already shifting towards cleaner energy. This coalition of cities, states, and the private sector has been called "We Are Still In." As New York City stated: "Let others endlessly debate the causes (or even the existence) of climate change. New York City has chosen, once again, to act—by continuing to reduce its contribution to climate change and, at the same time, taking decisive and comprehensive steps to prepare and adapt."[10]

While not all US cities discuss climate change, we note substantial commitment to addressing these issues among many cities. Some see mitigation and adaptation as opportunities for new economic strategies and argue that sustainable green technologies and green jobs could counterbalance the costs of GHG reduction.[11] We found that climate mitigation efforts were often a motivation for the creation of a municipal sustainability plan in the first place. Mitigation practices are relatively well-integrated into many cities' plans for sustainability. For this reason, further discussion of the actions that cities are taking to mitigate climate change is also integrated throughout the book but found primarily in Chap. 5 and Chap. 6.

Cities' Role in Climate Change Adaptation

Cities are motivated to act on climate change often because of concerns about the potential for a natural disaster or extreme weather event. As Seattle stated,

> flooding, heat waves, and extreme high tides are not new challenges in Seattle, and we have strategies for responding to them. However, climate change will shift the frequency, intensity, and timing of these events, and what we now consider an extreme event will become the new normal. If we are not prepared for these changes, the events will significantly impact our community's economy, infrastructure, and health.[12]

Indeed, cities have become early responders to the challenges and opportunities of climate change for two reasons: first, urban areas have large and growing populations that are vulnerable to climate variability and change for many reasons; and second, cities depend on extensive infrastructure systems and the resources that support them and these systems are also vulnerable to the impacts of climate change.

However, climate adaptation has proved difficult for many cities to address and integrate holistically into their planning. There are many reasons for this. At some level, there may be trade-offs between allocating funds for mitigation or adaptation efforts, and money spent on adaptation might seem like "giving up" and admitting that global mitigation efforts are insufficient. Climate change impacts are regionally specific, so adaptation efforts must be tailored for localized impacts of climate change. This is especially challenging because predicting the localized effects of climate change is a weakness of current scientific modeling. The uncertainty and unpredictability of climate change impacts lead some question if there is sufficient certainty to make major investments. Finally, climate change risk, uncertainty, and impacts broadly affect so many aspects of urban systems and life.

Despite these challenges, there is a widespread positive, can-do attitude that many cities display around climate change. This was the case for Philadelphia's plan, which recognizes that climate adaptation "creates opportunities for the city to make smart investments that will yield multiple benefits for years to come."[13] Denver makes a number of compelling arguments as to why they should undertake climate adaptation strategies: "It is unlikely that greenhouse gas emissions will be stabilized or reversed in the near term: Proactive planning is more effective and less costly than responding reactively to climate change impacts as they happen: Climate readiness is a potential competitive advantage for Denver, and can generate additional community benefits."[14]

Many cities leading in climate change adaptation are already feeling the effects of climate change. In 2012, Hurricane Sandy was called the "worst natural disaster to ever hit New York City," and was a stark reminder about the vulnerability of infrastructure to storm surges (see Box 4.2).[15] West Palm Beach lists climate change as one of three main obstacles to the city's economic growth, and US Senator Bill Nelson from Florida has frequently referred to South Florida as "Ground Zero" for climate change impacts, given concerns about sea level rise, flooding, hurricanes, and freshwater supply.[16] Figure 4.5 shows the key paths to urban climate resilience. We found that many cities contextualize climate adaptation as "resilience" or "climate resilience;" however we caution that this focus may leave out issues of equity and holistic planning, which are characteristics of a sustainability approach (Fig. 4.5).

Box 4.2   Best Practices in Planning: A Stronger, More Resilient New York City

On October 29, 2012, Hurricane Sandy slammed into New York City. The rain poured down, 80 mph winds took down power lines and trees, and the storm surge flooded streets, tunnels, and subway lines throughout Manhattan (Fig. 4.3). The flood caused Con Edison's electronic substations to short out, leaving 800,000 city residents without power. Forty-four people died and hundreds were injured. Total property damage in the city exceeded $19 billion. It was a brutal wake-up call to the vulnerabilities cities face because of climate change.

The impact of the storm spurred the city's 2013 plan, *A Stronger, More Resilient New York*. It builds on PlaNYC's framework to tackle issues of adaption and resiliency related to climate change impacts affecting New York City (Fig. 4.4).

City officials used the Sandy experience to not only justify preparedness efforts taken hitherto but also as an impetus to redouble the city's climate adaptation efforts. The detailed plan seeks to strategically rebuild and increase the resilience of the city, considering neighborhood-level assessments of exposure, vulnerability, and adaptation opportunity.

The city will leverage federal recovery money, funds from a city capital program, and utilities to cover projected costs of $19.5 billion over ten years to complete outlined projects. Broad actions include repairing homes and streets damaged by the hurricane, elevating electrical infrastructure, retrofitting hospitals and nursing homes, improvements to transportation and water infrastructure, restoring wetlands and sand dunes, and building and researching floodwalls.

With more than 250 specific initiatives to reduce the city's vulnerability to coastal flooding and storm surge, this is the most concrete, developed adaptation plan that we have found for any US city. However, it is concerned strictly with flooding—a reasonable outcome given the impact of Hurricane Sandy. Yet, New Yorkers will face other climate-related impacts as well, such as extreme heat, related poor air quality, and health risks associated with mosquito-borne illnesses, like West Nile Virus.

(*continued*)

Box 4.2   (continued)

Fig. 4.3 The Hugh L. Carey tunnel flooded during Hurricane Sandy. (Source: "Northern Access to Brooklyn-Battery Tunnel flooded," Wikimedia Commons, created October, 30 2012, accessed April 11, 2018, https://upload.wikimedia.org/wikipedia/commons/0/01/Hugh_L._Carey_Tunnel_during_Hurricane_Sandy_vc.jpg)

Fig. 4.4 Resilient New York (Source: Adapted from City of New York and PLANYC, "A Stronger, More Resilient New York" (June 2013, page 2), accessed April 11, 2018, https://www.nycedc.com/resource/stronger-more-resilient-new-york)

Source:
The City of New York, *A Stronger More Resilient New York* (2013) https://www.nycedc.com/resource/stronger-more-resilient-new-york February 1, 2018.

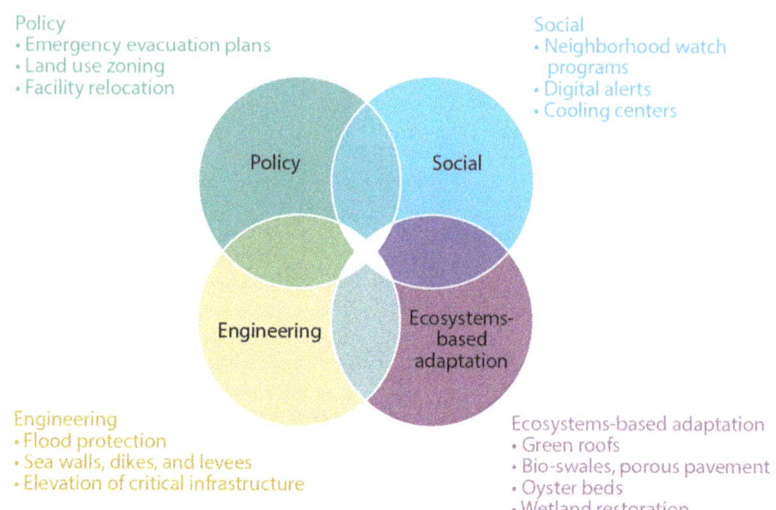

Fig. 4.5 Urban resilience to climate change. (Source: Adapted from City of New York and PLANYC, "A Stronger, More Resilient New York" (June 2013), accessed April 11, 2018, https://www.nycedc.com/resource/stronger-more-resilient-new-york)

Currently about 100 US cities have developed plans specifically for climate adaptation.[17] However, given funding and staff shortages, and a multitude of other pressing demands, few of these plans are truly comprehensive and action-oriented. Instead, plans tend to be overarching, big picture documents that do not yet propose a specific work plan. Many cities approach climate change adaptation by focusing on disaster preparedness either because they realize the importance of doing so, or because there are state mandates to create disaster response plans. In this process, cities conduct climate change risk and vulnerability assessments. These assessments generally use regional climate modeling data to provide a more detailed review of the possible impacts to natural and human systems. Understanding areas of vulnerability can sometimes uncover the inequities of climate change: some populations (like the elderly or those with asthma) might be more sensitive to exposures than others, and some populations (like low-income families) may have less resilience or adaptive capacity to recover after a disaster.

Based on information learned in planning for disaster response, some cities have generated a climate adaption plan that specifies actions to reduce climate-related vulnerabilities and respond to impacts when they do occur. These plans tend to focus on the idea that proactive planning will be more cost-effective than a reactive approach (responding to damage after it has occurred). Yet because climate change science is rapidly evolving and uncertainty still exists, we encourage cities to prioritize projects that allow for future modifications and for an adaptation strategy that is revisited and evolves as new information becomes available.[18]

Portland, Oregon, is a city that stands out for integrating climate change adaptation into its comprehensive sustainability plan, noting that "climate protection must be inextricably linked with actions to create and maintain jobs, improve community livability and public health, address social equity and foster strong, resilient natural systems."[19] We have found that for most cities that discuss adaptation in their plans for sustainability, the focus is often on coordinating local and regional agencies, calls for further study, or for relatively generic extensions of existing stormwater management or urban heat island amelioration projects. We see adaptation to climate change as being in a nascent stage. For these reasons, this chapter will focus primarily on actions cities are taking to adapt to a changing climate.

Taking Action on Climate Adaptation

A major challenge in preparing for the impacts of climate change is that it is a "wicked" complex problem. Many climate change impacts are cascading and interdependent: for instance, extreme heat events contribute to air quality problems, and rising sea levels exacerbate the flooding problems caused by more intense storm events. Additionally, multiple climate impacts affect the same systems. For instance, in some places, climate resilient buildings should be built to withstand floods, use materials that ameliorate the urban heat island effect, and conserve both water and energy. Table 4.1 summarizes examples of how cities are implementing climate adaptation.

While recognizing these interconnections and complexities, we organize our discussion of climate adaptation by focusing on three areas: (1) the built environment and infrastructure, (2) human systems, and (3) natural systems.

Adapting the Built Environment and Infrastructure

Buildings and other infrastructures are affected by climate change in a variety of ways. The vulnerability of these structures and potential impacts vary by use and type but also by age and location. New buildings and

Table 4.1 Examples of adaptation for climate change

Cities	Adaptation strategies implemented
Phoenix, AZ, Boston, MA, Philadelphia, PA, and New York City, NY	These cities have integrated climate change impacts into public health planning and implementation activities that include creating more community cooling centers, neighborhood watch programs, and reductions in the urban heat island effect
San Diego, CA	Local governments around the metro area partnered with the port, the airport, and more than 30 organizations with direct interests in the Bay's future to develop the San Diego Bay Sea Level Rise Adaptation Strategy. The strategy identified key vulnerabilities for the Bay and adaptation actions that can be taken by individual agencies, as well as through regional collaboration
Chicago, IL	Through a number of development projects, the city has added 55 acres of permeable surfaces since 2008 and has more than four million square feet of green roofs planned or completed
Lewes, DE	In partnership with Delaware Sea Grant, ICLEI-Local Governments for Sustainability, the University of Delaware, and state and regional partners, the City of Lewes undertook a stakeholder-driven process to understand how climate adaptation could be integrated into the hazard mitigation planning process. Recommendations for integration and operational changes were adopted by the City Council and are currently being implemented
Portland, OR	Updated the city code to require on-site stormwater management for new development and redevelopment. Provides a downspout disconnection program to help promote on-site stormwater management
Boulder, CO, New York City, NY, and Seattle, WA	Water utilities are using climate information to assess vulnerability and inform decision-making
Philadelphia, PA	The Philadelphia Water Department began a program to develop a green stormwater infrastructure, intended to convert more than one-third of the city's impervious land cover to "Greened Acres": green facilities, green streets, green open spaces, green homes, and so on, along with stream corridor restoration and preservation

Source: National Climate Assessment Report. 2014. at https://nca2014.globalchange.gov/report/response-strategies/adaptation

infrastructure can be designed with climate change in mind. However, cities are constrained by their existing building and infrastructure inventory, upon which they will still rely for decades to come. For these reasons, the poor condition of existing, aging infrastructure, including roads, bridges, railroad lines, water and wastewater pipelines, and electrical power networks, impacts the vulnerability of these systems to climate change.

Many cities have prioritized adaptation measures by focusing on the vulnerability of vital infrastructure, such as hospitals. Necessary measures are locally variable. For example, in Los Angeles, Providence Hospital used HEPA filters (initially purchased for use in the event of a pandemic flu) to deal with heavy particulate matter from smoke caused by wildfires.[20] A combined heat and power (CHP) system, installed by Greenwich Hospital in New Haven, was installed as an energy-saving measure that produces heat and uses the systems' thermal output for hot water and space heating. The system continued to operate during Hurricane Sandy in 2012, when the area experienced widespread power outages, proving that investment in this technology could offer multiple benefits.[21] Following the flooding of Hurricane Katrina, the Veterans Hospital in New Orleans was rebuilt in a less-flood-prone location, and all mission-critical mechanical and electrical infrastructures (like the HVAC system, kitchen, emergency department, and patient beds) are on upper floors, at least 20 feet above flood elevation.[22] These and other preparations have been undertaken to give the facility a seven-day "defend in place" capability.

Another focus is on creating resilient municipal buildings. For example, in 2017, New York City released preliminary Climate Resiliency Design Guidelines as a means to broadly incorporate the projected impacts of climate change into the design, construction, and renovation of all city buildings.[23] This step is informed not only by a general understanding of risk but specifically by the region's experiences with flooding and devastation following Hurricane Sandy. The Guidelines are the first of their kind to comprehensively address multiple climate risks across its capital program, the largest in the country.[24] Research has shown that when cities set such requirements for municipally controlled property, the practice is often adopted by private sector as well.[25]

Cities also confront the climate change impacts affecting their infrastructure systems. These include energy, water and wastewater, transportation, public health, banking and finance, telecommunications, food and agriculture, and information technology, among others. Already climate change is causing damage to infrastructure including roads, buildings, and industrial facilities and is also increasing risks to ports. Almost 40 percent of the US population lives in coastal counties which could be impacted by sea level rise. Flooding along rivers, lakes, and in cities following heavy downpours, prolonged rains, and rapid melting of snowpack is exceeding the limits of flood protection infrastructure designed for historical conditions. Extreme heat is damaging transportation infrastructure such as roads, rail lines, and airport runways. The 2014 National Climate Assessment Report noted that power outages and road and bridge damage are among the infrastructure failures that have occurred during these extreme events.[26] The study also notes that infrastructure is highly interconnected: climate-related disruptions of services in one infrastructure system will almost always result in disruptions in one or more other infrastructure systems. Miami Beach has launched a $400 million Sea-Level Rise Plan that consists of a series of stormwater pumps, improved drainage systems, elevated roads, and higher seawalls. Currently the city is raising 100 miles of roads by two feet, and the new wastewater treatment plant was constructed five feet higher than initial plans (Fig. 4.6).

Although many people first think about rising temperatures in relation to climate change, water is where cities are most likely to first feel the effects of climate change. Climate change is already having measurable effects on the amount, distribution, and timing of precipitation and the availability of water. Below, we examine how cities are preparing their infrastructure and built environment for the climate change impacts of flooding—in the form of changing precipitation and rising sea levels—and droughts. (We also note that some cities experience water challenges on two extremes: flooding and drought!)

Adaptation to Flooding
Climate change is expected to increase the frequency and intensity of storms across the entire United States. However, the Northeast has recently seen a greater increase in extreme precipitation than any other region in the United States—the region experienced more than a 70 percent increase in the amount of precipitation falling in "very heavy events" (defined as the heaviest 1 percent of all daily events) between 1958 and 2010. The frequency of these heavy downpours is projected to continue to increase over the remainder of the century.[27] As we will discuss in more detail in Chap. 7, more intense storms overwhelm the nation's already aging water infrastructure, disrupt and damage city infrastructure, and degrade water quality in nearby waterbodies.

For example, flooding is the top hazard in Louisville due to its location on the banks of the Ohio River and the presence of 11 major stream systems (for a total of 790 stream miles). As a result, about 15 percent of the

Fig. 4.6 The city of Miami Beach has been raising the height of roads to reduce the damage done by periodic flooding. (Source: Lisa Benton-Short.)

metro area lies within a floodplain. Between 2000 and 2017, the Federal Emergency Management Administration (FEMA) paid $35 million in flood-insurance payouts for Louisville infrastructure projects. Concern about flooding and water quality in surrounding rivers spurred the creation of the city's Multi-Hazard Mitigation Plan.[28]

Additionally, almost 40 percent of the US population——some 130 million people—live in coastal counties. Coasts are affected by climate change in a variety of interconnected ways. Sea level rise is caused by the thermal expansion of seawater due to warmer temperatures and a net increase of water due to melting ice. Sea level rise will increase saltwater intrusion in proximate aquifers, groundwater, and estuaries, affect coastal wetlands vegetation, and increase coastal erosion.[29] The Intergovernmental Panel on Climate Change projects a global average rise in sea level of about two feet by 2100.[30] The combination of sea level rise and changing precipitation patterns, which include larger, more intense storms, means that many cities must prepare for more frequent and severe flood events.[31]

Between 2000 and 2015, a major flooding event affected over half of nearly 2000 cities surveyed.[32] Not surprisingly, the most common climate change adaptation practices we have identified among US cities involve preparation for more frequent large storm events and flood prevention. There are many risks that flooding presents to a city including public health and safety hazards, interruptions in key services, and damage to buildings and infrastructure. In addition, floods can disrupt transportation and hamper emergency services and evacuation efforts. Because gasoline and diesel pumps and sump pumps require electricity to operate, a power failure during a flood could limit access to fuel for operating cars, running generators and contribute to water damage in buildings.[33]

Many cities have addressed moderate flooding and heavy storm events by planning to supplement their existing stormwater management system with green infrastructure, along with efforts to improve water quality of nearby lakes and rivers. The trend towards application of green infrastructure within stormwater management is discussed in more detail in Chap. 7. However, cities facing more extreme flooding have frequently developed more extensive plans to mitigate flooding and damage to their communities. We explore several of these plans and approaches below.

San Francisco's climate action strategy assessed the impacts of sea level rise on the city based on two different sea level rise scenarios over the next 50 years. Researchers concluded that the city would experience an increased likelihood and intensity of storm surges, high tide flooding, and shoreline erosion.[34] The report estimates the economic impacts on people, transportation, and property. On the low end, a 3-foot (1.0 meter) sea level rise could cause $50 billion in damages to property and displace some 220,000 residents; at the higher end, a 4.5-foot (1.4 meter) sea level rise could create $62 billion in damages and displace almost 270,000 residents. The neighborhood most affected is the Embarcadero Waterfront, the city's commercial and tourist center. By 2100, the study predicts \$4 billion worth of Waterfront property to be at risk.[35] Putting dollar amounts on these scenarios has helped motivate mitigation and adaptation responses to climate change.

Charleston, South Carolina, is another coastal city in which most elevations are near sea level. In 2015, it released its "Sea Level Rise Strategy" which they describe as an "overall strategy and guiding framework to protect lives and property, maintain a thriving economy, and improve quality of life by making the City more resilient to sea level rise and recurrent flooding."[36] In Charleston, the sea level has already risen over one foot in the last 100 years. The National Oceanic and Atmospheric Administration (NOAA) estimates a sea level rise of two to seven feet in Charleston over the next 100 years. Charleston experienced an average of 2 days of tidal flooding per year in the 1970s, but by 2045 it is projected that number could reach 180 days of flooding per year.

Charleston has developed several strategies to adapt to these changes. The city plans to invest in infrastructure to enhance drainage and store water and will use building codes and ordinances to assure that new buildings in the city follow flood-resistant construction practices and are built one foot above the designated base flood elevation. The city created the Charleston Resilience Network, a working group of public and private stakeholders, to improve resilience planning and response, and has pledged to work more closely with neighboring jurisdictions, because "seas do not respect civic boundaries."[37] The plan proposes further preparedness strategies including installing flood gauges in areas prone to flooding, improving real-time information sharing between public safety officials, acquiring public safety and rescue equipment to manage flooded areas, and developing clear and immediate communication methods to reach the public in an emergency.

New Orleans is trying to make itself more resilient to storms and hurricanes in the wake of catastrophic flooding by Hurricane Katrina in 2005, which affected over 80 percent of the city and left entire neighborhoods uninhabitable.[38] The city is now re-envisioning its relationship with water. New Orleans uses Rotterdam in the Netherlands—another city below sea level—as a model. The city plans to use canals, green space, and green infrastructure as a sponge to hold excess water and prevent flooding, as Rotterdam has. The plan envisions an "integrated living water system" that will use strategic parklands, wetlands, waterways, and retrofitted stormwater infrastructure to store stormwater and prevent flooding in other areas of the city.[39] The idea is to switch the paradigm from seeing water as something that the city needs to "pump away" quickly, to one that sees water as an asset. This new approach to urban water management should lower infrastructure costs, reduce flood risk to people and property, temper soil subsidence, and transform unsightly infrastructure into attractive amenities that enhance neighborhoods and improve quality of life.[40] An example is the project proposed for the Gentilly neighborhood, which was heavily impacted by flooding. A $141 million dollar Housing and Urban Development grant will be used to reengineer how water flows through this low-lying neighborhood and "restore functional water features to the urban grid" by adding green infrastructure to public places, schoolyards and parks, maximizing the water storage capacity of open spaces, and transforming street medians into stormwater swales (see Fig. 4.7).[41]

Drought

Mountainous snowpack is the source of drinking water and hydropower for many cities in the western United States. However, climate change is predicted to reduce the accumulated snowpack and change the time of snowmelt. Some models predict reductions of the average snowpack by about 28 percent by the 2020s and 40 percent by the 2040s in the state of

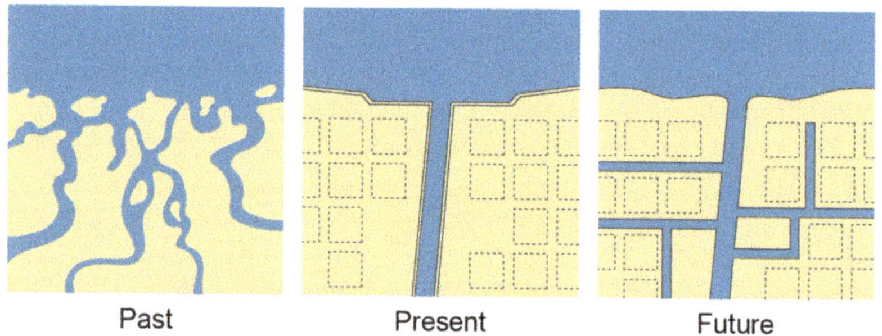

Fig. 4.7   A neighborhood in New Orleans redesigned to embrace water as an asset. (Source: Adapted from the design of Architects Waggonner and Ball in "Gentilly Resilience District: Fact Sheet" City of New Orleans (March, 2018) accessed April 7, 2018, https://www.nola.gov/resilience/resources/fact-sheets/gentilly-factsheet/ and from Waggonner and Ball "Greater New Orleans Urban Water Plan", accessed April 7, 2018, http://www.wbarchitects.com/urban-design/greater_new_orleans_water_management_strategy/)

Washington. Seattle is undertaking research on future energy demands, impacts on hydroelectric generation, and salmon survival. The city prioritizes investments in water conservation programs that would reduce per capita water use and constructing adaptive water capacity.[42] In 2017, Seattle's City Light (the city's public electric utility) began rolling out its smart-metering system that can detect system overloads and help prevent blackouts during extreme heat events.

Denver, located in a semi-arid climate, generally receives only about 15 inches of precipitation per year.[43] Reduced snowpacks and earlier snowmelt will also negatively affect Denver, leading to droughts. In this region, snowpacks feed streamflow, and as these snowpacks melt earlier in the spring, it could reduce the water available in reservoirs in the summer, when consumer demand is the highest.[44] The city partnered with Denver Water to develop a series of water conservation campaigns encouraging residents to "Use only what you need," and is providing rebates for high-efficiency fixtures (like toilets) and landscape irrigation products.[45] The city reports that residents are using an average of 20 percent less water than when these efforts started, even as population has increased. The city's Climate Adaptation Plan proposes to continue to conserve water, build recycled water systems, and secure new water supplies.[46]

Human Systems

Cities must also consider climate adaptation strategies to protect the health and well-being of their residents. Climate change impacts discussed throughout this chapter directly or indirectly impacts residents' health,

Box 4.3   Best Practices in Implementation and Results: Water Conservation in a Thirsty Los Angeles

Los Angeles' water supply challenges are legendary enough to be the central plot line in Hollywood movies (see the 1974 film noir classic *Chinatown*). Recent studies show that climate change is threatening water supplies further.[a] Currently, 85 percent of the metro area's water supply came from imported sources whose supplies are depleting.

(*continued*)

Box 4.3   (continued)

Understanding the importance of a coordinated, multi-departmental response to this problem, the mayor established a Water Cabinet to coordinate water policy and management. The city is taking a collaborative, integrated approach to managing all the City's water resources and integrating them within a large sustainability agenda. The result will be a series of plans and actions, organized under the umbrella *One Water Plan LA 2040*. In this way, the city will integrate efforts in wastewater and stormwater management, water recycling, and conservation.[b]

Between 2015 and 2017, Los Angeles has successfully reduced per capita potable water use from 131 to 104 gallons per capita per day, a 20 percent decrease, showing that even in thirsty Los Angeles, change can happen. Los Angeles has increased its commitment to water conservation measures and forbids hosing down sidewalks as well as outdoor watering within two days after a rain. Residents have also been encouraged to shower for only five minutes, install high-efficiency toilets, and turn off the water while brushing their teeth.

Other projects include the Purple Pipe Recycled Water Project which enables residents to use recycled water for irrigation and industrial purposes. It also features public engagement activities like free landscaping classes that feature draught-tolerant "California Friendly® Plants" and incentives to "Cash in Your Lawn," a program which reimburses homeowners who remove their water-thirsty lawns and replace them with drought-resistance plantings (xeriscaping) or artificial turf.[c]

Sources:

[a]Michael E. Mann and Peter H. Gleick, "Climate change and California drought in the 21st century," *Proceedings of the National Academy of Sciences of the United States* 112 no. 13 (2015): 3858–3859, https://doi.org/10.1073/pnas.1503667112

[b]"One Water LA," City of Los Angeles, accessed March 15, 2018, https://www.lacitysan.org/san/faces/home/portal/s-lsh-es/s-lsh-es-owla?_adf.ctrl-state=2qhj32cth_5&_afrLoop=4194785176667671#

[c]"Cash for Grass Rebate Program," Los Angeles County Waterworks District, accessed January 29, 2018, https://dpw.lacounty.gov/wwd/web/Conservation/CashforGrass.aspx

safety, income, and quality of life. In this section, we examine some ways in which climate change may bring new health challenges or exacerbate existing ones. Warmer weather will expand the range of mosquitoes and other disease vectors which raises new public health concerns in some areas. Increased pollen and poorer air quality may result in increased asthma rates and other respiratory ailments. Harmful algal blooms are also more prevalent in warmer waters. Increasing numbers of extreme events and even rises in temperature can increase the likelihood of anxiety and post traumatic stress disorder (PTSD).[47] In response to these changes, the

Box 4.4   Best Practices in Equity: Mapping Climate Change Vulnerability in Washington, D.C.

According to the 2016 *DC Climate Change Adaptation Plan*, vulnerability to climate change occurs as a result of a combination of exposure, sensitivity, and adaptive capacity. In order to understand where vulnerability is highest, the District has undertaken a number of steps to evaluate its vulnerability to climate change and to better plan and prepare for increased flooding (due to both heavier precipitation and sea level rise) and extreme heat. The plan was the result of several studies and reports that inventoried the city's built infrastructure (including energy, transportation, water, and telecommunication) and community resources (such as emergency and medical services, schools, and public housing). The city also considered the geographic distribution of vulnerable residents—those with less capacity to respond to disasters or who could be more sensitive to these events—including low-income residents and senior citizens. With this information, they then modeled future scenarios of flooding and extreme heat events to "stress test" the District's infrastructure and resources under these conditions.

Through this process, the city identified five priority neighborhoods for climate change adaptation in the city, by evaluating and ranking the comparative risk to infrastructure, public facilities, and community resources based on the likelihood of exposure to climate change impacts and the consequences of a failure or disruption (Fig. 4.8). Each of the five priority areas is at risk of flooding and has a concentration of both highly vulnerable populations and vital city infrastructure and support services.

(*continued*)

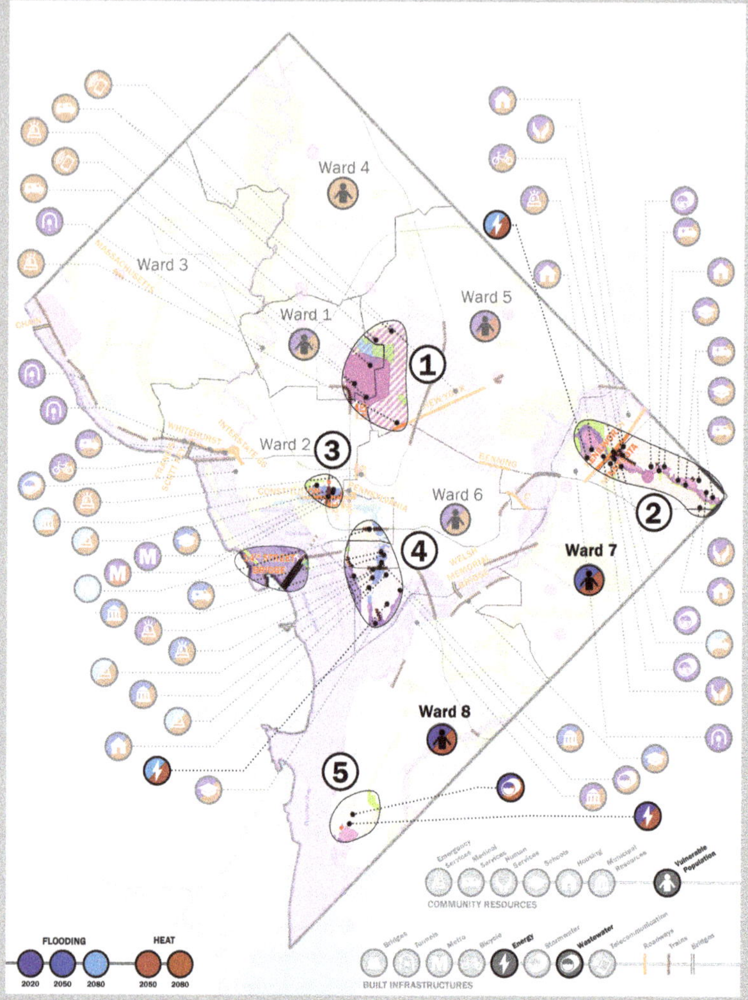

Fig. 4.8 A vulnerability map of Washington, D.C. This map of Washington, D.C. highlights neighborhoods that are more vulnerable to both flooding and heat events due to climate change. Maps such as these help cities prioritize vulnerability and target investments. (Source: courtesy of DC Department of Energy & Environment, Perkins + Will and Kleinfelder, 2016. Vulnerability & Risk Assessment, page 12 at https://doee.dc.gov/sites/default/files/dc/sites/ddoe/publication/attachments/150828_AREA_Research_Report_Small.pdf)

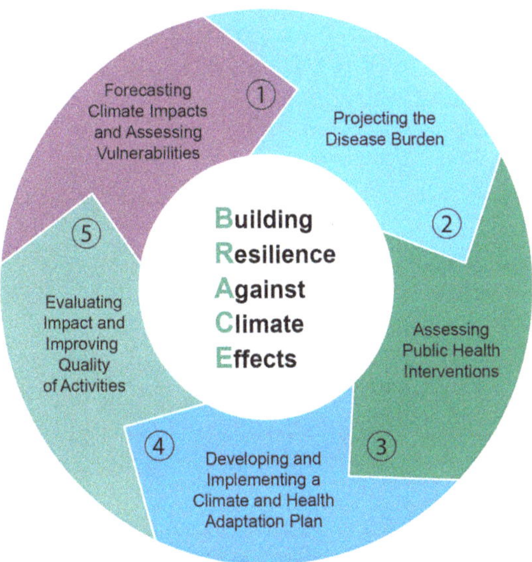

Fig. 4.9   The Center for Disease Control's BRACE program. The Center for Disease Control recommends cities become resilient against climate change by following these steps. (Source: Based on a diagram from the Centers for Disease Control "CDC's Building Resilience Against Climate Effects (BRACE) Framework," (last modified October 2015), accessed December 17, 2017, https://www.cdc.gov/climateandhealth/BRACE.htm)

US Center for Disease Control has published a five-step process, called BRACE, Building Resilience Against Climate Effects, to help health officials plan for the health effects of climate change (Fig. 4.9).[48]

Extreme Heat

The urban heat island effect refers to the fact that cities exhibit higher temperatures than the surrounding suburbs and rural areas (sometimes as much as 10 °F warmer) due to (1) less natural vegetation, (2) the presence and morphology of buildings and materials that absorb and store thermal energy, and (3) the emission of waste heat from buildings and vehicles. Climate change will likely mean that cities become even hotter, particularly during the summer months. Heat waves could be more intense and last longer.

Heat waves can be deadly. In 1995 a heat wave struck the city of Chicago. For over a week in July, the temperature reached over 100°F every day. By July 20, over 700 people died. Many cities in the Midwest and Eastern United States are planning to respond to the impacts of increased temperatures on its residents. More hot days may arrive together as heat waves, increasing the risk of residents experiencing heat-related health problems such as dehydration, heat exhaustion, and heat stroke.[49] In response, many cities have focused on the health impacts related to heat waves and respiratory diseases.

However, we point out that the impacts of extreme heat are uneven across the city, with some residents more vulnerable to health impacts than others. These include the elderly, the very young, people with low socio-economic status (under the poverty level), and people who do not have access to air conditioning.[50] Compounding the issue is that during some heat waves, power outages significantly broaden the vulnerable population. Efforts to address this problem include establishing "cooling stations"—air-conditioned public buildings such as libraries and schools specially opened and staffed to provide water and respite to those who do not have air conditioning in their homes. These efforts can be aided by GIS and mapping, which informs city officials where vulnerable populations are concentrated, and where access to "cooling stations" may be difficult to get to. One city that has done an excellent job learning more about how to address heat problems is Louisville (Box 4.5).

Box 4.5   Emerging Trend: Heat Assessment and Management in Louisville

With the help of foundation support, in 2016, Louisville commissioned the first comprehensive heat management assessment undertaken by a major US city in order to better prepare for the effects of

(continued)

Box 4.5   (continued)

climate change induced heat waves and the urban heat island effect. Researchers used a regional climate model to estimate the impact of different strategies the city could use to mitigate excessive temperatures in the Louisville Metro area. The study highlighted the use of three best practices:

1. Prioritize the use of cool materials (i.e. roofing and surface paving engineered for high surface reflectance and reduced energy storage) in industrial and commercial zones with a lot of impervious cover and few inexpensive options for vegetation.
2. Utilize tree planting and other vegetative strategies in residential areas, where population exposure to heat is greatest, lower-cost planting opportunities exist, and these can dovetail with stormwater management priorities.
3. Support energy efficiency programs already prioritized through city sustainability efforts and better integrate these with urban heat management objectives.

Source:
"Louisville Urban Heat Management Study, Draft for Public Comment," Urban Climate Lab of the Georgia Institute of Technology for the Louisville Metro Office of Sustainability: April 2016, https://louisvilleky. gov/sites/default/files/advanced_planning/louisville_heat_mgt_revision_ final_prelim.pdf

Adapting Natural Systems

Not only humans are impacted by climate change; ecological systems are also changing. We already see that plant and animal communities are experiencing shifts in ranges and abundance. The ability of ecological communities to adapt to these changes is also hampered by many other human impacts such as land use change, invasive species, and overharvesting. We must be prepared to adapt to changes in ecological communities. Although some think of cities as separate from the natural environment, this is of course not the case. Cities are in fact intertwined with natural systems.

Concern about the impacts of climate change on the natural environment motivates awareness of this issue in many cities, particularly those that rely on environmental tourism. Miami Beach, for instance, cites the city's vulnerability to climate change "given its location, elevation, and strong economic and social ties to a healthy environment" as a main motivation of its sustainability activities.[51] Similarly, Juneau, Alaska, has experienced a decrease in annual snowfall from approximately 109 inches to 93 inches and the rapid retreat of the Mendenhall Glacier.[52] Beyond the impacts to tourism, Juneau is also concerned about impacts to its hydropower resources, and to salmon and other marine fish and wildlife that are important to the economy.[53] Even smaller resort cities such as Aspen and Vail, whose economies are dependent on snowfall, could see major impacts. Some resort cities are adapting by boosting summer sports and music festivals to attract tourists for reasons other than snow.

Despite the many vital environmental services provided to society by natural systems, climate change adaption strategies in these areas are lagging behind. Below, we examine challenges raised in two contexts: (1) the impacts of climate change on the urban forest, which we rely on to ameliorate the urban heat island and other services, and (2) the increase in wildfires due to climate change and other practices.

The Urban Forest and Urban Heat Island

Urban street trees and the urban forest are a commonly utilized best practice for reducing the urban heat island effect (discussed earlier in this chapter) and minimizing climate change impacts such as poor air quality and intense stormwater runoff. Many cities encourage tree planting and new technology is allowing cities to create thermal maps to prioritize neighborhood tree planting priorities. Chicago provides a 50 percent rebate to residents for purchases of street trees and native plants. They emphasize native plants because the city is also home to numerous native species of flora and fauna and is located in one of the major North American bird migration routes.[54] We discuss such efforts in more depth in Chap. 8.

In planning these investments, it is crucial to recognize that "urban trees and forests can also be vulnerable to climate change through shifts in tree habitat suitability, changes in pests and diseases, and changes in extreme weather events."[55] Thus, in the face of warming temperatures amplified by the urban heat island effect, simply planting native trees may be insufficient to secure the long-term stability of a cities' urban forest. Studies examining shifts that have already occurred in plant distribution indicated that many cities have already lost at least one historical tree species (one that grew there ~200 years ago), with cities in the southeastern United States hardest hit.

One study predicts that on average, cities could lose six native trees if climate change trends continue, and suggest that "strategies employing green infrastructure must identify tree species that are likely to remain well adapted to urban climates many years into the future."[56] To this end, Chicago piloted a project to better understand the vulnerability of their urban forest to climate change. They found that most trees have low to moderate vulnerability, but non-native invasive species were generally least vulnerable. This study suggested that adaptation in urban areas might include utilization of new species or cultivars.[57]

These findings are somewhat counterintuitive; many urban forestry programs call for increased use of native species, often citing their tolerance of drought and habitat benefits. However, climate change complicates these decisions. We recommend that cities thoughtfully consider tree species for their planting programs in light of climate change and other objectives. This is especially the case, since tree planting is not a short-term fix but a long-term investment, over a tree's entire life cycle.

Wildfire

Wildfire has made headlines across the western United States in recent years due to a combination of climate change (increasing heat and drought), increases in the wildland-urban interface, and fire suppression strategies that have inadvertently led to a build-up of fuels. Between 1970 and 2003, there was a 650 percent increase in burned area in western coniferous forests. Modeling indicates that climate change is a significant factor contributing to this increase. Experts project future increases in wildfires, clearly necessitating preparations for this new reality.[58] To date, wildfire response has been mostly reacting to active threats and reducing fuel loads through active management of wild and prescribed fires.

The mounting impacts of wildfires include costs of management, property damage, air quality impairments, and threats to water quality within watersheds due to soil instability. Climate adaptation calls for a shift in strategies that focus on wildfire preparedness including mapping and discouraging development in fire hazard zones, rating homes for survivability, and developing the disaster response capacity of communities.[59] San Diego and Santa Fe both enforce strict brush management and other fire safety regulations to protect their communities from wildfire.

But as 2017 showed, few communities are safe from wildfires. Recent fires were started by human activity (tossing a cigarette, leaving a campfire unattended, etc.). However, these fires were made worse by hot, dry conditions that followed a rainy winter (which built up vegetation as fuel) and the fact that there are now more people and structures in areas that were once largely uninhabited. It is sure to generate controversy, but cities and county governments could consider restricting new suburban development in areas particularly vulnerable to wildfires (e.g. areas on the fringe of the metro area).

WHAT'S MISSING: ADAPTATION FOR AIR QUALITY AND EQUITY CONCERNS

Climate change will bring increased temperatures which are also associated with poor air quality. Ground-level ozone is created through reactions between volatile organic compounds and nitrogen oxides—which are emitted by automobiles, among other sources. This reaction is heat dependent, so ozone levels tend to rise as temperatures increase. Ground-level ozone irritates the respiratory system, aggravates asthma and other chronic lung diseases like emphysema and bronchitis, and can cause permanent lung damage.[60] The EPA notes that ground-level ozone is projected to increase in the 19 largest urban areas of the Southeast.[61]

However, our research discovered that cities do not pay sufficient attention to the impact that higher temperatures will have on air quality problems and thus on human health. Many cities address air quality by implementing strategies around transportation and energy. A few cities are targeting investment in green spaces and green infrastructure in areas of the city that are particularly hot (or suffer from the urban heat island effect). But in general, cities have insufficiently considered the ways in which climate change will exacerbate existing air pollution problems and health impacts.

In addition, many cities have not sufficiently addressed equity in relation to climate change. Seattle, Portland, and Providence are cities that have recognized that the uncertainty and risk associated with climate change disproportionately affects the most vulnerable populations, including lower income, recent immigrant, and older residents, who may lack the resources to respond to changing conditions (see Box 4.6). However, we note that there is tremendous room for improvement in this area.

Box 4.6   Best Practices in Equity: Providence, Rhode Island

Providence, Rhode Island has made it clear that equity is important when planning climate adaptation. Providence Director of Sustainability Leah Bamberger stated: "In Providence, like many cities in the US and around the world, frontline communities of color bear the burden of our environmental issues. They are often faced with poor air and water quality, toxic industries in their backyards, and risks like flooding that will be exacerbated by the impacts of climate change." She noted that the most important element of engagement is trust:

> I've learned that even if you check all the boxes for community engagement best practices (hold meetings in the neighborhoods, provide transportation, child care, food, translation services, compensate community members for their expertise, etc.), you are not going to get meaningful participation unless there is trust. As long as community members believe that their perspectives and voices don't really matter in determining outcomes, most will not participate…Why should anyone spend an evening at a community meeting when their voice is the one that is always marginalized?

Source:
"In Providence, Fighting Climate Change Starts With Racial Equity," National League of Cities, September 28, 2017, https://citiesspeak.org/2017/09/28/in-providence-fighting-climate-change-starts-with-racial-equity/

SUMMARY

The most recent decade was the nation's warmest on record. Temperatures in the United States are expected to continue to rise. Because human-induced warming is superimposed on a naturally varying climate, the temperature rise has not been, and will not be, uniform or smooth across the country. The hydrologic system is very sensitive to changes in temperatures, so floods, droughts, and changes in precipitation may be the first way most people experience climate change.

Climate change will challenge cities in different ways for the foreseeable future. Cities will need to adopt new strategies and overcome barriers such as limited funding and policy and legal impediments. Complicating these efforts is uncertainty of the localized impacts of climate change and the fact that there is no "one-size-fits-all" adaptation approach. However, opportunities still exist for productive lesson learning across regions and sectors, which is why sharing best practices is essential.

The good news is that more cities are addressing these adaptation and mitigation challenges. Those cities which have strong leaders on climate have completed climate change vulnerability assessments and are making no-regrets plans for climate adaptation, building upon steps already underway to manage stormwater or reduce the urban heat island effect with green infrastructure. Table 4.2 summarizes important trends and best practices.

Table 4.2   Best practices in climate adaptation

Infrastructure and the built environment
- Identify where infrastructure is most vulnerable (mapping) to heat, flooding, sea level rise, drought, and so on
- Engage multiple stakeholders to identify vulnerable infrastructure (airports, ports, highways) in planning
- Invest in upgrades or relocate critical infrastructure such as electrical substations or water systems
- Integrate state and regional agencies and organizations in hazards/disaster planning
- Update city codes to facilitate changes to infrastructure or buildings

Human systems
- Map the urban heat island and the location of residents vulnerable to extreme heat
- Integrate climate change into public health planning
- Carefully consider climate change impacts on vulnerable populations, including lower income, recent immigrant, and older residents
- Build trust so community members believe that ideas and voices will be heard in planning process

Natural systems
- Identify how ecosystems, vegetation, and other species will be impacted by changes due to climate change
- Use building codes and zoning to minimize risk in areas prone to wildfire

Climate   129

Notes

1. Rajendra Pachauri, Leo Meyer, and Core Writing Team, "Climate Change 2014 Synthesis Report" (The Intergovernmental panel on climate change, 2014), http://www.ipcc.ch/report/ar5/syr/.
2. The New York Times, "With Death Toll at 30, Storm Makes 2nd Landfall," *The New York Times*, August 29, 2017,https://www.nytimes.com/2017/08/29/us/hurricane-harvey-storm-flooding.html.
3. Aldo Svaldi, "Hailstorm That Hammered West Metro Denver May 8 Is Costliest Ever for Colorado," *The Denver Post*, May 23, 2017, https://www.denverpost.com/2017/05/23/hailstorm-costliest-ever-metro-denver/.
4. National Oceanic and Atmospheric Administration, "2017 Was 3rd Warmest Year on Record for U.S." (United States Department of Commerce,January8,2018),http://www.noaa.gov/news/2017-was-3rd-warmest-year-on-record-for-us.
5. Pachauri, Meyer, and Core Writing Team, "Climate Change 2014 Synthesis Report."
6. Pachauri, Meyer, and Core Writing Team.
7. Denver Environmental Health, "City and County of Denver Climate Adaptation Plan," 2014, 6, https://www.denvergov.org/content/dam/denvergov/Portals/771/documents/Climate/Climate_Adaptation_Final%20with%20letter.pdf.
8. Harriet Bulkeley and Michele Betsill, "Cities and Climate Change: Urban Sustainability and Global Governance," *Routledge*, 2005.
9. Rosina Bierbaum, Daniel Brown, and Jan McAlpine, "Coping with Climate Change National Summit Proceedings," *University of Michigan Press*, 2008, 356.
10. The City of New York, "PlaNYCA, Stronger More Resilient New York," 2013, http://s-media.nyc.gov/agencies/sirr/SIRR_singles_Lo_res.pdf.
11. Ted Nordhaus and Michael Shellenberger, "Break Through: From the Death of Environmentalism to the Politics of Possibility," *Environmental Change in Polar Regions*8, no. 3 (2008), http://digitalcommons.wcl.american.edu/cgi/viewcontent.cgi?article=1074&context=sdlp.
12. Seattle Office of Sustainability and Environment, "Seattle Climate Action Plan," June 2013, http://www.seattle.gov/Documents/Departments/OSE/2013_CAP_20130612.pdf.
13. The Mayor's Office of Sustainability and ICF International, "Growing Stronger: Toward A Climate-Ready Philadelphia," November 2015, https://beta.phila.gov/media/20160504162056/Growing-Stronger-Toward-a-Climate-Ready-Philadelphia.pdf.

14. Denver Environmental Health, "City and County of Denver Climate Adaptation Plan."

15. The City of New York, "PlaNYC A Stronger More Resilient New York."

16. Jenny Staletovich, "At a Rare Field Hearing, U.S. Sen. Bill Nelson Calls Miami Beach Ground Zero for Sea Level Rise," Miami Herald, accessed March 4, 2018, http://www.miamiherald.com/news/local/environment/article1963249.html.

17. Maria Gallucci, "6 of the World's Most Extensive Climate Adaptation Plans | InsideClimate News," Inside Climate News, June 20, 2013, https://insideclimatenews.org/news/20130620/6-worlds-most-extensive-climate-adaptation-plans.

18. Seattle Office of Sustainability and Environment, "Seattle Climate Action Plan."

19. City of Portland Bureau of Planning and Sustainability, "City of Portland and Multnomah County Climate Action Plan 2009," 2009, https://www.portlandoregon.gov/bps/article/268612.

20. US Climate Resilience Toolkit, "Health Care Facilities Maintain Indoor Air Quality Through Smoke and Wildfires," January 17, 2017, https://toolkit.climate.gov/case-studies/health-care-facilities-maintain-indoor-air-quality-through-smoke-and-wildfires.

21. U.S. Climate Resilience Toolkit, "Hospital Plans Ahead for Power, Serves the Community Through Hurricane Sandy | U.S. Climate Resilience Toolkit," U.S. Climate Resilience Toolkit, January 17, 2017, https://toolkit.climate.gov/case-studies/hospital-plans-ahead-power-serves-community-through-hurricane-sandy.

22. U.S. Climate Resilience Toolkit, "After Katrina, Health Care Facility's Infrastructure Planned to Withstand Future Flooding | U.S. Climate Resilience Toolkit," U.S. Climate Resilience Toolkit, January 17, 2017, https://toolkit.climate.gov/case-studies/after-katrina-health-care-facilitys-infrastructure-planned-withstand-future-flooding.

23. The City of New York, "Mayor Announces New Resiliency Guidelines," The Official Website of the City of New York, April 28, 2017, http://www1.nyc.gov/office-of-the-mayor/news/271-17/mayor-new-resiliency-guidelines-prepare-city-s-infrastructure-buildings-for.

24. The City of New York.

25. Joop F. M. Koppenjan and Bert Enserink, "Public–Private Partnerships in Urban Infrastructures: Reconciling Private Sector Participation and Sustainability," *Public Administration Review* 69, no. 2 (March 1, 2009): 284–96, https://doi.org/10.1111/j.1540-6210.2008.01974.x.

26. National Climate Assessment, "Infrastructure," 2014, https://nca2014.globalchange.gov/highlights/report-findings/infrastructure.

27. U.S. Climate Resilience Toolkit, "Northeast," November 29, 2017, https://toolkit.climate.gov/regions/northeast.

28. City of Louisville, "Sustain Louisville: Louisville Metro Sustainability Plan," March 2013, https://louisvilleky.gov/sites/default/files/planning_design/general/sustain_louisville.pdf.

29. Robert J. Nicholls and et al., "Sea-Level Rise and Its Impact on Coastal Zones," *Science* 328, no. 1517 (June 18, 2010), https://doi.org/10.1126/science.1185782.

30. Pachauri, Meyer, and Core Writing Team, "Climate Change 2014 Synthesis Report."

31. OA US EPA, "Climate Impacts on Coastal Areas," Overviews and Factsheets, accessed March 3, 2018, /climate-impacts/climate-impacts-coastal-areas.

32. ICMA, "Local Government Sustainability Practices, 2015," 2016, https://icma.org/sites/default/files/308135_2015%20Sustainability%20Survey%20Report%20Final.pdf.

33. The Mayor's Office of Sustainability and ICF International, "Growing Stronger: Toward A Climate-Ready Philadelphia."

34. The City and County of San Francisco, "San Francisco Climate Action Strategy 2013 Update," 2013, https://sfenvironment.org/sites/default/files/engagement_files/sfe_cc_ClimateActionStrategyUpdate2013.pdf.

35. The City and County of San Francisco.

36. City of Charleston, "Sea Level Rise Strategy," December 2015.

37. City of Charleston, 11.

38. Plyer, Allison, "Facts for Features: Katrina Impact" (The Data Center, August 26, 2016), https://www.datacenterresearch.org/data-resources/katrina/facts-for-impact/.

39. Waggonner & Ball Architects and Ball, "Greater New Orleans Urban Water Plan," Living With Water: A New Vision for Delta Cities, accessed March 3, 2018, http://livingwithwater.com/.

40. City of New Orleans, "Resilient New Orleans," 2015, http://resilient-nola.org/wp-content/uploads/2015/08/Resilient_New_Orleans_Strategy.pdf.

41. City of New Orleans, "Gentilly Resilience District," February 2017, https://www.nola.gov/resilience/resources/fact-sheets/gentilly-factsheet/.

42. Seattle Office of Sustainability and Environment, "Seattle Climate Action Plan."

43. Denver Environmental Health, "City and County of Denver Climate Adaptation Plan."

44. Western Water Assessment, "Colorado Climate Change Vulnerability Study," ed. Eric Gordon and Dennis Ojima, 2015, http://wwa.colorado.edu/climate/co2015vulnerability/co_vulnerability_report_2015_final.pdf.

45. Denver Water, "Use Only What You Need," accessed February 17, 2018, https://www.denverwater.org/about-us/history/use-only-what-you-need.

46. Denver Environmental Health, "City and County of Denver Climate Adaptation Plan."

47. Centers for Disease Control and Prevention, "Mental Health and Stress-Related Disorders," December 11, 2014, https://www.cdc.gov/climate-andhealth/effects/mental_health_disorders.htm.

48. National Center for Environmental Health, "CDC - Climate and Health - CDC's Building Resilience Against Climate Effects (BRACE) Framework," Centers for Disease Control and Prevention, accessed March 4, 2018, http://www.cdc.gov/climateandhealth/BRACE.htm.

49. The Mayor's Office of Sustainability and ICF International, "Growing Stronger: Toward A Climate-Ready Philadelphia."

50. The Mayor's Office of Sustainability and ICF International.

51. The City of Miami Beach, "Sustainability Plan Energy Economic Zone Work Plan," November 12, 2009, http://www.miamibeachfl.gov/green/scroll.aspx?id=63975.

52. Juneau Commission on Sustainability, "Climate," City/Borough of Juneau, n.d., http://www.juneau.org/sustainability/climate-action-plan/.

53. Juneau Commission on Sustainability.

54. City of Chicago, "City of Chicago's Sustainable Backyard Program: NATIVE PLANTS," 2011, https://www.cityofchicago.org/dam/city/depts/doe/general/NaturalResourcesAndWaterConservation_PDFs/Sustainable%20Backyards/nativeplantsmergedv3.pdf.

55. Kevin Lanza and Brian Stone, "Climate Adaptation in Cities: What Trees Are Suitable for Urban Heat Management?," *Landscape and Urban Planning* 153 (September 1, 2016): 74–82, https://doi.org/10.1016/j.landurbplan.2015.12.002.

56. Lanza and Stone.

57. Leslie Brandt et al., "A Framework for Adapting Urban Forests to Climate Change," *Environmental Science & Policy* 66 (December 1, 2016): 393–402, https://doi.org/10.1016/j.envsci.2016.06.005.

58. US Climate Resilience Toolkit, "Health Care Facilities Maintain Indoor Air Quality Through Smoke and Wildfires."

59. Tania Schoennagel et al., "Adapt to More Wildfire in Western North American Forests as Climate Changes," *Proceedings of the National Academy of Sciences* 114, no. 18 (May 2017): 4582–90.

60. US EPA, "The Ozone Problem," Overviews & Factsheets, accessed February 17, 2018, https://www3.epa.gov/region1/airquality/oz_prob.html.

61. US EPA, "Climate Impacts in the Southeast," Overviews and Factsheets, accessed February 17, 2018, https://19january2017snapshot.epa.gov/climate-impacts/climate-impacts-southeast_.html.

CHAPTER 5

Transportation

TRANSPORTATION: AN INTRODUCTION

The automobile has shaped US cities for over a century. The car has dominated urban design, and vast amounts of land have been set aside for roads, highways, and parking garages (Figs. 5.1 and 5.2). There are television shows, movies, and songs about cars. For decades, getting a driver's license has been a benchmark of teenage independence. Americans venerate cars and have come to depend on them but do not acknowledge the substantial costs—environmental, social, and economic—that come with it.

There are broad environmental impacts of our car dependency. Almost 30 percent of the GHGs emitted in the United States are from transportation, and the largest sector of these emissions is from cars and light trucks.[1] In addition to being a major contributor to climate change, traditional fuel burning cars contribute to local air pollution problems.[2] Oils, gas, and heavy metals from brakes collect on paved surfaces and are then washed into nearby streams and rivers when it rains.

Equity and public health impacts arise from our car culture. The health impacts of air pollution—asthma, lung cancer—are not trivial.[3] The Massachusetts Institute of Technology calculates that 53,000 Americans die prematurely every year from vehicle pollution, losing ten years of life on average compared to their lifespans in the absence of tailpipe emissions.[4] These losses are not equally born. Many major urban highways are located in low-income communities or communities of color, so these populations are disproportionately exposed to high levels of air pollution.

© The Author(s) 2019

M. Keeley, L. Benton-Short, *Urban Sustainability in the US*,

https://doi.org/10.1007/978-3-319-93296-5_5

Fig. 5.1   Interstate 405 in Los Angeles infrastructure for automobiles is considerable; this stretch of the 405 in Los Angeles is 16 lanes across. (Source: Lisa Benton-Short.)

There are safety issues as well: many US cities are not safe for pedestrians. In 2015, over 5000 pedestrians were killed by car crashes and another 129,000 were sent to the emergency room.[5] Cars are also a hazard to those driving them. In 2015, more than 35,000 people were killed in motor vehicle crashes.[6] Transportation access is also a problem. With so much money and space devoted to infrastructure for automotive transportation, people seeking other forms of transit are left stranded. This is particularly true for the youngest and oldest community members as well as lower-income individuals who may not be able to afford the costs of a car.

There are many economic costs hidden in our transportation choices as well. The costs of climate change adaptation and the health costs related to poor air quality and our sedentary lifestyles are rarely connected to car transportation but should be. We experience congestion, which costs time and money. We must also consider the costs of building and maintaining roads, bridges, and highways; the United States has largely invested in these instead of public transit. However, as a country, we have not kept up with the costs of maintaining these systems. The 2017 American Society of

Fig. 5.2   The amount of land used for cars and trucks includes parking lots and parking garages. Parking lots are impermeable surfaces, which contribute to stormwater runoff. (Source: Lisa Benton-Short.)

Civil Engineers Infrastructure Report Card gave the United States an overall grade of D+.[7] They estimate it will cost \$4 trillion to upgrade properly. One out of every five miles of highway pavement is in poor condition, and the nation's roads have a significant and increasing backlog of rehabilitation needs. Bridges are also in bad shape. The average bridge is 43 years old, and more than nine percent of all bridges are structurally deficient.

Even as we recognize the negative impacts of our reliance on cars, it can be hard to envision how to change this relationship. However, there are possibilities for more sustainable forms of transportation. Let us first examine where things currently stand.

Although twenty-first-century automobiles produce 60–80 percent less pollution than they did in the 1960s, more people are driving more cars more miles. In 1970, Americans traveled one trillion miles in motor vehicles; by 2000, they drove more than three trillion miles. But there has been good news; the number of vehicle miles traveled (VMT) seems to have flattened somewhat. In 2016, it was estimated Americans' VMT was approximately 3.2 trillion miles (for a sense of scale, 3.2 trillion miles is roughly the same distance as 337 round trips from Earth to Pluto).[8] The small growth in vehicle miles traveled between 2000 and 2016 is a positive development.

Another positive finding is that there is significant variation in the miles driven per capita in cities across the country, which indicates that geography, land use, investment in public transportation, and transportation policy, among other variables, do affect driving patterns (Fig. 5.3). Portland established a particularly ambitious goal of reducing the city's per capita daily VMT by 30 percent from 2008 levels by 2035.[9] They analyzed driving patterns and found significant variation in the VMT per person *within* their city. This level of geographic analysis provides planners with important insight as they develop targeted transportation and land use policy. It also further highlights the fact that even very localized conditions can impact a person's VMT.

At the end of the day, reducing VMT will require behavior change of citizens at an individual level. However, cities can support these efforts

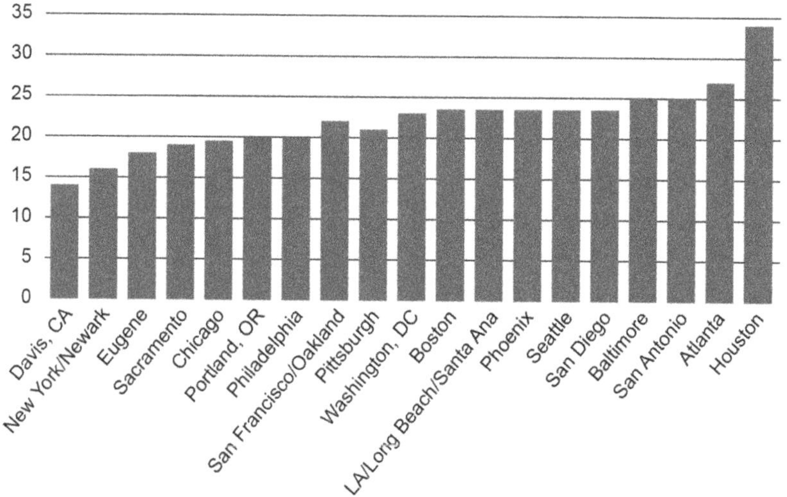

Fig. 5.3 Comparing daily vehicle miles traveled in selected US cities (2007). (Daily Source: Adapted from City of Philadelphia, Office of Sustainability, "Greenworks, a Vision for a Sustainable Philadelphia," (2008, page 65), https:// beta.phila.gov/media/20160419140515/2009-greenworks-vision.pdf)

through education, outreach, the provision of infrastructure to increase walking and bicycling comfort and safety, and investments in high-quality, fast, and frequent bus and rail service.

What steps should we take to reduce VMT in the United States? Peter Newman and Jeffrey Kenworthy, experts in sustainable transportation, advise us to resist the temptation to focus on incremental technical changes to solve our transportation challenges. Minimizing traffic impacts with buffers and noise walls or even the expansion of roads and highways just shifts the problem elsewhere. Easing air pollution by designing efficient, low-emission vehicles only extends automobile dependence. Instead, Newman and Kenworthy favor a much larger rethinking and willingness to make bigger changes such as radically rethinking land use, re-investing public transportation, and redesigning cities to promote non-automobile forms of mobility. In this chapter, we will see that cities at the cutting edge of planning for transportation sustainability are indeed heeding this advice, although many cities do still focus on increasing the purchase or use of fuel-efficient vehicles.

The mayor of Bogotà, Enrique Peñalosa, stated that a city can be made for people or for cars but not both, and his point shows who won out in American cities.[10] The vision for a sustainable transportation system is the reverse of most urban realities in the United States where, for the past century, we have privileged the automobile at the expense of public transit and active transport (walking and biking). Instead, a sustainable transportation system will prioritize foot travel, then cycling, then public transport and/or ride-sharing, and finally private motor vehicles (Fig. 5.4). In city centers, space will be allocated to pedestrian zones, street cafes, and markets instead of parking garages and congested city streets. Public transportation will be an easy and convenient choice, not just for commuting, but for accomplishing most daily tasks. When people do use cars, they will travel in low-emission or zero-emission vehicles that emit very few pollutants.

At a fundamental level, sustainable transport goes beyond moving vehicles. Transportation should be a means to improve the health and quality of life for people.[11] World Resources Institute president, Andrew Steer, noted: "If you get green transportation right, it pays for itself in terms of economics, in terms of environment, and in terms of human health and well-being. It's a wonderful win-win-win."[12]

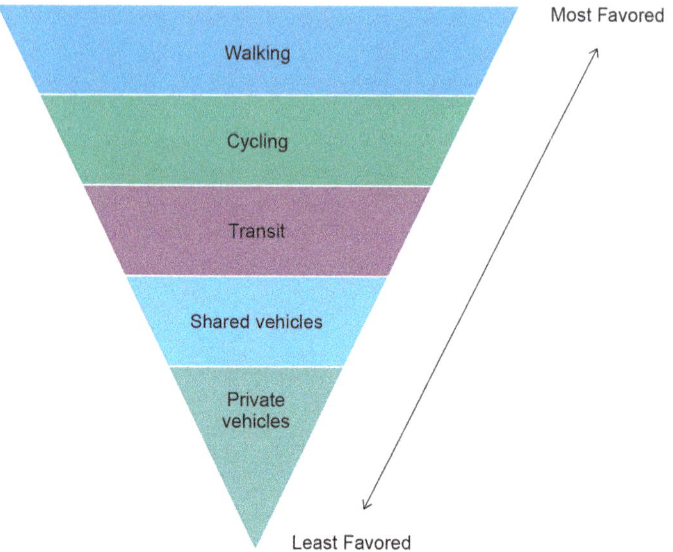

Fig. 5.4 A sustainable transportation hierarchy. (Source: Adapted from descriptions of sustainable transportation modes from numerous sources.)

CITIES' ROLE IN SUSTAINABLE TRANSPORTATION

Traditionally, cities have left the transportation agenda to state and federal agencies, or regional transit agencies.[13] This is because of the importance of federal funding for the construction of transportation infrastructure and of regional planning for highway networks. However, even as many cities recognize the importance of a holistic, regional approach to improved transportation, cities are increasingly taking ownership of this important topic. Cities have identified the importance of dependable, efficient public transit in making cities attractive places to live and work. They appreciate the leadership role and cost savings they can gain through fuel-efficient municipal fleets.

We must first understand the severe funding challenges relating to transportation infrastructure that cities face. An estimated 32 percent of urban roads are in poor condition. This is an indicator of our national backlog of basic maintenance and improvements of road, bridge, and tunnel infrastructure.[14] In part for this reason, cities like Grand Rapids prioritize basic street and traffic signal maintenance within sustainability plans, and Madison has adopted a practical "fix it first" policy, prioritizing road maintenance over construction of new lanes or road miles.[15]

Even systems with good public transportation networks are under significant strain and struggle with challenges related to deferred maintenance and perpetual budget shortfalls. Despite an increasing demand (10.5 billion trips in 2015), the nation's transit systems have been so chronically underfunded that most infrastructure is aging and needs repair. Across the country, transit systems have a backlog of deferred maintenance. There are substantial costs to the decline of our public transportation system. Closures, accidents, and inefficiencies cost individuals and companies money and reduce the efficiency of the US economy.

Defining and securing permanent funding for transit planning and improvements is a continual challenge.[16] The poor state of public transit in the United States stands in stark contrast to that in European cities which experience continued investment. Some cities are even expanding public transit networks to increase regional connectivity. For example, Paris is undergoing a \$36 billion project called the Grand Paris Express that creates four new rail lines and 68 stations throughout Île de France to better connect the outer metro area to important centers like airports and stadiums.[17] As a result of these investments, people in most European cities rely heavily on public transport, and it is a vital part of urban public life. While some US cities are reinvesting in their public transit systems and enjoying increased ridership, many Americans still have inadequate access to public transit. As we identified in Chap. 3, in the absence of federal or state funds, many cities are turning to public-private partnerships to improve or expand transportation infrastructure.

Box 5.1   Emerging Trend: Leveraging Public-Private Partnerships for Infrastructure Development

Despite their global popularity, public-private partnerships (PPPs) are less common in the United States, particularly with regard to transportation infrastructure. Some see them as an important tool for addressing the backlog of US infrastructure problems due to deferred maintenance of roads, local streets, bridges, tunnels, airports, and water and wastewater systems. In addition to simply restoring those facilities to a state of good repair, reconstruction today would benefit from an array of innovative technologies, new materials, and new designs not available at original construction.

(*continued*)

Box 5.1 (continued)

Others view PPPs more cautiously. On one hand, critics question relinquishing control over core government services and worry about the long-term effects on service, fees, and access for all. While private funding might seem like an immediate solution for the chronic under-funding of governments, PPPs are not free money. Private companies seek to recoup investments through fees over the long term, so the price for improvements must be paid at some point by someone. Further, infrastructure has been called a natural monopoly, which means that government regulation and control of public-private part-nerships is crucial. Thirty-four US states have adopted PPP-enabling laws designed to create the stable legal and institutional framework necessary to attract the long-term investment required to deliver many infrastructure services. In the best case, PPPs are a helpful and poten-tially cost-effective bundling of all elements of project, from design, financing, and construction, through operations and maintenance.

One recent example is the massive $1.6 billion redevelopment of Penn Station in New York City. In 2017, Governor Cuomo announced plans for the station's extensive renovation which includes many surrounding streets. The project will consist of a new 255,000-square foot terminal for the Long Island Railroad and Amtrak, called Moynihan Train Hall. This new hall will increase Penn Station's floor space by more than 50 percent. An additional 700,000 square feet will be developed for mixed-use commercial, retail, and dining spaces. Other changes include upgraded lighting and signage, and new digital screens.

The project is a collaboration between Empire State Development and three private partners—Related, Vornado, and Skanska—which collectively have contributed about $1.2 billion to the project. An additional $420 million comes from New York's three major transit agencies (MTA, Port Authority, and Amtrak), along with federal grants. The three private partners will lease and operate the 700,000 square feet of commercial and retail space that will be part of the new train depot. If all goes according to plan, the new transit hub will open by the end of 2020.

Source:

Patrick Lynch, "New Renderings of Penn Station's $1.6 Billion Renovation Released as Project Gets Greenlight," Arch Daily, June 19, 2017, https://www.archdaily.com/873993/new-renderings-of-penn-stations-1-dollars-6-cents-billion-renovation-released-as-project-gets-greenlight

Another trend is our growing understanding of the linkages between transportation and land use, and the importance of dense, walkable, vibrant neighborhoods to provide desirable places to live and make public transportation a viable and practical transportation option. As cities seek to provide more public transportation options in the form of rail or bus rapid transit programs, they must also be sure to align these improvements with neighborhoods that will provide the ridership to support these investments. Indeed, there is a growing wave of people who are eschewing long commutes in favor of more walkable urban living. Millennials seem less inclined to purchase cars and have been the early adopters of ride-share and bikeshare programs; empty nesters are also returning to the city.

Cities cite a variety of rationales for their focus on transportation within their plans for sustainability. Cities clearly recognize that transportation is a significant contributor of greenhouse gas emissions, and in many cases is a leading source. Charleston estimated that 40 percent of its GHGs came from transportation.[18] Our research finds that despite the connections between transportation and climate change, they tend to be treated separately within sustainability planning documents. This could be the result of the very different agencies that manage these systems. Yet, we identify this as an area where synergy and systems thinking could and should be enhanced.

Reducing emissions positively impacts local air quality and public health. Philadelphia and Washington, D.C. are trying to reduce the number of American Lung Association "Code Red and Orange air quality days," which indicate unhealthy ground-level ozone and particulate levels. When pollution reaches these levels, children, active adults, and people with respiratory disease, such as asthma, should avoid prolonged outdoor exposure.[19]

There are other connections between encouraging alternative transportation and health: walking and biking are parts of a healthy active lifestyle. Physical exercise can help combat obesity, a major health problem. Washington, D.C. has launched a "Healthy by Design" program incorporating infrastructure for pedestrians and bicyclists in affordable housing projects throughout the city so that these benefits are available to all residents regardless of income or ability.[20]

Finally, there is a connection between transportation, energy use, and economics. Economists have long criticized private automobiles for inefficient combustion, noting that much of the cost of fuel is wasted. Some cities are now rethinking the fuel efficiency of their city fleets as a way of saving money and see improved transportation as a key to supporting a more robust economy.[21] Cities appreciate the cost savings they can gain through fuel-efficient municipal fleets, and dependable, efficient public transit makes them more attractive places to live and work. There are significant economic incentives for cities to develop strong public transportation systems. A study of 3000 cities across the world from 2003 to 2014 found that cities with subways received 15 percent more foreign direct investment than those without them.[22] This finding demonstrates that good public transportation can engender economic benefits.

Equity implications of transportation—access to jobs, healthcare, healthy foods, and other amenities—is an area where cities should show greater consideration, especially given the racial and socioeconomic segregation that we discussed in Chap. 2. There are some exceptions. Burlington stands out as a city that prioritizes affordable transportation for all residents and raises the concern of residents who are "mobility impaired" and lack access to needed services and job opportunities.[23] Miami Beach more specifically defines groups that must receive special consideration when considering accessibility of public transit to also include "non-drivers, senior citizens, and/or disabled."[24] While identifying the mobility challenges of specific groups is a best practice, we urge cities to place more effort on meeting these needs.

The Center for Neighborhood Technology and TransitCenter collected bus and rail service data from over 800 transit agencies in the United States; the site allows users to map areas in cities across the country that are underserved by transit.[25] Even in cities with some rail options—buses are often the only travel option available to some residents.[26] Thus, in all cities it is essential to identify ways to make bus transportation, which is a much less costly undertaking than rail, an attractive and viable option for their residents and visitors. A trend on the horizon will be to more actively incorporate transportation costs into the cost of living, particularly for low-income residents. People that use public transportation save more than $10,000 a year on average.[27]

Cities must consider other shifts in transportation as well, given the rise of the sharing economy and "smart city infrastructure." Transportation network companies (like Uber and Lyft) and bikesharing programs are rapidly reshaping the future of urban transportation. These new services offer transportation alternatives in areas underserved by public transportation. However, as we discussed in Chap. 3, cities must quickly develop regulatory structures for this new kind of business, including those to protect drivers who comprise a growing number of contingent laborers. The first studies published on these innovations suggest unintended consequences such as negative impacts on public transportation ridership and accessibility challenges for community members without smartphones or credit cards. Autonomous cars will be another opportunity and challenge on the horizon. We encourage cities to monitor the implications of new innovations and adjust policy accordingly.

TAKING ACTION ON TRANSPORTATION

We have identified two very different strategies that cities are utilizing to achieve more sustainable transportation solutions. The first approach relies on behavior change of citizens to decrease the number of vehicle miles traveled. Cities can use education and incentives to encourage walking, biking, or using public transportation, but the provision of alternative infrastructure and changes to development patterns are ways that cities can have the greatest impacts. A second set of strategies use an incremental approach and do not seek to change our current automobile-based culture. Instead, these strategies rely primarily on technological innovations in engine and alternative fuel technologies to allow for vehicles with reduced ecological footprints.

Dense Urban Neighborhoods and Sustainable Transportation

Many city leaders realize that thoughtful urban planning lies at the heart of better, more sustainable transportation. Dense, walkable, mixed-use development is the cornerstone of sustainable transit for two reasons. First, it enables many people to simply walk to accomplish daily tasks. Second, accessing public transportation by foot (in the first and last legs of a commute) has been identified as crucial to developing a committed ridership base, that is, riders that provide sustained funding for public transportation by using this transportation mode not just for regular commutes but for other tasks and at other times as well.

As New York City noted, streets that better accommodate people bring multiple benefits. More people on foot support sustainable modes of transportation, leads to improved public health, and increase sales for local businesses.[28] Walkability results in higher neighborhood housing values and reduces neighborhood abandonment and crime.[29] For these reasons, dense, walkable urbanism is raised as a best practice at different points throughout this book (see particularly Chap. 3). Walkability is such an important feature that a Seattle-based company, *Walk Score*, capitalized on this by creating an index available on its website and through an app that allows you to look up the "walkability" score for your neighborhood.[30] It has become common for real estate advertisements to include the walkability score as an amenity.

In efforts to advance both walkability and support public transportation, Portland, Oregon has advocated for its "20 minute neighborhood concept," which is the idea that people should "be able to walk almost everywhere essential in 20 minutes or less."[31] The city set a goal of creating "vibrant neighborhoods where 80 percent of residents can easily walk or bicycle to meet all basic daily, non-work needs and have safe pedestrian or bicycle access to transit."[32] As of 2017, 65 percent of Portland's residents fall under this category.[33] The city has mapped its neighborhoods for walkability and has laid out many steps to achieve their goal. These include establishing a "balanced funding mechanism for creating walkable neighborhoods" and identifying land use changes to create bikeable and walkable neighborhoods but also improve the quality of that experience.[34]

Creating more inviting and safe streetscapes is another element of walkable neighborhoods. St Louis plans to make sure that bridges are accessible to pedestrians and is creating a unified plan for streetscape improvements such as traffic calming measures.[35] New York specifically calls to increase the number of benches lining sidewalks and intersections that feature pedestrian countdown signals.[36] San Jose wants to install cooling facilities along sidewalks that will provide shade for pedestrians and cyclists, given the often sweltering summer temperatures experienced in that city.[37] A number of cities, such as Madison, now have programs that assure that school children have safe and walking routes to school. This can include establishing citywide "walking school buses" that consist of chaperones walking groups of children to school.[38]

Finally, as noted earlier, centering dense, walkable, and mixed-use communities around public transportation nodes is particularly important, as attracting ridership is vital to the economic sustainability of these systems. Transit-oriented development (TOD) is a strategy to accomplish this (see Box 5.2 and Table 5.1). For this reason, TOD is at the forefront of planning strategies to make public transportation options economically viable and reduce VMT in cities.

Box 5.2   Best Practices in Planning: Transit-Oriented Development in Arlington

One of the earliest and most often cited examples of transit-oriented development (TOD) is the Rosslyn-Ballston Corridor in Arlington, Virginia. This development concentrates high-density, mixed-use development along a major transit corridor outside of Washington, D.C. Planning for and implementation of these strategies has a long history. Crucially, in the 1960s, as the rail lines were being planned, Arlington county lobbied against the easier aboveground option that would run adjacent to an existing highway, and instead for an underground line that would run through existing town centers. They were successful.

Fig. 5.5   Arlington's Transit-Oriented Development Corridor, with a view towards downtown Washington, D.C. The axis is approximately 3 miles long. As with many TOD projects, higher density surrounds the Metro stops and bus lines. (Source: "Transit Oriented Development," Wikipedia/ Wikimedia Commons (Arlington County, created November 30, 2010), accessed April 11, 2018, https://upload.wikimedia.org/wikipedia/ commons/b/b3/Arlington_County_-_Virginia.jpg)

(*continued*)

> **Box 5.2   (continued)**
>
> Then, in the 1980s, following extensive study and community input, the county implemented what they call a "bull's-eye approach," which targets the tallest and most dense development within one-quarter mile of each Metrorail station. These areas are zoned to provide for a mix of office, hotel, retail, and residential development.
>
> Between 1990 and 2000, the population increased by nearly 107 percent within a quarter-mile radius of the Rosslyn-Ballston metro stations, accounting for 28 percent of the county's overall growth. Today, the corridor is home to seven mixed-use, walkable, and bicycle-friendly Metro transit villages, 36 million square feet of office space, 6 million square feet of retail space, and over 47,000 residential units (Fig. 5.5).
>
> Source:
>
> "Rosslyn-Ballston Corridor," Arlington Projects and Planning, accessed January 28, 2018, https://projects.arlingtonva.us/planning/smart-growth/rosslyn-ballston-corridor/

Currently, there are dozens of TOD projects around the United States including the Del Mar Station in Pasadena, Atlantic Station in Atlanta, Mizner Park in Boca Raton, Horton Plaza in San Diego, and Mockingbird Station in Dallas—all cities traditionally associated with low-density sprawl. Cities like St. Louis and Chicago have recently announced strategies to design standards, change zoning laws, and provide incentives to developers to encourage denser development of housing and retail near transit stations. Table 5.2 highlights common ways to increase walkability.

That said, we must add that there are also projects that have received incentives and special permitting as "TOD" but have failed to encourage public transportation ridership and reduce VMT. These projects feature a number of different shortcomings including offering insufficient high-quality public transit options, neglecting the streetscape and qualities that encourage walkability, or an insufficient diversity of uses, among others. The good news is that there are many examples of successful projects and also studies of failures to learn from. However, cities should take the time to assure that TOD incentives are awarded to projects that respond to local needs and include the TOD components necessary to be successful.

Table 5.1   Transit-oriented development

Components of transit-oriented development
- Walkable design with pedestrian as the highest priority
- Train station as prominent feature of town center
- Public square fronting train station
- A regional node containing a mixture of uses in close proximity (office, residential, retail, civic)
- High-density, walkable district within 10-minute walk circle surrounding train station
- Collector support transit systems including streetcar, light rail, and buses
- Designed to include the easy use of bicycles and scooters as daily support transport
- Large ride-in bicycle parking areas within stations
- Bikeshare rental system and bikeway network integrated into stations
- Reduced and managed parking inside 10-minute walk circle around town center/train station
- Specialized retail at stations serving commuters and locals including cafes, grocery, dry cleaners

Benefits of transit-oriented development
- Higher quality of life with better places to live, work, and play
- Greater mobility with ease of moving around
- Increased transit ridership
- Reduced traffic congestion, car accidents, and injuries
- Reduced household spending on transportation, resulting in more affordable housing
- Healthier lifestyle with more walking and less stress
- Higher, more stable property values
- Increased foot traffic and customers for area businesses
- Greatly reduced dependence on foreign oil, reduced pollution, and environmental damage
- Reduced incentive to sprawl, increased incentive for compact development
- Less expensive than building roads and sprawl
- Enhanced ability to maintain economic competitiveness

Source: Transit Oriented Development Institute, at http://www.tod.org/home.html January, 2018

We note that there is another planning term associated with dense, walkable urban development. "Traditional Neighborhood Design" is a design-based approach which features concepts along the lines of New Urbanist principals such as walkable neighborhoods with stores, schools, and public spaces within walking distance of residences. Charleston is using these principles to encourage walkability using characteristics of traditional town centers.[39]

Reinvesting in Public Transportation
Many cities aim to make public transit the preferred mode of transportation for an increasing number of residents by improving connectivity and

Table 5.2   Ten steps to walkability

1. Mix the uses
2. Offer parking, but incentivize non-automobile use
3. Invest in public transit
4. Welcome bikes and car shares
5. Protect the pedestrian (make it safe!)
6. Provide spaces of play and relaxation
7. Plant trees
8. Make sure area is inclusive of all needs and users
9. Ensure affordable housing
10. Make the space interesting

Source: Based on Jeff Speck, 2012. *Walkable City: How Downtown can Save America One Step at a Time.* New York: North Point Press

accessibility through efficient, integrated, and affordable transit systems.[40] Achieving these ends will require significant investments. While some cities have extensive existing rail systems that they would like to better maintain or expand, others are exploring the creation of rail, streetcar, or rapid bus transit systems from key well-traveled areas such as an airport, a convention center, an arts district, or a sports center.

As cities prioritize transit investments, a best practice is to consider the features of transit most valued by the public. Multi-city user surveys indicate that expedient transit times and greater frequency of service are the most sought after public transportation features, as opposed to more aesthetic or experiential conveniences, like more comfortable seats or Wi-Fi access.[41] Sometimes a small change can make a big difference—for example, a bus that comes every 10 minutes instead of every 20 minutes may attract significantly more riders. Other practical improvements, including sheltered stops, and countdown clocks are also important. Chicago has invested in technology to provide customers with real-time transit information for trains and buses, through their website, smartphone applications, text messaging, and on-street displays.[42] Other cities are using similar apps and other technologies.

Urban Rail

Many cities are investing again in rail systems. Philadelphia is a good example of a city that has a tripartite approach to managing its rail infrastructure. First, the city hopes to improve rider experience and safety through basic steps like performing regular maintenance and cleaning

Box 5.3   Best Practices in Governance: Collaboration, Funding, and Evaluation in Madison

Madison, Wisconsin offers several best practices in governance. First, in the hopes of fostering better collaboration between city agencies, departments and committees, the city has called for quarterly transportation meetings for all department heads related to transportation and the co-location of transportation-related departments. They are further considering creating a position for communication liaisons between departments. These efforts recognize that sustainable transportation solutions will require better collaboration between departments. As we seek to identify and implement projects that provide multiple benefits, cities need innovative solutions to address the challenge of coordinating these efforts.

Madison is also exploring financial strategies to encourage the use of public transportation. Typically, cities construct and repair roads using federal or state dollars or out of their general tax revenue. In this way, the United States has effectively subsidized cars, because car drivers do not pay the full cost of this form of travel. However, Madison is considering ways to put more of the costs of road construction and maintenance on those who use them, or on properties that generate trips. The creation of a "Transportation Utility" that assesses fees for road use would reduce the subsidies provided to car drivers by requiring them to pay for related infrastructure. Ironically, users of public rail transit generally do bear infrastructure costs of track maintenance, as these are generally paid for by user fees rather than tax dollars. Madison has also lobbied state and federal decision-makers to reallocate highway money to alternative transportation.

Finally, Madison recognizes the need for concrete goals and targets for increasing alternative transportation, yet currently lacks the measures to create these. In response, the city will conduct a city-wide transportation survey that establishes methodology and standards for tracking mode-share, vehicle miles traveled, and other important transportation data. Measuring non-motorized flow/traffic numbers, as well as motorized traffic, on major pedestrian/bicycle arterials and collectors will more effectively help them plan for investment in the future.

Source:

The City of Madison, "The Madison Sustainability Plan: Fostering Environmental, Economic, and Social Resistance," 2011, https://www.cityofmadison.com/sustainability/documents/SustainPlan2011.pdf

stations more regularly.[43] Second, the city is trying to secure more investment for its current transit infrastructure such as updating train control computers.[44] Finally, the city is developing plans to expand its subway and light rail system.[45]

Washington, D.C. has the nation's second biggest heavy rail transit system (Metro), yet faces enormous challenges as it seeks to address a series of safety concerns, rebound from decades of deferred maintenance which now require service disruptions over the course of years to address, and recover community trust.[46] While management problems were also to blame, the primary challenge has been a lack of funding for proactive improvements and maintenance over the system's 40-year existence. A system that opened to such fanfare in 1976 is now crumbling.[47] Washington's Metro system extends beyond the city into Virginia and Maryland and is governed by a fractious 16-member board representing all jurisdictions, a particular challenge.[48] The Metro system has been forced to raise fares and reduce service frequencies, and the system has seen a decline in ridership since 2009.[49]

In 2016, Metro launched a maintenance program with the less-than-inspirational title, "Back to Good" during which they would have to shut down entire portions of the Metro system to assure safety. Bemoaning the state of Metro has become a D.C. pastime, and users vent their frustration on a rogue Twitter account called @unsuckdcmetro. After more than a year of intensive upgrades, Metro Board Chairman Jack Evans wryly noted, "we fixed the 13 or 15 worst parts of the system, and now we have a system that has a lot of bad parts, but not the worst parts. And so, the ongoing maintenance will continue for the rest of eternity."[50] However, things are looking up for Metro. Until 2018, Metro was the only major transit system in the United States without a dedicated source of funding. That changed, with Virginia, Maryland, and Washington, D.C. together pledging $500 million per year.[51] They also expect to receive $150 million from the US Congress in 2018.

While cities with older rail systems suffer from age and maintenance issues, other cities are building new light rail lines and systems. Phoenix's light rail system, which opened in 2008, already runs 20 miles through the middle of the city and is expanding quickly.[52] The city hopes to extend the system an additional 66 miles by 2034. Rapid expansion of the program and ties to downtown densification and redevelopment projects are seen as keys to the systems success.

Similarly, the City of Charlotte extended its light rail system by 9.3 miles, connecting it to Chapel Hill. Indeed, our research shows that the most successful light rail projects are designed to be expedient and include features like a dedicated right-of-way or connect to large ridership genera-tors, like universities and hospitals. The new line has attracted higher-density, mixed-use development along the corridor.[53] That said, some of the developments along this line feature a high number of parking spaces and parking garages (considered a *worst* practice in transit-oriented development, we should note). Developers argue the market is not ready for apartments and commercial buildings with less parking, even next to mass transit, and that they find it difficult to get funding for projects from lenders if they do not include enough parking.[54] These perspectives high-light some of the deep structural challenges that must be addressed to make urban rail and TOD projects viable and reduce VMT.

Even Los Angeles, the quintessential automobile-centric city known for monumental traffic jams, has made changes. Los Angeles is recognized as an automobile capital because of its size, dependence on automobiles, network of freeways, and its general lack of public transportation. However, in the 1990s, a modern rail transit network was built using many old tran-sit right-of-ways, relics of an early twentieth-century streetcar system. Today, the Metro system consists of six lines, serving 93 stations and that carry some 360,000 riders daily (Fig. 5.6). In addition, at all metro sta-tions, information is available in multiple languages. Surely if Los Angeles can invest more in public transit, every city can!

Improved Bus Service

Rail projects can be costly, take years to materialize, and are fixed in place once built. Many cities have instead sought to provide public transporta-tion options through improved bus service, which they can implement at a fraction of the cost and time of a rail system. The latest trend is bus rapid transit, which features expedited travel and reduced waiting times using strategies such as dedicated travel lanes and traffic light right-of-ways. Pre-paid cards, or other options that allow people to pre-pay before boarding, also speed up trips. Several cities are using GIS mapping to optimize bus routes and assess information such as the geographical distribution of tran-sit users to understand and document the impacts on car use in the city.[55]

Interestingly, many of the best bus rapid transit systems (BRT) are found in developing cities such as Curitiba (Brazil), Bogotá (Colombia), Guatemala City (Guatemala), Quito (Ecuador), and the São Paulo (Brazil) metro region. These systems have been in place for well over a decade—Curitiba's has been open since 1974—and may provide US cities with best practices.[56]

Fig. 5.6 Light rail in Los Angeles, a city once known for only automobiles. (Source: Lisa Benton-Short.)

Cities have also begun to enact strategies to make public transit more visible, inviting, and user-friendly. Such changes are seen as necessary because buses generally have a poor public image.[57] Cities are upgrading waiting areas and installing more lighting. Anchorage has developed an "Adopt-A-Stop" program, which leverages the muscle power and vigilance of community groups to maintain bus stops across the city.[58] In New York City, companies such as Chariot have launched their own "on-demand" private bus system (with plush leather seats) and hope to attract the hipster crowd.

Some people are reluctant to use buses because it can be difficult to understand their schedule and exact route. In response to these reservations, some cities are simplifying bus route numbering, developing trip-planning resources, installing monitors, and featuring apps that provide real-time information on bus arrival.[59]

Biking Is Back

Riding a bike can be a healthy, an effective, and an affordable mode of transportation.[60] For these reasons, many cities are trying to encourage bicycling by providing safe, convenient infrastructure and educating the community about bicycling options.

In order to make biking a viable mode of transit for more Americans, it needs to be safer. The experience of many cities in northern Europe indicates that improved infrastructure and education can make bicycling safer.[61] In 2010, the rates of cyclist fatality and serious injury (controlled for miles traveled and exposure) were four to five times higher in the United States than in the Netherlands, Denmark, and Germany.[62] Delineated bike lanes improves safety, particularly those protected from car traffic, and is a best practice for promoting biking. Another best practice is to develop bike plans with community involvement and create a unified approach to visually delineate bike lanes and trails within the city, so these are clear to all users.[63] Cities like Minneapolis have become certified as "Bicycle Friendly Communities" by the League of American Bicyclists for steps they have taken to provide safe bicycle access in their cities.[64]

Many cities in the United States have set ambitious goals for expansion of their network of dedicated bicycle infrastructure. Washington, D.C. is focusing its expansion in the cities' lowest-income neighborhoods east of the Anacostia River, which are not coincidentally also the most geographically isolated and transit-poor areas of the city.[65] Philadelphia and other communities along the East Coast are collaborating on the East Coast Greenway project, a 3000-mile-long network of bike trails and bikeable roads from Northern Maine to Key West.[66]

Finally, cities have taken numerous steps to increase biking convenience. Installing bike racks, especially at transit nodes, is a first step. Many cities are encouraging or partnering with companies to develop bikeshare programs. Bikeshare programs are generally designed for short-term use (under an hour or so) and allow users to pick up and drop off bicycles at different docking stations throughout the city (Fig. 5.7). These programs have a variety of pricing schemes. Often the shortest term (around 30 minutes) is free or very inexpensive, especially with a subscription. Bikes are available to serve several users each day. The National Association of City Transportation Officials reports that between 2010 and 2016, more than 88 million trips were made on a bikeshare bike in the United States.

Fig. 5.7 (a) Washington, D.C.'s bikeshare program began in 2013. Bikeshare uses a bike docking system. By 2018, the program had almost 4000 bikes and 450 stations around the D.C. metro area, a result of increasing popularity. (b) Dockless bikes. In 2017 D.C. began a trial period allowing five dockless bike companies to begin service. Today there are several thousand dockless bikes on the streets of D.C. (Source: Lisa Benton-Short.)

While some cities such as New York have developed substantial and thriving bikeshare programs, other systems in Baltimore and Seattle have faltered. The reasons for failing systems may include an insufficiently dense network of docking stations where demand exists, a hilly geography like that in Seattle, or theft and damage to bikes as experienced in Baltimore. Many point to the need of increasing investment in the system and expanding ridership beyond young white urban professionals to other city demographics. This would both provide a larger base of users and share bikeshare benefits more equitably. The San Francisco Bay Area program has features that increase equity: there are discounted memberships for qualified residents and the ability to register in person and pay without credit or debit cards.[67]

The new trend in bikeshare is "dockless" options which provide more flexibility to users. A user finds and unlocks a "dockless" bike with a cell phone app, and the bike can be returned anywhere since the system operates without any stations or docks.[68] They have advantages for users over traditional bikeshares in terms of convenience, since it avoids the problem of finding open docks. And, they can be rolled out much more quickly because there is no need for planning and construction of docking stations. However, Beijing, where many start-up companies have already entered the dockless market, has faced challenges with the distribution of these bikes, resulting in some cases with bikes piling up and blocking side-walks.[69] Cities like Boston, Baltimore, and Washington, D.C. have cautiously phased in a selected number of private dockless bikeshare companies for a trial period, under the condition that data is shared with city planners so that usage, success, bottlenecks, and other potential challenges can be identified and a more informed strategy set in place.[70]

Increased Fuel Efficiency

While the most sustainable transportation options are by foot, bike, and public transit, the truth is that much of American land use, urban design, culture, and proclivities are still automobile driven.

Within this context, cities are also pursuing more incremental approaches to transportation sustainability by promoting the uptake of alternative fuel vehicles and policies to encourage driving efficiency. We explore these below.

Improving Public Fleet

Cities are focusing on the fuel efficiency of their own public fleets. This is logical: not only can improvements here translate to cost savings for cities, but they also represent concrete purchasing decisions that municipalities directly control to reduce GHG emissions and improve local air quality. Changing their public fleets to alternative fuels or zero-emission vehicles can demonstrate the efficacy and reliability of new technologies and utilize a city's purchasing power to drive uptake.

Cities such as New York are practicing a strategy to "reduce, replace, retrofit, and refuel vehicles."[71] The first strategy is to reduce the size of the city fleet. A second strategy is to replace less fuel-efficient vehicles with more efficient models. For instance, Shoreline, Washington, requires all new fleet vehicles be alternatively fueled, or rated by EPA for 45 MPG or higher, and Chicago will replace three percent of on-road fleet vehicles with green vehicles annually.[72] San Jose has an ambitious goal of 100 percent of its public fleet vehicles running on alternative fuels by 2020. As of 2018, the city reports that 41 percent of their fleet runs on alternative fuel, most running on biodiesel.[73]

Retrofitting and refueling vehicles is another avenue to achieving a more efficient fleet. Philadelphia notes that 70 percent of its fleet uses diesel, which includes specialized vehicles like city buses and trash and recycling trucks.[74] Retrofitting diesel vehicles with oxidation catalysts is relatively affordable and improves air quality by converting carbon monoxide, hydrocarbons, and particulate matter to carbon dioxide and water without having to change fuels.[75] Philadelphia also plans to develop a compressed natural gas facility that will allow the city to begin replacing diesel trash trucks with those that run on natural gas.[76]

Box 5.4   Best Practices in Innovation: Tulsa's Public Fleet

Tulsa, Oklahoma is improving the fuel efficiency of its public fleet. Their sustainability plan features several best practices in improving the fuel efficiency of its public fleet, framing these as smart cost savings measures, given the rising cost of fossil fuels.

First, Tulsa believes it can "right-size" its fleet over five years, reducing it by 550 vehicles (22 percent) and decreasing the number of vehicles assigned to individuals, without compromising service. This is a strong example of a considered, measurable goal with a concrete deadline. This is a best practice that many cities have not fully incorporated into their plans for sustainability.

Tulsa is also implementing several innovative strategies to increase the net fuel efficiency of its fleet and better align vehicle procurement with the city's overarching sustainability goals. It uses fleet data management software to track the overall cost of ownership of fleet vehicles (including fuel costs). This will inform replacement priorities, with the least efficient vehicles removed from the fleet first. The city plans to make dashboard data and summaries about fleet energy usage readily available to city administrators. They hope this information creates a culture shift in the administration and makes it easier to evaluate needed vehicle size, uses, and fuel efficiency before purchasing new city vehicles. Finally, the city is looking to use compressed natural gas (CNG) and hopes to lead the region in adopting CNG as a cost-effective, secure, and locally sourced transportation fuel. In 2016, Tulsa attained CLEAN Fleet Certification (CFC) from the Coalition for Green Fleet Management and was ranked the #13 Greenest Fleet in North America by the 100 Best Fleets Organization.

Source:

City of Tulsa, "City of Tulsa Sustainability Plan: Resource Efficiency, Clean Energy, and Leading Growth in the New Economy," October 27, 2011, pages 101–106.

Infrastructure, Education, and Incentives

Infrastructure provision is a common mechanism cities use to support the uptake of electric vehicles and other alternative fuel vehicles through their communities—for public uses and for private citizens alike. Austin and New York City are placing hundreds of plug-in stations for electric vehicles around the city. New York City is also streamlining the installation of home charging stations, while Madison is pioneering solar charging stations for electric vehicles.[77] Another innovation can be seen in regional collaboration to improve infrastructure for electric vehicles.

While many actions to promote alternative fuel vehicles are based on provision of new infrastructure, education and incentives also play a role. Madison and Charleston propose developing incentives such as free or "preferred parking" for alternative fueled vehicles, or "graduated parking rates based on fuel efficiency/emissions."[78] Philadelphia proposed that electric and hybrid taxis might have priority for taking on passengers at the airport. Charleston announced that it would conduct research on the possibility of assessing property tax on cars based on emissions rather than value.[79]

Driving Efficiency

Another approach is to increase the efficiency of car transport by decreasing congestion and solving parking problems in order to minimize car idling. To put this into perspective, nationally, an estimated $160 billion was wasted in time and fuel in 2015 due to congestion and traffic delays.[80] Beyond the aggravation of congestion and traffic delays, vehicles emit more when they are idling. An idling engine can produce up to twice as many exhaust emissions as an engine in motion.

Many cities propose prohibitions on idling engines as a way to increase car efficiency and decrease emissions of carbon dioxide, nitrogen oxides, and other volatile organic compounds (VOCs). Some cities are adopting an anti-idling policy for government vehicles such as school buses, given the sensitive populations they serve. Washington, D.C. proposes to use technology that allows police cars to run important functions without the engine running and will phase in these technologies first in areas with high asthma rates.[81] Other best practices include increased on-street loading zones and targeting enforcement efforts in particular neighborhoods with identified air quality concerns.[82] New York City has a three-minute idling limit enforceable by traffic tickets and fines.[83]

Some cities are using new technologies to install traffic signal timers that better synchronize with traffic flows.[84] The hunt for parking spaces and double parking is another major source of congestion. Several cities publicize or have invested in parking apps that help people identify convenient, available and less expensive parking. Madison is one of these, and the city promotes a "Smart Park" policy to inform drivers of available parking, "so that unnecessary miles (with associated pollution and congestion) aren't driven looking for a parking spot."[85] Another option is encouraging flexible work hours, which allows drivers to avoid driving at high-traffic times or telecommuting.

Several cities are exploring the possibility of creating a regional congestion fee for travel during peak hours."[86] The largest and best known of these programs is in London, which designated a "Congestion Zone" around the downtown in 2003. Drivers that enter the Congestion Zone are charged $16 dollars a day. Since the congestion charging scheme began, it has resulted in a 10 percent reduction in traffic volumes, and an overall reduction of 11 percent in vehicle miles traveled. To date, congestion pricing is highly unpopular in the United States. Steadfast critics resist any infringement on their "freedom" to drive, resent being nickeled and dimed, and have exerted political pressure that, so far, has made this option less politically viable.

It is important to highlight that efforts to reduce congestion by adding and widening highways have had unanticipated effects. Comparisons between the amount of newly constructed roads and highways and the total vehicle miles traveled in different US cities indicate that road construction actually increases the amount that people choose to drive.[87] This finding confirms the "fundamental law of highway congestion" and is based on the economic concept of induced demand: increasing the supply of something (like roads) makes people want more. We question whether efforts to increase driving efficiency or ways to make it easier to park will actually reduce wastes of time and fuel; we are concerned that some of these techniques might actually encourage more people to take to their cars.

What's Missing: Even Completer Streets

We argue that cities need to take this moment to fundamentally re-envision city streets for sustainability. A movement for "Complete Streets" recognizes that street design in the United States has prioritized the experience of motorists above all other users, and seeks to change this by enabling safe and convenient travel for all users including pedestrians, bicyclists, bus riders, motorists, children, older adults, and the disabled.[88] Best practices include separated bike lanes, bus lanes, transit prioritization, wider side-walks, and pedestrian bump outs for safe street crossing (Fig. 5.8). New York City has made tremendous progress pioneering and implementing complete streets and measuring a host of their benefits—from increased bike ridership to reduced commercial vacancy.[89] While many cities are making progress in this area, we are surprised that it is not more central to most cities sustainable transportation efforts.

Fig. 5.8 A Completer Street. This photo shows best practices in integrating pedestrian, bike, public transit, trees, and permeable pavement in Berlin, Germany. Many US cities could learn from this example to create "Completer Streets" that consider not only transportation but also multiple benefits such as enhanced green space and walkability. (Source: "Complete Street (DSC_4942)" digital image taken July 10, 2014, posted to Flickr by Eric Sehr, https://www.flickr.com/photos/ericvery/15470445801 (accessed April 10, 2018), licence at https://creativecommons.org/licenses/by-sa/2.0/)

We also argue that this is the time for not just "Complete Streets" but even "*Completer* Streets." Thus far, the Complete Streets movement is mostly about sustainable transportation—designing for safety of all users and facilitating expedited bus transportation. We call for a broader understanding of the benefits that street space can provide in our cities for two reasons. First, streets are under the control of local authorities, so improvements in these areas are a way that cities can weave features providing multiple services and benefits within the existing urban fabric. Second, opportunities exist for sustainability benefits that move beyond transportation. Swales and pervious pavements can help manage storm-water. Street trees and low albedo (reflective) surfaces can help reduce the urban heat island effect and improve air quality, and thus can be particularly important in places we are seeking to encourage more physical activity.

The truth is that many cities have strong street tree programs and are even considering how streets can help management stormwater. (An example is Chicago's Green Alleys program which retrofits alleyways with permeable pavements.) However, a "Completer Streets" movement could unify these strategies and integrate them into routine practice. Over the past years, many cities, such as Louisville, Atlanta, San Francisco, and Boston, have created street design manuals for Complete Streets that formalize these changes. We see the need to create a similar design manual that includes a wider swath of best practices, as a way to scale these up from demonstration to citywide implementation. A reconceptualization of streets as places that provide multiple benefits is a straightforward way for cities to integrate these amenities into existing urban fabric.

Summary

Cities today have a central role in creating the infrastructure and developing a culture that promotes sustainable transportation options. Some strategies represent smaller, incremental steps, but many of the strategies we examined hold promise for major transformations in creating sustainable transportation and demonstrate that cities are engaged in rethinking transportation and sustainability in the twenty-first century. Table 5.3 summarizes the important trends and best practices.

Table 5.3   Best practices in transportation

Creating walkability

- Consider "20-minute neighborhood" concept
- Create inviting and safe streetscapes
- Zone to promote transit-oriented development (TOD)
- Improve sidewalk connectivity and amenities, particularly near transit corridors and mixed-use neighborhoods

Public Transit

- Reinvest in public transportation
- Improve bus service and systems
- Reduce travel time and increase frequency of service to enhance rider experience
- Consider bus rapid transit
- Consider how public transit integrates with car shares and bikeshares

Biking

- Support and expand bikeshare programs
- Enhance safety through separated or dedicated bike lanes
- Invest in bike infrastructure in low-income neighborhoods
- Collect data to determine how best to combat sites with frequent crashes

Increase fuel efficiency

- Retrofit diesel vehicles with oxidation catalysts
- Install infrastructure for electric and hybrid vehicles (plug-in stations, preferred parking)
- Tax vehicles based on emissions rather than value
- Establish anti-idling laws
- Centralize fleet and charging departments for fuel used
- Optimize green fleet replacement schedules

NOTES

1. United States Environmental Protection Agency, "Sources of Greenhouse Gas Emissions: Transportation Sector Emissions," April 14, 2017, https://www.epa.gov/ghgemissions/sources-greenhouse-gas-emissions#transportation.
2. United States Environmental Protection Agency, "Smog, Soot, and Other Air Pollution from Transportation," accessed April 2, 2018, https://www.epa.gov/air-pollution-transportation/smog-soot-and-local-air-pollution.
3. World Health Organization, "Ambient Air Pollution: Health Impacts," accessed March 28, 2018, http://www.who.int/airpollution/ambient/health-impacts/en/.
4. Jennifer Chu, "Study: Air Pollution Causes 200,000 Early Deaths Each Year in the U.S.," MIT News, 2013, http://news.mit.edu/2013/study-air-pollution-causes-200000-early-deaths-each-year-in-the-us-0829.
5. Centers for Disease Control and Prevention, "Motor Vehicle Safety: Pedestrian Safety," August 9, 2017, https://www.cdc.gov/motorvehicle-safety/pedestrian_safety/index.html.

6. National Highway Traffic Safety Administration, "Traffic Fatalities up Sharply in 2015" (United States Department of Transportation, August 29, 2016), https://www.nhtsa.gov/press-releases/traffic-fatalities-sharply-2015.

7. American Society of Civil Engineers, "2017 Infrastructure Report Card."

8. Doug Hecox, "3.2 Trillion Miles Driven On U.S. Roads In 2016," U.S. Department of Transportation Federal Highway Administration, February 21, 2017, https://www.fhwa.dot.gov/pressroom/fhwa1704.cfm.

9. City of Portland, "The Portland Plan April 2012," 2012, 42, http://www.portlandonline.com/portlandplan/index.cfm?c=58776.

10. Livable Streets, "Urban Happiness with Enrique Peñalosa," n.d.

11. Sarah Parsons, "4 Big Ideas to Revolutionize Transportation," World Resources Institute, 2013, http://www.wri.org/blog/2013/01/4-big-ideas-revolutionize-transportation.

12. Parsons.

13. Hayley Richardson, "All Transportation Is Local," accessed November 28, 2017, http://www.nlc.org/article/all-transportation-is-local.

14. American Society of Civil Engineers, "2017 Infrastructure Report Card."

15. The City of Madison, "The Madison Sustainability Plan: Fostering Environmental, Economic, and Social Resistance," 2011, 27, https://www.cityofmadison.com/sustainability/documents/SustainPlan2011.pdf.

16. Sustainable DC, "Sustainability DC," 2012, 80, https://sustainable.dc.gov/sites/default/files/dc/sites/sustainable/page_content/attachments/DCS-008%20Report%20508.3j.pdf.

17. The Economist, "Bicycles and Bans Are Reshaping the City," September 14, 2017, https://www.economist.com/news/europe/21728997-motorists-denounce-hipster-takeover-bicycles-and-bans-are-reshaping-city.

18. Charleston Green Committee, "Charleston Green Plan," 2007, 15, http://www.charlestongreencommittee.com/charlestongreenplan2010.pdf.

19. Sustainable DC, "Sustainability DC," 87.

20. Sustainable DC, 32.

21. City of Burlington, "The Burlington Legacy Project," 2000, https://www.burlingtonvt.gov/sites/default/files/CEDO/Legacy_Project/Legacy%20Action%20Plan.pdf.

22. Pierre-Henri Bono et al., "Métros et attractivité internationales des villes" (Sciences Po LIEPP Policy Brief, December 2017), https://spire.science-spo.fr/hdl:/2441/1nc1j3sifu9p2pr7v2hj7cpd05/resources/liepp-pb36-bono-et-ali.pdf.

23. City of Burlington, 13.

24. The City of Miami Beach, "Sustainability Plan Energy Economic Zone Work Plan," November 12, 2009, 12, http://www.miamibeachfl.gov/green/scroll.aspx?id=63975.
25. All Transit, "Potential Uses," accessed January 26, 2018, https://alltransit.cnt.org/potential-uses/.
26. City of Newport News, "Roadmap to Sustainability," February 2013, 92, https://www.nngov.com/DocumentCenter/View/1586.
27. City of Chicago, "2015 Sustainable Chicago Action Agenda," September 2012, 16, https://www.cityofchicago.org/content/dam/city/progs/env/SustainableChicago2015.pdf.
28. The City of New York, "PlaNYC A Greener, Greater New York," 2011, 42, http://www.nyc.gov/html/planyc/downloads/pdf/publications/planyc_2011_planyc_full_report.pdf.
29. John I. Gilderbloom, William W. Riggs, and Wesley L. Meares, "Does Walkability Matter? An Examination of Walkability's Impact on Housing Values, Foreclosures and Crime," *Cities* 42, no. Part A (February 1, 2015): 13–24, https://doi.org/10.1016/j.cities.2014.08.001.
30. Walk Score, "Walk Score," accessed January 26, 2018, https://www.walkscore.com/.
31. City of Portland, "The Portland Plan April 2012," 40.
32. City of Portland Oregon and Multnomah County, "Climate Action Plan: Local Strategies to Address Climate Change," June 2015, 26, https://www.portlandoregon.gov/bps/article/531984.
33. City of Portland Oregon and Multnomah County, "Climate Action Plan Progress Report," April 2017, 2, https://multco.us/file/62269/download.
34. City of Portland, "The Portland Plan April 2012," 42.
35. City of St. Louis Planning Commission, "City of St. Louis Sustainability Plan," February 6, 2013, 40, https://www.stlouis-mo.gov/government/departments/mayor/documents/upload/STL-Sustainability-Plan.pdf.
36. The City of New York, "PlaNYC," 95.
37. The City of San Jose, "San Jose's Green Vision," 2007, 12, http://www.globalurban.org/San_Jose_Green_Vision.pdf.
38. The City of Madison, "The Madison Sustainability Plan," 57.
39. Charleston Green Committee, "Charleston Green Plan," 72.
40. City of Chicago, "2015 Sustainable Chicago Action Agenda," 16, 82.
41. American Society of Civil Engineers, "2017 Infrastructure Report Card."
42. City of Chicago, "2015 Sustainable Chicago Action Agenda," 17.
43. City of Philadelphia, "Greenworks Philadelphia," 2009, 65, https://beta.phila.gov/documents/greenworks-progress-reports/.
44. City of Philadelphia, 66.
45. City of Philadelphia, 66.

46. Cynthia Shahan, "5 Largest Public Transit Systems In US (Infographic)" (Clean Technica, August 30, 2014), https://cleantechnica.com/2014/08/30/largest-public-transit-systems-us-infographic/.

47. John Rennie Short, "Why Is the U.S. Unwilling to Pay for Good Public Transportation?," The Conversation, April 1, 2016, https://theconversation.com/why-is-the-u-s-unwilling-to-pay-for-good-public-transportation-56788.

48. Gulliver, "How to Fix Washington, DC's Unloved Metro," *The Economist*, March 17, 2016, https://www.economist.com/blogs/gulliver/2016/03/subway-systems-problems-run-deep.

49. Gulliver.

50. Martine Powers, "Metro's Wild Year Included a Paint Debate," Washington Post, December 31, 2017, http://thewashingtonpost.newspaperdirect.com/epaper/viewer.aspx?issue=105820171231000000000001001&page=28&article=6aa748be-2d75-4cf5-a361-ae631000a364&key=F9O%2BUQI5QRpiTD5fKvCtFw%3D%3D&feed=rss.

51. Robert McCartney, "Metro Gets Third and Final 'Yes' as Maryland Commits to Its Full Share of Dedicated Funding," *Washington Post*, March 22, 2018, sec. Transportation, https://www.washingtonpost.com/local/trafficandcommuting/metro-gets-3rd-and-final-yes-as-maryland-commits-to-its-full-share-of-dedicated-funding/2018/03/22/ecd63946-2dfa-11e8-8ad6-fbc50284fce8_story.html.

52. Patrick Sisson, "Perfecting Public Transportation: 10 U.S. Cities Getting Public Transportation Right," Curbed, January 24, 2017, https://www.curbed.com/2017/1/24/14361030/best-cities-public-transportation-light-rail-bus.

53. Eli Portillo, "Along the Blue Line Extension, New Developments Are Taking Shape," News, The Charlotte Observer, January 24, 2016, http://www.charlotteobserver.com/news/business/biz-columns-blogs/development/article55922980.html.

54. Eli Portillo, "Charlotte's Light Rail Was Supposed to Change Our Attitude about Cars. It Hasn't.," News, The Charlotte Observer, accessed November 29, 2017, http://www.charlotteobserver.com/news/business/biz-columns-blogs/development/article149577004.html.

55. The City of Austin, "Rethink For A Bright Green Future," 2008, 11.

56. Drew Reed, "How Curitiba's BRT Stations Sparked a Transport Revolution—a History of Cities in 50 Buildings, Day 43," *The Guardian*, May 26, 2015, https://www.theguardian.com/cities/2015/may/26/curitiba-brazil-brt-transport-revolution-history-cities-50-buildings.

57. Charleston Green Committee, "Charleston Green Plan," 96.

58. Municipality of Anchorage, "Adopt-A-Stop Checklist," Municipality of Anchorage, accessed November 29, 2017, https://www.muni.org/Departments/transit/PeopleMover/Pages/AASCheck.aspx.

59. The City of Madison, "The Madison Sustainability Plan," 19; City of Chicago, "2015 Sustainable Chicago Action Agenda," 26.
60. City of Chicago, "2015 Sustainable Chicago Action Agenda," 17.
61. John Pucher and Ralph Buehler, "Safer Cycling Through Improved Infrastructure," *American Journal of Public Health* 106, no. 12 (December 2016): 2089–91, https://doi.org/10.2105/AJPH.2016.303507.
62. Ralph Buehler and John Pucher, "Trends in Walking and Cycling Safety: Recent Evidence From High-Income Countries, With a Focus on the United States and Germany," *American Journal of Public Health* 107, no. 2 (February 2017): 281–87, https://doi.org/10.2105/AJPH.2016.303546.
63. Charleston Green Committee, "Charleston Green Plan," 97.
64. Liz Murphy, "Bicycle Friendly Communities," Text, League of American Bicyclists, May 14, 2013, http://bikeleague.org/community.
65. Sustainable DC, "Sustainability DC," 83.
66. East Coast Greenway Alliance, "East Coast Greenway—Home," accessed November 29, 2017, https://www.greenway.org/.
67. Ford GoBike, "Bike Share for All," accessed November 29, 2017, http://www.fordgobike.com/pricing/bikeshareforall.
68. Vock Daniel, "Dockless Bike Shares Are Here. Are Cities Ready for Them?," Governing, October 2, 2017, http://www.governing.com/gov-dockless-bikeshare.html.
69. Javier C. Hernández, "As Bike-Sharing Brings Out Bad Manners, China Asks, What's Wrong With Us?," *The New York Times*, September 2, 2017, sec. Asia Pacific, https://www.nytimes.com/2017/09/02/world/asia/china-beijing-dockless-bike-share.html.
70. Luz Lazo, "Dockless Bike-Share Companies Race to Washington," *Washington Post*, September 19, 2017, sec. Transportation, https://www.washingtonpost.com/local/trafficandcommuting/dockless-bike-share-companies-race-to-washington/2017/09/19/a7e2c346-9a33-11e7-b569-3360011663b4_story.html.
71. The City of New York, "PlaNYC," 125; The City of New York, "NYC Clean Fleet," December 2015.
72. City of Shoreline, "Shoreline Environmental Sustainability Strategy," July 14, 2008, 24, http://cosweb.ci.shoreline.wa.us/uploads/attachments/pds/esc/COMPLETE_FinalSESStrategy2008July.pdf; City of Chicago, "2015 Sustainable Chicago Action Agenda," 18.
73. The City of San Jose, "Goal 8: Ensure That 100 Percent of Public Fleet Vehicles Run on Alternative Fuels," San Jose, California, January 2018, 8, http://www.sanjoseca.gov/index.aspx?NID=2953.
74. City of Philadelphia, "Greenworks Philadelphia," 30.

75. Hakan Caliskan and Kazutoshi Mori, "Environmental, Enviroeconomic and Enhanced Thermodynamic Analyses of a Diesel Engine with Diesel Oxidation Catalyst (DOC) and Diesel Particulate Filter (DPF) after Treatment Systems," *Energy* 128, no. Supplement C (June 1, 2017): 128–44, https://doi.org/10.1016/j.energy.2017.04.014.
76. City of Philadelphia, "Greenworks Philadelphia," 31.
77. The City of New York, "PlaNYC," 126; The City of Madison, "The Madison Sustainability Plan," 38.
78. The City of Madison, "The Madison Sustainability Plan," 33; Charleston Green Committee, "Charleston Green Plan," 106.
79. Charleston Green Committee, "Charleston Green Plan," 106.
80. American Society of Civil Engineers, "2017 Infrastructure Report Card," 1.
81. Sustainable DC, "Sustainability DC," 19.
82. Sustainable DC, 32.
83. The City of New York, "PlaNYC," 127.
84. Salt Lake City Division of Sustainability, "Sustainable Salt Lake: Plan 2015," 2015, 9, http://www.slcdocs.com/slcgreen/sustainablesaltlake_plan2015.pdf.
85. The City of Madison, "The Madison Sustainability Plan," 28.
86. Sustainable DC, "Sustainability DC," 86.
87. Gilles Duranton and Matthew Turner, "The Fundamental Law of Road Congestion: Evidence from US Cities," *American Economic Review* 101, no. 6 (October 2011): 2616–52.
88. Smart Growth America, "National Complete Streets Coalition," accessed March 20, 2018, https://smartgrowthamerica.org/program/national-complete-streets-coalition/.
89. New York City Department of Transportation, "Measuring the Street: New Metric for 21st Century Streets," 2012, http://www.nyc.gov/html/dot/downloads/pdf/2012-10-measuring-the-street.pdf.

CHAPTER 6

Energy

ENERGY: AN INTRODUCTION

In the urban context, energy is used for two broad purposes: transportation (including cars, trucks, planes, and trains, which is discussed in Chap. 7) and the generation of electricity, which powers industry, homes, and commercial buildings and is the focus of this chapter. It is estimated that globally, cities consume more than two-thirds of the world's energy and emit more than 70 percent of the world's GHGs.[1] For this reason, the urban-energy nexus is critical.

In the United States, a significant amount of energy is used to generate electricity. Today's US electricity system is a complex network of power plants, transmission and distribution wires, and end users of electricity. Most Americans receive their electricity from centralized power plants that use a wide variety of energy resources to produce electricity, including coal, natural gas, nuclear energy, or renewable resources such as water, wind, or solar energy. Since 2015, a significant amount of new energy generation capacity in the United States has come from renewable energy sources which have rapidly become the most economically competitive energy choice. Yet the majority of electricity in the United States is still derived from fossil fuels given the legacy of fossil fuel power plants in this country.

Energy is a major sustainability challenge. Although the United States produces a good deal of its own energy, it must rely on imported fossil fuels to meet domestic demand. Producing energy from fossil fuels releases pollutants and carbon dioxide into the air and dependence

© The Author(s) 2019

M. Keeley, L. Benton-Short, *Urban Sustainability in the US*,

https://doi.org/10.1007/978-3-319-93296-5_6

on these fuels leaves us vulnerable to global volatilities and price fluctuations. It is imperative that cities take action to meet the rising energy needs of their populations while maintaining a healthy living environment and avoiding catastrophic climate change.[2]

Fossil Fuels

The story of urban development in the United States is largely one of harnessing fossil fuel energy resources: first coal, then oil, and more recently natural gas. The nation's economy grew wealthy on carbon-based energy, but there was little thought given to how these practices impacted health and the environment.

Oil, coal, and natural gas are called fossil fuels because all three are derived from plant materials and living organisms which converted into hydrocarbons over millions of years. The type of fossil fuel formed depends on the nature of the organic material buried, the specific environmental conditions (types of sediment), and the time involved. Natural gas is trapped methane; crude oil is the residual sludge, and coal is highly compressed organic matter—mostly plants—that decomposed less than the others. Today, the three major fossil fuels—petroleum, natural gas, and coal—account for most of US energy production (Fig. 6.1).[3] Because fossil fuels contain high levels of carbon, they release carbon dioxide (CO_2) into the atmosphere when they are combusted along with particulate matter, nitrogen oxides, sulfur dioxide, mercury, and heavy metals.

Coal In 2016, coal generated 30 percent of all energy, most of that for electricity.[4] In addition to emitting greenhouse gases and other air pollutants, coal extraction also has environmental impacts (surface mining more visibly damages ecosystems but underground mining can create land subsidence and underground fires), as well as social impacts (mining work is hazardous and long-term health consequences are common).

Oil The United States has less than 5 percent of the world's population but consumes 20 percent of its oil.[5] The United States depends on imported oil for almost 25 percent of its petroleum.[6] In the United States, oil has become central for all forms of industrial production and transport. Many argue that without cheap oil, the US economy would grind to a halt. While public debate has focused on the need to reduce coal, there has been less discussion about reducing the use of petroleum, and very few

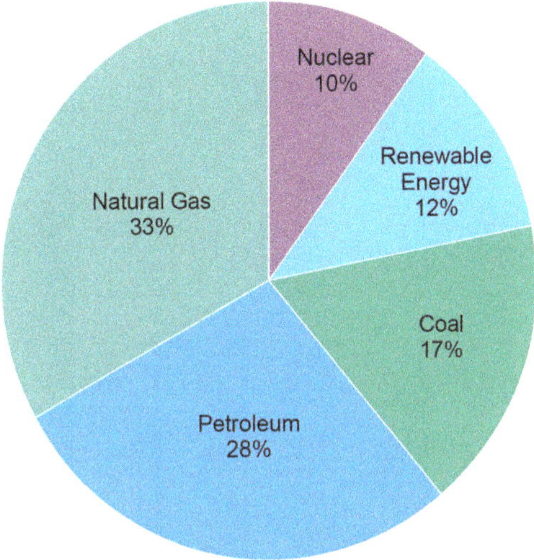

Fig. 6.1 Sources of energy production in the United States. (Source: Adapted from "U.S. Energy Facts Explained" U.S. Energy Information Administration, (last updated May 19, 2017), accessed March 20, 2018, https://www.eia.gov/energyexplained/?page=us_energy_home)

have suggested phasing out of petroleum by-products such as plastic chairs, cosmetics, and synthetic carpets.

Natural Gas Natural gas is largely methane and is called a "cleaner" fossil fuel because when burned, it emits less CO_2 and other air pollutants than other fossil fuels. Natural gas has become the leading source of energy production in the United States, and 97 percent of it is produced domestically.[7] Natural gas is also used for heating and cooking.

It is widely understood that fossil fuels have negative environmental and social impacts (Table 6.1). For decades, progress in addressing these has been hampered by the assumption that economic growth is dependent on current energy sources. Indeed, early in the industrial revolution, smoke stacks and the attendant poor air were a sign of success and economic prosperity. While some critics are still concerned that efforts to reduce fossil fuels, to conserve energy, or to switch to renewables could negatively impact economic growth, the good news is that cost-effective sustainable options—renewable energy—are available and many cities are making efforts to support uptake.

Table 6.1   The impacts of fossil fuel use

Extracting fossil fuels

- Ecosystem degradation and destruction
- Injury or death of workers
- Land subsidence
- Underground fires in coal mines
- Fires and explosions of oil wells (i.e. Deepwater Horizon in 2010)
- Impact on wildlife (pipelines, oil spills)
- Hydraulic fracturing (hydro-fracking) contaminates water and may be causing earthquakes
- Political impacts of oil dependency can include instability, and even war

Burning fossil fuels

- Gas emissions that include carbon dioxide, nitrogen oxides, sulfur oxides, and GHGs
- Emissions create air pollution that causes health impacts such as asthma or damages ecosystems (i.e. ozone poisoning)
- Emissions contribute to climate change
- Oil spills impact marine and coastal ecosystems
- Widespread traffic congestion
- Traffic accidents: Injuries and death

Renewable Energy

A renewable energy future is absolutely essential, yet the inertia of "business as usual" has stalled the development of renewable energy until relatively recently. Renewable energy such as solar, wind, and geothermal have become cost competitive with fossil fuels and offer tremendous potential to create a nonpolluting, more sustainable energy system. Many cities are making efforts to increase the use of renewable energy sources and have set ambitious targets for the proportion of electricity emanating from renewable sources including:

- Solar power
- Biofuels (wood and biomass)
- Wind
- Hydropower

Solar Solar energy, once slow to develop due to a lack of consistent government support, has seen tremendous gains in the last ten years. In the United States, markets for solar energy are maturing rapidly, and solar electricity is increasingly economically competitive with conventional energy sources. There are several types of solar energy systems, including photovoltaic (which converts sunlight directly), parabolic troughs (which concentrate energy to drive a generator), and solar water heaters. Solar power is more affordable, accessible, and prevalent than ever before. Solar installations have grown seventeen-fold in the last ten years, and the costs of installing PV panels had dropped by more than 60 percent, making solar installations affordable to many.[8] Homes around the country have solar panels and solar water heaters. Moreover, the solar industry is a proven incubator for job growth throughout the nation. As of 2017, solar jobs have increased about 168 percent since November 2010, with over 250,000 solar workers in the United States—this far outpaces job growth in conventional energy such as coal and oil.[9] While solar power is still a small part of total energy, its growth puts it on target to be one of the larger sources of renewable energy by 2040.[10]

Biofuels Biofuels are those made from solid, liquid, or gas biomass derived from living matter. In the United States, the most touted biofuel is ethanol made from corn. Recently farmers have benefited from the boost that ethanol has given to corn prices, but this trend is unlikely to be sustainable in the long term. The sustainability of energy produced by ethanol has been questioned. It may cost more and use more fossil fuels to produce than it returns as renewable energy, once all inputs are considered.[11] Using corn for energy production contributes a relatively large carbon footprint, increases food prices, and is an inefficient use of prime agricultural land. Seeking a nonfood crop that can be grown on marginal land (so agricultural lands can be used more efficiently) may be a more responsible approach to increase available biomass energy.

Wind While Europe leads the world in using wind energy, the United States has been actively investing in wind farms and capacity has been growing rapidly. Texas, Iowa, and California have been leaders in wind power, and recently many states have begun to add wind power to their energy portfolio. It is important to note that the wind industry also already employs more than people than coal.[12]

Hydropower The force of falling water can be used to drive turbogenerators, which in turn supplies electricity. In the United States, hydroelectric dams provide about 6.5 percent of electrical power and are generated from 300 large dams concentrated in the Northwest and Southeast.[13] While waterpower is a largely nonpolluting, renewable energy source, harnessing it with hydroelectric dams still involves ecological, social, and cultural trade-offs. Impoundments created behind the dam drown habitat and farmland. Dams can also impede or prevent the migration of fish, even when fish ladders are provided. Ecological consequences extend throughout river systems. Many experts believe that the United States has brought its hydropower to capacity. The trend now is to remove many of the smaller, legacy dams that impede the natural flow of rivers. As prices for renewable energy continue to fall, renewables are increasingly becoming an economical energy choice for American homeowners and businesses. The most significant hurdle to affordable solar and wind energy remains the soft costs—like permitting, zoning, and hooking a system up to the power grid. Part of the problem has been that renewable energy has been chronically underfunded, while fossil fuels have been subsidized for decades. Programs and policies to overcome the soft costs of renewable energy will help level the playing field and speed our uptake of renewable energy sources.

Another important barrier to an increased reliance on renewable energy is the periodicity of many of these energy sources. Solar panels produce energy when the sun is shining; wind turbines turn at the whim of winds. With renewable energy, power generation does not necessarily line up with times of power demand. Traditional fossil fuel burning power plants are unable to turn on and off quickly to "fill in" in response to this periodicity. For these reasons, developing advanced electricity storage capacity and updating the electrical grid will be important steps in phasing in renewable energy.

The United States has already seen emissions from fossil fuel combustion decrease as a result of multiple factors including substitution from coal to natural gas consumption in the electric power sector, warmer winter conditions that reduced demand for heating fuel in the residential and commercial sectors, and a slight decrease in electricity demand.[14] Many US mayors including those from Pittsburgh, San Diego, Austin, and Charlotte pledged to reduce carbon emissions, and the private sector is already shifting towards cleaner energy. There is an interdependent connection among energy, air pollution, and climate change, and much of what cities are doing to further sustainable energy will help address these other problems.

Cities' Role in Sustainable Energy

Cities act within a national energy framework including regional infrastructure systems and energy price fluctuations beyond their control. However, municipal governments are playing an increasingly central role in sustainable energy strategies. Many cities set their own targets for per capita energy use reduction or to increase the percentage of energy obtained from renewable sources. A small but growing number of cities (most of them small-sized) have already switched to 100 percent renewable energy, with zero net carbon emissions. Cities achieve these goals by changing practices in the buildings and utilities that they operate or by wielding power as a major consumer of electricity. Many cities are able to find considerable energy and cost efficiencies by better managing their energy-intensive water utilities, replacing street lights with high-efficiency fixtures, and in municipal purchasing policies that prioritize energy-efficient appliances and materials. Cities also influence the behavioral choices of citizens and businesses and educate the community about weatherization and sustainable energy options. Finally, cities can help finance projects in the private sector by offering incentives or low-interest loans to enable sustainable energy projects that offer savings in the long run but have high upfront costs.

Yet a challenge is that there is no universal solution to energy. Many energy strategies must be localized as cities' geographies determine their energy needs, optimal efficiency strategies, and opportunities for alternative energy production. The energy demand profiles in cold versus hot climates is very different. Significant variation in energy use exists even between neighborhoods in the same city. Studies of San Francisco show that average household carbon footprints vary according to "income, vehicle ownership, household size, home size, carbon intensity of electricity production, population density, and other factors."[15]

Cities are addressing energy for three main reasons:

1) Economic savings,
2) Improving air quality and public health
3) Mitigating climate change and reducing GHGs

For example, Philadelphia acknowledges the role of energy—first water power, and then fossil fuels—as a key to its successful industrial past, but highlights that success moving forward will require a sustainable energy economy and a reduced vulnerability to rising energy prices.[16] Chattanooga shares this perspective: "There is wide scale support for energy conservation within the community, especially with today's fluctuating energy costs."[17]

Still other cities see the need to reduce fossil fuel use in order to reduce air pollutants such as photochemical smog. Smog represents one of the most challenging air pollution problems for many US cities and is directly linked to increases in childhood asthma and respiratory tract infections. The EPA estimates that nearly four in ten people in the United States live in areas with unhealthy levels of ozone pollution. In Los Angeles, Denver, and Houston, residents have experienced long-term exposure to smog.

Many cities also have agendas to reduce greenhouse gas emissions (climate mitigation). For example, Pittsburgh has transformed itself over the past three decades since the collapse of the steel industry. The city estimates that over 13,000 Pittsburghers are now employed in the renewable energy sector.[18] In 2017 Pittsburgh's Mayor Bill Peduto announced a goal of complete reliance on renewable electricity sources for municipal operations by 2030 saying, "This is where the world's going…The only thing we can do is be a part of it—and lead it—like we did in the past in this country."[19]

The good news is that cities are playing an increasingly central role in sustainable energy strategies.[20] Nearly every city we have examined addresses energy as a major component of their plans for sustainability.

TAKING ACTION ON ENERGY

Energy conservation and the investment in renewable energy are the two most significant ways cities are taking action on energy. We first discuss energy conservation and efficiency efforts focused on both existing buildings and new construction. We then discuss how cities are developing alternative energy through policies, programs, and procurement power. Strategies here include innovative purchases of renewable energy, small-scale energy distribution, and using technology to create smart grids.

Energy Conservation and Efficiency

In the United States, buildings account for approximately 40 percent of all energy use.[21] Buildings have broader environmental impacts as well—about 40 percent of all extracted materials contribute to the built environment per year in the United States, and construction and demolition wastes together comprise one-third of landfilled materials.[22] Buildings also contribute 38 percent of carbon dioxide emissions and 12 percent of total water consumption. The siting of buildings can also have far-reaching impacts, such as its influence on transportation behavior, the landscape, and its connections to the electric, gas, and water grids.[23]

For these reasons, investing in sustainable building practices is a critical way that cities can move towards a more sustainable use of resources, including energy. Nearly every US city has policies and programs in place to encourage energy conservation.

Finally, it is important to realize that existing buildings are often already green and efficient. At a fundamental level, keeping and reusing old buildings has the environmental benefits of reuse and is one of the most environmentally sound things a person or community can do—more than building or buying anything new that claims to be green (Box 6.1).

Box 6.1   Best Practices in Innovation: Historic Buildings Are Green Buildings

Green building is an important element of urban sustainability, yet it is vital to consider the role that historic building preservation—which on the surface can seem the antithesis of cutting-edge green building techniques—plays in sustainability. Charleston's plans for sustainability often consider historic preservation. Beyond attracting tourists and establishing a unique sense of place, Charleston sets forth that "historic structures are inherently sustainable" because traditional construction practices used local materials, and focused on structural architectural practices to maximize ventilation, cooling, and lighting.[a] Indeed, there are a variety of energy-related benefits that rise from maintaining and reusing old buildings[b]:

1) **Embodied energy**—Continuing to use old buildings maximizes our use of the embodied energy of these structures. This is a recognition of the energy and carbon that was devoted to their construction.
2) **Environmental impacts**—Continued use of historic buildings also avoids the environmental impacts associated with the construction of new buildings including extraction, processing, and transportation of new materials.

(*continued*)

Box 6.1 (continued)

3) **Energy efficiency**—Some older buildings were constructed using techniques of "passive design." This approach achieves energy efficiency by taking advantage of sun energy for lighting and heating, natural air movement for cooling, etc.) These design approaches mean that some older buildings require less operating energy than new buildings. For example, data from the US Energy Information Administration (EIA) demonstrates that commercial buildings constructed before 1920 use less energy, per square foot, than buildings from any other decade of construction.[c]

4) **Density, transportation, and conserving land**—Older communities are often denser, more centrally located in cities, or are located on existing transportation corridors. These features reduce building users' use of cars and vehicle miles traveled. For this reason, reuse of existing structures is a key principle of smart growth.

These many benefits highlight the fact that at least in some cases, historic buildings are green buildings.

Sources:

[a]Charleston Green Committee, "Charleston Green Plan," April 2007, 2, accessed March 7, 2018, http://www.charlestongreencommittee.com/charlestongreenplan2010.pdf

[b]Tom Mayes and the National Trust for Historic Preservation, "Why do Old Places Matter?, January 9, 2017, accessed April 1, 2018, https://savingplaces.org/stories/why-do-old-places-matter

[c]Preservation Green Lab, "The Greenest Building: Quantifying the Environmental Value of Building Reuse" (National Trust for Historic Preservation, 2011, page 8), https://living-future.org/wp-content/uploads/2016/11/The_Greenest_Building.pdf

Energy Conservation and Efficiency of the Existing Building Stock
In most cities, building turnover rates are relatively low. For this reason, consideration of the energy efficiency of the existing building stock is key to reducing energy usage. For example, New York City estimated that buildings already in existence today would still account for at least 85 percent of the city's building stock in 2030.[24] Renovation, retrofit, and

refurbishment of existing buildings represent an opportunity to upgrade energy performance and decrease energy demand. This can involve measures ranging from superficial, low-cost measures/modifications to full overhauls or replacement of major systems. Retrofitting existing buildings additionally saves embodied energy (the energy required to extract, manufacture, and delivery building materials and construct the building) and avoids the waste of building demolition. Energy efficiency retrofits can reduce the operational costs, particularly in older buildings.[25]

Programs for Businesses and Homeowners
Energy audits, conducted at the building and system scale, are an important best practice used to identify and prioritize energy efficiency actions. Many power companies will conduct an energy audit to identify which retrofits will be most impactful.

In Cambridge, MA, a citywide analysis of home energy efficiency found that a few commonly available data points could be used to identify a small percentage of homes where retrofits could be most impactful. Researchers utilized information on gas bills (used in that city primarily for heating), the size and volume of buildings, and weather data to model benefits from low-cost retrofits. These simply included adding insulation, sealing drafty windows and doors, and installing new double-pane windows. The analysis found that such retrofits conducted in only 16 percent of buildings in the city would reduce the city's natural gas usage by 40 percent.[26] These findings underscore the variance that exists in the energy efficiency of the existing building stock and opportunities that exist for strategic improvements that maximize energy efficiency at a minimal cost. Common upgrades in homes and commercial buildings are indeed relatively inexpensive, and include practices such as the replacement of lighting, climate control, and other energy-consuming appliances with more efficient versions, as well as improved insulation and windows.[27]

Boston's Residential Energy Efficiency Program, launched in 2010, provides all residents free home energy audits.[28] During audits, residents are provided free LED light bulbs and "smart" advanced power strips.[29] Unlike programs in other cities that target homeowners, Boston's program is available to renters, who do not need landlord permission to participate. This is an important feature, making energy savings available to those who rent. Boston's program has been well studied and provides useful insight into the incentives that influence uptake of energy efficiency best practices. Their findings show the effectiveness of rebates, as two-thirds of those who implemented energy best practices would not have done so without this incentive.[30]

Because energy audits and identifying modest retrofits are often inexpensive and effective, a number of city policies are trying to motivate change in the private sector. Denver and Chicago both require large commercial and residential buildings to benchmark and report energy use to the city.[31] In Chicago, this requirement has resulted in 85 percent of large buildings reporting energy use to the city.[32] Chicago additionally offers training and guidance to help building owners comply with these requirements. Portland, Oregon, is another city whose energy programs have been a model (Box 6.2).

Box 6.2   Best Practice in Education and Communication: Portland's Home Energy Score Ordinance

In January 2018, Portland implemented an ordinance requiring homeowners selling their single-family home to share a "Home Energy Report and Score" to potential buyers when they list their residence for sale. The city enacted this ordinance because information on energy efficiency in homes is inconsistent and unavailable in most real estate markets.[a] Portland compares the score to a "miles-per-gallon rating" for a car and notes that the "Home Energy Score is an easy way for sellers, buyers, real estate professionals and builders to get directly comparable and credible information about a home's energy performance across the housing market."[b]

The city has a website guiding sellers, buyers, real estate agents, and builders through the new process. Sellers must have their home assessed by a professional Home Energy Assessor and display the Home Energy Score in any listing or public posting about the house. The website also guides sellers through methods they could use to improve their scores, if they choose. Similarly, the website helps home buyers interpret scores, and alerts them to how they could wrap energy improvement projects into home financing. The 2018 ordinance is an outcome of their 2009 plan that set a goal to help residents make informed decisions about the energy efficiency and energy costs associated with ownership of prospective homes.

Sources:

[a]"What's the Score?" City of Portland, 2018, https://www.pdxhes.com/

[b]City of Portland, "What's the Score?"

Energy Equity

Many cities have weatherization and energy efficiency retrofit programs that are specifically aimed at low-income residents. Austin, Madison, and Philadelphia, for example, offer weatherization assistance programs to "make sure all people feel the effects of energy improvements."[33]

From 2013 to 2016, Washington, D.C. spent $81 million on energy efficiency and renewable energy services for low-income residents in single-family homes and multifamily buildings.[34] Going forward, businesses will also be eligible for funding. In a strategic move that certainly increased program visibility among target communities, the city paid for Ben's Chili Bowl—an icon of the city's African American community—to install energy-efficient lighting. The long-lasting lighting will reduce energy use by approximately 50 percent and save the business about $1200 in energy costs yearly.[35] Washington, D.C. has also installed 158 solar photovoltaic systems on roofs of low-income residents.[36] Efforts such as these led to Washington, D.C. being named the world's first LEED Platinum City in 2017 (see Box 6.3).

Box 6.3   Best Practices in Implementation and Results: Washington, D.C., the World's First LEED Platinum City

In 2017, Washington, D.C. became the first LEED for Cities Platinum certified city in the world. LEED (Leadership in Energy and Environmental Design) is the most widely used green building rating system in the world and is designed to help buildings achieve high performance in key areas of human and environmental health.

LEED for Cities was launched in 2016 and enables cities to measure and communicate sustainability outcomes in many areas including energy, water, waste, transportation, and human experience (which includes education, prosperity, equity, and health and safety). Cities benchmark and track performance using Arc, a digital platform that uses data to provide greater transparency into sustainability efforts and helps cities make more informed decisions.

(continued)

Box 6.3 (continued)

Between 2010 and 2017, Washington, D.C. retrofitted and modernized 16 public schools and 5 recreation centers to at least the LEED Gold standard. The District also entered into one of the largest municipal on-site solar projects in the United States, completed the largest wind power purchase agreement deal of its kind ever entered into by an American city, and is on track to derive at least one-half of the entire city's electricity from renewable resources by 2032.

Washington, D.C.'s LEED Platinum certification recognizes the city's leadership in reducing greenhouse gas emissions, supporting clean energy innovation, and focusing on inclusive prosperity and livability in all eight wards. "Washington, DC is setting the bar for smart cities all around the world by leveraging technology and data to achieve sustainability and resiliency goals, creating healthy and safe communities where citizens can thrive," said Mahesh Ramanujam, President and CEO at US Green Building Council and Green Building Cities Initiative.

Source:

"Washington, DC Named First LEED Platinum City in the World," D.C. Department of Energy, Thursday August 31, 2017, at https://doee. dc.gov/release/washington-dc-named-first-leed-platinum-city-world

Another energy equity program is a federal program, the Property Assessed Clean Energy (PACE) program, which allows local and state governments to fund upfront energy improvement costs on private property, which is then paid back over time by the property owners with their property tax bills.[37] The rationale of this program is that energy improvements could occur without burdensome upfront costs, and repayments could occur as property owners realize financial savings from the energy upgrades. While this seems beneficial in principle, we note that the program has increasingly come under fire from those who are concerned that homeowners are taking out loans they cannot afford on the advice of contractors eager to profit from the installation work.[38] Cities should proceed with caution.

Box 6.4   Best Practices in Equity: Low-Income Solar

Too often, options for going green are reserved for the wealthy. This is because switching to smart heating systems, solar, or wind power can have expensive start-up costs. Further, cost savings are often unavailable to renters because installing alternative energy systems is often a low priority for building owners, even if some subsidy is available. As cities move towards renewable energy, they must ensure equity of these systems and their benefits as well.

In 2017, the California Solar Energy Industries Association and the California Environmental Justice Alliance co-sponsored a bill to increase access to clean energy for low-income and disadvantaged communities across California. The innovative new $1 billion program, California's Multifamily Affordable Housing Solar Roofs Program, is funded by the statewide greenhouse gas cap-and-trade program. The program will provide up to $100 million annually for ten years to incentivize installations of solar on multifamily low-income housing properties across California. It is expected to reach renters in more than 200,000 units. The program will cover the costs of outfitting low-income properties with solar, so savings can be passed along to renters living there. The law notably allows tenants to receive credits for electricity produced by the systems, thereby allowing them to directly benefit from the solar installation.

In addition to reducing electric bills for residents, the legislation provides low-income properties with self-reliance during storms or other natural disasters that may disrupt out the electrical grid, providing yet another benefit to the installation of solar power.

Other states such as Massachusetts and New York have experimented with low-income solar grant programs, though most of them have still targeted those owning, not renting, single-family homes. California's program is the first to target renters.

This program may provide multiple benefits, including:

- Reducing emissions of GHGs
- Reducing energy costs for low-income families
- Providing energy during disruptions to the electrical grid

(continued)

> **Box 6.4   (continued)**
>
> Source:
> Nicole Caldwell, "California To Invest $1 Billion In Solar For Low-Income Housing Units," *Greenmatters*, accessed February, 20 2017, http://www.greenmatters.com/living/2017/11/02/ZSWXp8/california-low-income-solar

Public Buildings

Many cities are encouraging the installation of energy efficiency retrofits in public buildings, both to reap available financial savings and to demonstrate these best practices in their communities. Charleston has implemented an innovative program to increase energy efficiency in public schools. Beginning in 2008, schools could opt in to an energy efficiency program. In return for participation, each school receives 20 cents for every dollar saved (up to $3000 per participating school) to spend any way they like.[39] The results have been impressive: the Charleston County School District saved 25 percent on energy consumption and the sensors and other equipment installed are expected to save more than $9 million over 20 years.[40]

Another best practice is Ann Arbor's long-term Municipal Energy Efficiency Fund, established in 1988. This revolving fund provides upfront capital for municipal energy efficiency projects, and then collects 80 percent of the resulting energy cost savings over the next five years. This "payment from savings" model has motivated department heads and facility managers to implement best practices, and the repayments through savings have been sufficient to maintain sufficient money to continue funding energy efficiency projects. The Fund has financed a variety of projects including "light emitting diode (LED) traffic and pedestrian lights, street light improvements, parking garage lighting, a building-level boiler, two electric vehicles, and rooftop photovoltaic (PV) cells."[41] More importantly, the Fund also demonstrates that energy efficiency can pay for itself in the long term.

Other cities accomplish similar ends using energy savings performance contracts. In this approach, an energy service company plans and renovates existing facilities to increase energy performance. Generally, the energy service company guarantees that planned improvements will generate enough energy savings to cover the cost of the project over the contract term. Richmond public schools used this approach to undertake a $6.1 million dollar project to update ten school district buildings with efficient HVAC, lighting, and water management equipment.[42]

Green Building and New Construction
In addition to retrofitting buildings, the rise of green building standards has revolutionized the construction industry. "Green building" is a broad term with multiple meanings. One definition is "structures designed to increase efficiency of resource use, including energy, water, indoor environmental quality, siting, infrastructure and pollution."[43] Alternative definitions prioritize occupant health, reducing the impacts of the built environment on the natural environment, or focus on considerations over a building's full life cycle including design, construction, operation, maintenance, and removal.[44] Regardless, green buildings are an important shift in building and construction activities.

The rise of green building has been important for several reasons. First, cutting-edge buildings have utilized new energy and resource-efficient technologies and demonstrated their efficacy. This provides builders with practical experience in installing these systems and brings them into the mainstream. Second, municipalities around the country have begun to change their building codes to encourage green buildings. This is necessary because in some cases, building codes actually prohibit or otherwise complicate use of these new technologies.

A number of green building certification systems now exist, including the US Green Building Council's Leadership in Energy and Environmental Design (LEED) rating system, the National Association of Home Builders' National Green Building Standard, and Energy Star. While these systems were developed for use in project planning, many municipalities have incorporated these metrics into their green building incentives and requirements.

Some cities have changed their building codes to smooth the way for, or require, green building. San Francisco requires that all municipal buildings over 5000 square feet meet the LEED Gold certification requirements.[45] Shoreline, Washington, requires that all new city construction achieve at least the LEED Silver standard.[46] In 2017, Shoreline revised its zoning and engineering standards to provide clear guidance and incentives for green building.[47] Among other changes, the revised standards waive application fees in part or full for buildings that are certified as "green" through one of the three green building programs, and allow builders to depart slightly from code regulations to meet green building goals.[48]

Another example is Santa Fe, which passed the Sustainable Land Development Code in 2015 requiring new residential buildings in the city

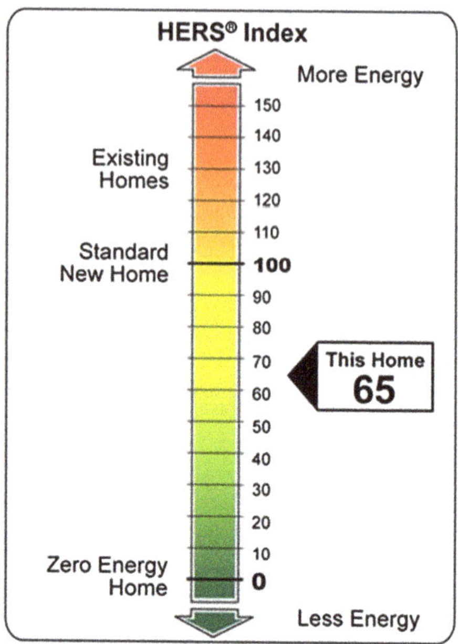

Fig. 6.2 The RESNET Home Energy Rating System (HERS) Index is used to communicate the relative efficiency of a home to builders, developers, and consumers. The scale is set with 100 being equal to the efficiency of a standard new home, and 0 being a home that produces as much energy as it consumes. (Source: By Florida Solar Energy Center [Public domain], via Wikimedia Commons https:// upload.wikimedia.org/wikipedia/commons/5/51/RESNET_HERS_Index.jpg)

to achieve a HERS rating of 70 or less. The HERS rating (established by the Residential Energy Services Network) is a nationally recognized system of rating a home's energy efficiency by comparing the house to a "reference home" built to meet the 2006 International Energy Conservation Code standards, and which would have a HERS rating of 100 (Fig. 6.2).[49]

Green buildings can also be promoted through incentives such as expedited permitting, or density and height bonuses. Cities can also provide financial incentives for green building, including tax credits or fee reductions or waivers during the permit review process.

Renewable and Alternative Energy

In 2016, approximately 15 percent of electricity consumed in the United States came from renewable energy sources including hydroelectric, wind, biomass, solar, geothermal, and co-generation.[50] This percentage is growing, even in the absence of large-scale federal policies and financial support,

Fig. 6.3 Electric cars can charge at this charging station, installed in Washington, D.C. (Source: Lisa Benton-Short.)

because these technologies are increasingly cost competitive with conventional power sources.[51] Cities also recognize other benefits of alternative energy, including energy independence and providing local jobs. Aspen, Colorado, Burlington, Vermont, Greensburg, Kansas, Rockport, Missouri, and Kodiak Island, Alaska, already source 100 percent of their energy from alternative sources (while this is impressive, we also note that these are cities with small populations). Currently there are 26 cities in the United States that have pledged to go to 100 percent clean energy, and many others are moving towards that goal by establishing intermediate targets (Fig. 6.3).[52]

Many cities rely on a combination of two overarching strategies for alternative energy: large-scale alternative energy procurement and distributed energy generation. In large-scale alternative energy procurement, cities either instruct their municipally-owned utilities to construct major alternative energy projects or they develop agreements with outside energy providers to purchase alternative energy. On the other hand, distributed energy generation relies on a variety of small-scale technologies that generate electricity where it will be used. An example includes solar panels on homes. In some cases, excess energy that is generated in this distributed fashion can also be sold back or "fed back" into the electric grid, providing a further incentive for installation of these systems.

Box 6.5   Best Practices in Implementation and Results: Austin's Pecan Street Project

In the 1990s, Austin vowed to become the "Clean Energy Capital of the World" and to grow in a more responsible way. Austin has set renewable energy goals, including the installation of 165 wind turbines that power 20,000 homes, and has committed to a 20 percent renewable electricity supply by 2020, with the most successful utility-sponsored green building program in the country. So far, the utility has saved enough energy to eliminate the need for additional coal-burning power plants. In 1991, Austin adopted the nation's first green building program. LEED Silver Certification is required on all city buildings, and residents and contractors are encouraged to build green. To date, Austin Energy Green Building has rated more than 10,000 homes and 15,000,000 square feet of commercial structures, and as many as one-third of all single-family homes and apartments built in Austin are now green-rated homes. Additionally, most of the new commercial and multifamily buildings downtown and in large-scale developments are green building-rated. The program has successfully avoided more than 20,000 metric tons of greenhouse gas emissions in the last ten years.

The city also partnered with Austin Energy, the University of Texas, the Austin Technology Incubator, the Greater Austin Chamber of Commerce, and the Environmental Defense Fund to create the Pecan Street Demonstration, a smart grid research project integrated into a new community being built on the site of Austin's former airport. The idea was to install a functioning open platform Energy Internet to test products and gather real-time energy consumption and generation data on more than 1000 homes. The platform included smart appliances, over 200 roof-installed PV solar panels, and 69 electric vehicles. The system also includes a variety of consumer behavior interventions such as pricing models, real-time feedback on energy use, and incentive programs. The project has produced many insights into the future of the Energy Internet and the impacts of distributed solar power and electric vehicles on the power grid. Among these:

(continued)

Box 6.5   (continued)

- Cost savings was of limited interest among this group of consumers, who responded better to messaging about optimizing home energy and appliance systems.
- In this location, although south-facing PV solar generated more energy, west-facing systems generated energy at times that better paralleled demand.
- PV solar paired with storage can mediate the variability of solar power that otherwise could pose a challenge to the electricity grid.
- There is currently a lack of commercially available cost-effective products to allow consumers to use electric vehicles as storage devices.
- Electric vehicle owners in this study were willing to charge vehicles at off-peak times when motivated through variable pricing models.

By using smart meters and sensors to detect and communicate changes in the use of electricity and gas, utilities are able to manage electricity demand and encourage sustainable practices. The Pecan Street research project also found that homes with residential solar and electric vehicles generate fewer greenhouse gas emissions and use less water than homes powered solely by the grid.

Source:

"About," Pecan Street, accessed February 2018, http://www.pecanstreet.org/

Alternative Energy Procurement

Burlington, Vermont, the first US city to draw 100 percent of its power from renewable sources, consciously developed a diverse energy portfolio.[53] The publicly owned utility draws power from a dam on the Winooski River, four wind turbines on nearby Georgia Mountain, and a massive solar panel array constructed at the airport. And about half of the city's electricity demand is met by burning pine and timber slash, which is sustainably harvested locally.

> **Box 6.6   Best Practices in Innovation: Cruise Ships Plug into Juneau**
>
> Every summer, Juneau's downtown cruise ship dock welcomes hundreds of thousands of happy tourists eager to visit. But this type of tourist economy has environmental costs. Cruise ship engines burn diesel fuel, spewing not only greenhouse gas emissions but also sulfur oxides, nitrogen oxides, and particulate matter. When ships are at dock, they must leave their engines running to provide power to the ship. A mid-size cruise ship's diesel engine can use 150 tons of fuel each day, and some estimate that one cruise ship can emit as much particulate matter as a million cars in a day.
>
> Juneau, in partnership with Princess Cruise Lines, has taken the lead in an innovation that allows ships to "plug in" to shoreside power—rather than run their polluting diesel engines—when they are docked. Using power from the city's grid instead of the engines to power the ship's onboard services reduces emissions while docked. This means less GHG emissions and improved local air quality.
>
> Cruise ships were not previously built with the capability of plugging into shoreside power, so older vessels must be retrofitted to access the new systems. Princess Cruise Lines has converted most of their ships with this infrastructure. Other cruise lines are considering this investment. The ground-breaking technology has now grown to include systems in Seattle, Vancouver, Los Angeles, San Diego, and San Francisco, and is planned to roll out in other ports that have made commitments to shore power programs, including New York.

An interesting feature of renewable energy is its regionalization: the availability, cost, and suitability of alternative energy sources are uneven, and therefore, strategies for increasing the alternative energy within a city's portfolio must also be localized. Perhaps nowhere is that clearer than Hawaii, where a focus on alternative energy is driven both by concerns of climate change-related sea level rise and the cost and vulnerability of oil which must be shipped to the island. In Hawaii, tropical temperatures make ocean thermal energy conversion possible. This technique "takes advantage of the temperature differences between sun-warmed surface water and cold deep water to generate electricity".[54] A temperature difference of at least 80 degrees Fahrenheit is sufficient to boil some liquids and create steam to make electricity. Although this technology only works in tropical waters, Hawaiian Electric and private companies are also experimenting with more widely transferable technologies that harness wave energy using systems of underwater buoys.

Many cities are currently unable to meet goals for renewable energy locally. Aspen, for instance, generates a significant portion of its energy locally through hydropower. However, when the city considered increasing its hydropower capacity, residents were concerned about the effects this measure would have on water resources and wildlife. Instead, the city created a purchase agreement to bring in energy from hydropower, wind, and biogas from afar.[55] Power purchase agreements allow municipalities flexibility as they seek to integrate renewable power into their energy portfolios. Las Vegas, now the largest US city to run municipal buildings and equipment on 100 percent renewable energy sources, used a power purchase agreement with the state utility NV Energy, to receive clean energy from the Boulder Solar plant.[56]

Cities also support alternative energy through municipal aggregation programs. Cleveland coordinates a community aggregation program which allows residential and small commercial customers of the Cleveland Electric Illuminating Company to leverage their power as a group to purchase green electricity at a price lower than otherwise possible. Customers can choose the percentage of green energy (0, 50, or 100 percent) they would like to purchase. Cleveland believes that this program provides their residents with price protections, while they support renewable energy and help reduce the city's carbon footprint.[57]

Box 6.7   Emerging Trend: Benefiting from State Energy Policies

While cities are taking action on energy, they also rely on state and federal policy and programs to help drive change. California has progressive renewable energy plans that benefit many of its cities. In

(*continued*)

Box 6.7 (continued)

2002, the state established the California Renewable Portfolio Standard (RPS) to drive investment in clean energy. Subsequent amendments to the law have set increasingly ambitious targets. Today, the state is generating enough electricity from renewable sources to power more than five million homes, and that number is expected to nearly double by 2030. The state continues to meet its goals for renewable energy setting records in rooftop solar arrays, hydropower, and wind power generation. In 2015 the most recent RPS amendment requires all utilities in the state to source half of their electricity sales from clean, renewable sources—wind, solar, and geothermal by 2030. In 2017 a new amendment to the RPS sets the goal of 100 percent renewable energy by 2045; the bill passed the state legislature. These ambitious goals mean growing investment in solar, wind, and other renewables.

Solar electricity production now contributes about ten percent of California's total electricity. Additionally, California has instituted the California Solar Initiative, a financial incentive program that offers homeowners a tax rebate on top of a small federal tax credit. It is the most ambitious solar program in the nation.

And wind energy continues to grow rapidly. California's size and diversity of terrain has enabled the state to develop several large wind energy sites that together house more than 13,000 wind turbines. In 2007 California received about 2.6 percent of the state's power from wind; by 2016 that had increased to nearly 7 percent. Additionally, hundreds of homes and farms are using smaller wind turbines to produce electricity. Geothermal has also seen growth and now produces about 6 percent of electricity generation with most of that based north of San Francisco.

While cities may not be able to control state efforts, they can and should take advantage of statewide policies and programs, making sure they promote and make their residents aware of these opportunities to invest in renewable energy.

Source:

"Renewables Portfolio Standard (RPS)," California Energy Commission, accessed November 1, 2017, http://www.energy.ca.gov/portfolio/

Distributed Generation

Cities are also encouraging the adoption of small-scale alternative energy systems to achieve their alternative energy goals. These systems also have the potential to serve as localized back-up power systems in the case of emergencies and regional power outages. Net-metering is a system offered by some states or utilities that allows customers who generate excess electricity to sell it back into the grid.[58] Provisions of these programs, however, vary greatly across the country.

Photovoltaic (PV) solar panels and solar water heating systems are easily integrated into even dense urban areas as rooftop units. PV solar panels are relatively easy to install, and the efficiency of these systems is increasing at the same time they are becoming more affordable. Chicago may be known as the Windy City, but its sustainability plan notes that the city is also well-suited to produce solar energy throughout the year.[59] To promote more solar, the city plans to reduce the time and paperwork involved in the solar permit approval process for small-scale solar installations.

In 2016, San Francisco became the first major US city to require 15–30 percent rooftop PV solar or green roofs on all new buildings.[60] This ordinance is in part made possible by a California state requirement that 15 percent of the roof area of all new buildings be "solar ready."[61] The idea is that creating clear and unshaded space for photovoltaics is relatively easy during the planning and construction phase but much harder to retrofit later. Indeed, there is little downside to making new buildings "solar ready" as it adds almost no additional construction costs.[62]

Wind power has also dramatically increased in the past ten years, but most wind farms are distant from urban areas, so while they might contribute renewables to the energy supply, they are generally not *in* cities. Wind energy has not been widely adopted in cities because of challenges and concerns related to installation space, low and turbulent urban wind-speed characteristics, vibration, noise, safety, shadow flicker (periodic shadows cast by the rotating blades of wind turbines), and aesthetics.[63] However, novel urban applications do exist. Lackawanna, New York developed a wind farm on an urban brownfield site—the old Bethlehem Steel Plant. In 2012, the old mill site was redeveloped with a bike path, community center, and 14 wind turbines, which produce $190,000 in tax revenue for localities.[64] The windfarm project is known as Steel Winds (Fig. 6.4).

There are also new small-scale wind electric systems for homes. These wind turbines can be mounted on roofs, lower electricity bills by 50–90 percent, and are a source of power during utility outages.[65] Most of the

Fig. 6.4 A view of the Steel Winds windfarm project in Lackawanna, New York, looking towards the city of Buffalo. (Source: "Steel Winds" Wikipedia/Wikimedia commons photo by Ken JP Stuczynski (Created October 11, 2007), accessed April 1, 2018, https://upload.wikimedia.org/wikipedia/commons/9/91/Steel_Winds_ 2007.png)

small-scale wind turbines are vertical turbines that have clean, aerodynamic lines and are both quiet and affordable. For example, the Aleko company sells a wind turbine for use in homes, boats, and telecommunications towers for a modest $159.00.[66]

A myriad of other alternative energy sources are available as well, such as biomass, geothermal, wave and tidal energy, methane gas sequestration from wastewater treatment plants, landfill-gas-to-energy systems, and trash-to-energy. These sources are often of medium scale (systems providing energy for multiple buildings) and take advantage of particular, local opportunities for energy generation. Many of these alternative sources are effectively utilized through district heating and cooling systems. District systems allow multiple buildings or even neighborhoods to be supplied with heating, cooling, and/or power through an underground distribution system.[67]

Another source of energy is co-generation or combined heat and power (CHP). Co-generation captures the large quantities of heat that is otherwise lost or wasted during power generation and industrial processes. The captured heat is then used to heat buildings. Typically, most co-generation facilities can power a few buildings, and they are not yet widespread across the United States. However, the US Department of Energy has set a goal of having co-generation constitute 20 percent of generation capacity by 2030.[68] Several universities including NYU have co-generation. NYUs CoGen plant provides electricity to 22 NYU buildings, distributes hot and chilled water to 37 buildings on campus, and is expected to save the university \$5–8 million in energy-related costs per year.[69] The CoGen plant helped NYU reduce its GHG emissions by 20 percent.[70] Another example is at New York City's Co-op City, the world's largest cooperative housing development. The development has two gas turbines and one steam turbine that produce around 40 Megawatts of electricity,[71] up to 16 Megawatts of which can be exported to the grid to generate revenue.[72] Steam generated by exhaust heat keeps residents warm in winter and——via absorption chillers——cool in summer, too.[73] The benefits of co-generation are promising: many will reduce air pollutants and greenhouse gases and can save money.

WHAT'S MISSING: CARBON NEUTRALITY AND THE SMART GRID

An emerging trend that many cities are considering is pledging to become carbon neutral. The concept "carbon neutral" or having a net zero carbon footprint refers to achieving net zero carbon emissions by offsetting any carbon released with an equivalent amount of sequestered or offset carbon. There are three main ways to achieve zero carbon.

The first is *reducing* or limiting energy usage and emissions from transportation (by walking, using bicycles or public transport, avoiding flying, using low-energy vehicles), as well as from buildings, equipment, animals and processes.

A second way is to obtain electricity and other energy from a *renewable energy* source, either directly by generating it (e.g. installing solar panels on the roof) or by selecting an approved green energy provider, and by using low-carbon alternative fuels such as sustainable biofuels.

A third way involves *sequestering carbon or buying carbon offsets*. Sequestered carbon can include planting trees, or funding carbon projects that would prevent future greenhouse gas emissions. It can also mean buying carbon credits. Carbon offsets enable organizations to reduce their environmental impact by supporting projects that reduce, absorb, or prevent carbon and other emissions from entering the atmosphere. A carbon offset is created when one ton of greenhouse gas is captured, avoided, or destroyed in order to compensate for an equivalent emission made. An example of a carbon credit could be investing in a sustainable forestry project in the Pacific Northwest or a biogas project from farms in the region.

Being carbon neutral is increasingly seen as a social responsibility. Companies such as Google, Dell, and PepsiCo have pledged to achieve carbon neutrality; countries such as Iceland, Sweden, Scotland, and Costa Rica have as well. In the United States cities such as Greensburg, Kansas, Boulder, Minneapolis, and San Francisco join a growing list of companies, countries, and cities with ambitious energy targets.

Going carbon neutral will require fundamental changes in our relationship to energy, and the emergence of a smart grid will be an essential part of this transformation. Over the past five years, the price of solar and wind power has decreased rapidly. This has spurred a dramatic change in the nation's energy portfolio. Wind and solar power are highly variable and need more sophisticated control systems to facilitate the connection of sources to the energy grid. Decentralized generation further challenges our aging electricity network. In response, we argue that cities need to take a more active role in piloting the Smart Grid or "Energy Internet." A Smart Grid is an electrical grid which includes a variety of operational and energy measures including smart meters, smart appliances, renewable energy resources, and energy-efficient resources that relay information to users and energy producers such as power companies. According to the US Energy Independence and Security Act of 2007, a Smart Grid is characterized by the:

1. Increased use of digital information and dynamic optimization to improve reliability, security, and efficiency of the electric grid.
2. Better integration of distributed power generation and renewable resources.
3. Development and incorporation of demand response, demand-side resources, and energy efficiency resources.
4. Deployment of "smart" technologies (real-time, automated, interactive technologies that optimize the physical operation of appliances and consumer devices) for metering, communications concerning grid operations and status, and distribution automation.
5. Usage of electricity storage systems including plug-in electric and hybrid electric vehicles.

A first step in this direction is "smart meters" which provide homes and businesses with detailed information about their energy use, which helps consumers identify ways of conserving energy and reaping financial savings.[74] In one version of a smart grid, information (likely in the form of cost) flows between the utility and its customers, enabling real-time management of the home's electricity consumption. The idea is that if customers know that energy is cheaper in the middle of the night when demand is low, they will shift some energy uses to that time. This is called "demand side management," which either reduces the consumption of electricity or can help synchronize demand and supply by shifting non-critical usage of electricity from peak to non-peak time periods.

Already, electricity transmitters have developed programs that compensate large customers for temporarily reducing their electricity usage during periods of high demand, or other system challenges.[75] Smart Grids could greatly expand this. Power would be flexibly priced according to availability (for instance, systems relying on solar power would have lower prices during the day). This information could be communicated to appliances, set, for instance, to automatically run a load of dishes when a low price is reached.

Energy storage is another important topic, because of the variable nature of solar and wind energy. The role that energy storage can play in systems dominated by variable alternative energy is highlighted by conditions in Kodiak Island, Alaska. The island's power now comes from a combination of hydro and wind power.[76] The local electric co-op sought to end reliance on diesel generators given the vulnerability to high and variable diesel prices, despite concerns about power variability and industrial demand for sudden bursts of large amounts of power. Kodiak has successfully addressed these needs through battery capacity and other innovations, including a flywheel energy storage system.

While it may take another decade or two for the entire energy grid to "smarten up," utility companies and cities around the United States have begun pilot programs to test the technology before rolling it out nationwide. Cities that have pilot "smart grids" include Austin, Boulder, Fort Collins, Maui, Sacramento, San Diego, Tempe, and Worcester, Massachusetts.[77] San Diego was one of the first cities to partner with Google's Smart Meter Initiative which allows users to connect their smart meters to the internet to track their power usage.[78]

Summary

Nearly every US city has policies in place to support the energy efficiency of existing buildings or energy conservation generally, although these programs may not yet be at a large enough scale to make significant change, nor sufficiently targeted to address the least energy-efficient buildings or the homes of low-income residents. Rapid and widespread advances in green buildings and alternative energy are underway and hold tremendous promise. Municipalities are developing innovative policies and programs to capitalize on regionally and locally appropriate strategies. Table 6.2 summarizes best practices.

Table 6.2 Best practices in energy

Energy conservation and efficiency of existing buildings

- Provide information about energy efficiency for all home sales
- Provide free home audits, as well as free energy-efficient power cables and bulbs
- Support subsidies and low-interest loans to subsidize high front-end costs of modernization
- Ensure that loan programs are structured to achieve energy and cost savings and do not take advantage of vulnerable populations

Green building in new construction

- Change building codes to smooth the way for or require green building
- Promote green building through incentives such as expedited permitting or density and height bonuses

Renewable and alternative energy

- Seek out municipal aggregation programs
- Approve net-metering, which allows customers to sell excess energy back to the grid
- Require newly constructed buildings be "solar ready"
- Invest in district heating and co-generation to make use of heat lost during power generation and industrial processes

Modernizing the energy grid

- Develop a smart grid and distribute smart meters
- Pilot decentralize smart systems
- Set up utilities to use the Energy Internet, to feed electricity price information to smart devices
- Foster distributed energy storage to accompany distributed power generation

---

NOTES

1. C40 Cities, "Why Cities? Cities Have the Power to Change the World," accessed March 5, 2018, http://www.c40.org/why_cities.
2. Jasper Rigter, Deger Saygin, and Ghislaine Kieffer, "Renewable Energy in Cities" (The International Renewable Energy Agency, 10/16), http://www.irena.org/-/media/Files/IRENA/Agency/Publication/2016/IRENA_Renewable_Energy_in_Cities_2016.ashx.
3. U.S. Energy Information Administration, "Electricity Explained: Electricity in the United States," May 10, 2017, https://www.eia.gov/energyex-plained/index.cfm?page=electricity_in_the_united_states.
4. U.S. Energy Information Administration.

5. Worldometers, "US Population (LIVE)," March 5, 2018, http://www. worldometers.info/world-population/us-population/; U.S. Energy Information Administration, "Frequently Asked Questions: What Countries Are the Top Producers and Consumers of Oil?," October 17, 2017, https://www.eia.gov/tools/faqs/faq.php?id=709&t=6.

6. U.S. Energy Information Administration, "Frequently Asked Questions: How Much Oil Consumed by the United States Comes from Foreign Countries?," April 4, 2017, https://www.eia.gov/tools/faqs/faq. php?id=32&t=6.

7. U.S. Energy Information Administration, "Electricity Explained: Electricity in the United States"; U.S. Energy Information Administration, "Natural Gas Explained: Where Our Natural Gas Comes From," October 25, 2017, https://www.eia.gov/energyexplained/index.cfm?page=natural_gas_ where.

8. United States Department of Energy, "Solar Energy in the United States," 2017, https://energy.gov/eere/solarpoweringamerica/solar-energy-united-states.

9. The Solar Foundation, "National Solar Jobs Census," 2017, https:// www.thesolarfoundation.org/national/.

10. Wesley Reisser and Colin Reisser, *Energy Resources: From Science to Society*, First Edition (Oxford, New York: Oxford University Press, 2018).

11. National Geographic, "Biofuels: Biofuels Offer Plant-Based Solutions to the Earth's Growing Energy Problems," *National Geographic*, accessed February 28, 2018, https://www.nationalgeographic.com/environment/ global-warming/biofuel/.

12. Climate Nexus, "What's Driving the Decline of Coal in the United States?," January 25, 2017, https://climatenexus.org/climate-issues/ energy/whats-driving-the-decline-of-coal-in-the-united-states/.

13. U.S. Energy Information Administration, "Frequently Asked Questions: What Is U.S. Electricity Generation by Energy Source?," April 18, 2017, https://www.eia.gov/tools/faqs/faq.php?id=427&t=3.

14. United States Environmental Protection Agency, "Inventory of U.S. Greenhouse Gas Emissions and Sinks," 4/17, https://www.epa. gov/ghgemissions/inventory-us-greenhouse-gas-emissions-and-sinks.

15. Daniel M. Kammen and Deborah A. Sunter, "City-Integrated Renewable Energy for Urban Sustainability," *Science* 352, no. 6288 (May 20, 2016), https://doi.org/10.1126/science.aad9302.

16. City of Philadelphia, "Greenworks Philadelphia," 2009, 4, https://beta. phila.gov/documents/greenworks-progress-reports/.

17. Chattanooga Green Committee, "The Chattanooga Climate Action Plan," February 24, 2009, 30.

18. Anne Hidalgo and William Peduto, "Opinion | The Mayors of Pittsburgh and Paris: We Have Our Own Climate Deal," *The New York Times*, June 7, 2017, sec. Opinion, https://www.nytimes.com/2017/06/07/opinion/the-mayors-of-pittsburgh-and-paris-we-have-our-own-climate-deal.html.

19. Adam Smeltz, "Peduto Announces Executive Order on Climate Change," *Pittsburgh Post-Gazette*, June 3, 2017, http://www.post-gazette.com/local/city/2017/06/02/Mayor-Bill-Peduto-Pittsburgh-executive-order-climate-change-trump-paris-accord/stories/201706020174.

20. Rigter, Saygin, and Kieffer, "Renewable Energy in Cities."

21. Architecture 2030, "Why the Building Sector?," 2017, http://architecture2030.org/buildings_problem_why/.

22. Charles J. Kibert, "Policy Instruments for a Sustainable Built Environment," *Journal of Land Use & Environmental Law* 17, no. 2 (2002 2001): 380.

23. Lucas Reijnders and A. van Roekel, "Comprehensiveness and Adequacy of Tools for the Environmental Improvement of Buildings," *Journal of Cleaner Production* 7, no. 3 (March 1, 1999): 221, https://doi.org/10.1016/S0959-6526(99)00080-3.

24. New York City Mayor's Office of Long-Term Planning and Sustainability, "Overview of the Greener, Greater Buildings Plan," October 2014, http://www.nyc.gov/html/gbee/downloads/pdf/greener_greater_buildings_plan.pdf.

25. Office of Energy Efficiency and Renewable Energy, "Retrofit Existing Buildings" (United States Department of Energy), accessed February 28, 2018, https://energy.gov/eere/buildings/retrofit-existing-buildings.

26. Mohammad Javad Abdolhosseini Qomi et al., "Data Analytics for Simplifying Thermal Efficiency Planning in Cities," *Journal of The Royal Society Interface* 13, no. 117 (April 1, 2016): 20150971, https://doi.org/10.1098/rsif.2015.0971.

27. Commission for Environmental Cooperation, "Best Energy Management Practices: In 13 North American Municipalities," accessed January 27, 2018, http://www3.cec.org/islandora/en/item/11410-best-energy-management-practices-in-13-north-american-municipalities-en.pdf.

28. CharlestonWISE, "CharlestonWISE Impact Project," 2010, http://www.charlestonwise.com/Impact.aspx.

29. Renew Boston, "No-Cost Energy Visits from Renew Boston" (City of Boston, January 11, 2017), https://www.boston.gov/departments/environment/no-cost-energy-visits-renew-boston.

30. Pamela Stazesky, Markeisha Grant, and Colleen Manning, "Renew Boston Residential Energy Efficiency Program Evaluation Report" (Goodman Research Group, Inc., October 2012), http://www.grginc.com/documents/PUBLICMassEnergyEvaluationReport.pdf.

31. City of Chicago, "2017 Chicago Energy Benchmarking Report," 2017, https://www.cityofchicago.org/content/dam/city/progs/env/EnergyBenchmark/2017_Chicago_Energy_Benchmarking_Report.pdf; Department of Public Health and Environment, "Energize Denver: Energy Efficiency in Large Buildings" (City and County of Denver), accessed March 5, 2018, http://www.denvergov.org/content/denvergov/en/environmental-health/environmental-quality/Energize-Denver.html.

32. City of Chicago, "2017 Chicago Energy Benchmarking Report," 2.

33. City of Philadelphia, "Greenworks Philadelphia," 26–27; The City of Madison, "The Madison Sustainability Plan: Fostering Environmental, Economic, and Social Resistance," 2011, 35, https://www.cityofmadison.com/sustainability/documents/SustainPlan2011.pdf; The City of Austin, "Rethink For A Bright Green Future," 2008, 8.

34. Sustainability DC, "Sustainable DC 2016 Detailed Progress Report," 11, accessed February 28, 2018, http://www.sustainabledc.org/in-dc/planprogress/.

35. Sustainable DC, "Sustainability DC," 2012, 59, https://sustainable.dc.gov/sites/default/files/dc/sites/sustainable/page_content/attachments/DCS-008%20Report%20508.3j.pdf.

36. Sustainable DC, "Sustainable DC Detailed 2017 Progress Report," 2017, 7, http://www.sustainabledc.org/in-dc/planprogress/.

37. Office of Energy Efficiency and Renewable Energy, "Best Practice Guidelines for Residential Property Assessed Clean Energy Financing" (US Department of Energy), accessed January 27, 2018, https://energy.gov/eere/slsc/property-assessed-clean-energy-programs.

38. Liz Farmer, "This Clean Energy Home Loan Program Has Problems. California's Trying to Fix Them," *Governing: The States and Localities*, December 13, 2017, http://www.governing.com/topics/transportation-infrastructure/gov-clean-energy-home-loan-program-problems.html.

39. Diette Courrégé, "Schools' Goal: Energy Savings," *The Post and Courier*, July 4, 2008, https://www.postandcourier.com/news/schools-goal-energy-savings/article_e2550982-658d-5392-94f2-471a1e391d62.html.

40. South Carolina Energy Office, "South Carolina School Success Stories," 18, accessed February 28, 2018, http://www.energy.sc.gov/files/SCSchoolSuccessstories_0.pdf.

41. Energy Sector Management Assistance Program, "Good Practices in Energy Efficiency, Ann Arbor, Michigan (USA): A Municipal Energy Efficiency Fund," September 2011, 1, https://www.esmap.org/node/1299.

42. Grant Capital Management, "Case Studies: Richmond Public Schools—Energy Performance Contract Project," accessed January 31, 2018, http://www.grantcapitalmgmt.com/case-studies-richmond-maryland-schools-energy-performance-contract-project.php.

43. Rebecca C. Retzlaff, "The Use of LEED in Planning and Development Regulation: An Exploratory Analysis," *Journal of Planning Education and Research* 29, no. 1 (September 1, 2009): 67, https://doi.org/10.1177/0739456X09340578.

44. Charles Kibert, "Green Buildings: An Overview of Process," *Journal of Land Use and Environmental Law* 19, no. 2 (2004): 491; Pat Murphy, "LEEDing from Behind: The Rise and Fall of Green Building" (Community Solutions, May 2009), 2.

45. Municipal Green Building Task Force, "City of San Francisco- Green Building Requirements for City Buildings" (Database of State Incentives for Renewables & Efficiency, September 20, 2016), http://programs.dsireusa.org/system/program/detail/5906.

46. City of Shoreline, "Shoreline Environmental Sustainability Strategy," July 14, 2008, 14–15, http://cosweb.ci.shoreline.wa.us/uploads/attachments/pds/esc/COMPLETE_FinalSESStrategy2008July.pdf.

47. City of Shoreline, "Deep Green Incentive Program (DGIP)," May 2017, 2, http://www.shorelinewa.gov/Home/ShowDocument?id=31411.

48. City of Shoreline, 2.

49. Santa Fe County, "Santa Fe County's New Energy Efficient Building Code for New Home Construction: A Guide for Homeowners and Home Builders," 2016, 1, https://www.santafecountynm.gov/media/files/Green%20Building%20Code/HERS-Compliance-Guide-01-16.pdf.

50. U.S. Energy Information Administration, "Electricity Explained: Electricity in the United States."

51. Rigter, Saygin, and Kieffer, "Renewable Energy in Cities."

52. Sierra Club, "100% Commitments in Cities, Counties & States," accessed January 27, 2018, https://www.sierraclub.org/ready-for-100/commitments.

53. Colin Woodard, "America's First All-Renewable Energy City," *Politico Magazine*, November 17, 2016, https://www.politico.com/magazine/story/2016/11/burlington-what-works-green-energy-214463.

54. Hawaiian Electric Company, Inc., "Ocean Energy," 2018, https://www.hawaiianelectric.com/clean-energy-hawaii/clean-energy-facts/renewable-energy-sources/ocean-energy.

55. Grace Hood, "It's Not Easy, But Aspen Moves Toward 100 Percent Renewable Energy," *Morning Edition* (National Public Radio, July 5, 2017), https://www.npr.org/2017/07/05/535578438/aspen-moves-toward-its-goal-of-supporting-100-percent-renewable-energy.

56. Hayley Miller, "The City Of Las Vegas Is Now Powered Entirely By Renewable Energy," *Huffington Post*, December 20, 2016, sec. Politics, https://www.huffingtonpost.com/entry/the-city-of-las-vegas-is-now-powered-entirely-by-renewable-energy_us_58594291e4b0b3ddfd8ea4e8.

57. City of Cleveland, "Advanced and Renewable Energy," accessed January 27, 2018, http://www.city.cleveland.oh.us/CityofCleveland/Home/Government/CityAgencies/OfficeOfSustainability/AdvancedAndRenewableEnergy.

58. Solar Energy Industries Association, "Net Metering," 2017, https://www.seia.org/initiatives/net-metering.

59. City of Chicago, "2015 Sustainable Chicago Action Agenda," September 2012, 13, https://www.cityofchicago.org/content/dam/city/progs/env/SustainableChicago2015.pdf.

60. City and County of San Francisco, "San Francisco Better Roofs," January 2017, http://sf-planning.org/san-francisco-better-roofs.

61. State of California, "2013 Building Energy Efficiency Standards-Reference Ace: Section 110.10 Mandatory Requirements for Solar Ready Buildings," 2013, https://energycodeace.com/site/custom/public/reference-ace-2013/index.html#!Documents/section11010mandatoryrequirementsforsolarreadybuildings.htm.

62. The City of Minneapolis Sustainability Office, "Minneapolis Climate Action Plan: A Roadmap to Reducing Citywide Greenhouse Gas Emissions," June 28, 2013, 22, http://www.minneapolismn.gov/www/groups/public/@citycoordinator/documents/webcontent/wcms1p-113598.pdf.

63. Kammen and Sunter, "City-Integrated Renewable Energy for Urban Sustainability."

64. United States Environmental Protection Agency, "Success Stories- Siting Renewable Energy on Contaminated Land: Steel Winds, Lackawanna, New York. Development of Wind Power Facility Helps Revitalize Rust Belt City," May 2012, https://www.epa.gov/sites/production/files/2015-04/documents/success_steelwinds_ny.pdf.

65. United States Department of Energy, "Electricity and Fuel: Small Wind Electricity Systems," accessed March 2, 2018, https://www.energy.gov/energysaver/buying-and-making-electricity/small-wind-electric-systems.

66. Aleko, "Vertical Wind Power Generator - 10 Watt Nominal - 15 Watt Maximum - 12 Volt," accessed March 2, 2018, https://www.alekoproducts.com/Vertical-Wind-Generator-10W-to-15W-12V-p/wgv15w12v-ap.htm.

67. Behnaz Rezaie and Marc A. Rosen, "District Heating and Cooling: Review of Technology and Potential Enhancements," *Applied Energy*, (1) Green Energy; (2)Special Section from papers presented at the 2nd International Energy 2030 Conf, 93 (May 1, 2012): 2–10, https://doi.org/10.1016/j.apenergy.2011.04.020.

68. Office of Energy Efficiency and Renewable Energy, "20% Energy Efficiency by 2030: Increasing Wind Energy's Contribution to U.S. Electricity Supply" (United States Department of Energy), accessed March 2, 2018, https://www.energy.gov/eere/wind/20-wind-energy-2030-increasing-wind-energys-contribution-us-electricity-supply.

69. New York University, "NYU Switches on Green CoGen Plant and Powers Up for the Sustainable Future," January 21, 2011, https://www.nyu.edu/about/news-publications/news/2011/january/nyu-switches-on-green-cogen-plant-and-powers-up-for-the-sustainable-future.html.

70. NYU Web Communications, "Energy," accessed March 29, 2018, http://www.nyu.edu/content/nyu/en/life/sustainability/areas-of-focus/energy.

71. William Pentland, "Lessons from Where the Lights Stayed on during Sandy," *Forbes*, October 21, 2012, https://www.forbes.com/sites/williampentland/2012/10/31/where-the-lights-stayed-on-during-hurricane-sandy/#5e97733c7074.

72. Siemens AG 2016 Power and Gas Division, "Make the Most of Fuel: Combined Heat and Power Portfolio" (Siemens, 2016), https://www.siemens.com/content/dam/webassetpool/mam/tag-siemens-com/smdb/power-and-gas/brochures/chp/siemens-chp-brochure-sep17.pdf.

73. Siemens AG 2016 Power and Gas Division, 3–5.

74. Wendy Sunshine, "The Pros and Cons of Smart Electricity Meters" (The Balance, February 19, 2018), https://www.thebalance.com/pros-and-cons-of-smart-meters-1182648.

75. EnerNOC, "Business in the Mid-Atlantic Reduce Energy Spend and Earn Money with EnerNOC" (Enel Group), accessed January 27, 2018, https://www.enernoc.com/resources/datasheets-brochures/faq-pjm-demand-response.

76. Margaret Kriz Hobson, "Renewables: On Kodiak Island, Flywheels Are in, and Diesel Is 99.8% Out" (E&E News, June 10, 2016), https://www.eenews.net/stories/1060038577/.

77. Alex Kingsbury, "10 Cities Adopting Smart Grid Technology" (US News, February 19, 2010), https://www.usnews.com/news/energy/slideshows/10-cities-adopting-smart-grid-technology?onepage.

78. Greener Building, "Google Partners with Eight Utilities in Smart Meter Projects to Track Energy Use Online" (Green Biz, May 20, 2009), https://www.greenbiz.com/news/2009/05/20/google-partners-eight-utilities-smart-meter-projects-track-energy-use-online.

CHAPTER 7

Water

Water: An Introduction

A fresh and dependable supply of water is critical to sustaining life and supporting healthy communities, economies, and environments. In every US city, there are two main and often related water challenges: (1) supplying sufficient quantities of high-quality water to residents and consumers and (2) assuring that water quality in nearby waterbodies, like rivers and lakes, is not overly impacted by wastewater and stormwater runoff. This chapter examines both supply and quality issues and how cities are planning for and implementing more sustainable water systems.

Water Supply

In 2014, more than 100,000 residents of Flint, Michigan, were potentially exposed to high levels of lead in their drinking water.[1] As many as 12,000 of those were children who are particularly susceptible to the detrimental effects of lead.[2] The crisis emerged after the city switched its drinking water supply from Lake Huron and the Detroit River to the Flint River.[3] This water was improperly treated, causing lead from aging pipes to leach into the public water supply. The Flint water crisis was a failure of governance and technology that had serious health implications. It also highlighted the fact that drinking water safety is a much wider problem, affecting other cities as well.

M. Keeley, L. Benton-Short, *Urban Sustainability in the US*,
https://doi.org/10.1007/978-3-319-93296-5_7

Wastewater treatment and stormwater management problems have caused a different set of issues, such as a 2014 toxic algae bloom in Lake Erie that disrupted the water supply for half a million people in Toledo.[4] And recently in West Virginia, 300,000 people were without tap water after a chemical spill.[5] These threats to our water demonstrate the vulnerability of this essential resource and are a powerful reminder that many Americans have long taken their water for granted.

In the last decade, droughts have also caused concern about water supply, triggered irrigation bans, and contributed to widespread wildfires throughout Southern California. Laws and traditions allocate water to satisfy economic or political interests, yet often fail to see water systems in the context of larger physical processes. For example, political borders divide watersheds arbitrarily. As population and water use have increased, serious disputes have arisen over allocations, causing conflict. Shortages have occurred in expected regions, such as the deserts of the southwestern United States, but also in unexpected areas, such as the humid southeastern states, where recent population growth, suburban development, and a lack of water conservation have depleted supplies. In coastal areas, overdrawing water from aquifers can lead to saltwater intrusion, ruining the aquifer.

Further, there is an increasing understanding that climate change will significantly impact precipitation patterns and water resources. Uncertainty about the extent and severity of these impacts represents a major challenge for planners, and climate change is likely to exacerbate existing water infrastructure deficiencies. For instance, models predict that much of the Midwest and Eastern United States will experience more frequent and severe storm events. Existing antiquated stormwater infrastructure was not designed to manage these larger events. Coastal areas in particular are vulnerable to flooding due to a combination of rising sea levels and storm events. Other areas, particularly in the Southwest, can expect increased drought associated with altered precipitation patterns, increased temperatures, and evaporation, which will stress water resources at the same time that continued population growth is expected. A National Resources Defense Council report concludes that one out of every three counties in the United States will likely face water shortages due to climate change.[6] The greatest risk of shortage will concentrate in 13 states: Arizona, Arkansas, California, Colorado, Florida, Idaho, Kansas, Mississippi, Montana, Nevada, New Mexico, Oklahoma, and Texas. Figure 7.1 shows the probability of water resources at risk.

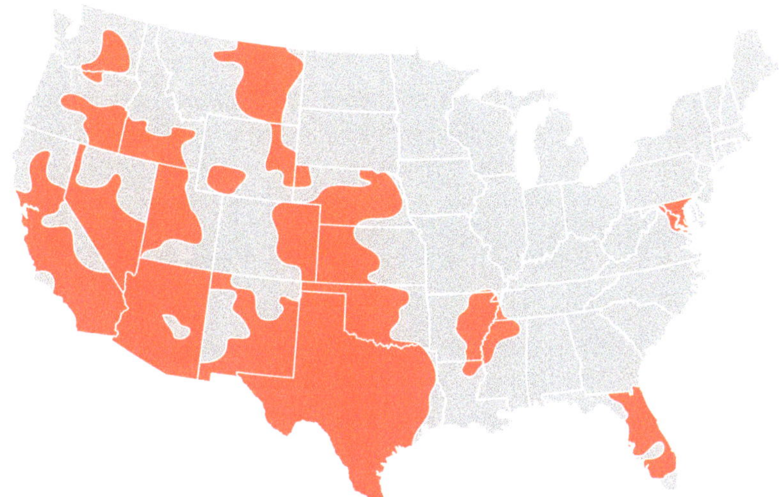

Fig. 7.1 Watersheds at risk for increased drought due to climate change. (Source: Adapted from several reports from the U.S. EPA "Drought Resilience and Water Conservation" https://www.epa.gov/water-research/drought-resilience-and-water-conservation)

The connection between climate change and water is a significant one, and it presents a challenge in how to discuss the issue in this book. We focus on potential changes in water supply due to climate change in the climate chapter (Chap. 4). In this chapter, we focus more on more general water infrastructure, supply, and quality issues that transcend the issue of climate change.

Water Quality

As the United States industrialized throughout the twentieth century, water quality of the nation's rivers, lakes, and estuaries degraded and became a subject of public concern. In 1972, the United States passed the Clean Water Act (CWA) to restore integrity to waterbodies throughout the country. As a result, the nation's waters have seen significant improvements, particularly in ameliorating pollution at point sources. Point source pollution emanates from specific locations, like industrial plants, sewage treatment plants, and outfalls.

However, some 45 years after the passage of the CWA, approximately 40 percent of US freshwater remains polluted and fails to meet CWA goals of "fishable and swimmable waters." Today, non-point source pollution—runoff from farms and from cities—is the leading cause of water pollution. The diffuse nature of these sources makes them more difficult to control, so they remain the largest source of water quality issues.

One type of non-point pollution, urban stormwater runoff, impacts water quality in several ways. First, urban stormwater picks up pesticides, fertilizers, and pet waste from lawns and gardens as well as salts, antifreeze, oil, and heavy metals (from brakes) off of road surfaces. In many areas, stormwater is then carried in a separate storm sewer and released directly and entirely untreated into a nearby waterbody. In addition to pollutants themselves, elevated water temperatures and extreme peaks in water volume lead to "Urban Stream Syndrome." This is a term used to describe the ecological degradation of streams in urban areas characterized by "elevated concentrations of nutrients and contaminants, altered channel morphology, and reduced biotic richness with increased dominance of tolerant species."[7]

Urban stormwater contributes to another challenge for water quality as well. Over 700 US communities, mostly concentrated the Northeast and Great Lakes and Pacific Northwest, rely at least in part on combined sewer systems (Fig. 7.2). Unlike separate sewers, in which sewage and stormwater are conveyed in separate systems, combined sewers carry raw sewage and stormwater together in one pipe to a sewage treatment plant. Crucially, these systems are designed to overflow into nearby waterbodies when the capacity of the system is exceeded. In some places, an overflow can be triggered by as little as 1/10″ of rain. These overflows, called Combined Sewage Overflows (CSOs), release untreated raw sewage and stormwater into rivers or lakes (Figs. 7.3 and 7.4).

There are other threats to water quality as well. Improperly disposed-of chemicals and pharmaceuticals, animal and human wastes, wastes injected underground, and naturally occurring substances also have the potential to contaminate drinking water. Drinking water that is not properly treated or disinfected, or that travels through an improperly maintained distribution system, may also pose a health risk. Finally, there is a risk from intentional contamination of drinking water. In a post 9/11 world, drinking water utilities find themselves facing new responsibilities due to concerns over water system security and threats of infrastructure terrorism.

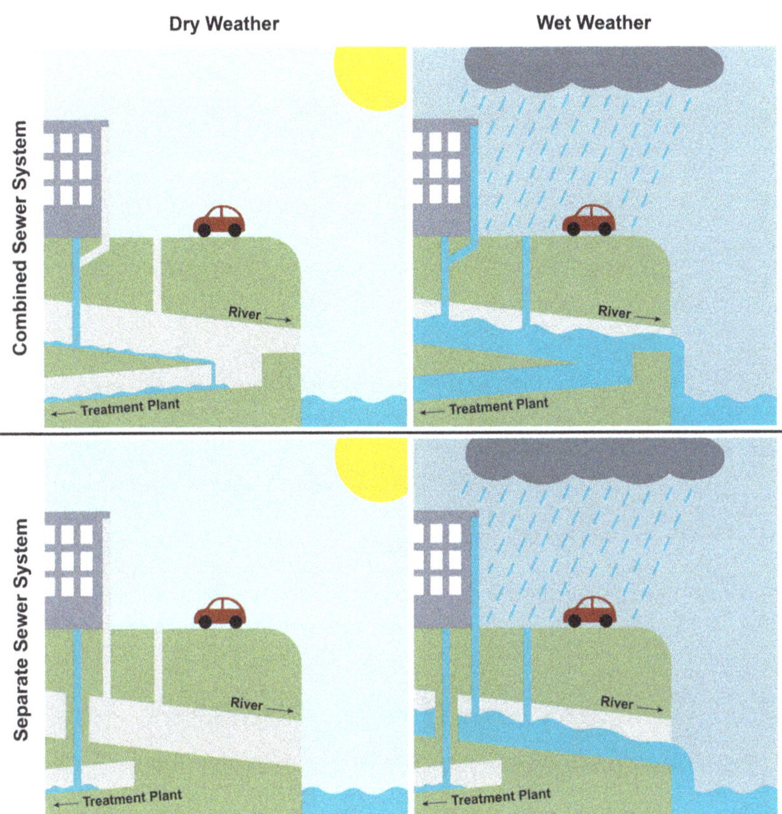

Fig. 7.2 Combined and separate sewer systems during dry and wet weather. During dry weather, both combined and separate systems convey wastewater to wastewater treatment plants. However, during wet weather, combined systems (carrying both wastewater and stormwater) are designed to overflow into nearby waterbodies when system capacity is exceeded. Separate systems continue to convey wastewater to treatment plants and divert all stormwater directly into rivers. While separate systems prevent untreated sewage from entering waterbodies, stormwater still enters rivers carrying trash and pollutants from streets. (Source: Authors.)

Fig. 7.3 On the Cincinnati waterfront, residents and visitors are reminded that the Ohio River is subject to combined sewer overflows. (Source: Lisa Benton-Short.)

Cities' Role in Water Management

US cities have been active in water management for more than 200 years. Philadelphia was the first US city to take on water supply as a municipal responsibility in 1801 in response to cholera epidemics ravaging the city. Presciently, in the nineteenth century, Philadelphia renaturalized the land surrounding the Schuylkill River which was both the most industrialized waterway in the country and the source of the city's drinking water. This effort created the 110-acre Fairmount Park in the middle of Philadelphia which few people recognize as a legacy of actions to protect the city's water supply.[8] The city has installed extensive water supply and water treatment infrastructure since then and has undertaken many efforts to provide residents with high-quality drinking water. This has been in part financed and directed through federal government actions to monitor and regulate how modern cities use and treat their water resources. Yet, Philadelphia's forward thinking on issues of water management has continued. One example of this was the early creation of an Office of

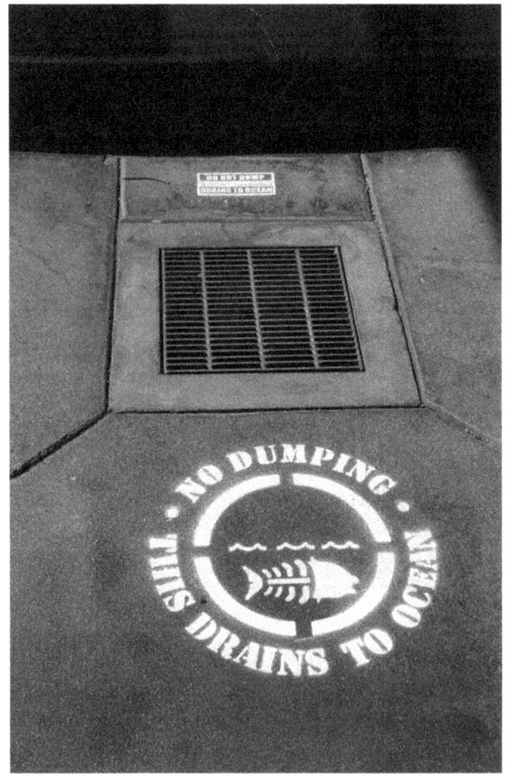

Fig. 7.4 A sign educating residents of San Diego. In a separate sewer system, stormwater from streets can carry trash or pollutants directly into waterbodies such as rivers, lakes, or oceans. Many cities such as San Diego are raising awareness about this problem by placing reminders not to dump. (Source: Lisa Benton-Short.)

Watersheds within the water department to coordinate management efforts with the upstream municipalities whose actions affect Philadelphia's drinking water supply.

Philadelphia's experiences highlight the fact that US cities must manage water resources crucial to the economic and environmental success of their cities while balancing needs and demands at the following three scales: (1) city policies and infrastructure created in response to local needs, (2) regional governance and coordination within a watershed, and (3) federal regulations and funding for infrastructure or pollution prevention. We explore these below.

There are many stresses on municipal water supply and treatment systems: population growth, aging infrastructure, climate change, increasingly complex water quality issues, and financial constraints continue to challenge our planning for "sustainable" water systems. In the United States, water infrastructure both supplies clean drinking water and removes waste. Many cities rely on water pipes and mains that are over 100 years old, and this infrastructure is nearing the end of its useful life. In 2017, the American Society of Civil Engineers gave the nation's drinking and wastewater systems grades of "D" and "D+," respectively, and estimated the investments necessary to maintain and expand service over the next 25 years at about $1.25 trillion.[9] This deficit is the result of decades of underinvestment in the nation's infrastructure.

Funding for infrastructure remains a critical challenge. Due to funding rules that constrain utilities and a need to keep water affordable for consumers, water utilities are inadequately funded at a time when costs for maintenance and treatment are rising with increasingly stringent environmental regulations. Most urban residents do not pay the "full cost" of water; water bills cover the expense of water delivery, but do not cover the maintenance or expansion of the water systems. As a result, many cities confront aging water infrastructure but have been unable to find the economic or political will to invest in the millions or billions of dollars needed for upgrades or expansion.

At the same time, many cities see the economic importance of water in their cities. Miami Beach, with its vibrant tourism industry, plans to improve water quality in order to "avoid economic costs of pollution mitigation and remediation, preserve the values of waterfront properties, and support water-related recreational activities crucial to the local economy."[10] Burlington similarly sees Lake Champlain, the waterfront, and the Winooski River Corridor as the centerpieces of an urban natural environment and part of their regional identity.[11]

Some cities are trying to re-attract water-heavy industry into their region as a way to stimulate economic growth.[12] Some water managers in the Great Lakes region predict that looming water shortages in arid states could soon reverse population and job loss in their region.[13] Finally, many cities recognize the energy intensiveness, and thus the management costs of their massive and diffuse water provision and sewer systems.[14] Water conservation strategies and decentralized stormwater management can reduce some of these expenses.

While local governments have some authority over water (such as land use decisions), water flows within watersheds that rarely conform to political boundaries. Thus, the only way to comprehensively address water issues is through an integrated water resources management strategy that often involves numerous jurisdictions. This makes water a regional issue as well, and one that requires effective coordination and cooperation across the watershed. Yet current water management practices are complicated by fragmentation of responsibility, such as varying levels of government sharing diverse management responsibilities; the presence of multiple jurisdictions within a single watershed; and the distinctive interests and management goals of stakeholders operating in a single municipal area.[15] It is also made more complicated by organizational barriers that impair coordinated land and water management.[16]

Consider Washington, D.C. DC Water distributes drinking water, and collects and treats wastewater (according to federal regulation) from the combined sewers in the city and neighboring counties in Maryland and Virginia. While some cities have fully public water departments and a few rely on private companies for these services, DC Water is an independent authority of the District of Columbia, which means that while the D.C. Mayor appoints the agency's Board of Directors, its finances are not tied to D.C.'s overall budget.[17] The District of Columbia Department of the Environment (DDOE) manages the city's separate storm sewers and complies with federal regulations regarding rivers in the city. Washington, D.C. lies within the Chesapeake Bay watershed, along with six states, so the city and DC Water must also work with municipal and state governments throughout the watershed to address concerns about the health of the vital Chesapeake Bay Estuary, which is vulnerable to pollution from all of these sources within its watershed. Such complexities are common within water management across the urban United States, since rivers often define political boundaries, yet watersheds transcend them.

Finally, water management is also significantly shaped by federal regulations, including The Safe Drinking Water Act, which regulates drinking water treatment and quality, and The Clean Water Act, which controls the pollutants that can be discharged into the nation's waters. Through this regulatory framework, utilities and municipalities that manage water resources are highly constrained, having legally mandated levels of water supply and quality they must achieve, and limits in how they raise funds.

The National Pollutant Discharge Elimination System (NPDES) is a permit program under the Clean Water Act that regulates point source polluters, including municipal stormwater discharge. More than 3700 US municipalities must fulfill strengthened federal requirements to manage separate storm sewers and combined sewer overflows.[18] With compliance lagging, a number of municipalities are under negotiated consent orders, which are legally binding agreements with set frameworks and timetables for reducing discharges into receiving waterbodies, often through enhanced maintenance practices and capital improvement projects. These programs require municipalities to expand the scope of their stormwater management programs from collecting and conveying runoff to comprehensively redress the ecological impacts of stormwater volumes and pollutants, including those caused by combined sewer overflows (CSOs). As a result, many cities' goals and actions for improving water supply and quality come from national mandates.

TAKING ACTION ON WATER

We have identified two major ways cities are taking action to develop more sustainable water systems: (1) water supply, security, and conservation; and (2) water quality and pollution reduction.

Water Supply, Security, and Conservation

Securing an adequate water supply is a concern for many cities, even those outside of the desert Southwest. In the humid South Atlantic, Atlanta faces ever-increasing water problems due to its distance from major waterways. The metro area had a population of 3.0 million in 1990; it nearly doubled to 5.7 million in 2017.[19] An increase in population impacts its daily draw on the water reserve; in 1990 the city consumed 320 million gallons, and by 2010 it was 510 million gallons. With an additional 2 million residents projected by 2030, water use is expected to rise to more than 700 million gallons a day.[20] In 2007, a major drought brought Atlanta's water supply to the brink of failure. Officials admitted that there were only three months left of stored freshwater to supply the city.

Atlanta's primary source of water has been Lake Lanier. The state of Georgia has attempted to limit the amount of water released from the lake. The river system also serves the states of Alabama and Florida, and these states fear that Atlanta's increasing use of water upstream will harm ecosystems in their states. Court cases have ensued: Alabama sought to prevent Atlanta from continuing to withdraw water from Lake Lanier. The case is still under review, but if Atlanta is denied use of the lake, the city's water supply could be reduced by roughly 40 percent. While we tend to think of "water wars" in the arid West, this is an example of how increased demand for water, even in areas that tend to have high rainfall, can be politically charged.

Desalination (desal)—removing salts from ocean water—is another potential option for cities facing extreme and persistent water shortages, particularly in California. However, the process is extremely energy intensive, and as a result, at least four times the cost of urban water.[21] Scientists are also concerned about the possible impacts that concentrated salt water discharged from desal plants could have on aquatic ecosystems. Still, the increased pressure to find freshwater has driven technology investment in the desalination industry. In the early 2000s, there were more than 20 *proposed* desal plants in California. Local concern about the energy usage intensity and environmental impacts of these plants has significantly delayed construction, and so far only two have been constructed. The Carlsbad desal plant in San Diego became operational in 2015 after 14 years of construction and planning at a cost of $1 billion.[22] The plant provides 50 million gallons of water per day to the San Diego's water distribution system.

Water Efficiency and Conservation

One way to stretch existing water supplies is to focus on water efficiency, which occurs at a number of scales. Water losses from aging infrastructure are a significant and costly challenge. For example, Atlanta is estimated to lose about ten billion gallons per year due to main breaks and undetected system leaks.[23]

Cities are encouraging the use of water-efficient fixtures and appliances in their jurisdictions. Shoreline, Washington, is trying to identify and address barriers to water-saving technologies within building codes and other regulations.[24] Another regulatory solution comes from Austin, Texas, which proposed to require that all new Austin Green Building-rated projects install water-efficient fixtures.[25] A 2014 report noted that the city reduced its gallon per capita per day from 163 gallons to 125 gallons.[26] Santa Fe has strengthened water conservation standards for its parks department and requires irrigation certification from commercial and residential landscapers.[27] Santa Fe will also adopt new technologies that track water use and may "require water conserving retrofits upon the sale of a residential or commercial building."[28] Similarly, St. Louis plans to make data on water usage available by property.[29] This is a successful approach that encourages consumers and businesses to measure their conservation efforts in comparison to others. Other common options include rebates, incentive programs, and recognition for water conservation efforts.[30]

In drought-prone areas, cities are promoting xeriscaping. The term xeriscape is derived from the Greek word *Xeros* meaning dry. A xeriscaped yard is "not a rock or cactus garden but a well thought-out plan to conserve water through creative landscaping and native plants."[31] The Arlington, Texas website highlights the need for xeriscaping: "During the summer months, as much as 50% of water used at a residence is applied to a landscape."[32] To inspire residents, Arlington and Dallas, Texas, maintain a two-acre demonstration garden featuring native and other plants adapted to the local climate as well as landscaping materials that can conserve water (Fig. 7.5). A number of cities, including Chandler, Arizona, Albuquerque,

Fig. 7.5 A xeriscape demonstration garden in Dallas. (Source: "The Xeriscape Demonstration Garden at the headquarters of Denver Water in Denver, Colorado" Wikipedia/Wikimedia Commons photo by Jeffery Beal (created July 24, 2015), accessed April 1, 2018, https://upload.wikimedia.org/wikipedia/commons/a/a7/Xeriscape_Demonstration_Garden.JPG)

New Mexico, and Ft. Collins, Colorado, utilize "cash for grass" rebate programs that reward homeowners who replace grass with water-efficient vegetation, or install conservation landscaping practices.

However, we were surprised to find that few cities integrated water conservation programs into their sustainability plans. This does not necessarily mean that conservation activities are lacking. Many city water department websites feature information about water conservation incentives for installing low-flow toilets or shower heads with mandatory water restrictions. However, integrating water conservation more holistically in sustainability planning could benefit cities and enhance conservation efforts, especially given the many connections that exist between this topic and others commonly raised in sustainability plans including green building practices, land use, and green space.

Water Reuse Systems

One form of water conservation is to reuse water (water recycling). Water reuse generally refers to projects that use technology to treat water according to the water quality requirements of its planned reuse.[33] While recycling water for drinking water requires intensive and specialized treatment processes, water that will be reused for landscape irrigation needs little or no treatment. Golf courses, large parks, and green areas are increasingly being irrigated with reclaimed water. Recycling water not only conserves a vital resource, but it can also provide financial savings. And, of course, water reuse is a natural part of the hydrologic cycle.

The most basic water recycling systems tend to be decentralized systems, which collect and recycle water at a house or business. These systems collect "greywater" generated from sources such as baths, showers, sinks, washing machines, and dishwashers. Water from toilets and urinals contains more nutrients, bacteria, and viruses and is called "black water." Dirtier black water is excluded from greywater systems and treated separately. Greywater systems generally use collected water for purposes other than human contact or consumption, such as landscape irrigation, toilet flushing, or industrial processes. In addition to saving water, these systems also save energy through reductions in water treatment and distribution.

Box 7.1   Best Practices in Multiple Benefits: Dallas and Trinity River Wetlands

The city of Dallas and the US Army Corps of Engineers are harnessing the natural processes of wetlands to mitigate flooding, improve water quality, and enable wastewater reuse. They are creating a 271-acre wetland, stretching 11 miles through downtown Dallas along the Trinity River (Fig. 7.6). This project will reverse the straightening and canalization of the Trinity River which occurred in the 1920s.[a] The project has converted a golf course and a capped landfill into floodplain wetlands, and this more naturalistic riparian system will reduce flooding in Dallas.[b]

In addition to capturing floodwaters, the wetland system is fed year-round by recycled water. During dry periods, the Trinity River is comprised almost entirely of this treated wastewater. Effective treatment is of paramount concern, as the Trinity River is also the primary water source for downstream users, including Houston and other more rural communities.[c]

Fig. 7.6   Trinity River in Dallas. (Source: Wikipedia commons at https://upload.wikimedia.org/wikipedia/commons/f/f9/View_from_Reunion_Tower_August_2015_07.jpg)

(*continued*)

Box 7.1   (continued)

This example shows that cities can use wastewater effluent as a resource rather than a waste product; this could become a vital water management strategy to meet increasing demands for water. Water shortages complicate water management, and western water law, which gives use rights based on prior appropriation (to whoever first puts water to beneficial use) means that water withdraws and the inputs are closely monitored for permit compliance.

The project is also being celebrated for creation of an ecologically diverse wetland ecosystem and the educational and recreational opportunities this provides for urban residents. Thirty-one miles of recreational trails will be built, allowing residents to walk, hike, bike, and explore this wetland ecosystem.[d]

Sources:

[a]US Army Corps of Engineers, "Fact Sheet on Dallas Chain of Wetlands," January 29, 2015, http://www.swf.usace.army.mil/Portals/47/docs/PAO/DFE/PDF/1-29-2015_Lower_Chain_of_Wetlands_Fact_Sheet.pdf

[b]Roy Appleton, "Trinity River Wetlands Construction Brings Dallas Floodway Extension Project Closer to City's Core" (Dallas News, 2013). https://www.dallasnews.com/news/news/2013/02/03/trinity-river-wetlands-construction-brings-dallas-floodway-extension-project-closer-to-citys-core

[c]Trinity River Authority of Texas, "Trinity River Basin Master Plan," 2016, http://serv.trinityra.org/reports/BasinSummaryReports/Master_Plan_2016_Final.pdf

[d]US Army Corps of Engineers, "Dallas Floodway Extension Project," accessed January 4, 2018, http://www.swf.usace.army.mil/Missions/Water-Sustainment/Dallas-Floodway-Extension/

A more intensive process is large-scale water recycling, which centrally captures and reclaims previously used water, sometimes redistributing it for large-scale irrigation, using it to replenish a ground water basin, or even fully treating it to potable standards.

Some municipalities have already invested in large, community-scale water reuse systems. In California, San Jose and neighboring communities have already heavily invested in water recycling and distribute recycled

Box 7.2   Emerging Trend: Residential Scale Greywater Systems

The use of small-scale greywater systems is increasing in the United States, driven in part by droughts in the desert southwest. In these areas, residents immediately see the benefits of greywater systems in their homes, which allow them to maintain their landscapes despite local watering restrictions on the use of potable water for this purpose. Yet, there are many barriers to wider uptake of small-scale greywater systems. In many communities, the implementation of greywater systems is complicated by antiquated ordinances and permit requirements. Plumbing contractors, inspectors, and regulators may additionally be unfamiliar with these newer approaches, making them more expensive and troublesome.

As greywater systems become more common—in part due to the trailblazing of LEED and other green building programs—these barriers are being broken down. Several states including California, Washington, and Florida have updated building codes in the last decade to allow greywater reuse. Municipalities are additionally crafting ordinances that more easily allow for greywater systems. Some are even requiring that all new construction buildings are "greywater ready" (already containing the basic pipe infrastructure for greywater), as these systems are more cost-effectively integrated into a building during construction. Another best practice is to provide training about greywater systems for policymakers and regulators.

Berkeley, California is one of a growing number of cities to allow the construction of qualified small-scale greywater systems meeting the California Plumbing Code without permits. They also provide guidance to homeowners about the use of these systems—such as being cautious when using detergents or bleaches in sinks or the laundry that might harm landscape plants, and not using greywater on vegetable gardens.

Source:

"Energy & Sustainable Development" City of Berkeley, Office of Energy and Sustainable Development, accessed January 4, 2018, https://www.cityofberkeley.info/Planning_and_Development/Energy_and_Sustainable_Development/Graywater_Collection_Systems.aspx

water through 110 miles of pipeline for irrigation, cooling buildings, and industrial processes.[34] San Jose's sustainability plan sets several goals associated with water recycling, including adding new pipelines to expand the water recycling system and connect new users. Similarly, Austin has a 50-mile system of "purple pipes" (to visually differentiate them from potable water) that carry reclaimed water recycled from wastewater.[35] This water can be used for non-potable applications and costs about one-third the price of potable water.

San Diego, which currently imports about 90 percent of its water from the Colorado River and other sources, is considering various options to meet growing demands for potable water and decrease the city's reliance on outside water.[36] The city has already constructed a water reclamation plant that treats up to 30 million gallons of wastewater per day. The water is redistributed through 79 miles of pipe, and is used for irrigation, landscaping, and industrial use.

The term direct potable reuse means that wastewater is treated and then returned directly into the drinking water distribution system or into pipelines to a drinking water treatment plant. While some cities like San Diego are considering this approach, concern about public perception has delayed these efforts. While some critics deride this as "toilet to tap," direct potable reuse systems already exist worldwide and in a few US cities. In 2013, the Colorado River Municipal Water District opened a direct potable use system that treats two million gallons of wastewater to drinking water standards per day.[37] The system was ten years in design and uses a variety of technologies including microfiltration, reverse osmosis, and ultraviolet disinfection to prepare water. The water district reports that it was less difficult than expected to gain community support for the project, but this was certainly impacted by the dire drought the area faced.

Water Quality and Pollution Reduction

Many cities have established goals for water quality based on requirements in the federal Clean Water Act for good reason. Despite 40 years of work, the basic goals of fishable and swimmable waters remain unmet for 40 percent of the nation's waterbodies. Pollution remains a big challenge for most US cities as water quality is not in compliance with the Clean Water Act or

NPDES permit requirements. For instance, Chattanooga acknowledges that many of the area's streams and creeks have been listed as impaired.[38]

As we noted earlier, point source pollution has been dramatically reduced and controlled (see Box 7.3). Today, the challenge comes from non-point pollution, particularly from urban stormwater runoff. As a result, many cities frame water issues specifically around stormwater and have been actively updating or creating stormwater management plans to protect local surface waters.

One challenge for cities and water departments is that the public does not understand how combined sewer systems operate or the consequences of stormwater on water quality. The financial burden of upgrading stormwater management systems to comply with increasingly stringent federal water quality standards has largely fallen to cities, municipal water departments, and their customers. These upgrades can be extremely costly—in the billions of dollars. Communicating the need for improved stormwater

---

Box 7.3   Best Practices in Implementation and Results: The Cuyahoga 50 Years After the Fire

In June 1969, the Cuyahoga River in Cleveland caught on fire. The river, polluted with kerosene and other flammable materials, was probably ignited by a spark from a passing train. *Time Magazine* coverage of the incident described the Cuyahoga as the river that "oozes rather than flows" and in which a person "does not drown but decays." Impressively, the river actually *repeatedly* caught fire during this point in its history, but the incident and the famous photograph of the river on fire became a pivotal part of the emerging environmental movement. The memorable 1969 fire sparked legislation inluding the Great Lakes Water Quality Agreement and the Clean Water Act of the 1970s. A concerted effort to improve water quality followed, and the federal government directed large amounts of money to clean up point sources of pollution like municipal wastewater and pollution from industrial sources.

Although much healthier now, some sections of the river remain impaired. For example, most of the river remains unacceptable for recreational use due to the high concentrations of *Escherichia coli* (*E. coli*),

(*continued*)

Box 7.3   (continued)

a bacterial species indicative of fecal contamination. Contaminant and bacteria levels are high as the river still receives discharges of stormwater, combined sewer overflows, and incompletely disinfected wastewater from urban areas. These impacts are the result of suburbanization in metro Cleveland, where former open spaces and farmland have been replaced with impervious surfaces such as rooftops, driveways, parking lots, sidewalks, and lawns. On a more optimistic note, continued investments, first in managing point source industrial pollution, and more recently in managing non-point source stormwater and related pollutants, have improved river conditions. Water quality specialists have recently found some freshwater mussels and sport fish like the walleye, which had been absent from the river for some 100 years.

Source:

"Cuyahoga River Fire," Ohio History Connection, accessed April 8, 2018, http://www.ohiohistorycentral.org/w/Cuyahoga_River_Fire

Read the 1969 article:

Times Magazine, "America's Sewage System and the Price of Optimism," *Time Magazine* Friday, Aug. 01, 1969 (Vol 94 no 5), http://content.time. com/time/magazine/article/0,9171,901182,00.html

management to the public is a continual challenge. Yet, it is necessary for several reasons. First, improved stormwater management will require broad land use change, including on private property. Second, residents must be willing and motivated to pay the higher fees associated with improved stormwater management. For this reason, public education and awareness is a necessary part of implementing water sustainability.

In the next section, we examine three strategies that cities are using to improve water quality of nearby waterbodies to meet Clean Water Act and NPDES permit requirements.

Changing Management Practices

One federally-required step in overhauling urban stormwater management practices falls under the category of pollution prevention or "good housekeeping." By better managing the pollution that collects on streets, parking lots, and other paved surfaces, the pollution load and environmental damage caused by stormwater from these surfaces can be reduced.

These actions address a number of issues, but an area of particular concern is road salt (sodium chloride), which is the inexpensive and effective street deicing chemical applied in most of the Midwest and Northeastern United States during the winter months.[39] As a result of these deicing practices, melt water from roads sometimes contains acutely toxic chloride concentrations which then flow into lakes, streams, and the groundwater.[40] Chloride accumulates in waterbodies and the environment generally, as it is not altered or taken up by any biological or chemical process. As a result, chloride concentrations are rising in lakes across the country with research indicating that if salinity continues to increase at its present rate, many surface waters in the Northeastern United States would not be potable for human consumption and would become toxic to freshwater life within the next century.[41]

Madison is working to develop methods for reducing its salt usage at a time in which salt demand is increasing (for example, salting bike paths).[42] The city is changing its own road maintenance practices to use less road salt. Best practices include applying salt liquids to roads *before* snow and ice events and varying levels of winter maintenance based on need, prioritizing areas such as: hills, intersections, high volume streets, and roads in proximity to schools and hospitals. However, drivers expect roadways to be safe and open during and immediately after snowfall, and the city notes that this expectation will have to change before meaningful reductions in salt application will be achieved.[43] The city is also educating residents on proper salt application techniques.[44] Their "Salt Wise" program suggests that residents shovel more to reduce ice, evenly scatter salt, and to switch to a different ice melter blend when temperatures drop below 15 degrees because salt alone is ineffective. They advertise that "less salt = healthier waters."

Upgrades to "Grey" Infrastructure

Conventionally, stormwater infrastructure has been designed to prevent flooding and convey rainfall and snowmelt away from built areas as quickly as possible through pipes, tanks, or underground storage facilities (known as "grey" infrastructure). Investment and improvements in separate sewer systems, existing combined sewer systems, and wastewater treatment plants has led to dramatic improvements in local river and lake water quality since the 1970s. Some cities continue to prioritize optimization of existing "grey" infrastructure systems to improve stormwater management. For instance, many cities propose upgrades to existing water treatment plants to reduce nitrogen discharges and achieve secondary treatment standards.[45]

Although America's cities have a long history of conventional sewage infrastructure, advances in modern sensors, data acquisition systems, and remote actuators hold potential for real-time adaptive management and "smarter" infrastructure.[46] Infrastructure is often thought to be static, and therefore unable to adapt as climate patterns and land use within a sewer-shed changes. However, technically-advanced and low-cost sensors, wireless data acquisition systems, and cloud-hosted real-time data systems make it possible to understand system performance in a nuanced way. An increasing number of commercial and open-source platforms allow users to monitor precipitation, soil-moisture, water flow, and model system performance. Perhaps, the biggest environmental benefits come from the availability of low-cost, remote actuators (such as valves, gates, and pumps) that can be used to retrofit existing systems and temporarily optimize capacity (enhanced inline storage) or other system features based on weather forecasts or real-time data. This allows managers to strategically and remotely close off or reduce flow in parts of the system and use excess capacity in pipes to reduce combined sewer overflows and urban flooding.

Box 7.4   Best Practices in Innovation: South Bend's Smart Grey Infrastructure

South Bend, Indiana, has invested about $6 million in "CSOnet," a system of smart wireless sensors retrofitted into the city's 500-mile sewer system and 36 combined sewer outfalls.[a] The sensors have allowed the city to find the location of underutilized pipe with existing capacity. They then installed "smart" valves that can remotely divert water into these pipes when needed to act as overflow reservoirs at key points in the system. System managers noted that this "smart" system saved the city upward of $110 million over constructing new underground water storage capacity and prevented hassle to residents from tearing up streets.[b] Thus, the program was an economic win for the city, which was able to meet its water management needs while avoiding millions of dollars in capital expenditures

(*continued*)

Box 7.4 (continued)

associated with conventional sewer work. The project employed a local South Bend-based company that supplied the sewer optimization technology. When first implemented, it was "the largest cyber-physical embedded sensor network in the world" and has since been the subject of a National Science Foundation-funded study to enhance the system, further bolster its capacity to manage severe weather events, and to learn lessons for applications in other cities.[c]

Sources:

[a]"CSONet," City of South Bend, Indiana, accessed February 22, 2018, https://www.southbendin.gov/government/content/csonet

[b]City of South Bend, Indiana, "CSONet".

[c]Jim Lynch, "NSF Awards $1.8M to Help Develop Smart Stormwater System" *The University Record, University of Michigan,* (October 12, 2017), accessed February 22, 2018, https://record.umich.edu/articles/nsf-awards-18m-help-develop-smart-stormwater-system

Green Infrastructure

In an attempt to find cost-effective solutions for stormwater management challenges, cities have begun to take a closer look at the water management services provided by vegetation.[47] Urban-compatible (site-scale) green infrastructure elements include street trees and other vegetation, green roofs, green façades, permeable pavements, rain gardens, and stormwater treatment swales (see Box 7.5 for descriptions of these techniques). Such decentralized efforts provide a "greening" option even in dense and largely built-out urban areas where available land is scarce or expensive.[48] Advocates of green infrastructure often point to the multiple benefits this provides, including energy savings, mitigation of the urban heat island effect, reduction of air pollution, wildlife habitat creation, and provision of an aesthetically-pleasing amenity.[49] We discuss the connection between green infrastructure and green space in Chap. 8.

In order to keep stormwater out of combined systems, municipalities have started to examine the efficacy and cost-effectiveness of "grey-green hybrid" systems that integrate decentralized green infrastructure throughout an area serviced by existing "grey" infrastructure to manage runoff. Since 2007, the EPA has issued a series of memorandums giving technical

Box 7.5 Emerging Trend: Green Infrastructure

Green Infrastructure provides multiple benefits in cities. Below, we explore design considerations, benefits, and challenges associated with four common types of green infrastructure.

Green roofs have waterproof layers and a soil-like substrate that allows plants to grow on the roof of buildings. Extensive green roofs have thin substrate layers and can only support specialized, drought-tolerant plants, like sedum (Fig. 7.7a). Despite thin soil layers, these green roofs still act like a sponge when it rains, retaining and detaining stormwater. Intensive green roofs have thicker soils but are more expensive to construct because of their weight. They can support a wide variety of vegetation—even gardens and trees. Given this variety of vegetation, they might contribute more valuable habitat or even vegetable gardens, but their impacts on water quality and quantity depend on soil type, fertilization, and watering regimes. While green roofs can be installed on most roof types, including pitched or peaked roofs, for a variety of reasons, they are most economical to build on larger, new construction. Additionally, some green roofs systems feature many layers of waterproofing, root barriers, and drainage or water storage layers. We caution that when one considers the full life cycle of some of these resource intensive roofs, they may not necessarily be environmentally beneficial.

Rain gardens or bioswales are both forms of stormwater bioretention (Fig. 7.7b). At the most fundamental level, they are depressions in the landscape where stormwater from nearby surfaces collects until it can infiltrate into the soil. Bioretention is generally the simplest and most inexpensive type of green infrastructure. These areas can be planted with moisture-tolerant or native plants, which provide habitat, aid in maintaining water infiltration rates, and can mitigate pollution from stormwater runoff contaminated with nutrients from pet waste, oils, or heavy metals from road surfaces. Alternatively bioretention systems can be planted with turfgrass and disappear into lawns. Sometimes, the soils underneath a bioretention

(continued)

Box 7.5 (continued)

system are amended with organic material or sand in order to increase the rate at which water can infiltrate. Finally, in dense urban areas, rain gardens often feature overflow devices, which prevent water from particularly large events from flooding the area and connect the system to the sewer. In a few scenarios, where stormwater infiltration is not desirable, a form of bioretention might still be used. In these cases, the system is constructed to prevent infiltration and is connected directly to the sewer system, but still benefits the stormwater system through evapotranspiration and flow delays.

Permeable pavements allow water to infiltrate through them into reservoirs underneath the pavement surface. Permeable pavements are available in many surface types, including brick or concrete pavers (which can have grass or other vegetation growing between them) or permeable concrete or asphalt (which look like rougher versions of traditional applications and are permeable because they are made only with large particles—the fine particles are sifted out before the material is mixed) (Fig. 7.7c). However, the most important part of permeable pavement systems is the reservoir below the pavement, which holds water temporarily, until it can infiltrate into the soil or move into the sewer system. Advantages of permeable pavements can include reduced winter maintenance. This is because water is never standing on the pavement surface so ice does not form. However, inappropriate maintenance practices can damage these systems or cause environmental problems. For example, sanding and salting are normal road treatments during snowstorms, but sand would clog holes in pervious pavements and decrease infiltration rates, while salt would move into the soil and groundwater.

Trees provide many benefits in urban areas. They shade streets, sidewalks, and buildings, and their process of transpiration has a cooling effect. In this way, they combat the urban heat island effect and improve air quality (Fig. 7.7d). Tree canopies intercept and hold water, which divert some water from the sewer system. Trees also use many gallons (sometimes hundreds of gallons) of water per day, depending on tree species and size. The benefits that trees provide in the landscape and tree lifespan are improved with carefully constructed planter boxes that provide adequate rooting and prevent soil compaction.

(continued)

Box 7.5   (continued)

Planter boxes can also be constructed as bioretention systems. Trees—and particularly those that produce berries and nuts—provide valuable habitat in the city. However, close attention should be placed on tree selection, because some trees can also be a nuisance in urban environment. Leaves, berries, and nuts must be removed; some species produce pollen that cause common allergies; and trees planted in the wrong place can buckle sidewalks or threaten power lines.

Fig. 7.7 Types of Green Infrastructure   (a) Extensive green roof, (b) Bioswale, (c) Permeable pavement, (d) Street trees. (Sources: "Green Roofs" the U.S. EPA at https://www.epa.gov/region8/building; "Green Infrastructure," the U.S. EPA, accessed December 17, 2017, https://www.epa.gov/green-infrastructure/what-green-infrastructure#bioswales; Wikipedia/Wikimedia Commons https://upload.wikimedia.org/wikipedia/commons/b/bf/Permeable_Pavement_%2815456488240%29.jpg; and Lisa Benton-Short.)

credibility to green infrastructure, and it has begun to promote urban applications of decentralized green infrastructure as "a more cost-effective, sustainable path to clean water."[50]

Yet, green infrastructure techniques require a substantially different set of implementation, operation, and maintenance approaches than traditional grey infrastructure. Green infrastructure fundamentally involves land use changes, multiple stakeholders, community outreach and buy-in, frequent decentralized maintenance regimes, and technical skills different than those associated with traditional "grey" stormwater management systems.[51]

Perhaps for these reasons, many cities are still at the stage of developing water quality monitoring and reporting protocols or are at the "data gathering and research" stage of considering green infrastructure. Cities often begin their foray into green infrastructure through the implementation of some green infrastructure pilot projects, as Madison first did. Today, Madison is over half way to its goal of creating 1000 rain gardens around the city through several programs, including installations in city parks, greenways, and private properties.[52] Grand Rapids set a goal of using pervious pavements in at least five percent of reconstructed streets, alleys, and parking lots.[53] By 2015, the city exceeded their goal, with the percentage of projects using pervious pavements reaching 23 percent.[54]

While the potential role of green infrastructure is increasingly recognized, there is still a need for comprehensive policy mechanisms to coordinate such investments and achieve wide-scale application.[55] Some cities are considering using streams, ponds, and wetlands to treat and detain stormwater prior to its release into a waterway.[56] Portland, Oregon for example, is creating "networks of streams, rivers, and open spaces that naturally manage stormwater."[57]

Chicago has implemented a number of fascinating programs, including incentive programs for green roofs and a municipal "green alley" program. Green alleys are made of highly reflective recycled materials that reduce the urban heat island effect, and the pavement used is permeable to allow stormwater to filter through and into the soil below, instead of draining to the sewer system.[58] Washington, D.C., Louisville, and Kansas City have all made legally binding commitments to utilize site-scale stormwater best practices such as rain gardens, vegetated swales, permeable pavement, and green roofs to meet stormwater management goals established in consent decrees.[59] Philadelphia's green infrastructure approach deserves particular mention (Box 7.6).

**Box 7.6   Best Practices in Multiple Benefits: Green Infrastructure
and Philadelphia's Water Department**

Philadelphia is a pioneer in green infrastructure implementation, in large part due to the leadership of the Philadelphia Water Department (PWD). First, the agency has a long history of considering land–water interconnections within its system and throughout the region. The PWD developed the Office of Watersheds in 1999 to better integrate the formerly separate operations of CSO management, stormwater management, and source water control watershed-wide (beyond city limits). Second, the PWD has defined its mission broadly, stating that "government agencies (must) break out of their traditional roles of providing narrowly defined services."[a] Thus, they actively sought to extend their mission beyond water management to contribute to and connect with other city goals.

In order to comply with the federal Clean Water Act, PWD examined the costs and benefits of various CSO management options using a sustainability framework. This approach compared not just costs of potential projects, but included an assessment of wider social, economic and environmental benefits of each option. As a result, green infrastructure compared favorably to grey alternatives primarily due to reductions in heat-stress mortality, improved aesthetics and property value, and increased recreational opportunities.

Based upon these findings, in 2009, the PWD created a green infrastructure-based Long Term Control Plan which will be the single largest investment in the Philadelphia's environment over the next 25 years, and is much more than just a water quality improvement program. Philadelphia's "Green City, Clean Waters" plan sets out an agenda spending $2.4 billion between 2011 and 2026, 67 percent of which will be spent on green infrastructure techniques.[b] It is a commitment to reshape the city by developing the most extensive urban network of green infrastructure in the United States. Philadelphia's objective is to create 9500 "Greened Acres" over 25 years. The city will convert nearly 15 square miles of impermeable surfaces so that these manage one inch of rainfall on-site and reduce overflows by 85 percent through projects on both public and private properties. The city owns approximately 45 percent of impervious

(continued)

Box 7.6   (continued)

surfaces in areas served by combined sewers and will integrate green infrastructure into capital improvement projects on city-owned streets, sidewalks, and properties.[c] Other public land projects include open space preservation and stream restoration. One innovative approach is modifying Philadelphia's vacant land to better manage stormwater, thus using vacant land as a resource. The PWD is further creating requirements and incentives for green stormwater management on private property.

In the first years of the program, the focus was on organizational repositioning, establishing monitoring baselines, and setting up regulatory and incentive frameworks. As of October 2017—six years into the 25-year planning period—the city celebrated the creation of 1000 "Greened Acres" with a City Hall celebration called "1,000 (Green) Thank Yous" *which* was a "tribute to the dedicated coalition that's working to protect Philadelphia's water."[d]

Philadelphia's leadership in green infrastructure embodies the best of sustainability planning and action:

1) Philadelphia Water Department extended it mission beyond water management to think more holistically about how its actions can support broader city sustainability goals.
2) The PWD coordinates across agencies and breaks down silos.
3) Their approach clearly connects stormwater and green infrastructure to the multiple benefits these will provide Philadelphia residents.

It is in our estimation the ultimate sustainability "success story."
Sources:
[a]Philadelphia Water Department, "Philadelphia Combined Sewer Overflow Long Term Control Plan Update" accessed July 3, 2017, http://www.phillywatersheds.org/ltcpu/LTCPU_Section01_Introduction.pdf

[b]Kevin DeGood, "Clean Water Infrastructure, the Cost of Inaction," Center for American Progress, last modified November 4, 2013, https://www.americanprogress.org/issues/economy/report/2013/11/04/78526/clean-water-infrastructure

(*continued*)

WHAT'S MISSING: INTEGRATING WATER HOLISTICALLY

Given the scope and scale of water issues, and the many ways cities are implementing more sustainable water practices, we were surprised to find water underrepresented in many comprehensive sustainability plans. While nearly all US cities include water within sustainability planning documents at some level, we have found, with a few exceptions, that water issues are rarely a major focus. Instead of discussing water supply and quality in a holistic way, many cities appeared to focus only on their most pressing water topic. For example, New Orleans focuses on vulnerability to floods from hurricanes and says very little about water supply while drought-prone Phoenix focuses on water supply but only mentions water quality of its rivers in passing. There could be several reasons for this. For instance, a number of cities have separate plans to manage water issues, as is the case for many cities facing court orders to better manage stormwater and comply with the Clean Water Act and NPDES program.

Despite the existence of these separate water plans, we argue the integration of water issues within larger holistic planning exercises is crucial for several reasons. First, water quantity and quality are fundamentally tied to land use practices throughout a watershed. This interconnectedness means that holistic planning is essential for effective management and planning should involve actors outside the water sector. This is epitomized by trends in the use of green infrastructure for stormwater management, which holds the additional promise of environmental, public health, and economic benefits, yet brings a myriad of new challenges in its implementation. Second, scientists believe that changes in precipitation frequency and intensity will be the first ways that many people experience climate change.

Third, as discussed above, watersheds often transcend political boundaries, which means that water problems and solutions must involve actors from multiple municipalities to be truly effective. Watershed planning is an approach that addresses complex water quality and quantity issues that are affected by land use and water management practices throughout the whole watershed. This approach is necessary due to the integrated nature of water resources, the scope and scale of related challenges, and the many stakeholders who must not only be involved but also invested in sustainable management of this resource. Although this is clearly an area in which more attention is needed, we provide three examples below of unique and effective watershed management.

New York City is known for its efforts to protect water quality in the entire Delaware Watershed, which serves as the city's source of drinking water. Through upstream investments, and "a delicate balance between urban/rural and upstate/downstate interests," the city secures such high-quality drinking water for its residents that filtration of the water is unnecessary.[60] In this case, a long-term strategy for protecting water quality upstream is far more cost-effective than constructing a new filtration plant for the city that would cost billions of dollars.[61] Trade-offs and tensions do exist, however. Upstream residents in the Catskill Mountains have accepted land use limitations in exchange for compensation from the city.

Colorado has addressed the pressure to provide water for growing populations in cities such as Denver, Boulder, and Fort Collins by creating "basin roundtables" for each of the nine watersheds in the state.[62] Roundtable members include representatives from all municipalities in the watershed, the water conservation district, water utility, and representatives of agricultural, recreational, industrial, and environmental interest groups. The basin roundtables develop assessments of water needs, including municipal, industrial, and agricultural consumptive needs and environmental and recreational needs, and of available water and proposed projects for more sustainable water management.

In Milwaukee, a partnership of stakeholders known as "Sweet Water" (Southeastern Wisconsin Watersheds Trust) was established in 2008 to coordinate stormwater management efforts and improve water quality throughout the region.[63] This unique partnership includes a diverse set of stakeholders including municipalities, businesses, utilities, and nongovernmental organizations.[64] It was created because leaders realized that effective management would require a different approach than business as usual.[65] The group has found it effective to work together solving common problems, supporting innovations in new technologies and green infrastructure and in raising public awareness about stormwater and the impacts it has on the watershed. Stakeholders acknowledge the importance of relationships and ongoing communication to address problems that span jurisdictions and purviews and see Sweet Water as an important vehicle to addressing challenges in a cohesive and cost-effective fashion.[66]

It is clear that water managers must work across disciplines and political boundaries. They must learn to plan with new levels of uncertainty, and they would benefit from collaboration with others working on climate change adaptation measures. For all these reasons, water is an issue that should figure more prominently within sustainability plans, even when other planning documents on the topic exist. Otherwise, an opportunity to engage in inter-agency planning and synergies around issues of water has been missed.

SUMMARY

Water management is framed by local needs, regional watershed features, and federal regulations. However, management is also complicated by fragmented responsibility, climate change, aging infrastructure, and, in some places, increased use from population growth. Cities are taking action in numerous ways as they move towards more sustainable water practices. Table 7.1 highlights important trends and best practices.

Table 7.1 Best practices in water

Water efficiency

- Identify and address barriers to water-saving technologies
- Make data on water usage available for each property
- Promote the cost-effectiveness of smart irrigation and drought-resistant landscaping

Water reuse systems

- Provide training about greywater systems for policymakers and regulators
- Streamline permitting for straightforward, small-scale greywater systems
- Require that all newly constructed buildings are "greywater ready"
- Consider dual greywater infrastructures for major water users, including golf courses and industry

Water quality and stormwater management

- Reduce application of deicing salts
- Invest in "smart" stormwater management systems
- Promote green infrastructure solutions

Integrating water holistically

- Undertake watershed-scale planning that crosses regional and state boundaries
- Integrate planning efforts across departments

NOTES

1. Gianna Palmer, "Flint Water Crisis: Living One Bottle of Water at a Time," *BBC News*, January 22, 2016, sec. Magazine, http://www.bbc.com/news/magazine-35376517.

2. Maggie Fox, "Flint Water Crisis: Feds Expand Programs to Help Kids Affected by Lead," *NBC News*, March 2, 2016, https://www.nbcnews.com/storyline/flint-water-crisis/flint-water-crisis-feds-expand-programs-help-kids-affected-lead-n530556.

3. Merrit Kennedy, "Lead-Laced Water In Flint: A Step-By-Step Look At The Makings Of A Crisis," April 20, 2016, https://www.npr.org/sections/thetwo-way/2016/04/20/465545378/lead-laced-water-in-flint-a-step-by-step-look-at-the-makings-of-a-crisis.

4. Michael Wines, "Behind Toledo's Water Crisis, a Long-Troubled Lake Erie," *The New York Times*, August 4, 2014, sec. Environment, https://www.nytimes.com/2014/08/05/us/lifting-ban-toledo-says-its-water-is-safe-to-drink-again.html.

5. Heather Rogers, "Don't Drink the Water: West Virginia After the Chemical Spill," *Rolling Stone*, March 12, 2014, https://www.rollingstone.com/culture/news/dont-drink-the-water-west-virginia-after-the-chemical-spill-20140312.

6. Eric Young, "Report: More Than One out of Three U.S. Counties Face Water Shortages Due to Climate Change" (National Resources Defense Council, July 20, 2010), https://www.nrdc.org/media/2010/100720.

7. Christopher Walsh et al., "The Urban Stream Syndrome: Current Knowledge and the Search for a Cure," *Journal of the North American Benthological Society* 24, no. 3 (2005): 706–23.

8. Philadelphia Water Department, "History," 2017, http://www.phillywatersheds.org/your_watershed/history; Russell Weigley, *Philadelphia: A 300 Year History* (New York: W.W. Norton & Company, 1982).

9. ASCE, "Wastewater – 2017 Infrastructure Report Card" (American Society of Civil Engineers, 2017), https://www.infrastructurereportcard.org/wp-content/uploads/2017/01/Wastewater-Final.pdf; ASCE, "Drinking Water – 2017 Infrastructure Report Card" (American Society of Civil Engineers, 2017), https://www.infrastructurereportcard.org/cat-item/drinking-water/.

10. The City of Miami Beach, "Sustainability Plan Energy Economic Zone Work Plan," November 12, 2009, 10, http://www.miamibeachfl.gov/green/scroll.aspx?id=63975.

11. City of Burlington, "The Burlington Legacy Project," 2000, 37, https://www.burlingtonvt.gov/sites/default/files/CEDO/Legacy_Project/Legacy%20Action%20Plan.pdf.

12. City of St. Louis Planning Commission, "City of St. Louis Sustainability Plan," February 6, 2013, 186, https://www.stlouis-mo.gov/government/departments/mayor/documents/upload/STL-Sustainability-Plan.pdf.

13. Melissa Keeley et al., "Perspectives on the Use of Green Infrastructure for Stormwater Management in Cleveland and Milwaukee," *Environmental Management* 51, no. 6 (June 2013): 1093–1108, https://doi.org/10.1007/s00267-013-0032-x; Mark Caro, "Milwaukee Dives into Water Tech, Chicago Just Getting Feet Wet," *The Chicago Tribune*, June 12, 2015, http://www.chicagotribune.com/news/globalcity/ct-water-tech-hub-met-20150612-story.html.

14. City of Tulsa, "City of Tulsa Sustainability Plan: Resource Efficiency, Clean Energy, and Leading Growth in the New Economy," October 27, 2011, 12, http://cdn.cityoftulsa.org/parks/COT%20Sustainability%20Plan_FINAL.pdf.

15. Keeley et al., "Perspectives on the Use of Green Infrastructure for Stormwater Management in Cleveland and Milwaukee."

16. Patricia Gober et al., "Why Land Planners and Water Managers Don't Talk to One Another and Why They Should!," *Society & Natural Resources* 26, no. 3 (March 1, 2013): 356–64, https://doi.org/10.1080/08941920.2012.713448.

17. DC Water, "History," 2017, https://www.dcwater.com/history.

18. Robert Pitt et al., "Evaluation of NPDES Phase 1 Municipal Stormwater Monitoring Data" (National conference on Urban stormwater: enhancing the programs at the local level), accessed January 5, 2018, https://www.researchgate.net/publication/267835093_EVALUATION_OF_NPDES_PHASE_1_MUNICIPAL_STORMWATER_MONITORING_DATA.

19. Demographia, "US Metropolitan Area Population: 1990–2000," 2003, http://www.demographia.com/db-usmet2000.htm; Mark Niesse, "Census: Metro Atlanta's Population Expands to 5.7 Million" (The Atlanta Journal-Constitution, March 29, 2016), http://www.ajc.com/news/local-govt--politics/census-metro-atlanta-population-expands-million/lXg26y7C7f7WYymrtcvg0N/.

20. Jenny Jarvie, "Atlanta Water Use Is Called Shortsighted," *Los Angeles Times*, November 4, 2007, http://articles.latimes.com/2007/nov/04/nation/na-drought4.

21. Center for Sustainable Systems, "Fact Sheet" (University of Michigan, 2017), http://css.umich.edu/factsheets/us-water-supply-and-distribution-factsheet).

22. Bradley J. Fikes, "State's Biggest Desal Plant to Open: What It Means," *The San Diego Union-Tribune*, December 13, 2015, http://www.sandiegouniontribune.com/news/environment/sdut-poseidon-water-desalination-carlsbad-opening-2015dec13-htmlstory.html.

23. Andy Pierrotti, "Why Is Atlanta Losing Billions of Gallons of Water Each Year?" (11Alive News, October 3, 2016), http://www.11alive.com/article/news/local/investigations/why-is-atlanta-losing-billions-of-gallons-in-water-each-year/85-328291738.

24. City of Shoreline, "Shoreline Environmental Sustainability Strategy," July 14, 2008, 44–45, http://cosweb.ci.shoreline.wa.us/uploads/attachments/pds/esc/COMPLETE_FinalSESStrategy2008July.pdf.

25. The City of Austin, "Rethink For A Bright Green Future," 2008, 14.

26. The City of Austin, "Imagine Austin: Year 5 Progress Report," 2017, 17, ftp://ftp.ci.austin.tx.us/npzd/ImagineAustin/FINAL_Progress_Report_1709.pdf.

27. Sustainable Santa Fe Commission, "Sustainable Santa Fe Plan," April 2012, 23.

28. Sustainable Santa Fe Commission, 24.

29. City of St. Louis Planning Commission, "City of St. Louis Sustainability Plan," 184.

30. Sustainable Santa Fe Commission, "Sustainable Santa Fe Plan," 22; City of Tulsa, "City of Tulsa Sustainability Plan: Resource Efficiency, Clean Energy, and Leading Growth in the New Economy," 67.

31. Molly Hollar, "Wildscape Demonstration Garden," City of Arlington, TX – Water Utilities, accessed April 3, 2018, http://www.arlington-tx.gov/water/water-conservation/xeriscaping/smartscape-garden/.

32. City of Arlington, TX, "Xeriscaping," City of Arlington, TX – Water Utilities, accessed April 3, 2018, http://www.arlington-tx.gov/water/water-conservation/xeriscaping/.

33. United States Environmental Protection Agency, "Water Recycling and Reuse: The Environmental Benefits," September 28, 2017, https://www3.epa.gov/region9/water/recycling/.

34. The City of San Jose, "San Jose's Green Vision," 2007, 9, http://www.globalurban.org/San_Jose_Green_Vision.pdf.

35. Austin Water, "Reclaimed Water Program," accessed January 4, 2018, http://www.austintexas.gov/department/water-reclamation.

36. The City of San Diego, "Wastewater: North City Water Reclamation Plant," accessed February 14, 2018, https://www.sandiego.gov/mwwd/facilities/northcity.

37. Laura Martin, "Texas Leads The Way With First Direct Potable Reuse Facilities in U.S." (Water Online, September 16, 2014), https://www.wateronline.com/doc/texas-leads-the-way-with-first-direct-potable-reuse-facilities-in-u-s-0001.

38. Chattanooga Green Committee, "The Chattanooga Climate Action Plan," February 24, 2009, 61.

39. Hilary A. Dugan et al., "Salting Our Freshwater Lakes," *Proceedings of the National Academy of Sciences* 114, no. 17 (April 25, 2017): 4453–58, https://doi.org/10.1073/pnas.1620211114.

40. Rick Wenta and Kirsti Sorsa, "Road Salt 2013: Where's the Balance?" (Public Health Madison and Dane County, January 3, 2014), https://www.cityofmadison.com/engineering/stormwater/documents/RoadSaltReport2013.pdf.

41. Sujay S. Kaushal et al., "Increased Salinization of Fresh Water in the Northeastern United States," *Proceedings of the National Academy of Sciences* 102, no. 38 (September 20, 2005): 13517–20, https://doi.org/10.1073/pnas.0506414102.

42. Rick Wenta and Kirsti Sorsa, "Road Salt Report 2014" (Public Health Madison and Dane County, December 11, 2018), 9, http://www.publichealthmdc.com/publications/documents/RoadSaltRpt2014.pdf.

43. Wenta and Sorsa, 10.

44. WI Salt Wise Partnership, "Be Salt WIse!," 2015, https://www.wisaltwise.com/.

45. The City of New York, "PlaNYC A Greener, Greater New York," 2011, 64, http://www.nyc.gov/html/planyc/downloads/pdf/publications/planyc_2011_planyc_full_report.pdf.

46. Branko Kerkez et al., "Smarter Stormwater Systems" (ACS Publications, 2016), http://pubs.acs.org/doi/pdf/10.1021/acs.est.5b05870?src=recsys&.

47. Konstantinos Tzoulas et al., "Promoting Ecosystem and Human Health in Urban Areas Using Green Infrastructure: A Literature Review," *Landscape and Urban Planning* 81, no. 3 (June 2007): 167–78.

48. Franco Montalto et al., "Rapid Assessment of the Cost-Effectiveness of Low Impact Development for CSO Control," *Landscape and Urban Planning* 82, no. 3 (September 24, 2007): 117–31, https://doi.org/10.1016/j.landurbplan.2007.02.004.

49. Tzoulas et al., "Promoting Ecosystem and Human Health in Urban Areas Using Green Infrastructure"; P. Bolund and S. Hunhammar, "Ecosystem Services in Urban Areas," *Ecological Economics* 29 (1999): 293–301.

50. Lisa P. Jackson, "Remarks on Green City Clean Waters Partnership Agreement in Philadelphia" (The United States Environmental Protection Agency, April 10, 2012), https://archive.epa.gov/epapages/newsroom_archive/speeches/bbdcd9f00cafbe96852579ed0057486e.html.

51. David P. Dolowitz, Melissa Keeley, and Dale Medearis, "Stormwater Management: Can We Learn from Others?," *Policy Studies* 33, no. 6 (2012): 501–21; Keeley et al., "Perspectives on the Use of Green Infrastructure for Stormwater Management in Cleveland and Milwaukee."

52. Randy Rodgers, "Madison Colors Wisconsin Green" (Sustainable City Network, July 10, 2013), http://www.sustainablecitynetwork.com/topic_channels/policy/article_8b8345aa-e8e3-11e2-aed1-0019bb30f31a.html.

53. City of Grand Rapids, Office of Energy and Sustainability, "FY 2011 Through FY 2015 Sustainability Plan," 2011, 28.

54. City of Grand Rapids, Office of Energy and Sustainability, "FY2011-FY2015 Sustainability Plan 5th Year Progress Report," 2015, 63, http://grcity.us/enterprise-services/officeofenergyandsustainability/Pages/default.aspx.

55. Melissa Keeley, "The Green Area Ratio: An Urban Site Sustainability Metric," *Journal of Environmental Planning and Management* 54, no. 7 (2011): 937–58.

56. The City of New York, "PlaNYC," 66.

57. City of Portland, "The Portland Plan April 2012," 2012, 57, http://www.portlandonline.com/portlandplan/index.cfm?c=58776.

58. City of Chicago, "Green Alleys," accessed January 3, 2018, https://www.cityofchicago.org/city/en/depts/cdot/provdrs/street/svcs/green_alleys.html.

59. United States Environmental Protection Agency, "Consent Decrees That Include Green Infrastructure Provisions."

60. NYC Environmental Protection, "About Watershed Protection" (The City of New York), accessed January 4, 2018, http://www.nyc.gov/html/dep/html/watershed_protection/about.shtml.

61. Graciela Chichilnisky and Geoffrey Heal, "Economic Returns from the Biosphere," *Nature* 391 (1998): 629–30.

62. Colorado Water Conservation Board, "Basin Roundtables" (Department of Natural Resources), accessed January 4, 2018, http://cwcb.state.co.us/water-management/basin-roundtables/Pages/main.aspx.

63. Southeastern Wisconsin Watersheds Trust, Inc., "Sweet Water: Our Work," accessed January 4, 2018, http://www.swwtwater.org/our-work-1/.

64. Southeastern Wisconsin Watersheds Trust, Inc.

65. Keeley et al., "Perspectives on the Use of Green Infrastructure for Stormwater Management in Cleveland and Milwaukee," 1101.

66. Keeley et al., 1101.

CHAPTER 8

Urban Green Space

Urban Green Space: An Introduction

Cities are situated in broader physical processes and entangled in complex ecosystems. Nature is present in cities in both visible and invisible ways. Wildlife in a variety of forms continues to find ecological niches in the city. Urban parks—from large parks and natural areas to pocket parks and private backyards—provide habitat to a remarkable number of species. Small tot lots may be used by only neighborhood residents, while larger parks are often central features of a city. It is difficult to imagine New York without Central Park, Washington, D.C. without the National Mall, or Boston without its Emerald Necklace. Other natural features are important—the lakeside shore of Chicago, the beaches of Los Angeles and San Diego. There are more specialized forms of green space as well, like street trees and community gardens. In this chapter, we focus our discussion of urban green space on the many forms of vegetation within cities including parks, green space, street trees, and gardens.

Urban green space is a broad category that can be loosely defined as vegetated areas within an urban landscape.[1] The Environmental Protection Agency defines "green space" as a subset of "open space," and is "any piece of land that is completely or partly covered with grass, trees, shrubs or other vegetation and can include parks, community gardens and cemeteries."[2] Many cities take an expansive approach in classifying green space to include parks and trails, open space, tree canopy, urban gardens, vegetated medians, recreational areas, greenways, green roofs, and green infrastructure.

Urban vegetation is considered particularly important because of the many environmental, social, and economic benefits they provide.[3] For this reason, the US Mayors Climate Protection Agreement specifically suggests that municipalities maintain healthy urban forests and preserve open space.[4]

The ways in which cities plan for green space in sustainability plans can provide new insight on the values cities hold and the ways that they conceptualize green space as part of the urban landscape. For instance, wetlands reconstruction and stream restoration bring natural processes back to cities; large-scale parkway systems provide corridors for wildlife; green infrastructure is used to manage stormwater (green infrastructure is primarily discussed in Chap. 7). In this chapter, we focus on the following types of green space: parks; tree canopy and the urban forest; and community gardens and urban agriculture. We focus on small-scale urban green space here because it is integrated within the urban fabric and has the potential to impact every city neighborhood.

CITIES' ROLE IN GREEN SPACE

Cities have been proactively "greening" for more than a century. New York City's Central Park was designed by Frederick Law Olmsted and Calvert Vaux in 1857 to feel like a naturalistic escape from the city. The park embodied an egalitarian perspective that green space should be accessible to all people. This conception of a "public park" took off, and since the early twentieth century, cities have actively set aside spaces for parks, gardens, and waterfronts. The recent emergence of comprehensive sustainability planning has prompted cities to give renewed attention to these valuable resources.

Such efforts are simultaneously generalizable and highly localized. On the one hand, all cities have some forms of green space, open space, parks and recreational areas, and gardens. Many cities are taking action to plan wider eco-corridors, encourage native vegetation, increase the urban tree canopy in both number and diversity, foster urban forestry partnerships, update zoning codes to allow urban agriculture, and use green space as an educational tool.

On the other hand, cities occupy specific sites, which means there are local and regional variations in climate, culture, and environment. These can constrain efforts to "green" the city. One of the most significant features of urban sustainability is making cities more responsive to local environments and variations in temperature, rainfall levels, altitude, and biotic zone. Planting indigenous vegetation, encouraging local species, removing invasive species, and building within the context of local ecosystems connect cities to their immediate environment. For example, the classic English garden may be suitable for the cool, damp climate of England but is not the most ecologically sensitive design for gardens in hot, dry Phoenix. Not all cities can plan for the same types of parks and open spaces or utilize the same species of street tree because different geographies and environments call for different applications. From a human perspective, communities with different age, gender, or ethnic compositions should tailor their green space plans to local conditions and preferences.[5] Urban planning and design is now more imbued with a bioregional *awareness* and a sensitivity to the local environment and community, forging a much closer connection between cities and their particular sites.

Not only do cities plan differently for green spaces based on specific geographies, they may use many different terms in discussions of parks, green spaces, and open spaces in their jurisdictions. For example, many cities in the Southwest and in California do not use the term "green space."[6] These cities are located in desert environments where the natural vegetation is not necessarily "green." Instead, they use terms such as "open space" and "natural vegetation." In fact, the avoidance of "green" in these cities can be viewed as a positive trend because traditional "green" space would likely be energy and water intensive and therefore have a negative and unsustainable connotation within these geographies.[7] Therefore in these contexts, spaces that are green could actually be unsustainable, such as irrigated green lawns in Las Vegas.

A prominent and more sustainable strategy in desert cities is xeriscaping, which uses native and other drought-tolerant vegetation and landscaping that requires little or no irrigation. The use of local context (physical, social, economic) is an important factor in sustainability (and especially green space) planning.[8] Research suggests the importance of designing policy instruments for real world conditions rather than trying to make the existing world conform to a particular policy.[9] This means that local climactic conditions are more important than the popular notion of needing "green" spaces.

Green spaces figure prominently in many municipal plans for sustainability, perhaps because they provide so many benefits in urban areas (Table 8.1); however, we found most cities prioritize the environmental benefits of green spaces rather than their many economic and social benefits.

Green spaces are of course tied to the natural environment which makes these connections very straightforward.[10] In addition, many environmental benefits are available to all residents whether or not they use the green spaces.[11] The inclusive nature of these benefits is another reason why green spaces are commonly included in the sustainability plans. Common environmental benefits include:

- Cooling the city and reducing the urban heat island,
- Improving air quality,
- Acting as a carbon sink, and
- Providing habitat for species.

Yet research shows that green spaces can provide many economic benefits and cities are beginning to recognize these.[12] Some cities recognize the potential for green space to be a strategy for "economic development."[13] First, proximity to green spaces tends to raise property values.[14] Burlington, Chattanooga, and Grand Rapids, for example, say that urban gardens may boost the local economy through local production.[15] Still other cities see the potential of street trees to help residents save money in heating and cooling costs, as planting the right trees in the right locations around a building can result in both lowered cooling and heating costs.[16] These financial benefits are very tangible to most people, so it is no surprise that cities take notice.[17]

Another benefit of green space creation and maintenance is the creation of local jobs. For example, Philadelphia states that there are jobs "directly connected to the 'greening' of neighborhoods, such as planting trees [and] growing food in urban gardens."[18] Some cities also link green spaces with goals for job training programs which can help people develop skills for the workforce. For example, Earth Conservation Corps in Washington, D.C. trains unemployed, disadvantaged youth to work on a variety of environmental projects. The program helps the youth builds skills in environmental management such as wetland restoration, raptor rehabilitation, and tree planting while also teaching leadership and life skills. Explicitly connecting green spaces and jobs helps to break down the dichotomy of sustainability/environmental protection versus economic growth.[19]

Table 8.1 The benefits of green space and green infrastructure

Benefit category	Benefits	Examples of related actions from Sustainability plans[a]
Environmental	• Urban heat island regulation • Improve air quality • Wildlife habitat/biodiversity • Stormwater management • GHG sequestration • Walter filtration • Shade provision	• Revise parking requirements to provide for additional green space (City of Newport News) • Increase percent of low-maintenance and native plants used by the city by at least 25% (City of Grand Rapids) • Plant 8600 new trees citywide per year until 2032 (City of Washington, D.C.)
Economic	• Increase property values • Economic development • Energy savings • Promote tourism • Jobs and employment • Use naturally unbuildable property	• Incubate innovative new urban agriculture ventures to support entrepreneurship (City of St. Louis) • Identify and support the "use of naturally unbuildable properties… for agricultural use" (City of Madison)
Social	• Promote and enhance recreation and physical activity • Local healthy food • Community gatherings and social interaction • Education • Interaction with nature/time spent outdoors • Beauty and aesthetics • Promote walkability • Sense of place • Mental and spiritual health	• "Link all parks and open spaces to the maximum extent possible" (City of Madison) • "Coordinate a campaign to encourage citizens to help plant trees and care for the urban forest" and "continue tree planting programs in partnership with community organizations" (City of Austin) • Update the zoning code to allow urban agriculture and gardening broadly defined (City of St. Louis)

Source: By authors

[a]Most of the actions listed have multiple goals associated with them. We provide them here as examples with the category of benefit they seemed primarily associated with

Tourism is another economic benefit that can bring money to local economies, thus many cities advertise themselves, and their green spaces as tourist destinations.[20] Gardens, parks, and other natural amenities have become staples in ensuring the desirable image of a "green and sustainable city," helping to promote tourism.[21] Washington, D.C. understands that its iconic and historical green spaces, including the National Mall, the National Arboretum, and the Botanic Gardens, draw some 25 million tourists each year. Similarly, no visit to New York City is complete without a trip to Central Park.

In addition to economic benefits, there are numerous social benefits to investment in green space. Recreation and physical activity are growing in importance, particularly because Americans have become increasingly sedentary and obesity has skyrocketed to become one of the most prominent health issues in the country.[22] The Centers for Disease Control (CDC) credits a combination of a lack of physical activity and poor nutrition to the vast majority of obesity cases. Exercise has been proven to aid in reducing the risk for cardiovascular disease, heart attacks, strokes, and type 2 diabetes.[23] Parks and open spaces encourage walking, running, and both individual and group sports.[24] As Newport News highlights, "The city's many scenic parks are filled with every activity imaginable from hiking, camping, fishing, canoeing, golf and more fun-filled attractions that let you get up close and personal with nature and Virginia's wildlife."[25]

Facilitation of community gatherings, social interaction, and neighborhood cohesion are also benefits associated with green space. Parks and other public urban green spaces have an important function as community gathering places which are critical for nourishing a sense of community.[26] Green space can function as a form of social capital by providing a meeting place for users to develop and maintain neighborhood social ties.[27] Spending more time in nature as well as learning about its processes can foster a sense of respect, connection, understanding, and stewardship.[28]

For these reasons, many cities are now using green spaces as outdoor educational tools for both children and adults. Parks and trees can be used to teach about environmental stewardship and processes, and gardens can be used to teach about ecosystems, food, nutrition, and community.

Green spaces can also improve mental health and offer psychological and spiritual nourishment. Public green spaces are locations for passive recreation activities that include watching (people, children, nature), reading, resting, photography, enjoying scenery, and meeting friends. These activities "have been clearly expressed as opportunities for rest, relaxation and getting away from it all."[29] Daily urban life can be very stressful, and it has been shown that "natural" views can aid in attention, have restorative effects, mitigate mental fatigue, reduce aggression, facilitate recovery, and lower stress levels.[30] Studies also suggest that office workers with a view of nature are more productive, report fewer illnesses, and have higher job satisfaction.[31] Washington, D.C. and others explain the importance of green space to their residents, citing studies that demonstrate the ability of green space to help people recover more quickly from illness and to improve the productivity of students and workers.[32]

In summary, green space provides numerous environmental, economic, and social benefits in cities, and municipalities are increasingly cognizant of these. Yet, our research shows that to fully capture these multiple benefits, cities need to better recognize, value, and plan for the economic and social benefits green spaces provide.

Taking Action to Improve Urban Green Space

Green spaces are of varied character and provide multiple benefits in cities. Below, we consider approaches that cities are taking to use green spaces to achieve their sustainability goals within three broad strategies:

1. Parks, green space, and open space
2. Urban forests
3. Community gardens and urban agriculture.

Parks, Green Space, and Open Space

Many cities have taken action to protect existing parks, green space, and open space. Cities are also expanding and improving on their green space and linking individual parks and green spaces together to create connected park systems. Finally, cities are also creating new parks, often with creative and innovative design approaches.

Protecting Open Space

Urban growth is a pervasive feature of the past hundred years. While some cities have seen population increases, a major cause of land use change is suburban sprawl. Sprawl has occurred as urban residents moved outward in patterns of automobile-dependent suburban and exurban growth of decreasing density. Sprawl causes the metropolitan sphere of influence to lengthen its shadow across the landscape as farmland turns into tract housing, woods into subdivisions, and the prairie into gated communities. Open space has been lost; farmlands transformed. Reactions to this challenge have included efforts to curtail growth and protect open space.

Smart growth has emerged as a strategy to deal with the constant pull of development towards greenfield sites on the city's edge. Smart growth is a planning strategy that focuses development in areas with existing infrastructure to create more dense development, minimize infrastructure investments, and preserve open space and farmland. We discuss strategies for mitigating sprawl and creating dense development in Chap. 5.

Another way cities have reacted to protect open space is by establishing urban growth boundaries (UGBs). UGBs delineate land that should be densely used for housing, transportation, and employment. Growth occurs inside the UGB, while areas outside the UBG are preserved either for agriculture or in its natural state. UGBs can be an effective tool to limit urban sprawl and unplanned development because they direct growth into the core through redevelopment and infill and remove market pressure to develop open space at the city's periphery.

The state of Oregon was a pioneer in UGB, passing legislation in 1973 that required cities to develop a long-range plan for managing growth. The city of Portland was the first US city to establish a growth boundary in the 1970s.[33] The city's UGB protects farmland surrounding the city and tightly limits development in outlying areas. Because of the urban growth boundary, Portland has assimilated a sharply rising population while limiting encroachment on its valuable agricultural and natural lands. Portland's urban design provides affordable and accessible public transit located close to schools, businesses, and residential communities, and the city is working to connect the entire city with walking and bike paths. However, Portland's UGB has also experienced serious pushback and controversy. Critics note the challenge faced by low-income residents in the face of escalating home prices, and the limitations and economic burden placed on land owners outside the UGB, who are limited in future uses of their property.

Creating New Parks and Green Spaces

Many cities are successfully creating new parks and green spaces out of former industrial and brownfield sites (this is part of a larger trend of waterfront and brownfield reuse we discuss in Chap. 3). One of the most notable new parks created recently is Chicago's Millennium Park. For many years, part of the site now home to Millennium Park was a railyard along Lake Michigan controlled by the Illinois Central Railroad. In 1997, then Mayor Richard M. Daley put in motion plans to turn this space into a new urban park, in part by securing the air rights above the railyard. It took seven years to realize, but today, the 24.5-acre park is the centerpiece of the city, featuring state-of-the-art performance facilities, public artwork, and gardens (Fig. 8.1). During summer months, some art installations incorporate water. In the winter, an ice skating rink set up near Cloud Gate (locally known as the bean) is a major tourist attraction. There are strong indications that the park has contributed to a steady increase of tourists visiting Chicago each year, a value estimated at over $1.2 billion. Several studies estimate that the park has increased the value of residential development downtown by over $1 billion dollars. By any measure, Millennium Park is an urban planning success story.

Fig. 8.1 Chicago's Millennium Park. (Source: "Millennium Park, Chicago," Wikipedia/Wikimedia commons photo by J.Crocker (created October 13, 2005), accessed April 11, 2018, https://upload.wikimedia.org/wikipedia/commons/5/50/2005-10-13_2880x1920_chicago_above_millennium_park. jpg)

In 2009, the city of Irvine in California unveiled a new master plan for the site of the former El Toro Marine Corps Air Station, which closed in 1999.[34] At 1347 acres, the Great Park features a constructed two-and-a-half-mile canyon, a "daylighted" stream (removed from concrete conveyances and restored), a large lake, a great lawn, an aviation museum, a conservatory/botanical garden, a promenade, and a sports park. Ecologically, the park will be a vital link in a chain of land reserves stretching from the mountains to the sea. The park will also connect communities throughout the county by knitting together multi-use trails from all parts of the region.

Other recently built parks include Klyde Warren Park in Dallas; Railroad Park in Birmingham, Alabama; Campus Martius Park in Detroit; and Yards Park in Washington, D.C. (see Fig. 8.2). Many of these new urban

Fig. 8.2 Washington, D.C.'s new Yards Park acts as both a stormwater management system and a multi-use public space. During the summer, Canal Park fountains and food trucks make this a vibrant public space, and the park offers outdoor movies and sunset yoga. In the winter, the fountain area is converted to an ice rink. (Source: Lisa Benton-Short.)

parks have transformed underused industrial spaces and emphasize interaction, fitness, activities for families, and good food, featuring restaurant pavilions and dining.

Expanding and Improving Parks and Green Spaces
Another best practice is expanding and improving existing parks and green spaces. While we highlight some high-profile examples here, we note that parks of all sizes require ongoing maintenance to continue to serve as community amenities. Maintenance of a decentralized park system is a logistical challenge, and in times of financial hardship, may frequently be cut back. For these reasons, consideration of park quality, placement, and expansion requires increased attention.

The expansion and renovation of the 150-year-old Washington Park in Cincinnati illustrates several best practices.[35] The latest major improvements to the park in 2012 were the result of a partnership between the Cincinnati Park Board and the Cincinnati Center City Development Corporation. Together, the two organizations engaged in a community-based planning process. The vision which emerged from this process not only preserved unique park elements but added new amenities to provide green space access and connect the Over-the-Rhine neighborhood with the rest of the city. The park was expanded from six to eight acres. Additional park features included gathering spaces like a plaza for the existing Music Hall, and a large "civic green." Other elements that draw park users include a restored historic bandstand and performance stage, an interactive water park, a playground with climbing walls inspired by the city's architecture, and an underground parking garage.

Cincinnati's attentions have not just been on Washington Park. The city has also invested in a riverfront park which reconnects the central business district to the river and other riverfront parks. The design includes a series of terraces that accommodate seasonal flooding along the river edge, as well as areas lifted out of the floodplain. Cincinnati is not alone in its efforts to build new parks and green spaces. A major trend in planning is to interconnect parks and green spaces throughout urban areas.

Connecting Parks and Green Spaces
Urban ecologists, landscape architects, and designers now realize that metro areas are not comprised of fragmented, unrelated ecosystems but are in fact integrated structures. There are circulation and flows of energy, biophysical cycles, and species movement. Urban ecosystem fragments have been demonstrated to contribute to species preservation more "than

their limited size and disturbed state might suggest," making their planning and connectivity of vital importance.[36] As a result of recent research in the area, many cities are attempting to reconnect their green spaces, open spaces, parks, and green features.

Green space connectivity improves the habitat value of these systems and also increases the utility of these spaces as transit and recreation corridors for humans. The idea of thinking about city green spaces as a *system* has been taken to a new level, and Washington, D.C., Los Angeles, and San Francisco have led the way in demonstrating the benefits of such systems. Two other notable examples of reimaging the connectivity of green space are found in New York City's Highline and Atlanta's BeltLine (Box 8.1).

We also see examples of these aspirations in the city of Madison's goal to "link all parks and open spaces to the maximum extent possible."[37] Similarly, Austin aims to increase greenway and open space acreage along the Colorado River and local creek systems.[38] In 2017, Atlanta released the Atlanta City Design, which among other ideas includes building new parks, creating an integrated park system through system-wide planning and "re-wilding" parts of the Chattahoochee River waterfront.

Box 8.1   Best Practices in Innovation: Linear Parks

In 1934, an elevated rail line opened in Manhattan, New York, to deliver goods and material to factories and warehouses along its 13-mile route through Chelsea and the Meatpacking District. When the warehouses and factories closed, the rail line was no longer viable and made its last delivery in 1980. In 1999, the Regional Plan Association, commissioned by the railway line owners, CSX Railroad, suggested turning the narrow railroad into a pedestrian promenade. The first section of the linear pedestrian park was opened in 2009 and instantly became popular among locals and visitors. The route retains an industrial aesthetic with railroad tracks and movable seats on railroad car wheels yet softens this experience with extensive plantings of native vegetation and provides unique views of the city. The conversion of an abandoned railroad track into an urban public space and walking route is one of the more successful transformations in the shift from industrial to postindustrial. The Highline has been lauded for reimagining green spaces as both vertical and linear

(continued)

Box 8.1   (continued)

possibilities. It has helped to influence the design of other linear parks, such as Atlanta's Beltline Park.

The Atlanta BeltLine was first conceived as a 1999 master's thesis by Georgia Tech student Ryan Gravel. It evolved into a grassroots

Fig. 8.3   The New York City Highline pays homage to its industrial past by featuring railroad tracks in the design and native plants. (Source: Lisa Benton-Short.)

(*continued*)

Box 8.1 (continued)

campaign of local citizens and civic leaders and then became a robust new vision for an Atlanta dedicated to integrating transportation, land use, greenspace, and sustainable growth.

When completed, the BeltLine will be a more extensive park than the Highline. Following abandoned railroad corridors that encircled Atlanta, it will ultimately connect 45 neighborhoods via a 22-mile loop of parks, multi-use trails, and a streetcar line. It will open in phases with completion anticipated in 2030. As of 2018, the Atlanta BeltLine has already generated $3 billion in private economic redevelopment and provides a multitude of amenities such as the largest temporary public art exhibition in the south, an urban farm, free fitness classes, an arboretum, seven parks, four trails, and hundreds of affordable workforce homes.

Both the Highline and the BeltLine are innovations in park design which effectively reuse brownfield sites to provide multiple environmental, economic, and social benefits to their communities (Fig. 8.3)

Sources:

"Visit the High Line," Friends of the Highlight, accessed April 8, 2018, http://www.thehighline.org/visit

"The Atlanta BeltLine," Atlanta BeltLine, accessed April 8, 2018, https://beltline.org/about/the-atlanta-beltline-project/atlanta-beltline-overview/

However, there remain significant barriers to increasing greenspace connectivity. The complexity of mapping, inventorying, and analyzing existing and potential greenspaces to increase connectivity should not be underestimated. Fortunately, this type of analysis fits with the expertise of geographers who can bring sensitivity to scale and assessment using tools such as GIS and remote sensing. A new asset that is being used by cities in Maine are drones.[39] These tools can also assist in assessing green spaces and open spaces in the context of wider planning efforts.[40] For example, in some municipalities, private and unprotected areas can or could constitute an important component of network planning. From large parcels to run-of-the-mill backyards, the extent of private green space viewed cumulatively can be larger than that of public green space, yet many cities have little or no information on private green space, despite its potential importance.[41] Overarching assessments of green spaces, including privately owned ones, are essential for a full understanding of a municipality's green space.

The Urban Forest

Over the past 30 years, there has been an increased understanding of the many benefits of the urban forest. The urban forest has several components: street trees, trees in parks and other open space, and trees on private property. Much effort has been placed in locating existing trees and estimating their value, particularly in relationship to the environmental services they provide: urban heat island reduction, air quality improvements, and stormwater mitigation. Efforts to quantify the benefits of urban forests stem from the need to increase awareness for trees, convey their value within urban areas, and motivate improved management, especially in the face of climate change.

San Francisco notes the value and challenges of its trees: "Our urban forest is a valuable capital asset worth $1.7 billion. Like the public transit and sewer systems, it needs a long-term plan to ensure its health and longevity."[42] The need for coordinated efforts to maintain and enhance the urban forest is highlighted by the experiences of Milwaukee. The city had an estimated 55 percent canopy coverage in the 1960s and 1970s, 30 percent canopy coverage in 1990, and about 23 percent cover in 2013.[43] Much of this loss is the result of Dutch elm disease, a fungal disease that devastated the frequently planted elm trees in Milwaukee and across much of the eastern United States.

The impact of Dutch elm disease on urban forests highlights the need for improved planning. There are many considerations when planning for a sustainable urban forest. Diversification of planted species and use of disease resistance cultivars can reduce the loss of trees from disease. However, other factors are important to consider as well. In addition to serving as urban amenities, trees can provide disamenities (or contribute negatively) in the urban environment. For instance, the pollen of some trees causes allergies; tree maintenance—fall leaf pickup and life cycle needs such as watering during establishment, pruning, and eventual removal—incur cost; and trees and their roots can damage sidewalks, power and communication lines, and other infrastructure. Many of these disamenities can be limited by careful plant selection and planting the "right plant in the right place," an approach that identifies trees appropriate for a given area given each species' characteristics including mature size.

Below, we explore trends in the ways that cities are planning for and managing their urban forests.

Tree Planting Programs
Street trees provide multiple benefits including greenhouse gas sequestration, urban heat island amelioration, and stormwater management. Given these many benefits, it is not surprising that plans to increase the number of street trees or increase the percent cover of trees in cities are features of most city sustainability efforts.

The Milwaukee non-profit organization Greening Milwaukee has set a goal of reaching a citywide canopy rate of 40 percent. This is an ambitious goal that they hope to achieve in part by offering free saplings to residents each year. Research by the US Forest Service indicates that a 40–60 percent urban tree canopy is potentially attainable in areas that naturally support forest growth.[44] Lower tree canopy goals are appropriate for cities in other geographies. Their study recommends lower goals of 20 percent in grassland cities and 15 percent in desert cities.

Washington, D.C.'s canopy cover is currently 35 percent. The city has a goal to plant 8600 new trees citywide per year until 2032 with a target canopy cover of 40 percent.[45] The city's goal is significant for including not only quantity but quality of urban trees. The plan cites the importance of including a range of species in these plantings and including heat-tolerant species in preparation for climate change.[46] In 2011, Grand Rapids set a tree canopy goal of 40 percent by 2015.[47] The city has not met that goal in part because of an infestation by the emerald ash borer, a non-native, invasive beetle that killed many trees. In response, the city is now setting a goal to increase the *diversity* of tree species planted by 25 percent. Diversity of trees in urban areas plays an important role in the long-term sustainability of an ecosystem, especially given the uncertainties of climate change.

Philadelphia's urban forest goal is to increase tree coverage towards 30 percent in all neighborhoods by 2025. There are many positive aspects of this goal. The city has benchmarked their current tree canopy cover (16 percent), has set a quantitative and measureable goal, and has a timeline for completion. In terms of equity, this goal measures tree coverage by neighborhood rather than aggregating the whole city and includes a sub-goal to "prioritize tree planning in low-canopy, high-crime districts."[48] Philadelphia's 2013 Progress Report confirms that the city has used data from its Urban Tree Canopy Assessment to prioritize eight focus areas with low canopy cover.[49] Maps can show the presence (and absence) of tree cover by neighborhood and represent a best practice when it comes to where to focus money and efforts to increase the tree canopy.

Tree Inventory, Mapping, and Maintenance
As cities set tree canopy goals, try to manage their tree inventory, and track maintenance needs, measurement and mapping become a priority. For this reason, many cities undertake tree inventories. For instance, in 2014, San Francisco undertook a Street Tree Census, gathering information on age, location, species, and condition of street trees, in order to improve management. The census was followed by a Street Tree Financing Study, which evaluated the costs associated with street tree planting and maintenance. The city now features a searchable, interactive urban forest map (through OpenTreeMap), which details the location and size of each tree and quantifies (in dollars) the benefits that each tree provides (see Box 8.2).[50]

Another California city, Sacramento, gathers information about street trees and their maintenance in a database of approximately 100,000 public trees in parks, cemeteries, and medians.[51] Each time a public tree is planted, pruned, maintained, or removed and replaced, information in the database is updated. Collection of this detailed information is a best practice in urban forestry, as it provides data to determine condition and management needs. For instance, Sacramento's Neighborhood Pruning Program provides pre-emptive tree inspection and maintenance at regular intervals. To preserve its urban forest, Sacramento also now requires tree permits for pruning and removal of city trees and private protected trees. The city's database similarly allows for management and accountability within this program.

Box 8.2   Emerging Trend: Using Technology to Support Urban Forests

We have identified three important new ways technology can help support urban forests:

1) **Citizen Scientists**: (Also known as community science, crowd science, crowd-sourced science.) Nonprofessional scientists who conduct, in whole or in part, scientific research. Citizen science is described as "public participation in scientific research." Large

(*continued*)

Box 8.2 (continued)

volunteer networks can allow scientists to accomplish tasks that would be too expensive or time consuming to accomplish through other means. Examples include the annual bird and butterfly counts in many urban forests and parks.

Citizen scientists can also help cities inventory and direct urban forestry investments based on where environmental services were most needed as prioritized by community stakeholders. For example, the city of Baltimore used community partners to collect information needed to make these assessments and provided on-the-ground intelligence about neighborhood and block-level conditions that might affect implementation. Open maps and creative applications (both below) help make this possible.

2) **Open Maps and Open Data**: Another important trend is the use of open data and open maps. Open-source data is freely available for use. Most maps you think of as free actually have legal or technical restrictions on their use, constraining people from using them in creative, productive, or unexpected ways. For example, the data in Google Maps is proprietary and can cost money to use. Similarly, mapping software licensing fees can be costly for city partners, like non-profits. Cities that use open maps and open data can more easily involve citizens in a community mapping effort. Smart phones allow individuals to contribute to such mapping efforts because their "location services" can be used to pinpoint locations.

3) **Creative Applications**: Many cities use creative applications to publicize issues and generate community awareness. The state of Michigan has a "tree app" that allows anyone to log on and map trees. Another example comes from outside the United States in Melbourne, Australia. The city tagged street trees with ID numbers and email addresses so that citizens could more easily report problems or maintenance needs. The unintended but positive consequence of the program was that people wrote messages *to* the trees. The trees received thousands of messages: simple greetings, poetry, love letters, and existential questions. What began as a practical solution to streamline maintenance requests morphed

(*continued*)

Box 8.2   (continued)

into an initiative that led residents and managers alike to consider the most intangible benefits that trees in urban areas provide to communities such as psychological benefits and connections to seasonal cycles, nature, and earth systems.

Cities can and should look for ways to use new technologies to benefit their urban forests and engage citizens in these efforts.

Source:

Dexter Locke et al., "Applications of Urban Tree Canopy Assessment and Prioritization Tools: Supporting Collaborative Decision Making to Achieve Urban Sustainability Goals," *Cities and the Environment (CATE)*, September 27, 2013, http://digitalcommons.lmu.edu/cate/vol6/iss1/7/

Public Partnerships

Another common strategy related to the urban tree canopy is to create partnerships or programs to encourage residents to care for trees. In nearly every successful city tree program we have examined, partnerships between cities, local community groups, and non-profit organizations are central to program success. A best practice is New York City, which planted one million new trees by relying on partnerships to accomplish this ambitious goal (Box 8.3).

There are many reasons why public partnerships are so vital. First, in many cities, much of the urban forest is on private property. One estimate puts 71 percent of Los Angeles' urban forest on private property.[52] For that reason, the best opportunities for expanding the urban forest are frequently on private property, and these efforts similarly require buy-in from property owners.[53] Second, trees that are on public property are necessarily spread diffusely throughout the city, which complicates monitoring and maintenance. Third, in times of financial stress, the budget line for urban forest planting and maintenance are a lower priority than other, mandatory line items.

In many cases, non-profit organizations and community groups take charge of local programs. These take the form of park trusts, or "friends" of park organizations, or foundations which partner with city parks and recreation departments. The rise of public-private partnerships is increasingly important. In Washington, D.C., for example, the non-profit Casey

Box 8.3   Best Practices in Implementation and Results: Planting One Million Trees Ahead of Schedule in New York City

In 2007, New York City launched its MillionTreesNYC program to plant and care for one million new trees by 2020. In November 2016, the city celebrated the planting of its' one millionth tree, planted four years ahead of schedule. The million new trees expand the city's tree canopy by more than 20 percent.

Several aspects of this successful project are notable. New York City's approach to tree planting directly targets equity issues by bringing trees to those areas where the health benefits may be most needed, including neighborhoods with the highest asthma rates and fewest trees. This approach sets New York's program apart from those of many cities that seek to increase the tree canopy citywide, but do not necessarily ensure that communities in need are targeted. Notably, the MillionTreesNYC program is a successful public-private partnership between NYC Parks and Bette Midler's New York Restoration Project and relied on more than 50,000 volunteers. The city allocated more than $350 million towards the effort, but more than $30 million was also raised from private sources. Because fundraising has been so successful, the city will continue to plant an additional 150,000 new trees until 2020.

Sources:

"About MillionTrees NYC: I'm Counting on You," Million Trees NYC, accessed April 3, 2018, http://www.milliontreesnyc.org/html/about/about.shtml

The City of New York, "PlaNYC A Greener, Greater New York," 2011, http://www.nyc.gov/html/planyc/downloads/pdf/publications/planyc_2011_planyc_full_report.pdf

Trees is primarily responsible for all non-transportation-right-of-way tree plantings on public space. They support several city programs that offer discounted trees to residents by working directly with the homeowners. They also organize community tree planting and maintenance events. Community partners can also provide information about safety, traffic, and walkability at a local scale. Casey Trees has a GIS expert on staff, and the city relied on tree canopy research conducted by this organization to develop their goals for tree canopy increase.

Community Gardens and Urban Agriculture

For many people, the term "urban agriculture" itself is an oxymoron. Over the nineteenth and twentieth centuries, many Americans left behind agricultural roots and started new lives and livelihoods in cities. Today, most urban and suburban residents are very disconnected from food production. As scholar and urban agriculturist Tom Angotti wrote: "To most New Yorkers today, agricultural production is a mere abstraction, divorced from land, place and community."[54]

Yet community gardening in cities has a long tradition. During the First and Second World Wars, the Department of Agriculture encouraged individuals and families to plant gardens in surplus space (eventually called "victory gardens") to offset the food that was being diverted to the war effort.

In the last decades, cities have experienced another resurgence of urban gardening.[55] Many cities want to expand community gardens or provide more support to existing gardens. But urban agriculture takes other forms as well. There is a beehive on the roof of the Chicago city hall, and residents in many cities are keeping backyard bees and chicken coops. This resurgence of urban gardening is driven by a variety of different goals. First, small-scale community gardens are seen as a productive utilization of vacant lands, a way to improve community cohesion and educate residents about healthy food. Second, these techniques are framed as a way to address food insecurity and improve access to nutritious food for urban communities. Finally, some see large-scale urban agriculture as a way to provide green jobs either through innovations like hydroponics and vertical farming or by utilizing vacant or underutilized urban land.

However, Geographer Chiara Tornaghi cautions that "urban agricultural practices are being portrayed as benevolent and unproblematic, with the potential to partially solve" a multitude of urban problems.[56] We agree, and while we see successes and many opportunities for urban agriculture, we are mindful that the complexity of urban food systems and the resource-and-knowledge-intensiveness of urban agriculture are frequently overlooked.

In the next section we explore opportunities and challenges associated with agriculture in urban areas in two different scales. First, we examine community gardens, which we characterize as smaller-scale, often feature communal shared spaces, and emphasize recreational benefits and food self-sufficiency. Then, we look more closely at urban agriculture, which we see as either larger-scale or higher-tech operations which are entrepreneurially focused to provide job opportunities and local food options in urban areas.

Community Gardens: Providing Amenity, Education, and Nutritious Food
The 1970s marked a resurgence in the community garden movement as a way to clean up and stabilize vacant lots and foster stronger community bonds.[57] The potential of community gardens to provide nutritious foods and alleviate the food security of individuals and neighborhoods makes it a common feature in municipal sustainability plans. A study of mostly low-income community gardeners and home gardeners in San Jose, California, demonstrates the positive effect that participation in community gardens can have on access to fresh vegetables for this population. Study participants reported doubling their vegetable intake to a level that met the number of daily servings recommended by the US Dietary Guidelines.[58]

Many cities have set goals to create more community gardens or to increase the total agricultural area in their jurisdictions. There may be opportunities to create new gardens by identifying and supporting the use of naturally unbuildable properties adjacent to parkland, greenways, railroad right-of-way, former landfills, and so on for agricultural use.[59] Palm Springs intends to encourage temporary uses of vacant land within the city for demonstration gardens and community-supported agriculture alongside other uses like parks and renewable energy development.[60] We should note that while turning a brownfield site into a community garden has the potential to turn a disamenity into an amenity, it also raises important considerations for public health and safety, which must not be ignored.

Another way that cities plan to support urban agriculture is rezoning for inclusion of small-scale farming and gardening in the city, since zoning currently restricts this practice in many US cities.[61] This may require updating the zoning code, but it also may require broadening the definition of urban farming to include alternatives such as vineyards, orchards, or beehives.

Community gardens should ideally be supported in two ways. Both community grassroots (and sometimes guerrilla) action and commitment and institution-led support (provided by municipalities, non-profits, or agriculture extensions services) are important elements of success. We argue that both are essential for well-functioning community gardens and that municipalities must bear this in mind as they plan for enhanced urban gardening.

The success of community gardens clearly relies on community buy-in. Neighbors come together to turn vacant land into a community amenity. Community gardens are a place where neighbors gather, collaborate, help one another, and perhaps share tools and other resources. However, many gardens—and particularly food gardens—require daily and weekly maintenance throughout the entire growing season. To be successful, committed gardeners must weed, water, and watch for pest and disease problems. Such a voluntary, daily commitment cannot be orchestrated from the top down, no matter how well intentioned. Community investment in a garden is visible in other ways as well. Gardeners comment that fences are not necessary when a garden is run by people from the neighborhood, because it will be respected by fellow residents. However, "if it's something outsiders are running…of course people are going to steal stuff because it's outsiders doing things in your neighborhood."[62]

The importance of a committed grassroots effort in the face of daily maintenance needs is one reason that school gardens—though providing tempting educational benefits—are often unsuccessful. That is because the months during which vegetable gardens require the most care and provide the greatest harvest are precisely the months that school is not in session. Thus, even committed teachers or administrators (never mind the school children targets) are not available to attend to garden needs. We note with some irony that many cities discussed urban gardens as a teaching tool for city schools, yet—at least in plans we could find—did not suggest how this gap would be filled.

At a practical level, community gardens function best when they are supported by institutions that help meet their needs. Community gardens need access to water, tools, and materials to create raised beds and compost facilities. They have legal challenges and may need assistance with special permitting, property tax waivers, and land tenure (securing permissions to use land, or to create a land trust so that the garden can be maintained in the future, even if property values start to rise).

Access to technical expertise is crucial to the success of community gardens. Many urban soils—including those in gardens—have elevated levels of lead and other heavy metals.[63] Access to soil testing and advice on best practices—like raised beds—can prevent negative health outcomes (Fig. 8.4). Another example comes from an assessment of community gardens in New York City that highlighted common agricultural best practices that would improve yield in many gardens. These included (1) cover cropping to improve the soil, (2) rotating crops, (3) soil testing and applying only recommended soil amendments, and (4) enhancing habitat for insects and animals that could provide biological insect control.[64] Classes, training programs, and plant and pest clinics that gardeners can turn to for advice all contribute to more productive gardens. In many cities, these

Fig. 8.4 Raised garden beds with painted wooden edgings at Wise Words Community Garden in Mid-City, New Orleans. (Source: "Raised garden beds with painted wooden edgings at Wise Words Community Garden in Mid-City, New Orleans" Wikipedia/ Wikimedia Commons photo by Bart Everson (created July 31, 2010), accessed April 10, 2018, https://upload.wikimedia.org/wikipedia/commons/1/19/2010_WiseWords_community_garden_NewOrleans_4855100893.jpg)

roles are filled by non-profit organizations such as The Pennsylvania Horticultural Society in Philadelphia, Gardening Matters in Minneapolis, and DUG (Denver Urban Gardens) in Denver.

Urban Agriculture: an entrepreneurial venture
Urban agriculture is distinct from community gardening in two ways. First, it involves intensive plant cultivation or animal husbandry. Second, urban agriculture is an entrepreneurial venture, in which food is grown, processed, and distributed to provide jobs and economic opportunity in urban areas. Locally grown food can provide multiple benefits such as

reducing food miles traveled and GHG emissions, reducing produce waste, increasing freshness and nutritional values, and supporting the local economy.[65]

While there may be potential in some specific markets for urban agricultural economic ventures in cities, the relative high cost of land and of living-wage prices make it very difficult for urban agriculture to compete with conventionally grown agricultural products. Farms today take advantage of economies of scale, may have access to inexpensive water, are located where growing seasons are long, and may use very low-cost or exploited labor. This creates—artificially—low prices with which local products and workers paid a living wage must compete. Comprehensive analysis of commercial agriculture in North American cities indicates that in most areas, commercial agriculture in the city could never compete with factory farms in rural areas where "land is cheaper, farm machinery and chemical fertilizers can be widely used, and public subsidies and private financing are abundant."[66]

Despite these challenges, some cities are thinking creatively about how to support entrepreneurship and innovation in urban farming considering unique opportunities and needs in their area. One example is "ZFarming" a term for agricultural practices associated with buildings such as rooftop gardens, rooftop greenhouses, indoor farms, and vertical farming.[67] These experimental forms of urban agriculture require specialized technologies and, in some cases, the innovation of entirely new materials or cultivation techniques. High costs of these systems prohibit widespread applications and limit the utility of these systems to selling high-margin foods (like tomatoes, greens like baby spinach and kale, and heirloom vegetables). We also note that despite the reduction in food miles traveled and provision of green jobs, ZFarming practices may not necessarily be considered sustainable, given the inputs necessary for production in these spaces.

Some cities are thinking beyond the roof and pursuing urban agriculture because they have large amounts of vacant land available. In the Midwest, cities such as Cleveland and Detroit have experienced deindustrialization and population loss. These cities confront challenges related to managing vacant land and service provision over wide areas with reduced budgets. In response, they are radically reinventing the urban landscape, and large-scale urban agriculture is seen as one way to effectively manage this land. In this way, vacant land might be productively used. These efforts might provide local green jobs and improve community food security. At the same time, these cities also need to carefully consider if urban agriculture can and should be a permanent element in their cities (Box 8.4).[68]

Box 8.4   Best Practices in Multiple Benefits: Farming in Detroit

Detroit, birthplace of the American car industry (and nicknamed Motor City), boasted this country's highest median income and rates of homeownership in the 1950s. A city celebrated for creativity, it was known for industrial design and its music industry (the Motown Sound). At that time, it reached a peak population of almost two million people and was the fourth largest city in the country. However, deindustrialization devastated the city's economy; job loss and racial tension led to an exodus from the city and a 60 percent population decline. In 2013, the city declared bankruptcy in the largest municipal bankruptcy filing in US history.

Today, Detroit is home to a population of 673,000. It is the largest African American majority city in the United States (82 percent African American and 10 percent white).[a] It is also one of the most segregated and among the poorest cities in the United States, with a poverty rate of 40 percent.

The combination of economic and population decline, rising rates of poverty, and segregation have significant impacts on the landscape. It is estimated that there are more than 78,000 vacant buildings in the city. One-third of the city's enormous land mass is vacant. In several parts of central Detroit, nature has reclaimed the land and properties, overtaken by high grasses, resemble a prairie.

While Detroit faces multiple challenges, it has been recreating itself. One response to the excess of vacant land has been creative efforts of "adaptive reuse of the built-environment."[b] In this context, Detroit is experiencing a renaissance in urban gardening and urban agriculture. To facilitate this change, the city passed a new urban agriculture ordinance that legalized farming in the city of Detroit and complies with state law that protects farmers.

Today there are as many as 1500 community gardens and farms in the city, and many of these gardens sell produce to local businesses and farmers markets. Some also sell produce directly in low-income neighborhoods that lack grocery stores using a pay-what-you-can model or provide produce for local food pantries. Some of these farms are large-scale, covering several acres of once vacant land. For example, the Michigan Urban Farming Initiative is an all-volunteer non-profit organization that seeks to "use urban agriculture as a platform to promote education, sustainability, and community in an

(continued)

Box 8.4   (continued)

effort to empower urban communities, solve many social problems facing Detroit, and potentially develop a broader model for redevelopment for other urban communities."[c] Their production farm has grown over 50,000 pounds of produce since 2011. They have plans to develop a second community garden where people can grow their own food, renovate a nearby vacant building to create a community resource center and non-profit incubator, demolish a second vacant building so that its foundation can facilitate stormwater retention (for use in irrigation), and plant a 200-tree orchard covering 2 acres.

Detroit is rebuilding its identity around farming and in the process realizing multiple benefits: reclaiming vacant land, growing local food, and providing food to underserved areas. A partnership of organizations celebrates these transformative efforts, leading ten-mile roundtrip bicycle tours to urban farms and gardens.[d] At the conclusion of the tour, participants can eat in restaurants that feature produce from local farms (Fig. 8.5).

Fig. 8.5 The Michigan Urban Farming Initiative logo, depicting the Detroit skyline. (Source: "Michigan Urban Farming Initiative" Wikipedia/Wikimedia Commons (created September 4, 2017), accessed April 1, 2018, https://en.wikipedia.org/wiki/Michigan_Urban_Farming_Initiative#/media/File:MUFI_Logo.png)

(*continued*)

Box 8.4 (continued)

Sources:
[a]"QuickFacts, Detroit city, Michigan," The United States Census Bureau, accessed April 7, 2018, https://www.ccnsus.gov/quickfacts/fact/table/detroitcitymichigan/PST045216

[b]"About MUFI," The Michigan Urban Farm Initiative, accessed April 7, 2018, http://www.miufi.org/about

[c]The Michigan Urban Farm Initiative "About MUFI."

[d]"Urban Agriculture: Farm to Fork," Wheelhouse Detroit, accessed April 7, 2018, https://wheelhousedetroit.squarespace.com/urban-agriculture-farm-to-fork

Box 8.5 Emerging Trend: Here Comes the Agrihood

Community gardens are not a new idea, but a new variation on that theme combines community gardens and cooperative housing: an agrihood. Agrihoods are planned housing developments that are centered around a working farm, often using the sweat equity of residents to create a sustainable food system for the entire community. It is estimated there are some 100 agrihoods around the United States.

In Phoenix, Agritopia consists of 450 homes along with commercial, agricultural, and open space tracts. All are specifically designed to reduce physical, social, and economic barriers to relationships between neighbors. The central feature is an 11-acre certified organic working farm complete with lambs, chickens, a citrus grove, and rows of heirloom vegetables.

Forty minutes outside of Washington, D.C. in Loudoun County, Virginia, Willowsford spans over 4000 acres and is comprised of four distinctive yet interconnected "villages." Three hundred acres has been designated as farmland to cultivate more than 150 varieties of vegetables, herbs, fruit, and flowers and raise several breeds of livestock—many of which are sold to the community through its community-supported agriculture program.

(*continued*)

Box 8.5 (continued)

In Fort Collins, Colorado, a developer has proposed the Bucking Horse project. The 160-acre agrihood will feature a trail system, healthy retailers (think bike shop and yoga studio), community gardens, and a farm-to-fork restaurant that will serve up produce and other edibles grown on-site.

Agrihoods are not just on the urban periphery. In center cities, agrihoods are emerging on a smaller scale. In West Oakland, California, a repurposed warehouse space of the Pacific Cannery Lofts features a raised bed community garden of 30 plots shared with Ironhorse, an affordable rental community next door.

Sources:

Beth Buczynski, "12 Agrihoods Taking Farm-to-Table Living Mainstream," Charter for Compassion, May 14, 2014, https://charterforcompassion.org/shareable-community-ideas/12-agrihoods-taking-farm-to-table-living-mainstream

MegWhite, "Inside the Agrihood Trend," National Association of Realtors, May 2017, http://realtormag.realtor.org/home-and-design/feature/article/2017/05/inside-agrihood-trend

What's Missing: Equity in Green Space

Few cities have deliberately and effectively addressed equity in relation to green space. At one level, green space equity is a distributional justice issue. Research has shown that areas with lower socioeconomic status and/or a higher minority population often contain fewer green space resources than their higher socioeconomic and lower minority population counterparts.[69] (We note that this issue is complicated by changing demographic patterns in cities, and assumptions about the inequality paradigm of green space distribution are not always correct.)[70]

An inequitable distribution of parks, open spaces, gardens, or trees is of particular concern given the multiple benefits vegetation provides in urban areas. In this way, green space inequities perpetuate uneven social space.[71] For example, as we have explored in Chap. 5, communities of color often have disproportionate exposure to freeways and other sources of air pollution. These communities would then most benefit from reductions in the urban heat island effect and air quality improvements associated with green spaces and street trees.

We frequently observed cities making general statements about creating new park amenities or increasing the number of parks citywide—important goals, but goals that leave the question of equity to the side. However, some cities are leading the way in considering equity and green space. For example, Salt Lake City, Utah, aims to "provide equitable access to open space by completing trail networks, providing for multiple users and offering local open space."[72] St. Louis pledged to ensure all residents have access to parks, recreation facilities, and open spaces.[73] To reach this goal, the city will inventory neighborhoods for distribution and maintenance, and prioritize the creation of new public spaces within underserved neighborhoods. However many cities have not yet taken inventory or measured their tree canopies or green spaces which makes it difficult to assess the outcome of investments in these areas (Box 8.6).

Box 8.6   Best Practices in Planning: Benchmarking, Measuring, and Tracking

Sustainability and green space initiatives and goals are important parts of a city's sustainability plan. However, setting a goal or action is only half the battle. The real test comes in the form of showing that the goals are progressing in the direction they are supposed to and achieving their purpose.

Benchmarking, measuring, and tracking indicators do just this. However, a big challenge is that green spaces do not have standardized units of measure. Additionally, different forms of green space require different measurement. While on the surface, quantitative (measurable) goals seem the most robust, qualitative monitoring of maintenance, cleanliness, and attractiveness can also be very important. Several types of measurements of green space are considered best practices: measuring quantity of green space area, measuring quality, perceived benefits provided by green spaces, accessibility, and the distance residents must travel for access.

Often, city departments of parks and recreation have a baseline number for the acreage or number of parks and open spaces which are based on field observation. However, this can be quite time consuming and may not include all types of green spaces, such as trees or private green space. Another method that some cities may use to measure green space is remote sensing and GIS. Remotely sensed

(continued)

Box 8.6   (continued)

images are data recorded from a distance and include aerial photos and satellite images. The process is also time consuming and becomes less accurate with the more types of green space that one attempts to classify. A combination of remote sensing images and fieldwork may produce the best measurements.

Too few cities include benchmarking or measurement plans for their green spaces; without these, cities may not achieve desired goals.

Sources:

Huang, Yan, Yu, Bailang, Zhou, Janhuan, Hu, Chunlin, Tan, Wenqi, Hu, Zhiming, & Wu, Jianping, "Toward automatic estimation of urban green volume using airborne LiDAR data and high resolution Remote Sensing images," *Frontiers of Earth Science* 7, (2013): 43–54, doi:10.1007/s11707-012-0339-6

Shin, Dong-hoon, & Lee, Kyoo-seock, "Use of remote sensing and geographical information systems to estimate green space surface-temperature change as a result of urban expansion," *Landscape Ecology Engineering* 1, (2005):169–176, doi:10.1007/s11355-005-0021-1

Washington, D.C. set a goal of having "green and open spaces distributed more evenly in neighborhoods throughout the District" to help enable greater access for residents in their local areas.[74] The city's target to achieve this is to provide parkland or natural space within a ten-minute walk to all residents.[75] One short-term strategy to achieve this end is to create small parks and green spaces in areas with inadequate open space as well as investing in "mobile parklets."[76] Mobile parklets are an extension of the sidewalk that take the place of one or two parking spaces and provide additional public gathering space in dense urban areas. Several cities echo this goal of having residents live within a ten-minute walk of a park, recreation area, or open space, including Chicago and New York City.[77] We highlight that these goals are beneficial in that they include a specific and quantitative way to measure equity of green space access; however a more nuanced consideration of park spaces is crucial to the creation of equitable spaces.[78]

What is equally important, and perhaps far more inequitable than park distribution, are the issues of the quality, type, and size of parks as well as social access to these spaces. While the distance to and number of parks speaks to the spatial access of green space, features such as safety, traffic, and walkability refer to the "social access." For this important reason, amenities and quality should be examined from a perspective of equity as well.

Procedural justice—including all community members in the decision-making related to green space location, desired amenities, or safety—is an important element to this end. Procedural justice addresses the process of green space improvement or creation and is reflected in the implementation of deliberative and inclusionary processes and procedures which seek to actively engage the public.[79] Community involvement in park planning projects help to ensure that community needs are met and that new or improved "spaces are not perceived as inferior," unwanted, or unsafe.[80]

While few cities explicitly discuss these considerations within green space discussions in their plans for sustainability, we were impressed with Washington, D.C., which was candid about its park inequities. The city describes this legacy, admitting: "In the past, playgrounds, parks and schools were better maintained in wealthier neighborhoods" and that "the District needs to balance the maintenance and protection of natural resources with enhancing citywide access to green and open spaces so that all residents can enjoy the benefits of parks and natural areas."[81]

In addition to access to parks and trees, cities have opportunities to improve access to community gardens and urban agriculture. Santa Cruz, California, has developed an urban gardening program for people experiencing homelessness or poverty. They also use gardens as therapy for those with mental and physical disabilities, transitioning to life outside of prison, and for young people. So too does Santa Fe, New Mexico.[82]

There are several examples of cities integrating equity within green space strategies, but perhaps no city has done a better job than Philadelphia (Box 8.7). Equity is emerging as a critical issue and cities would be wise to pay more attention to this within the context of green space.

Box 8.7   Best Practices in Equity: Philadelphia Parks

The city of Philadelphia has many large and well-known parks including Fairmount Park and Pennypack Park, along with numerous smaller neighborhood squares and parks. Despite the presence of all of these greenspaces, the city also acknowledges that existing parks and open space are not distributed equally and some neighborhoods are woefully underserved. In response to this inequity, the city's sustainability plan articulated a goal of creating a park, greenspace, or open space within 10 minutes of 75 percent of residents. The city also plans to address this deficit by prioritizing new green space creation in the least served neighborhoods.

In 2017, the Philadelphia Office of Sustainability received funding to implement the first Greenworks Equity Index project, which identifies communities not currently benefiting from sustainability and improves outcomes in those areas. One part of the index used GIS to map open space and parks in the city, with their corresponding ten-minute service areas in pink. Areas in white are considered underserved and are not within a ten-minute walk of a park (see Fig. 8.6). Areas around Fairmont Park and Pennypack Park in Northeast Philly, Manayunk, and Germantown are much better served than many areas in Kensington and North and South Philadelphia. While this map is important, only those who know the city well would know how park acccess aligns with equity considerations in the city. From a planning perspective, this map would be more powerful if information on neighborhood socioeconomics was also displayed.

Our research found that few cities are making use of spatial technologies to identify equity issues generally and around green space investments specifically. And yet this technology can allow cities to better invest their limited funds in ways that will have the most benefits.

Sources:

City of Philadelphia, "Greenworks Initiatives Update," 2017, accessed March 9, 2018, https://beta.phila.gov/media/20180201155423/Sustainability-Greenworks-Initiatives-Update-2.2.2018.pdf

City of Philadelphia, "Greenworks Philadelphia," 2009, 46, accessed March 9, 2018, https://beta.phila.gov/documents/greenworks-progress-reports/

(continued)

Box 8.7   (continued)

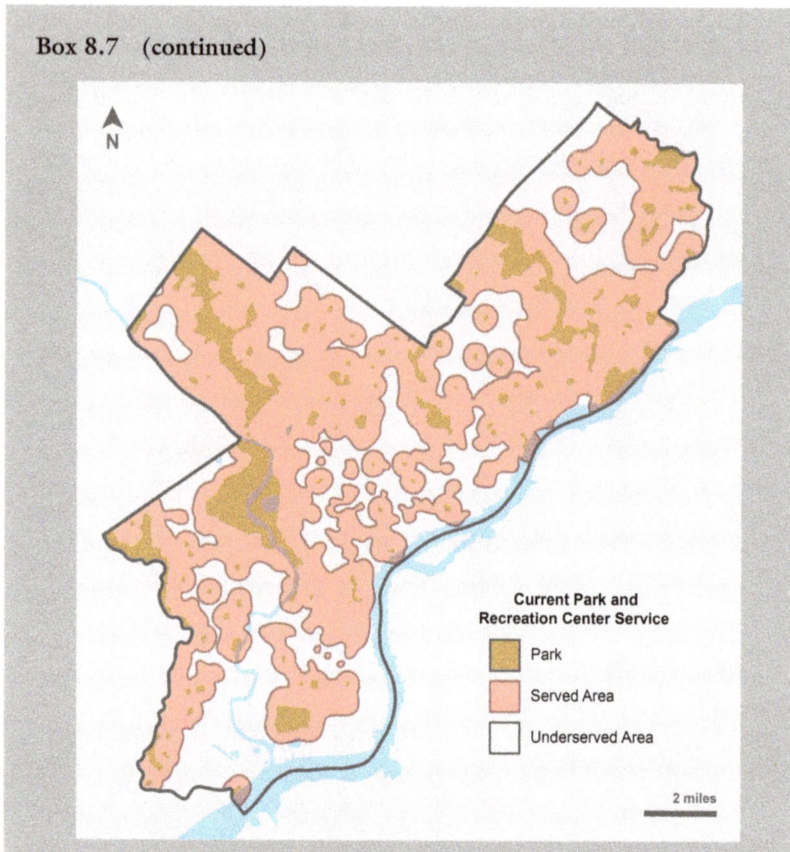

Fig. 8.6   Open space and parks in Philadelphia. Ten-minute walk radius service areas are colored pink; areas in white are considered underserved. (Source: Adapted from City of Philadelphia, "Greenworks Philadelphia," (2009, p 46) accessed March 9, 2018, https://beta.phila.gov/documents/greenworks-progress-reports/)

Summary

Green spaces come in diverse forms and sizes, and many cities are not only protecting their green spaces, they are actively engaged in expanding and improving them. We have found that green spaces—including parks, open space, the urban forest, community gardens, and urban agriculture—hold potential to provide multiple benefits in many cities. Table 8.2 summarizes the best practices.

Table 8.2   Best practices in urban green space

Parks, green space, and open space

- Protect open space through growth boundaries or other policy measures
- Use public-private partnerships to build, improve, or expand parks and green spaces
- Identify neighborhoods lacking in parks and green spaces and prioritize those for investment
- Plan improvements to parks that reflect neighborhood identity and take into account a diversity of residents and their needs
- Reimagine parks as linear (or other forms)
- Connect parks and green spaces to each other to enhance habitat and connectivity to bike and walking trails

Urban forest

- Expand urban forests and the urban tree canopy to realize multiple benefits that include reducing the urban heat island, providing amenities to residents
- Identify tree species that are likely to remain well adapted to urban climates many years into the future for tree planting programs
- Plant a diversity of trees to prevent diseases or pests from causing widespread destruction
- Partner with tree planting organizations
- Motivate volunteers
- Map and measure the existing tree canopy to manage long-term needs
- Identify neighborhoods lacking trees and prioritize those for investment

Community gardens and urban agriculture

- Identify underserved communities and prioritize these for investment in community gardens
- Recognize the multiple benefits of supporting community gardens to include access to healthy and affordable foods, job creation, and fostering community
- Help community gardens to access resources such as water, electricity, and permits
- Protect community gardens from development pressure and gentrification
- Consider opportunities and limitations to urban agriculture

NOTES

1. Oxford Dictionaries, "Green Space," 2015, https://en.oxforddictionaries.com/definition/green_space.
2. US EPA, "What Is Open Space/Green Space?," accessed February 21, 2018, https://www3.epa.gov/region1/eco/uep/openspace.html.
3. Benedict Wheeler, "Health-Related Environmental Indices and Environmental Equity in England and Wales," *Environment and Planning A: Economy and Space* 36, no. 5 (May 1, 2004): 803–22, https://doi.org/10.1068/a3691; Tuzin Baycan-Levent and Nijkamp, "Planning and Management of Urban Green Spaces in Europe: Comparative Analysis," *Journal of Urban Planning and Development* 135, no. 1 (March 1, 2009): 1–12, https://doi.org/10.1061/(ASCE)0733-9488(2009)135:1(1).

4. The United States Conference of Mayors, "The U.S. Mayors Climate Protection Agreement," 2005, http://www.mayors.org/climateprotection/documents/mcpAgreement.pdf.

5. Laura L. Payne, Andrew J. Mowen, and Elizabeth Orsega-Smith, "An Examination of Park Preferences and Behaviors Among Urban Residents: The Role of Residential Location, Race, and Age," *Leisure Sciences* 24, no. 2 (April 1, 2002): 181–98, https://doi.org/10.1080/01490400252900149; Ching-Hua Ho et al., "Gender and Ethnic Variations in Urban Park Preferences, Visitation, and Perceived Benefits," *Journal of Leisure Research* 37, no. 3 (September 1, 2005): 281–306, https://doi.org/10.1080/00222216.2005.11950054.

6. Lisa Benton-Short, Melissa Keeley, and Jennifer Rowland, "Green Infrastructure, Green Space, and Sustainable Urbanism: Geography's Important Role," *Urban Geography* 0, no. 0 (August 18, 2017): 1–22, https://doi.org/10.1080/02723638.2017.1360105.

7. Mark Roseland, *Toward Sustainable Communities: Resources for Citizens and Their Governments* (New Society Publishers, 2005).

8. Maria Conroy and Philip Berke, "What Makes a Good Sustainable Development Plan? An Analysis of Factors That Influence Principles of Sustainable Development," *Environment and Planning* 36, no. 8 (2004): 1381–96; Baycan-Levent and Nijkamp, "Planning and Management of Urban Green Spaces in Europe."

9. Zhenghong Tang et al., "Moving from Agenda to Action: Evaluating Local Climate Change Action Plans," *Journal of Environmental Planning and Management* 53, no. 1 (2011): 41–62.

10. City of Grand Rapids, Office of Energy and Sustainability, "FY 2011 Through FY 2015 Sustainability Plan," 2011.

11. Helen Woolley, *Urban Open Spaces* (Taylor & Francis, 2003).

12. Woolley; Michelle L. Bell et al., "Climate Change, Ambient Ozone, and Health in 50 US Cities," *Climatic Change* 82, no. 1–2 (May 1, 2007): 61–76, https://doi.org/10.1007/s10584-006-9166-7.

13. City of St. Louis Planning Commission, "City of St. Louis Sustainability Plan," February 6, 2013, https://www.stlouis-mo.gov/government/departments/mayor/documents/upload/STL-Sustainability-Plan.pdf.

14. Shah Md. AtiqulHaq, "Urban Green Spaces and an Integrative Approach to Sustainable Environment," *Journal of Environmental Protection* 02, no. 05 (July 13, 2011): 601, https://doi.org/10.4236/jep.2011.25069.

15. City of Burlington, "The Burlington Legacy Project," 2000, https://www.burlingtonvt.gov/sites/default/files/CEDO/Legacy_Project/Legacy%20Action%20Plan.pdf; Green Policy 360, "Chattanooga, TN Sustainability Plan," n.d., accessed January 19, 2018; City of Grand Rapids, Office of Energy and Sustainability, "Grand Rapids Sustainability Plan."

16. Michael Kuhns, "Planting Trees for Energy Conservation: The Right Tree in the Right Place" (Utah State University, Forestry Extension, 2014), https://forestry.usu.edu/files-ou/PlantingTreesEnergyConservation.pdf.

17. Kuhns.

18. City of Philadelphia, "Greenworks Philadelphia," 2009, 75, https://beta.phila.gov/documents/greenworks-progress-reports/.

19. Dante Chinni, "Environment vs. Economy in 2012," PBS NewsHour, August 26, 2011, https://www.pbs.org/newshour/politics/the-environment-vs-the-economy-in-2012.

20. Woolley, *Urban Open Spaces*.

21. Nicolae Cianga and Antoaneta Popescu, "Green Spaces and Urban Tourism Development in Craiova Municipality in Romania," *European Journal of Geography* 4, no. 2 (2013): 34–45.

22. Centers for Disease Control and Prevention, "Strategies to Prevent Obesity and Other Chronic Diseases: The CDC Guide to Strategies to Increase Physical Activity in the Community," 2011, https://www.cdc.gov/obesity/downloads/pa_2011_web.pdf.

23. Centers for Disease Control and Prevention.

24. Helen Woolley, "Freedom of the City: Contemporary Issues and Policy Influences on Children and Young People's Use of Public Open Space in England," *Children's Geographies* 4, no. 1 (April 1, 2006): 45–59, https://doi.org/10.1080/14733280600577368.

25. City of Newport News, "Roadmap to Sustainability," February 2013, 6, https://www.nngov.com/DocumentCenter/View/1586.

26. Donna L. Erickson, *MetroGreen: Connecting Open Space in North American Cities* (Island Press, 2006).

27. Andrew Lee and Ravi Maheswaran, "The Health Benefits of Urban Green Spaces: A Review of the Evidence," *Journal of Public Health (Oxford, England)* 33, no. 2 (June 2011): 212–22, https://doi.org/10.1093/pubmed/fdq068.

28. Francisco Gomez et al., "Green Areas, the Most Significant Indicator of the Sustainability of Cities: Research on Their Utility for Urban Planning," *Journal of Urban Planning and Development* 137, no. 3 (September 1, 2011): 311–28, https://doi.org/10.1061/(ASCE)UP.1943-5444.0000060.

29. Woolley, *Urban Open Spaces*, 9.

30. Haq, "Urban Green Spaces and an Integrative Approach to Sustainable Environment"; Baycan-Levent and Nijkamp, "Planning and Management of Urban Green Spaces in Europe"; Ken Willis and Bob Crabtree, "Measuring Health Benefits of Green Space in Economic Terms," in *Forests, Trees and Human Health* (Springer, Dordrecht, 2011), 375–402, https://doi.org/10.1007/978-90-481-9806-1_13; Xiaolu Zhou and

Masud Parves Rana, "Social Benefits of Urban Green Space: A Conceptual Framework of Valuation and Accessibility Measurements," *Management of Environmental Quality: An International Journal* 23, no. 2 (February 24, 2012): 173–89, https://doi.org/10.1108/14777831211204921.

31. Kathleen Wolf, "Trees, Parking and Green Law: Strategies for Sustainability" (Urban and Community Forestry – Policy and Law, 2004), https://www.naturewithin.info/Roadside/Trees_Parking_Green%20Law.pdf.

32. Sustainable DC, "Sustainability DC," July 2011, https://sustainable.dc.gov/sites/default/files/dc/sites/sustainable/page_content/attachments/DCS-008%20Report%20508.3j.pdf.

33. The Oregon Encyclopedia, "Urban Growth Boundary," March 17, 2018, https://oregonencyclopedia.org/articles/urban_growth_boundary/#.WspyitPwYdU.

34. The Orange County Register, "History of the El Toro Marine Corps Air Base and the Great Park Project.," January 6, 2006, https://www.ocregister.com/2006/01/06/history-of-the-el-toro-marine-corps-air-base-and-the-great-park-project/.

35. Washington Park, "Features of the Park," accessed February 21, 2018, https://washingtonpark.org/features-of-the-park/.

36. Hillary Rudd, Jamie Vala, and Valentin Schaefer, "Importance of Backyard Habitat in a Comprehensive Biodiversity Conservation Strategy: A Connectivity Analysis of Urban Green Spaces," *Restoration Ecology* 10, no. 2 (June 1, 2002): 368–75, https://doi.org/10.1046/j.1526-100X.2002.02041.x; Cy Jim, "Characteristics of Urban Park Trees in Hong Kong in Relation to Greenspace Planning and Development," *ActaHorticulturae*, 2004, http://agris.fao.org/agris-search/search.do?recordID=US201301057744.

37. The City of Madison, "The Madison Sustainability Plan: Fostering Environmental, Economic, and Social Resistance," 2011, 16, https://www.cityofmadison.com/sustainability/documents/SustainPlan2011.pdf.

38. The City of Austin, "Green Events Guidebook," 2017, 3, http://austintexas.gov/sites/default/files/files/CityStage/GreenEvents-Guidebook_2017.pdf.

39. Maine Association of Planners, "The View from Above: How Drones Are Adding a New Perspective in Planning," October 13, 2016, https://meplan.org/articles/4304779.

40. Erickson, *MetroGreen*.

41. Stephan Pauleit, "Perspectives on Urban Greenspace in Europe," *Built Environment* 29, no. 2 (2003): 89–93; Yan Huang et al., "Toward Automatic Estimation of Urban Green Volume Using Airborne LiDAR Data and High Resolution Remote Sensing Images," *Frontiers of Earth*

Science 7, no. 1 (March 1, 2013): 43–54, https://doi.org/10.1007/s11707-012-0339-6.

42. San Francisco Planning Department, "San Francisco Urban Forest Plan," 2014, 1, http://www.sf-planning.org/ftp/files/plans-and-programs/planning-for-the-city/urban-forest-plan/UrbanForestPlan-121814_Final_WEB.pdf.

43. Virginia Small, "Throw Some Shade: Milwaukee's Trees, Vital to Urban Well-Being, Are Vanishing," Wisconsin Gazette, 2016, http://www.wisconsingazette.com/news/environment/throw-some-shade-milwaukee-s-trees-vital-to-urban-well/article_f49400e8-7102-5732-87b2-203117c08ef9.html.

44. Ian Leahy, "Why We No Longer Recommend a 40 Percent Urban Tree Canopy Goal," *American Forests* (blog), January 12, 2017, http://www.americanforests.org/blog/no-longer-recommend-40-percent-urban-tree-canopy-goal/.

45. Sustainable DC, "Sustainability DC," 76.

46. Sustainable DC, "Sustainability DC."

47. City of Grand Rapids, Office of Energy and Sustainability, "Grand Rapids Sustainability Plan."

48. City of Philadelphia, "Greenworks Philadelphia," 58.

49. City of Philadelphia, "Greenworks Philadelphia: Progress Report," 2014, http://www.phila.gov/green/PDFs/Greenworksprogressreport.pdf.

50. OpenTreeMap, "San Francisco Urban Forest Map," accessed February 21, 2018, https://www.opentreemap.org/urbanforestmap/map/?

51. City of Sacramento, "Tree Programs," accessed February 21, 2018, https://www.cityofsacramento.org/Public-Works/Maintenance-Services/Trees/Programs.

52. E. Gregory McPherson and Louren Kotow, "A Municipal Forest Report Card: Results for California, USA," *Urban Forestry & Urban Greening* 12, no. 2 (January 1, 2013): 134–43, https://doi.org/10.1016/j.ufug.2013.01.003.

53. The City of New York, "PlaNYC A Greener, Greater New York," 2011, 29, http://www.nyc.gov/html/planyc/downloads/pdf/publications/planyc_2011_planyc_full_report.pdf.

54. T. Angotti, "Urban Agriculture: Long-Term Strategy or Impossible Dream?: Lessons from Prospect Farm in Brooklyn, New York," *Public Health* 129, no. 4 (April 1, 2015): 336–41, https://doi.org/10.1016/j.puhe.2014.12.008.

55. Chiara Tornaghi, "Critical Geography of Urban Agriculture," *Progress in Human Geography* 38, no. 4 (August 1, 2014): 551–67, https://doi.org/10.1177/0309132513512542.

56. Tornaghi.

57. Patricia Hynes and Genevieve Howe, "Urban Horticulture in the Contemporary United States: Personal and Community Benefits," 2002, http://www.nchh.org/Portals/0/Contents/Article0820.pdf.
58. S. Algert et al., "Community and Home Gardens Increase Vegetable Intake and Food Security of Residents in San Jose, California," *California Agriculture* 70, no. 2 (April 1, 2016): 77–82.
59. The City of Madison, "The Madison Sustainability Plan," 2011, 23.
60. The City of Madison, 26.
61. American Planning Association, "Urban Agriculture," 2011, https://www.jhsph.edu/research/centers-and-institutes/johns-hopkins-center-for-a-livable-future/_pdf/projects/FPN/Urban_Community_Planning/URBAN_AGRICULTURE_A_SIXTEENCITY_SURVEY_OF_URBAN_AGRICULTURE_PRACTICES_ACROSS_THE_COUNTRY.pdf.
62. Mahbubur R. Meenar and Brandon M. Hoover, "Community Food Security via Urban Agriculture: Understanding People, Place, Economy, and Accessibility from a Food Justice Perspective," *Journal of Agriculture, Food Systems, and Community Development* 3, no. 1 (August 2, 2016): 143–60, https://doi.org/10.5304/jafscd.2012.031.013.
63. City of St. Louis Planning Commission, "City of St. Louis Sustainability Plan."
64. Megan M. Gregory, Timothy W. Leslie, and Laurie E. Drinkwater, "Agroecological and Social Characteristics of New York City Community Gardens: Contributions to Urban Food Security, Ecosystem Services, and Environmental Education," *Urban Ecosystems* 19, no. 2 (June 1, 2016): 763–94, https://doi.org/10.1007/s11252-015-0505-1.
65. Renee Cho, "How Green Is Local Food?" (Earth Institute: Columbia University, September 4, 2012), http://blogs.ei.columbia.edu/2012/09/04/how-green-is-local-food/.
66. Angotti, "Urban Agriculture."
67. Dickson Despommier, "Farming up the City: The Rise of Urban Vertical Farms," *Trends in Biotechnology* 31, no. 7 (July 1, 2013): 388–89, https://doi.org/10.1016/j.tibtech.2013.03.008.
68. Kathryn J. A. Colasanti, Michael W. Hamm, and Charlotte M. Litjens, "The City as an 'Agricultural Powerhouse'? Perspectives on Expanding Urban Agriculture from Detroit, Michigan," *Urban Geography* 33, no. 3 (April 1, 2012): 348–69, https://doi.org/10.2747/0272-3638.33.3.348.
69. Katherine B. Vaughan et al., "Exploring the Distribution of Park Availability, Features, and Quality Across Kansas City, Missouri by Income and Race/Ethnicity: An Environmental Justice Investigation," *Annals of Behavioral Medicine* 45, no. 1 (February 1, 2013): 28–38, https://doi.org/10.1007/s12160-012-9425-y.

70. Vaughan et al.

71. Lisa Benton-Short and John Rennie Short, *Cities and Nature*, 2nd ed. (New York: Routledge, 2013), 242.

72. Salt Lake City Division of Sustainability, "Sustainable Salt Lake: Plan 2015," 2015, 11, http://www.slcdocs.com/slcgreen/sustainablesaltlake_plan2015.pdf.

73. City of St. Louis Planning Commission, "City of St. Louis Sustainability Plan," 47.

74. Sustainable DC, "Sustainability DC," 74.

75. Sustainable DC, "Sustainability DC," 77.

76. Sustainable DC, "Sustainability DC," 78.

77. City of Chicago, "2015 Sustainable Chicago Action Agenda," September 2012, https://www.cityofchicago.org/content/dam/city/progs/env/SustainableChicago2015.pdf; The City of New York, "PlaNYC"; Christina D. Rosan, "Can PlaNYC Make New York City 'Greener and Greater' for Everyone?: Sustainability Planning and the Promise of Environmental Justice," *Local Environment* 17, no. 9 (October 1, 2012): 959–76, https://doi.org/10.1080/13549839.2011.627322.

78. Hamil Pearsall and Joseph Pierce, "Urban Sustainability and Environmental Justice: Evaluating the Linkages in Public Planning/Policy Discourse," *Local Environment* 15, no. 6 (2010).

79. Mona Seymour, "Just Sustainability in Urban Parks," *Local Environment* 17, no. 2 (February 1, 2012): 167–85, https://doi.org/10.1080/13549839.2011.646968.

80. Heather Wright Wendell, Joni A. Downs, and James R. Mihelcic, "Assessing Equitable Access to Urban Green Space: The Role of Engineered Water Infrastructure," *Environmental Science & Technology* 45, no. 16 (August 15, 2011): 6731, https://doi.org/10.1021/es103949f.

81. Sustainable DC, "Sustainability DC," 34, 72.

82. City of Santa Fe, "Sustainable Santa Fe Plan," 2008, https://www.santafenm.gov/media/files/Public_Utilities_Environmental_Services/SustainableSFweb.pdf.

CHAPTER 9

Waste

WASTE AND REFUSE: AN INTRODUCTION

Americans generate a tremendous amount of waste, about 260 million tons of trash each year, more refuse per person than any other country in the world.[1] Solid waste is defined as material that, with no apparent, obvious, or significant economic or beneficial value to humans, is intentionally thrown away for disposal. Such a definition makes waste a relative concept: it is possible that one person can find value in what another considers worthless.

America's relationship to waste parallels our consumerism. In the 1950s, postwar economic prosperity created a "throw-away" culture, vastly increasing volumes of waste generated in the United States. New materials such as plastics, other synthetic products, and toxic chemicals made their way to landfills and industries redesigned products for short-term use. More recently, the "planned obsolescence" of electronics such as cell phones and computers has created an entirely new set of e-waste management challenges. Along similar lines, the packaging industry has also created innumerable goods with very short lives. Rather than seeking long-term reuse of limited natural resources, consumable or nondurable goods are designed to be thrown "away," following the American preference for convenience over conservation.

The US EPA classifies different types of solid waste sources: residential, industrial, commercial, institutional, and construction and demolition (Table 9.1). The destination of much of these wastes is a landfill, and while contemporary landfills operate under established standards for use and

281

M. Keeley, L. Benton-Short, *Urban Sustainability in the US*,
https://doi.org/10.1007/978-3-319-93296-5_9

Table 9.1 Sources and types of municipal solid wastes

Source	Typical waste generators	Types of solid waste
Residential	Single and multifamily dwellings	Food wastes, paper, plastics, textiles, leather, yard wastes, glass, metals, ashes, bulky items like refrigerators, tires, hazardous wastes
Industrial	Manufacturing, construction sites, power and chemical plants	Packaging, food wastes, construction materials, hazardous wastes, ashes, slag, scrap materials, tailings, special wastes
Commercial	Stores, hotels, restaurants, markets, office buildings	Paper, cardboard, plastics, wood, food wastes, glass, metals, special wastes
Institutional	Schools, hospitals, prisons	Same as commercial plus medical wastes
Construction and demolition	New construction sites, road repair, renovation sites, demolition of building	Wood, steel, concrete, dirt

Source: United States Environmental Protection Agency, "Advancing Sustainable Materials Management: 2014 Fact Sheet," accessed November 7 2017, https://www.epa.gov/sites/production/files/2016-11/documents/2014_smmfactsheet_508.pdf

disposal, they are not without environmental consequences. Landfills contribute to climate change by emitting large amounts of methane gas (a by-product of anaerobic bacterial processes) and they can also pollute groundwater. Furthermore, landfills waste precious resources and require a great deal of energy and money to manage not only during operation but also long after they have closed.

While landfills remain the management solution of choice for much of the United States, other options exist. Waste-to-energy incineration generates electricity through the controlled combustion of organic material at very high temperatures. This process allows for some energy recovery from waste but also contributes to air pollution (particularly fine particulates, heavy metals, and carcinogenic substances like dioxin). After incineration, toxic residues must be disposed of as hazardous waste. Other concerns include the cost of constructing incineration plants, the long-term contracts that cities must sign to get them built, and the potential disincentive this places on recycling goods in ways that recoup more than just imbedded energy.[2] Another landfill alternative is anaerobic digestion, a process which purposefully creates conditions for bacterial communities to break down biodegradable waste and sewage sludge to produce biogas for energy.

Although there are federal regulations surrounding the safe disposal of waste in landfills and incinerators in the United States, there are no federal requirements about waste generation, reuse, or recycling. Instead, waste is an issue that is managed at the state and local scale.

For this reason, it is difficult to generalize about waste in US cities due to great variation in waste management programs. Some cities have minimal recycling and diversion efforts in place. A best practice is offering curbside recycling for residential customers, and these programs feature two general types of recycling regimes. With single-stream recycling all recyclable materials including paper, cardboard, plastic, glass, and metal are mixed together for pickup. This method has logistical advantages for residents and cuts collection costs.[3] However, while these comingled materials are sorted at a processing facility, the process frequently results in misdirection of materials and many contaminants remain intermixed with recycled materials, often resulting in a low-grade product. The other option is dual-stream recycling (or source-separated recycling) where paper and cardboard are separated from glass, metal, and plastic containers by consumers.[4] Advocates for this strategy argue that lower levels of contamination lead to higher quality recovered material and lower processing costs, despite the logistical challenges of this approach. What is clear is that in the United States, a considerable amount of what ends up in landfills is either compostable, reusable, or recyclable (Fig. 9.1). For example, in 2017 food accounted for 21.6 percent of what was sent to landfills; yard trimmings and wood accounted for another 16 percent.

A few US cities and agencies are leading the way to new, more holistic and sustainable considerations of waste. The EPA has transitioned from focusing on waste management to discussions of "Sustainable Materials Management," (SMM).[5] SMM refers to the use and reuse of materials in the most productive and sustainable way across their entire life cycle. SMM conserves resources, reduces waste, slows climate change and minimizes the environmental impacts of the materials used. Along these lines, Palm Springs proposes a name change: shifting from the use of the term "waste management" to "resource management."[6] This change in terminology suggests a management approach that continues to place value on materials throughout their life cycle—including eventual reuse or recycling. We see some cities begin to adopt this perspective as they set ambitious "zero waste" goals.

A broader consideration of the life cycle of goods is certainly a vital first step in sustainable waste managment. An examination of a product's life cycle follows it from the raw materials used to produce it, through

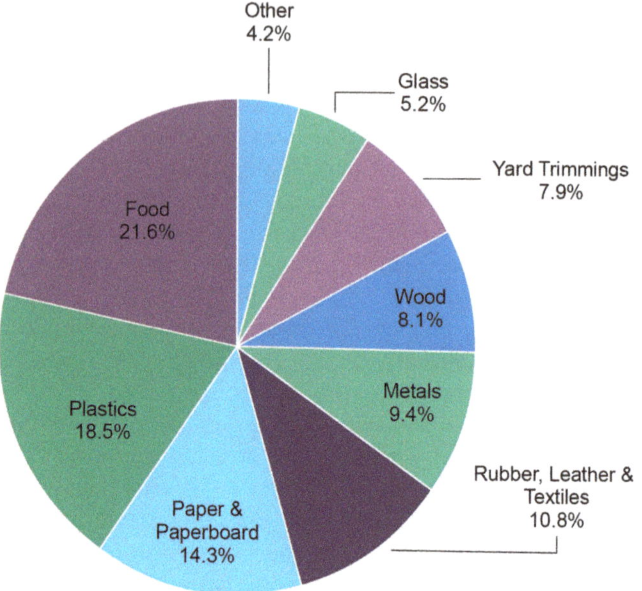

Fig. 9.1 Components of municipal solid waste that end up in US landfills. Nearly all of what Americans throw away is either compostable or recyclable. The fact that these materials end up in landfills underscores the challenge cities face implementing effective waste programs, but it also reveals the difficulty in changing behaviors and cultural values associated with waste. (Source: Adapted from data from the U.S. EPA "Recycling Economic Information (REI) Report" (2016), accessed April 1, 2018, https://www.epa.gov/smm/recycling-economic-information-rei-report and also https://www.epa.gov/landfills/municipal-solid-waste-landfills#whatis)

manufacturing, use, and ultimate disposal. Along the way, the product's environmental and social costs are considered, including transportation, waste, emissions, energy and water use, and labor costs. "Cradle to cradle" (C2C) is a term for a product that is taken back by the manufacturer at the end of its useful life, at which point its components or materials are used to make new products of equal or higher value. C2C production mimics natural cycles, minimizes environmental impact, aims for more sustainable production and increased social responsibility, along with a myriad of other benefits.[7] C2C moves us beyond our disposal-oriented society to a more sustainable closed-loop recirculation of materials.

In this chapter, we explore the ways in which cities are taking action on waste. We first discuss the role of cities in waste management and what they see as challenges. We then examine the most critical paths to achieving sustainability—reduction, reuse, and recycling—and highlight best practices from across the country.

Cities' Role in Waste Management

Unlike water or air pollution, waste and refuse are a particularly local issue. Significantly, waste must actively be collected to be disposed of by local governments. Coordinating regular collection over an entire city is a logistical feat. For example, New York City generates 14 million tons of waste and recyclables every year, which are hauled by 2000 city government and 4000 private trucks.[8] These trucks sometimes go as far as Virginia and South Carolina to unload.[9] Chicago generates more than 7.6 million tons of waste each year, 61 percent of which comes from construction and demolition, a fact most residents are likely unaware.[10] (Fig. 9.2.)

Waste management is connected to many aspects of sustainability, so cities sustainably managing their waste may receive positive externalities such as reduced greenhouse gas emissions and local financial benefits. Indeed, improved waste management can be a central component of efforts to reduce greenhouse gas (GHG) emissions and mitigate climate change. Solid waste results in GHG production in two ways. First, on its

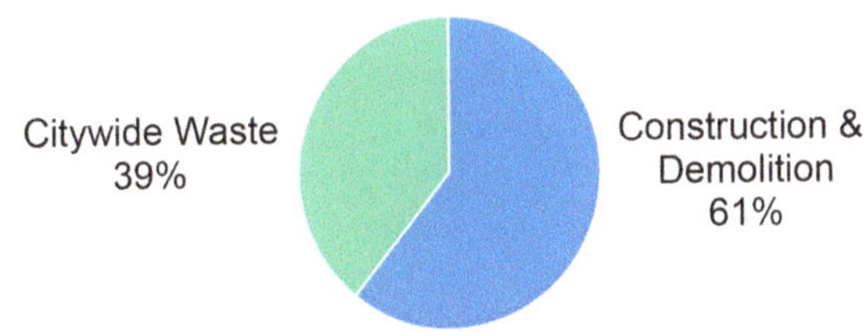

Fig. 9.2 Construction and demolition waste in Chicago. In many cities experiencing growth, construction and demolition may constitute a significant part of the waste stream. In Chicago, citywide waste accounts for 39 percent, while construction and demolition account for 61 percent of the waste stream. (Source: Adapted from the City of Chicago, "2015 Sustainable Chicago Action Agenda," September 2012, https://www.cityofchicago.org/content/dam/city/progs/env/SustainableChicago2015.pdf)

way to becoming waste, energy is expended during the materials manufacture, transportation, use, and disposal. Then, as it decomposes in a landfill, it produces the GHG methane. Reducing GHG from solid waste can be achieved in each step along the way from material manufacture to disposal/decomposition.[11] Many cities have now realized the potential to capitalize on reducing waste and GHG emissions at the same time. Santa Fe plans to establish new city purchasing policies to reduce waste and embodied energy, reduce GHG emissions, and provide preferences for vendors that take similar steps.[12] At the same time, they seek to enable consumers to themselves make more sustainable purchasing decisions through an educational brochure about reducing waste and emissions.

Cities have found it advantageous to promote the significance of waste in terms of their climate mitigation strategies. As Charleston noted, if it "reduces the waste stream by 50 percent from the projected 2030 amount, it could result in a reduction of 22,860 tons of CO_2e [carbon dioxide equivalents, which is a standard unit for measuring carbon footprints] in 2030 from projected" business as usual " 2030 level."[13] The benefits of reduced GHG emissions may further entice cities to reduce waste production.

Waste management is expensive. Residents of Charlotte, North Carolina, threw away an average of three pounds of solid waste per day, and by 2008, it cost the city some $37 million to send 1.5 million tons of material to landfills.[14] While Charlotte has set ambitious goals to reduce waste by 2050, at least half of the single-family residents in Mecklenburg County (where Charlotte is located) do not fully participate in the available recycling programs.

The costs associated with waste management are rising in many areas due to limitations in landfill space. In the last 30 years, many cities in the Northeast, New England, and mid-Atlantic have experienced a "garbage crisis." Many landfills in these areas have or will soon close as they reach capacity. Landfill closures create several challenges including higher fees for collection and disposal, difficulties transporting waste to more distant landfills, and securing the long-term safety of local landfills after they have reached capacity. There are ethical considerations as well, when one considers that transporting trash to distant landfills means that people in other states or countries now shoulder associated environmental and health consequences. More cities will be faced with "garbage crises" if waste management is not optimized.

Box 9.1   Best Practices in Planning: Redeveloping Freshkills Landfill in New York City

As the largest and most densely populated city in the Northeast corridor, New York City's challenges surrounding waste are well-known. In 2001, the Freshkills landfill on Staten Island was closed, after accepting approximately 150 million tons of solid waste over 50 years of operation. Towards the end of this time, Freshkills was the city's only landfill, and residents raised equity concerns about concentrating the disposal of all of the city's waste in just one area. Landfill closure, however, has resulted in the city's garbage being directed to private trash transfer stations concentrated in a few neighborhoods in the Bronx, Queens, and Brooklyn and then exported out of the city. This situation also raises issues of equity, since unpleasant smells, truck traffic, and associated air pollution are again concentrated in some areas of the city. Further, residents far from New York City bear the environmental and health burdens of the city's trash. It is also costly: the city spends more than $1 billion per year to export 3.2 million tons of city-collected waste. The city increasingly transports waste via rail or barge to reduce reliance on trucks which contribute to air pollution and GHG emissions. In these ways, considerations of the economics, equity, and pollution associated with waste removal have motivated the city to increase recycling and more equitably manage waste.

New York City also provides an example of inventive reuse of the now-closed Freshkills site. The city's sustainability plan highlights Freshkills conversion from the world's largest landfill to New York City's largest park, noting that eventually the park will be almost three times the size of Central Park, covering 2200 acres. It will take several decades to cap the landfill, manage landfill gases and leachate in a way that will protect ecological and human health, and construct park areas for active and passive recreation. For New York City, however, reuse of Freshkills presents an opportunity to provide unique recreation space in a densely populated region. It also highlights the work required to manage landfills even after their capacity has been reached and they have "closed" (Fig. 9.3).

(continued)

Box 9.1   (continued)

Fig. 9.3 Recently developed FreshKills Park in New York City, with a view towards downtown. (Source: "Downtown Manhattan view over Freshkills Park" Wikipedia/Wikimedia Commons photo (Created May 1, 2010), accessed April 1, 2018, https://commons.wikimedia.org/wiki/File%3ADowntown_Manhattan_view_over_Freshkills_Park.jpg)

Sources:
The City of New York, "PlaNYC A Greener, Greater New York," 2011, pages 39 and 137, http://www.nyc.gov/html/planyc/downloads/pdf/publications/planyc_2011_planyc_full_report.pdf

The Freshkills Park Alliance, "Frequently Asked Questions," accessed April 4, 2018, http://freshkillspark.org/the-park/faqs

The Freshkills Park Alliance, "The Park Plan," accessed April 3, 2018, http://freshkillspark.org/the-park/the-park-plan

While some cities focus on the costs of waste management, others frame their discussion in terms of the financial benefits of more efficient waste management practices. Some are beginning to see waste as an untapped resource. As part of the zero waste movement, cities must change how they think about waste. Rather than seeing materials as a by-product or waste to be disposed, zero waste thinking considers these same materials as a resource that can generate energy, create jobs, and spur economic development.[15] San Jose hopes that diverting waste from landfills will "show the world how environmental responsibility makes financial sense and stimulates economic opportunity."[16] San Jose wants to utilize its position in Silicon Valley to create innovative green technology, including the potential of "garbage to energy," increasing the economic prosperity of the city. These, however, are not the only financial reasons for cities to improve waste management.

Job creation is another financial benefit of changes in waste management systems. Many cities highlight the job creation expected from increased waste diversion and recycling. Portland considers waste reuse and recovery to be a green job that should provide a "living wage" to people in this profession. Another advantage of these jobs is that, given the logistics of moving waste and recycling, they will remain local or regional and cannot be moved elsewhere.

Consider the state of California, a recycling leader with a recycling rate of about 50 percent. However, the state still sends remaining solid waste to landfills or incinerators, missing opportunities to recover valuable material resources. In 2011, California Governor Jerry Brown signed AB 341, which requires that 75 percent of solid waste generated be source reduced, recycled, or composted by the year 2020. A recent report by CalRecycle estimated that if the state could achieve 75 percent recycling, it would translate into 100,000 jobs.[17] Another study by the BlueGreen Alliance estimates that 1.5 million new jobs would be created if the United States diverted 75 percent of the nation's waste.[18] This increase in jobs would not only address unemployment but also increase tax revenue for city governments.

As cities try to address these waste challenges, a clear first need is detailed information about waste streams, which is used to establish baselines and benchmarks, set goals, and measure progress. For instance, New York City has prioritized a waste life cycle study, that is, a comprehensive study of commercial waste collection focused on logistics, types, and quantities of waste collected throughout the city. Officials hope such a survey will identify additional markets for recycled materials to reduce the cost of waste reduction.[19] And, as the city noted, "once we are able to benchmark our waste generation and identify opportunities in our procurement practices for improvement, we will set targets to increase our diversion rate."[20]

Another challenge for cities is the "knowledge gap" between the significance of waste management and how it is understood by the city's residents. For many cities, waste management is a high-profile issue and a significant part of municipal operations, however, it is not a particular concern for many average citizens. Portland, for example, surveyed residents and discovered only one percent of respondents considered "Consumption and Solid Waste" as critical aspects of the city's sustainability efforts.[21] This finding highlights a perceptual challenge around waste: garbage is generated

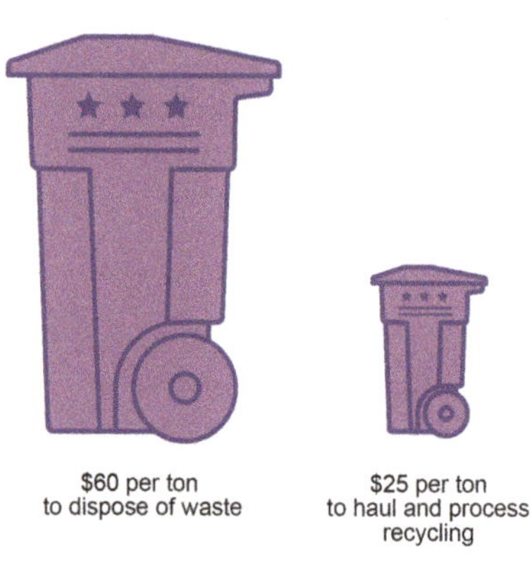

Fig. 9.4 Waste infographic. The financial benefits to recycling can be considerable. Increasingly, infographics are used in sustainability plans and educational materials as a way to better communicate dense and complex data, allowing a variety of audiences to understand this information. (Source: Adapted from data from Sustainable DC, "Sustainability DC," (Washington DC, July 2011), 88, https://sustainable.dc.gov/sites/default/files/dc/sites/sustainable/page_content/attachments/DCS-008%20Report%20508.3j.pdf)

and collected but then disappears. We rarely see or think of waste beyond our garbage cans or as impacting the environment.

Municipalities recognize that at a fundamental level, they must motivate behavior change among residents to address issues of waste. Cities are trying to engage residents and break the mundane routinization of our waste practices. For instance, municipal sustainability plans and websites use infographics to increase awareness of an issue that is often out of sight and out of mind. Washington, D.C. used infographics such as those shown in Fig. 9.4 to educate residents that if they increased recycling rates to 30 percent, the city could save $250,000 a year.

Taking Action on Waste

As cities strategize about how to more effectively address issue of waste and recycling, they must act to reduce, reuse, and recycle waste. Yet as the city of Santa Fe admitted, "the adage 'Reduce, Reuse, Recycle' is simple in concept, and yet a challenge to implement."[22] Our research shows that there are a variety of ways cities are reducing waste or reusing it. These include programs that ban non-recyclables, develop a community culture of reuse, and organize composting programs.

Reduce and Reuse

Traditionally, US cities have dealt with waste as an "end of the pipe" issue, rather than challenging the production of waste. However, the most effective way to address the problem of waste is to not create it to begin with. The EPA prioritizes reduction of consumption and reuse over recycling; source reduction is preferred since it reduces the use of raw materials and avoids the energy and pollution associated with transportation and even recycling itself (Fig. 9.5). However, underlying social and cultural values challenge efforts to reduce and reuse, and these continue to lag behind efforts to recycle.

Despite Americans' rich history of making reliable products and repairing those that are broken, most Americans today do not buy used or consider the benefits of purchasing reusable rather than disposable items, and cannot find or afford repair options. Indeed, our culture of reusing is disappearing; it is now difficult to find shoe repair stores or small appliance repair services that were once commonplace. Many people have discovered it is less expensive to purchase a new cell phone rather than repair a

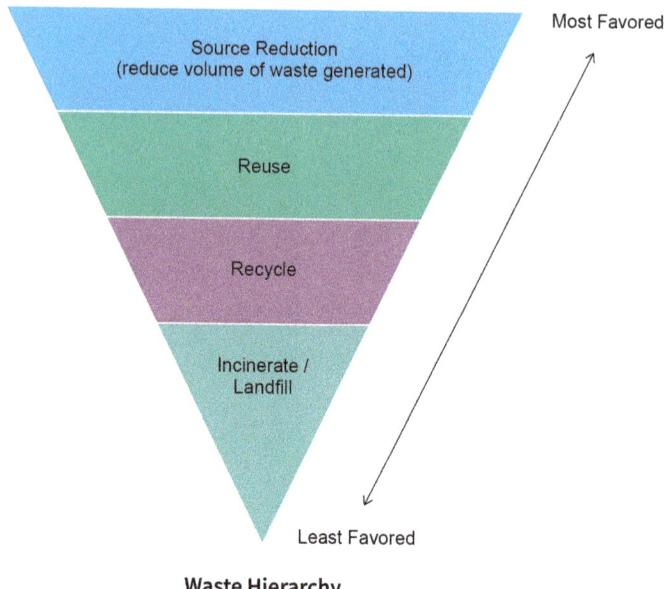

Fig. 9.5 The waste hierarchy, according to the US EPA. This hierarchy prioritizes reducing consumption over reuse and recycling with the least favorable waste management options being incineration and landfills. (Source: Adapted from the U.S. EPA "Sustainable Materials Management: Non-Hazardous Materials and Waste Management Hierarchy," accessed April 10, 2018, https://www.epa.gov/smm/sustainable-materials-management-non-hazardous-materials-and-waste-management-hierarchy)

broken one. Electronics companies, for example, have been criticized for "planned obsolescence," that is, the practice of limiting the useful life of a product so that consumers will be forced to replace it in just a few years. There are thousands of computers, cell phones, and other electronics that are thrown away each year, and many cities do not yet have robust electronic recycling programs. The proper disposal of electronics is critical because on the one hand they contain valuable material such as copper and gold that can be recovered, on the other hand some of the materials can be hazardous. Effective programs to manage e-cycling have the potential to close the digital divide: for example, Palm Springs suggests donating used computer electronics to the Computer Tech program at a local high school (Box 9.2 E-cycling).

Box 9.2   Emerging Trend: E-cycling

The use of electronic products has grown substantially over the past two decades, changing the way and the speed with which we communicate, get information, and consume entertainment. With the proliferation of computers, tablets, cell phones, and other electronics, dealing with "e-waste" is an emerging priority for municipalities. Compounding this problem is the relatively short life of many electronic products. Most cell phones and computers are tossed within two years of purchase. Americans generate an estimated 3.5 million tons of e-waste per year.

Electronics contain both valuable and hazardous materials, which mean they are dangerous to send to landfills and should be carefully recycled. Americans are already recycling about 40 percent of discarded electronics. In this way, recycling of used electronics can yield materials (e.g., gold, copper, glass, aluminum) that can be reused, reducing both the need for raw materials and disposal challenges.

In 2015, New York City and the state of New York banned electronics from the household waste stream to minimize the hazards of e-waste, with fines of $100 for improper disposal. Their website provides a list of places to donate or recycle electronics appropriately instead.

Cities have begun to recognize both the challenge and opportunity in e-cycling. New companies are emerging to handle electronic devices responsibly and securely, and there is an unmet need for electronic repair and refurbishment. Dealing sustainably with electronic products is likely to be a critical issue in the future (Fig. 9.6).

Sources:

"Basic Information about Electronics Stewardship," United States Environmental Protection Agency, accessed March 20, 2018, https://www.epa.gov/smm-electronics/basic-information-about-electronics-stewardship#01

"Electronic Disposal Information," The City of New York, accessed April 3, 2018, http://www1.nyc.gov/nyc-resources/service/4661/electronic-disposal-information

(*continued*)

Box 9.2   (continued)

Fig. 9.6   E-waste recycling in Ann Arbor, Michigan. Increasingly cities must deal with electronic waste—computers, cell phones, televisions are replaced frequently and there are few reuse or refurbish options. (Source: "An E-waste landfill in Ann Arbor, Michigan" Wikimedia commons (created April 21,2007), accessed April 10, 2018, https://commons.wikimedia.org/wiki/File%3AE-Waste_Landfill.jpg)

A fast-food society is a disposable society. Fast food restaurants embody a cultural value that embraces convenience and accepts the short-term duration of packaging and goods. Food arrives within minutes; the food wrappers and drink cups have a commercial lifespan of less than an hour, free plastic kids' toys are broken in days, but all of this survives intact in landfills for years. Changing this throw-away mentality has proven to be a big challenge. This is because "waste is a reflection of consumption patterns," as Palm Springs acknowledges.[23]

Cities need to place more attention on the vital role of consuming less and being thoughtful about the products we as consumers do choose to buy. The city of Portland has moved in this direction as it outlines:

> On one end of the spectrum are goods manufactured using energy-intensive processes, packaged with excessive materials, transported long distances and ultimately discarded after a short usable life. On the other end of the spectrum are goods manufactured using minimal energy and packaging, transported short distances and used for a long time because they are highly durable. By choosing products on the low-emission end of this spectrum, and reusing and recycling them appropriately, residents and businesses can substantially reduce emissions.[24]

Below are several ways that cities are taking action on reducing materials consumed and encouraging reuse within our society.

Banning Common Single-Use Items

Cities are beginning to ban products that they cannot recycle. Washington, D.C. and others have banned Styrofoam and non-recyclable plastic containers from food and retail outlets, and several cities have developed strategies to reduce the use of single-use plastic or paper bags as well.[25] These strategies involve working with stores to provide reusable bags to customers (especially to low-income residents) or by imposing a bag tax (or bag fee) on single-use bags. In 2010, Los Angeles passed a bag ban that requires stores to charge no less than 10 cents for bags provided at checkout, reducing plastic bag use from 2.2 million bags per year at the average grocery store to only 125,000.[26] Due to its success in Los Angeles, this policy was then adopted by the entire state of California in 2014. Washington, D.C.'s bag fee program has been lauded for its success as well, reducing single plastic bag use by 50 percent (Box 9.3).[27] These ordinances greatly reducing the waste strain put on landfills and increase cities' sustainability.

Other programs include those which reduce the use of plastic water bottles and paper. Chicago aims to make city processes as paperless as possible, New York City is educating residents they can opt out of unwanted subscriptions, while Newport News supports a "Day without Paper" in area schools. Paper-related ordinances will further reduce the amount of waste generated each year and bring cities closer to a sustainable way of living.

Box 9.3   Best Practices in Implementation and Results: Washington, D.C.'s Bag Tax

The sustainability plan for Washington, D.C. is ambitious in many ways. By 2032, the District aims to create five times as many jobs providing green goods and services, cut the citywide obesity rate by 50 percent, eliminate food desserts, reduce greenhouse gas emissions by 50 percent, cut citywide energy use by 50 percent, and make 100 percent of Washington, D.C. waterways fishable and swimmable. Improving water quality in the two rivers that surround the city, the Potomac to the west and the Anacostia to the east, is a big challenge. The long-neglected Anacostia River has numerous combined sewer outfalls that discharge untreated wastewater when it rains. It is severely polluted by sediment, nutrients, pathogens, and toxins. The river has also been plagued by trash—thousands of plastic bottles and plastic bags are washed into the river yearly from the surrounding suburbs and city sewer systems.

To combat the trash problem, Washington, D.C. launched a "bag fee." The bag fee aims to reduce litter and curb disposable plastic and paper bag use by charging $0.05 for single use bags at grocery stores and other venues. The bag fee discourages waste while raising funds to clean the river. Since the bag fee took effect, 80 percent of residents are using fewer disposable bags, and stream cleanup groups report 70 percent fewer bags collected in the Anacostia River. The bag fee has raised about $10 million for the Anacostia River Clean Up and Protection Fund. It has paid for six trash traps that have collectively removed more than 25,000 pounds of trash from Washington, D.C. waterways and funded more than 2300 feet of stream restoration projects, the installation of almost 1000 trees, 550 rain barrels, and 130 rain gardens that help capture polluted stormwater before it reaches the river.

D.C. has realized multiple benefits in this program: a change in consumer habits that generates less waste, a reduction of trash in the river, and raising money for further river cleanup and green infrastructure installations. D.C.'s bag fee has been heralded as one of the nation's most successful "bag laws"—and has become a familiar and accepted routine at cash registers across the city. In combination

(*continued*)

Box 9.3   (continued)

with other river restoration projects, the future of D.C.'s "forgotten river" is suddenly looking a little less bleak.

Source:
"Anacostia River Initiatives," DC Department of Energy and Environment, accessed April 4, 2018, https://doee.dc.gov/trashfreedc

Developing a Culture of Reuse and Closed-Loop Systems

Municipalities have also explored how city practices can support a culture of reuse. Tulsa plans to introduce an internal Quartermaster system, in which materials like basic repair, painting, cleaning, and safety supplies are purchased and stored centrally for departments to borrow and use when needed.[28] While framed as a cost-cutting measure, this may also reduce waste and allow for the reuse of some supplies. New York City intends to revise its procurement practices to include packaging reduction guidelines calling for elimination or minimization of packaging and using packaging that is recyclable or reusable, including pallets.[29] These plans aim to change the workplace culture among city employees to decrease waste produced by the city.

Palm Springs is among many cities educating residents about purchasing products that are more durable and have the potential to be repaired, reused, or recycled. Portland has two interesting, interrelated initiatives: "tool libraries" and "Repair PDX" (PDX is the transportation abbreviation for Portland). Instead of lending books, "tool libraries" lend common home improvement, automotive repair, and gardening tools so that residents do not necessarily need to buy them. The tool libraries and other locations around the city also host "Repair PDX," where people with small appliances, bikes, or clothing in need of repair learn from "volunteers who like to fix things."[30]

Washington, D.C., Austin, and Santa Fe want to encourage public/private partnerships with companies and non-profit organizations already providing reuse options such as Goodwill Industries, iOS World Books, Salvation Army, Open Hands, and Habitat for Humanity ReStore. Other cities have promoted online venues for residents to donate, buy, or sell unused supplies or have created their own systems, such as the NYC Stuff Exchange. New York City also has a *Materials for Arts* program, which has diverted over 8000 tons of arts materials to schools and cultural institutions,

Reuse programs can help businesses as well. New York City's *WasteMatch* program helps businesses and organizations in the city find used or surplus commercial goods and equipment. The city notes that this program has successfully diverted over 25,000 tons of materials since 1997.[31]

Composting Programs for Organic Waste

As noted earlier, a significant component of the US waste stream is biodegradable organic material such as food waste, yard waste, and tree trimmings. Natural processes cause organic material to biodegrade over time, creating nutrient-rich soils. However, landfills are compacted and capped such that that there is insufficient oxygen for bacterial aerobic respiration to occur, leaving the organic debris piled in landfills for years.

Composting involves decomposing food scraps and other organic wastes, like cardboard rolls and cotton rags, into a useful nutrient-rich substance called mature compost which can be used as fertilizer. Many residents with yards can compost by setting aside small areas for composting, but currently, the United States only composts about three percent of its food waste. These figures are expected to change though, as the topic of composting of food and yard waste is on the agenda of many cities. While yard waste composting (of leaves, twigs, and yard debris) is relatively straightforward, food composting can be more challenging due to issues like contamination with non-compostable products like plastics, managing vermin, and nuisances such as smells. Despite these obstacles, food composting poses particular environmental and financial benefits due to the high nutrient and carbon content of this type of waste. Composting is a straightforward solution to reduce the volume of waste buried in landfills and the moisture content of waste (which increases the viability of waste incineration), and, instead, produce a compost end product that can be used as fertilizer in municipal operations, sold to local farmers, or marketed back to the public.

Many cities do not have citywide composting programs or facilities. However, many are in the development phase of their composting programs and working to create the physical and institutional infrastructure necessary for a comprehensive approach to composting. Charleston's sustainability plan proposes to conduct waste audits to determine the proportion of organic waste currently in the waste stream, to review relevant laws and regulations which might hinder composting activities, and to develop an organic waste composting and mulching program for city operations.[32] Cities such as Palm Springs and Portland propose piloting a curbside food waste collection program for local restaurants or at large public facilities like the airport or convention center. Portland now requires all trash companies to offer composting.[33] Washington, D.C. has compost drop-off locations at farmers markets across the city, and Madison and St. Louis plan to require that events occurring in public spaces or buildings provide composting bins alongside those for recycling. New York is targeting organics recovery at the city's Hunts Point Food Distribution Center and providing incentives for the conversion of waste cooking oil from restaurants into biodiesel. San Francisco's composting efforts are perhaps the most developed and represent best practices.

Recycling

Recycling rates have risen steadily over the last several decades. In 1980, the United States recycled only 10 percent of waste; by 2017 this increased to 35 percent. However, this is still below many European countries—Sweden, for example, recycles more than 49 percent of its waste and the United Kingdom recycles 44 percent. In terms of both waste quantity and recycling, the United States is ranked among the worst for industrialized countries. Further, as we outline at the end of this chapter in the "What's Missing" section, the United States' recycling sector was thrown into turmoil in 2017. This is because we have inadequately assured the quality of recycled materials and developed diverse markets for these goods. The origins of this crisis are closely related to municipal recycling strategies and challenges we consider below.

The United States does not have federal regulations that require recycling at the municipal level; rather, these programs are left to states and municipalities to decide. Some cities have developed successful recycling programs and others have not. Seattle, Portland, Los Angeles, and Minneapolis have all achieved recycling rates of over 50 percent of their solid waste stream. Other cities still struggle to increase their diversion rate (the amount of waste that is recycled instead of sent to landfills). The presence of successful programs means that best practices exist from which others can learn. Cities that have mandatory curbside recycling and accept a variety of materials have the highest recycling rates, yet even with robust residential curbside recycling, challenges remain. Our research shows best practices in recycling in four areas: (1) education and outreach, (2) financial incentives, (3) recycling requirements, and (4) developing zero waste goals.

The Importance of Education and Outreach

New York City reports that despite 22 years of mandatory residential recycling and one-third of the residential waste stream recycled by curbside collection, residents still improperly sort recyclable goods.[34] It is clear that cities must continue education and outreach programs so that residents understand the importance of recycling, are motivated to do their part, and know how to do it properly. Portland, for example, is planning to label garbage bins throughout the city as "landfill" to remind people of exactly where their trash is headed and as push back against "out of sight out of mind" mentality.[35]

Other cities are introducing hands-on learning and games to educate the public on city recycling efforts. Newport News offers residents waste audits, so that they better understand consumption habits and how they should more appropriately use waste diversion services.[36] The city also plans to incentivize recycling through reduced user fees, recognition, and prizes such as discounts on restaurants. Philadelphia proposed a recycling competition between neighborhoods and will reward winning neighborhoods with a small donation to local community organizations.[37] Finally, some communities are trying to collect and share waste diversion data online, which helps the city, but also helps community-based organizations monitor effects of their recycling and outreach initiatives.

Another strategy is to enhance the physical infrastructure to support residential recycling. This can involve accepting more types of plastics for recycling, adding more bins, or increasing the size of recycling bins. For example, Philadelphia expanded plastic recycling to include #3–#7.[38] In its effort to raise its citywide diversion rate to 80 percent by 2032, New York City intends to "increase the size of recycling bins so individuals are psychologically more inclined to recycle."[39] To achieve this goal, the city plans to provide residential customers with larger recycling bins and will also expand recycling services to provide curbside three-track waste collection (waste, recyclables, and compost). In order to provide citywide composting service, the city must secure a 10- to 20-acre site to house a composting center, among other logistical challenges. Enhancements in infrastructure have the potential to greatly increase waste sustainability of these cities.

Create Financial Incentives

Some cities are embracing "Pay as you Throw Programs" (PAYT). This involves charging residents for waste going to landfills or incinerators but making recycling either free or cost significantly less. Cities that have prioritized the financial benefits of waste diversion, like Santa Fe, Philadelphia, St. Louis, and Washington, D.C., see the PAYT system as an incentive to increase participation in reduction, recycling, and reuse efforts. A recent EPA study concluded that after cities have introduced PAYT systems, the amount of solid waste going to landfills decreased an average of 17 percent[40] (Fig. 9.7).

The city of Charleston has higher per capita waste than similarly sized cities. In an effort to lower waste and increase recycling, the city embraced the PAYT system, calling it "the single most effective action that can increase recycling and diversion" because it allows businesses and residents to save money when they waste less and recycle more.[41]

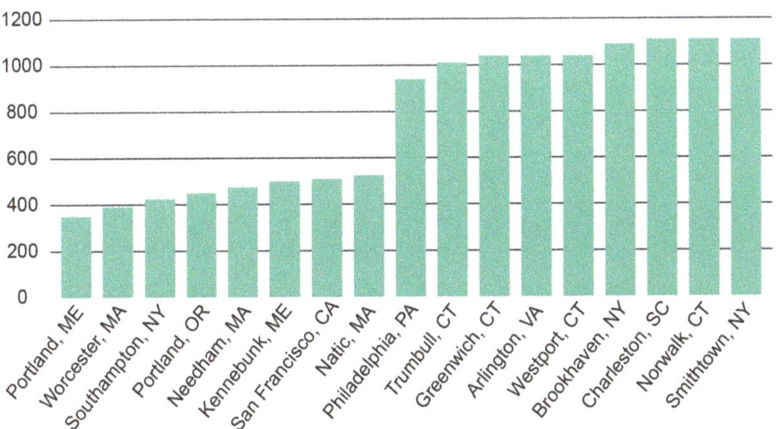

Fig. 9.7 Per capita annual waste (in pounds) for selected cities. This chart shows the difference between cities that have PAYT programs and those that do not. On the left are cities that have a PAYT program and weekly recycling. Those on the right only have weekly curbside recycling. These data indicate that residents that pay the true cost of waste disposal waste less. Charleston collected this information in their consideration of a PAYT program. (Source: Adapted from Charleston Green Committee, "Charleston Green Plan," (2007, page 111), http://www.charlestongreencommittee.com/charlestongreenplan2010.pdf)

PAYT systems are promising; however, it is important to keep in mind that there could be equity concerns with PAYT systems, as waste charges represent a higher proportion of the income of poorer households than wealthier households. For this reason, the PAYT system may have unintended consequences as the financial burden of high waste removal prices based on volume might result in illegal dumping of trash in parks, vacant lands, or alleys. Cities considering PAYT programs should consider the impacts of inequitable financial burdens and possible consequences.

Set Requirements for Recycling

Requiring participation in recycling programs is another option to increase waste diversion rates. Austin has tackled a particularly challenging problem with the implementation of a Universal Recycling Ordinance for all large multifamily properties and commercial businesses.[42] For a number of reasons, managing recycling in multifamily units is harder than for single-family homes. For instance, trash rooms throughout existing buildings may lack the space and infrastructure to collect separate streams of waste. Austin is phasing in this regulation for multifamily buildings of different sizes over several years. They will help building owners develop a waste management strategy and ensure that signage and the correct number of bins for recyclables and non-recyclables are available on-site.[43] Some cities have recycling programs aimed specifically at businesses. New York City simply states that they have "set recycling goals for City government and challenge corporations and institutions to meet or exceed those goals."[44] Santa Fe is currently exploring a carbon credit trading system for businesses tied to reductions in recycling-related carbon.

In addition to requirements for residents and businesses, many cities are considering requirements for management of construction waste as a way to re-capture the economic value of this material. A study in Chicago revealed that "over 60 percent of the waste generated in the city comes from construction and demolition projects."[45] This percentage could be even higher in cities experiencing high levels of growth and development and highlights the importance of this waste category. Portland has set a goal of recycling 75 percent of construction and demolition debris and prioritizing salvage and reuse activities.[46] While few cities have such ambitious goals, many are using ordinances and building codes to reduce construction and demolition waste.

Set Zero Waste Goals

An emerging trend within urban sustainability planning is establishing "zero waste" as a goal or waste management strategy. "Zero waste" is a broad term for more sustainable solid waste management practices that maximize diversion from landfills and reduce waste at the source. "Achieving zero waste will require radical changes in three areas: product creation (manufacturing and packaging), product use (use of sustainable, recycled, and recyclable products), and product disposal (resource recovery or landfilling)."[47] Several cities have set out goals to be "zero waste," although fewer cities have followed through with concrete goals and timelines to achieve this ambitious goal.

Box 9.4   Best Practices in Governance: Madison's Approach to Zero Waste

Madison, Wisconsin, has a goal to divert 75 percent of its waste from landfill sites by the year 2020 through programs for reducing, reusing, and recycling of materials, with the ultimate goal of zero waste by 2050. They plan to achieve more sustainable waste management by developing and implementing a zero waste plan in the city. Zero waste goal creation is a growing trend in the United States, but we highlight Madison's approach as a best practice because of the city's transparent collaboration with various agencies and community organizations.

Within Madison's plans for sustainability, the city has specified the lead agencies and vital partners that will work together to achieve established goals. Among these are the City of Madison Streets Division, Engineering Division Facilities & Sustainability Unit, Dane County, private disposal companies, the Wisconsin Department of Natural Resources, the University of Wisconsin-Madison and other large employers. In identifying and publishing this list of partners, the city has created a level of commitment and accountability. They work regionally with surrounding municipalities, the county, and state government. The Madison sustainability plan further envisions a partnership with the University of Wisconsin-Madison, other large

(*continued*)

Box 9.4   (continued)

employers and surrounding municipalities to "create and use a coherent visual system for identifying waste containers" such that recycling bins have a consistent look across greater Madison. As cities develop plans for complex problems like waste reduction, it is important to create accountability, partnerships, and a broad network of collaboration and support.

Source:

The City of Madison, "The Madison Sustainability Plan: Fostering Environmental, Economic, and Social Resistance," 2011, page 15, https://www.cityofmadison.com/sustainability/documents/SustainPlan2011.pdf

Some best practices exist as cities try to encourage close-looped materials systems in their communities. New York City aims to incentivize vendors to recover and reuse products after consumers are done with them. Washington, D.C. is looking to establish a citywide sustainable supply chain. They state: "this responsibility means manufacturers must consider reducing the use of toxic substances, designing for reuse and recyclability, or create take-back programs for consumers to return products when no longer useable."[48] Another approach to sustainable production currently undertaken by Chicago, NYC, and Palm Springs aims to develop or strengthen closed-loop systems within the business community, to make "one company's waste another company's resource."[49]

The state of California has played an important role in shaping municipal sustainability efforts. California's Integrated Waste Management Act (AB 939) required municipalities in the state to cut waste in half by 2000. The California Integrated Waste Management Board now promotes "Zero Waste California," a campaign to shift community goals from "reduce, reuse, recycle" to instead "zero waste." As a result, several cities including San Francisco, Los Angeles, San Diego, and San Jose have adopted "zero waste" initiatives (Box 9.5).[50]

Box 9.5   Best Practices in Governance: Getting to Zero Waste in San Francisco

San Francisco is recognized as a US leader in recycling and composting programs. In 2002, San Francisco set an ambitious goal of creating zero waste by 2020, meaning that they would not landfill or incinerate any waste material. Indeed, the city made zero waste a signature element of their climate action strategy known as the "0-50-100" campaign. Three pillars of this strategy are 0 waste, 50 percent sustainable trips, and 100 percent renewable energy for residential consumption.

To achieve this ambitious goal, the city outlined the following strategies:

- Ban the use of Styrofoam and other brands of polystyrene in city departments and by food service operators
- Ban the use of non-compostable bags
- Require events to offer recycling and composting
- Reduce packaging in collaboration with legislators, producers, wholesalers, retailers, and consumers
- Reduce carbon-intensive foods and reduce food waste through campaigns, legislation, and education
- Reduce consumption through campaigns, legislation, and education
- Implement a Construction and Demolition Debris Recovery Ordinance
- Expand produce responsibility laws
- Strengthen compliance with mandatory source separation

San Francisco has passed a number of ordinances, codifying more sustainable waste management efforts. In 2009, the city passed a Mandatory Recycling and Composting Ordinance (the first of its kind in the United States) that requires everyone in San Francisco to separate recyclables, compostables, and landfill-bound trash. Key in realizing this separation is the "Fantastic Three" residential curbside collection program that includes three bins—blue bins for recycling, green bins for composing (food scraps, yard trimmings, soiled

(*continued*)

Box 9.5   (continued)

paper), and smaller black bins for trash. Another ordinance requires every event held in San Francisco to offer recycling and composting at the event.

One of the less visible but important categories of waste is the debris produced by the construction industry. In 2006 the city passed an ordinance requiring the building trade to recycle at least two-thirds of its debris such as concrete, steel, and timber at a registered facility. Companies that fail to comply can have their registration suspended for six months. At the same time, the city prioritized using recycled materials for asphalting and gutters in public works projects. Creating a market for recycled materials is an important best practice in holistic considerations of waste management.

Funding for San Francisco's zero waste program are the fees customers pay for waste management. The cost of collecting compostable, recyclables, and landfill-bound materials has been comparable. The cost of sending materials to landfills include transportation and landfill management fees (called tipping fees). Recyclables processing costs are higher, but can be offset by selling these goods, yet prices vary depending upon demand and quality of the material. Compostable materials are processed and transformed into nutrient-rich compost, which is sold to local farms.

A broad array of policy innovations has helped San Francisco set the North American record for recycling and composting, with an 80 percent waste diversion rate in 2013. (This means only 20 percent of waste is landfilled or incinerated). San Francisco has shown that political determination and changing behaviors in how residents and business deal with garbage is effective. Whatever the results in 2020, San Francisco has set an example for other US cities to follow.

Source:
"Zero Waste—Frequently Asked Questions (FAQs)," San Francisco Department of the Environment, 2017, https://sfenvironment.org/zero-waste-faqs

What's Missing: Closing the Loop and Creating Demand for Recycled Materials

For many years, China has been the world's largest importer of many types of recycling, including nearly half of all plastic and paper products. The country has used these raw materials to support its prolific manufacturing sector although the situation clearly raises global equity issues. In 2017, China issued restrictions and outright bans on the import of over 24 types of recyclable materials, saying that it would no longer be the "world's garbage dump."[51] China stated that it made this policy move because many of the imported materials were poorly sorted (which complicates reuse), sometimes contaminated with hazardous substances (which compromise human health). Instead, China will increasingly rely on its own growing recycling stream for raw materials.

This change has had dramatic implications for recycling programs in the United States and highlights unsustainability in the current model. The value of many recyclables dropped drastically as US cities and recycling companies scramble to find new buyers for materials. The backlog of recycled material is so overwhelming that some states that had banned landfilling of recyclables (like California and Oregon) have had to again allow this practice.

What is clear is that the United States—long dependent on China's acceptance of our recycling—has insufficiently attended to several key aspects of more holistic waste management practices (as featured in C2C or zero waste strategies). Two interrelated approaches are necessary to increase the demand for recycled materials. This is essential, because the costs of a recycling program are directly related to the demand and the price at which raw recycled materials can be sold. When demand rises, recycling profit increases. On the flip side, without demand, material that has been "recycled" at the curbside may go directly to a landfill because there is no market for them.

The first important step is to improve the quality of recycled material by lowering contamination rates. High-quality materials with low contamination rates simply have more uses, so there is more demand for them. China, for instance, will still accept some of these materials. Achieving this goal will not be easy. In many cities, some 30 percent of what is thrown in recycling bins is not actually recyclable.[52] One industry insider calls it "wishful recycling."[53] There are trade-offs between the costs, efficiencies, and end product quality of different recycling systems. This is because end-of-the-pipe solutions to the contamination problem, such as increased mechanical and hand sorting, are expensive. Some cities are instead enforcing stricter laws about what should be put in recycling bins, moving to dual-stream recycling programs, or considering adding cameras to collection trucks to identify households that put trash in recycling containers.

The second needed approach is to create new markets—including domestic markets—for recycled materials. There is clearly a niche in some communities to process specific waste streams, including organics, construction debris, or higher-value glass and aluminum for local markets. Encouraging local companies to use recycled materials is certainly a strategy that would provide multiple benefits for communities. Along these lines, a strong example of innovation comes from Phoenix where the city has partnered with Arizona State University to fund a waste innovation hub, called the Resource Innovation and Solutions Network, focusing on a reimagination of waste as a resource and the development of a circular economy.[54] The hub hosts an incubator for entrepreneurs in waste-to-product innovation, connects with global partners, and tests practices within the city of Phoenix.

SUMMARY

Many cities are addressing the problem of waste and refuse in creative and compelling ways. Table 9.2 summarizes important trends and best practices.

Table 9.2   Best practices in waste management

Waste reduction and reuse

- Ban non-recyclable materials
- Set bag fees to reduce the use of plastic bags
- Establish comprehensive zero waste programs
- Challenge consumption and create a culture of reuse (i.e., establish and improve innovative reuse programs)
- Organize composting programs and establish curbside composting for residential areas
- Create new markets for recycled materials
- Develop a circular economy

Recycling

- Require recycling and composting at events and in public spaces
- Create pay-as-you-throw incentives
- Create more robust residential curbside recycling and reduce contamination rates
- Take notice of the emerging issue of e-cycling

Notes

1. US EPA, "Advancing Sustainable Materials Management: Facts and Figures," US EPA, September 22, 2015, https://www.epa.gov/smm/advancing-sustainable-materials-management-facts-and-figures.

2. Nate Seltenrich, "Incineration Versus Recycling: In Europe, A Debate Over Trash," Yale E360, August 28, 2013, https://e360.yale.edu/features/incineration_versus_recycling__in_europe_a_debate_over_trash.

3. Minnesota Pollution Control Agency, "Single Stream Recycling: What Questions Should You Be Asking?," accessed April 4, 2018, https://www.pca.state.mn.us/sites/default/files/081211rust.pdf.

4. Minnesota Pollution Control Agency.

5. United States Environmental Protection Agency, "Sustainable Materials Management Basics," November 2, 2017, https://www.epa.gov/smm/sustainable-materials-management-basics.

6. City of Palm Springs, "The Palm Springs Path to a Sustainable Community Draft," March 25, 2009, 39, http://www.palmspringsca.gov/home/showdocument?id=5610.

7. William McDonough and Michael Braungart, *Cradle to Cradle: Remaking the Way We Make Things* (New York: New York Point Press, 2002); Janine Benyus, *Biomimicry: Innovation Inspired by Nature* (New York: Harper Collins, 1997).

8. The City of New York, "Final Comprehensive Solid Waste Management Plan," September 2006, http://www1.nyc.gov/assets/dsny/docs/about_swmp_exec_summary_0815.pdf.

9. Ashley Milne-Tyte, "Carting New Yorkers' Trash to Landfills Is Expensive. One Solution: Make Less of It.," August 4, 2017.

10. Chicago Department of the Environment, "Waste Characterization Study," April 2, 2010, https://www.cityofchicago.org/content/dam/city/depts/doe/general/RecyclingAndWasteMgmt_PDFs/WasteAndDiversionStudy/WasteCharacterizationReport.pdf.

11. Sustainable Santa Fe Commission, "Sustainable Santa Fe Plan," April 2012, 9.

12. Sustainable Santa Fe Commission, 9.

13. Charleston Green Committee, "Charleston Green Plan," 2007, http://www.charlestongreencommittee.com/charlestongreenplan2010.pdf.

14. Jennifer Fairchild et al., "Sustain Charlotte 2014 Sustainability Report Card," 2014, http://www.sustaincharlotte.org/reportcard2014.

15. The City of New York, "PlaNYC A Greener, Greater New York," 2011, 137, http://www.nyc.gov/html/planyc/downloads/pdf/publications/planyc_2011_planyc_full_report.pdf.

16. The City of San Jose, "San Jose's Green Vision," 2007, 1, http://www.globalurban.org/San_Jose_Green_Vision.pdf.

17. CalRecycle, "AB 341 Goal: 75% Recycling by 2020," 2013, www.calrecycle.ca.gov/Actions/Document.ashx?id=3172.
18. BlueGreen Alliance, "Increasing Recycling Will Create Nearly 1.5 Million Jobs, Reduce Pollution," accessed February 3, 2018, https://www.bluegreenalliance.org/the-latest/increasing-recycling-will-create-nearly-1-5-million-jobs-reduce-pollution/.
19. The City of New York, "PlaNYC."
20. The City of New York.
21. City of Portland, "The Portland Plan April 2012," 2012, 25, http://www.portlandonline.com/portlandplan/index.cfm?c=58776.
22. Sustainable Santa Fe Commission, "Sustainable Santa Fe Plan," 25.
23. City of Palm Springs, "The Palm Springs Path to a Sustainable Community Draft," 39.
24. City of Portland, "The Portland Plan April 2012," 47.
25. Sustainable DC, "Sustainability DC," July 2011, 91, https://sustainable.dc.gov/sites/default/files/dc/sites/sustainable/page_content/attachments/DCS-008%20Report%20508.3j.pdf.
26. Lucy Bayly, "Ban the Bag? Why Plastic Bag Taxes and Bans Don't Always Work - NBC News," NBC News, May 28, 2016, https://www.nbcnews.com/business/business-news/ban-bag-why-plastic-bag-taxes-bans-dont-always-n580926.
27. Bayly.
28. City of Tulsa, "City of Tulsa Sustainability Plan: Resource Efficiency, Clean Energy, and Leading Growth in the New Economy," October 27, 2011, 93, http://cdn.cityoftulsa.org/parks/COT%20Sustainability%20Plan_FINAL.pdf.
29. NYC The Mayor's Office of Contract Services, "Environmental Preferable Purchasing," accessed February 6, 2018, https://www1.nyc.gov/site/mocs/resources/environmental-preferable-purchasing.page.
30. The City of Portland, "Building Community through Repair," accessed February 3, 2018, https://www.portlandoregon.gov/bps/article/655757.
31. The City of New York, "PlaNYC," 138.
32. Charleston Green Committee, "Charleston Green Plan," 131.
33. The City of Portland, "History of Portland's Garbage and Recycling System," accessed April 3, 2018, https://www.portlandoregon.gov/bps/article/109782.
34. The City of New York, "PlaNYC," 139.
35. City of Portland, "The Portland Plan April 2012," 49.
36. City of Newport News, "Roadmap to Sustainability," February 2013, https://www.nngov.com/DocumentCenter/View/1586.
37. City of Philadelphia, "Greenworks Philadelphia," 2009, 34, https://beta.phila.gov/documents/greenworks-progress-reports/.

38. City of Philadelphia, 34.

39. The City of New York, "PlaNYC," 139.

40. City of Philadelphia, "Greenworks Philadelphia," 38.

41. Charleston Green Committee, "Charleston Green Plan," 134.

42. The City of Austin, "Rethink For A Bright Green Future," 2008, 15.

43. Emterra Environmental USA, "Garbage & Recycling Services for Multi-Unit Residences," accessed February 3, 2018, http://www.emterrausa.com/multi-residential-waste-management.

44. The City of New York, "PlaNYC," 139.

45. The City of New York, 139.

46. City of Chicago, "2015 Sustainable Chicago Action Agenda," September 2012, 29, https://www.cityofchicago.org/content/dam/city/progs/env/SustainableChicago2015.pdf.

47. Sustainable DC, "Sustainability DC," 92.

48. Sustainable DC, "Sustainability DC," 92.

49. City of Chicago, "2015 Sustainable Chicago Action Agenda," 30.

50. California Department of Resources Recycling and CalRecycle, "Zero Waste Communities," accessed February 3, 2018, http://www.calrecycle.ca.gov/ZeroWaste/Communities/.

51. Kimiko de Freytas-Tamura, "Plastics Pile Up as China Refuses to Take the West's Recycling," *The New York Times*, January 11, 2018, sec. World, https://www.nytimes.com/2018/01/11/world/china-recyclables-ban.html.

52. Elizabeth Daigneau, "China's Foreign-Waste Ban Could Have Recycling Repercussions in America," Governing, accessed April 5, 2018, http://www.governing.com/topics/transportation-infrastructure/gov-china-ban-scrap-paper-plastic-recycling.html.

53. Jason Margolis, "Mountains of U.S. Recycling Pile up as China Restricts Imports," USA TODAY, accessed April 5, 2018, https://www.usatoday.com/story/news/world/2018/01/02/mountains-u-s-recycling-pile-up-china-restricts-imports/995134001/.

54. Arizona State University, "About Resource Innovation and Solutions Network," *Resource Innovation and Solutions Network* (blog), accessed April 5, 2018, https://sustainability.asu.edu/resourceinnovation/about-us/.

CHAPTER 10

Summary and Best Practices

Despite the challenges cities face in achieving a more sustainable future, the good news is that many US cities are not only planning for but taking action on sustainability. We organized the chapters in this book by specific topics, but in reality, achieving sustainability involves reaching across the silos of specific topics to holistically integrate planning and action in order to achieve multiple benefits. We thought it would be valuable to conclude by highlighting the cross-cutting strategies we explored throughout this book because they are essential to creating, implementing, and realizing sustainability.

Governance
- Organize, coordinate, and integrate between municipal agencies (inter-agency) and also with key community stakeholders and organizations; stakeholders often include:

  - Local businesses
  - Residents
  - Non-profit organizations
  - Community development groups

- Appoint leaders that are accountable
- Lead with incentives and education
- Embed sustainability into policies, practices, and values that guide day-to-day decision-making within local government

© The Author(s) 2019

M. Keeley, L. Benton-Short, *Urban Sustainability in the US*,

https://doi.org/10.1007/978-3-319-93296-5_10

- Develop transparency and accountability for the planning process and the plan

Planning Process
- Support planning efforts that are holistically integrated and move beyond compartmentalization of planning specialties
- Engage in a process that involves multiple municipal agencies
- Build community trust by communicating how their feedback affects the process
- Engage in a planning process that embraces public participation, involves important stakeholders (such as community groups and non-profits), and actually listens to what they say
- Inventory and benchmark current problems
- Identify solutions to those problems by learning from other cities yet being sensitive to local conditions
- Articulate and set measurable goals with a timeline for completion
- Create an action plan
- Evaluate progress on the plan
- Recognize achievements
- Reassess conditions and set new goals in an iterative process

Education and Communication
- Meet people where they are (both physically and conceptually)
- Talk to the community about the merits of investments in sustainability as well as results
- Disseminate information and reports in a timely way
- Use education and communication as an opportunity to drive change and implement new behaviors
- Make use of new technologies (such as apps and websites) to help disseminate information as well as educate and involve residents
- Motivate people to support sustainability strategies and be involved using competitions, rewards, and recognition
- Evaluate and show the risk of *not* taking an action
- Create reports, updates, and websites that are informative by accessible to a general audience (i.e. infographics)

Incorporating Equity
- Clearly articulate that equity is a critical part of a sustainable future and include this explicitly in any plan

- Integrate considerations of equity throughout all city services by structuring all goals in such a way that they increase equity
- Use GIS and other geospatial technologies to specifically identify vulnerable populations and specific inequities and make these widely available to inform all planning exercises
- Incorporate Health In All policies to assure that vulnerable populations such as those experiencing and have access to services homelessness, mental health issues, and/or addiction are included
- Discuss strategies to reduce poverty, inequality, and homelessness
- Examine barriers and opportunities to expand the supply of affordable housing
- Promote diverse and livable neighborhoods
- Plan for and prioritize investment in low-income and/or minority neighborhoods
- Set goals by neighborhood (instead of for the entire city) as a way to incorporate equity across any action

Implementation and Results
- Infuse sustainability into agency culture and community values
- Elect or select leaders that think holistically
- Hold leaders, structures, and systems accountable
- Seek creative ways to finance implementation of the plan
- Monitor progress, particularly when the goals are significant and the timeframes are long.
- Regularly disclose or report progress towards sustainability goals through a range of communication: stand-alone reports, annual reports, websites, and social media
- Understand and plan for risk—including climate change, hazards, and disasters
- Recognize financial and other benefits from sustainability projects and meeting goals
- Share the credit

Innovation
- Identify solutions that take into account a city's unique geography, environment, or socioeconomic context
- Try a novel approach to the problem
- Build on the ideas of others, but adapt to unique local situations

- Take full advantage of public-private partnerships but ensure equitable and favorable long-term outcomes
- Use social media
- Make use of "smart city" innovations to capture data to inform and improve service provision

Multiple Benefits
- View multiple benefits and holistic planning as a cost-effective way to achieve more than one goal
- Effectively convey the multiple benefits of a project or plan to all stakeholders and the public
- Use the multiple benefits of a project as a way to attract project partners and leverage project funding
- Create a job position for someone who will facilitate planning and communication across departments
- Realize that any individual agency has responsibility to community wellbeing that is broader than their specific mandate

Sustainability is, no doubt, the challenge for the twenty-first century. It is the most ambitious reimagining of the city to date. Can cities effectively deal with growth and urban sprawl? Can cities create a more just and equitable future? Can cities create an economy sufficient to provide all residents with basic needs such as food, shelter, and meaningful work? These are dramatic and important questions, and the faster we can move in that direction, the better. Fortunately, scholars and practitioners alike are undertaking exciting research on a variety of topics related to sustainable cities. We provide suggested readings on the following page.

Suggested Readings

Suggested Readings on Urban Sustainability in General

Angel, S. *Planet of Cities*. Cambridge, MA: The Lincoln Institute of Land Policy, 2012.

Beatley, T., ed. *Green Cities of Europe*. Washington, DC: Island Press, 2012.

Benton-Short, L. and Short, J. R. *Cities and Nature Second Edition*. New York: Routledge, 2013.

Birch, E. L. and Lynch, A. "Measuring U.S. Urban Sustainability," In *Moving to Sustainable Prosperity, State of the World 2012*, 77–86, The Worldwatch Institute. Washington, DC: Island Press, 2012.

Boone, C. and Moddares, A. *City and Environment*. Philadelphia: Temple University Press, 2006.

Douglas, I., Goode, D., Houck, M. and Wang, R., eds. *Routledge Handbook of Urban Ecology*. New York: Routledge, 2010.

Heynen, M., Kaika, M. and Swyngedouw, E., eds. *In The Nature of Cities*. New York and London: Routledge, 2006.

Niemelä, J., Breuste, J. H., Elmqvist, T., Guntenspergen, G., James, P. and McIntyre, N. E., eds. *Urban Ecology: Patterns, Processes, and Applications*. Oxford: Oxford University Press, 2011.

Peet, R., Robbins, P. and Watts, M. J., eds. *Global Political Ecology: A Critical Introduction*. New York: Routledge, 2010.

Portney, K. *Taking Sustainable Cities Seriously; Economic Development, the Environment and Quality of Life in American Cities*. Cambridge, MA: The MIT Press, 2003.

© The Author(s) 2019   317

M. Keeley, L. Benton-Short, *Urban Sustainability in the US*,
https://doi.org/10.1007/978-3-319-93296-5

Roberts, P., Ravetz, J. and George, C. *Environment and the City*. New York: Routledge, 2009.

Stefanovic, I. G. and Scharper, S. B. *The Natural City: Re-envisioning The Built Environment*. Toronto: University of Toronto Press, 2012.

The World Watch Institute. *Can a City Be Sustainable? (State of the World)*. Washington, DC: World Watch Institute, 2016.

SUGGESTED READINGS ON SUSTAINABILITY PLANNING

Benfield, F. K. *People Habitat: 25 Ways to Think About Greener, Healthier Cities*. Washington, DC: Island Press, 2014.

Hersh, B. *Urban Redevelopment: A North American Reader*. London and New York: Routledge, 2018.

Kelly, E. *Community Planning: An Introduction to the Comprehensive Plan, Second Edition*. Washington, DC: Island Press, 2010.

National Research Council. *Pathways to Urban Sustainability*. Washington, DC: The National Academies Press, 2010.

Tyler, N. and Ward, R. *Planning and Community Development: A Guide for the 21st Century*. New York: WW Norton, 2010.

Wheeler, S. M. *Planning For Sustainability: Creating Livable, Equitable, and Ecological Communities, Second Edition*. New York, NY: Routledge Press, 2013.

Zeemering, E. *Collaborative Strategies for Sustainable Cities: Economy, Environment and Community in Baltimore*. New York: Routledge, 2014.

SUGGESTED READINGS ON EQUITY

Abramsky, S. *The American Way of Poverty: How the Other Half Still Lives*. New York: Nation Books, 2014.

Dyson, M.E. *Come Hell or High Water: Hurricane Katrina and the Color of Disaster*. New York: Basic Civitas Books (A Member of the Perseus Books Group), 2006.

Hartman, C. and Squires, G. D., eds. *There Is No Such Thing as a Natural Disaster: Race, Class and Hurricane Katrina*. New York: Routledge, 2006.

Desmond, M. *Evicted: Poverty and Profit in the American City*. New York: Penguin Random House, 1994.

Gowan, T. *Hobos, Hustlers, and Backsliders: Homeless in San Francisco*. Minneapolis, MN: University of Minnesota Press. 2010.

Harvey, D. *Rebel Cities: From the Right to the City to the Urban Revolution*. New York: Verso, 2013.

Rothstein, R. *The Color of Law: A Forgotten History of How Our Government Segregated America*. New York: WW Norton & Company, 2017.

Adamson, J., Evans, M. M. and Stein, R., eds. *The Environmental Justice Reader.* University of Arizona Press, 2002.

Agyeman, J. *Introducing Just Sustainabilities: Policy, Planning and Practice.* London: Zed Books, 2013.

Bullard, R. D., ed. *The Quest for Environmental Justice: Human Rights and the Politics of Pollution.* San Francisco: Sierra Club, 2005.

Bullard, R. D., ed. *Growing Smarter: Achieving Livable Communities, Environmental Justice, and Regional Equity.* Cambridge, MA: MIT Press, 2007.

Holifield, R., Porter, M. and Walker, G. *Spaces of Environmental Justice.* Malden, MA: Wiley-Blackwell, 2010.

Pellow, D. N. and Brulle, R. J. *Power, Justice and the Environment: A Critical Appraisal of the Environmental Justice Movement.* Cambridge, MA: MIT Press, 2005.

Robbins, P. *Political Ecology: A Critical Introduction,* Second Edition. Chichester, West Sussex: Wiley-Blackwell, 2012.

Short, J. *The Unequal City: Urban Resurgence, Displacement and the Making of Inequality in Global Cities.* New York: Routledge, 2018.

Stein, R., ed. *New Perspectives on Environmental Justice: Gender Sexuality and Activism.* New Brunswick: Rutgers University Press, 2004.

Washington, S. H. *Packing Them In: An Archaeology of Environmental Racism in Chicago.* Washington, DC and Covelo, CA: Rowman and Littlefield, 2005.

The environmental justice website of the USA EPA is http://www.epa.gov/environmentaljustice/index.html

SUGGESTED READINGS ON SUSTAINABLE ECONOMY

Deitche, Scott. *Green Collar Jobs: Environmental Careers for the 21st Century.* Santa Barbara, CA: Praeger, 2010.

McClelland C. *Green Careers for Dummies.* Hoboken, NJ: Wiley, 2010.

Madrid, J. and Alvarez, B. *Growing Green Jobs in America's Urban Centers.* Washington, DC: Center for American Progress, 2011.

Makower, J. and Pike, C. *Strategis for the Green Economy: Opportunities and Challenges in the New World of Business.* New York: McGraw-Hill, 2009.

Tiscareño-Sato, G. *Latinnovating: Green American Jobs and the Latinos Creating Them.* Hayward, CA: Gracefully Global Group, 2010.

SUGGESTED READINGS ON CLIMATE CHANGE

Bloomberg, M. and Pope, C. *Climate of Hope: How Cities, Businesses, and Citizens Can Save the Planet.* New York, New York: St. Martin's Press, 2017.

Aerts, J., Botzen, W., Bowman, M., Ward, P. and Dircke P., eds. *Climate Adaption and Flood Risk in Coastal Cities.* London and New York: Routledge, 2011.

Bicknell, J., Dodman, D., Sattherwaite, D., eds. *Adapting Cities to Climate Change, Understanding and Addressing the Development Challenges*. London: Earthscan, 2009.

Bulkeley, H. *Cities and Climate Change*. London and New York: Routledge, 2012.

Foster, J., Winkelman, S. and Lowe, A. *Lessons Learned on Local Climate Adaptation from the Urban Leaders Adaptation Initiative*. Washington, DC: The Center for Clean Air Policy, 2011.

Ghosh, A. *The Great Derangement – Climate Change and the Unthinkable*. Chicago: The University of Chicago Press, 2017.

Girardet, H. *Cities People Planet: Urban Development and Climate Change*, Second Edition. Chichester, England: Wiley Academic Press, 2008.

Hughes, S., Chu, E. and Mason, S., eds. *Climate Change in Cities: Innovations in the Multi-level Governance* (The Urban Book Series). Cham, Switzerland: Springer International, 2018.

IPCC, Intergovernmental Panel on Climate Change, Climate Change 2014: Mitigation of Climate Change, 2014, http://www.ipcc.ch/report/ar5/wg3/

Rosenzweig, C., Solecki, W. D., Romero-Lankao, P., Mehrotra, S. and Dhakal, S., eds. *Climate Change and Cities, Second Assessment Report of the Urban Climate Change Research Network*. Cambridge: Cambridge University Press, 2018.

Stone, Jr. B. *The City and the Coming Climate: Climate Change in the Places we Live*. Cambridge: Cambridge University Press, 2012.

US Government. *U.S. Global Change Research Program, Climate Change Impacts in the United States: The Third National Climate Assessment, 2014*, https://www.globalchange.gov/browse/reports/climate-change-impacts-united-states-third-national-climate-assessment-0

Suggested Readings on Urban Transportation

Altoon, R. *Urban Transformations: Transit Oriented Development & The Sustainable City*. Victoria, Australia: Images Publishing Group, 2011.

Bohl, C. *Place Making: Developing Town Centers, Main Streets, and Urban Villages*. Washington, DC: Urban Land Institute, 2002.

Ditmar, H. and Ohland, G., eds. *The New Transit Town: Best Practices In Transit-Oriented Development*. Washington, DC: Island Press, 2004.

Gresco, T. *Straphanger: Saving Our Cities and Ourselves from the Automobile*. New York: Henry Holt, 2012.

Tumlin, J. *Sustainable Transportation Planning: Tools for Creating Vibrant, Healthy, and Resilient Communities*. Hoboken, NJ: John Wiley & Sons, 2012.

Newman, P. and Kenworthy, J. *The End of Automobile Dependence: How Cities are Moving Beyond Car-Based Planning*. Washington, DC: Island Press, 2015.

Schwartz, S. *Street Smart: The Rise of Cities and the Fall of Cars.* Philadelphia, PA: Perseus Group, 2015.

Speck, J. *Walkable City: How Downtown Can Save America, One Step at a Time.* New York, NY: Farrar, Straus and Giroux, 2013.

Suggested Readings on Energy

Reisser, W. and Reisser, C. *Energy Resources: From Science to Society.* New York: Oxford University Press, 2018.

Smil, V. *Energy and Civilization: A History.* Cambridge, MA: MIT Press, 2017.

Yergin, D. *The Quest: Energy, Security, and the Remaking of the Modern World.* New York: Penguin Books, 2012.

Suggested Readings on Water

Biswas, A., Tortajad, C. and Izquierdo-Avino, R. *Water Management in 2020 and Beyond.* Berlin: Springer-Verlag, 2009.

Cisneros, B. J. and Rose, J. B. *Urban Water Security: Managing Risks.* Leiden, The Netherlands: Taylor & Francis, 2009.

Craig, R. K. *The Clean Water Act and the Constitution: Legal Structure and the Public's Right to a Clean and Healthy Environment,* Second Edition. Washington, DC: Environmental Law Institute, 2009.

Desfor, G and Roger, K. *Nature and the City: Making Environmental Policy in Toronto and Los Angeles.* Tucson: Arizona University Press, 2004.

Engel, K., Jokiel, D., Kraljevic, A., Geiger, M. and Smith, K. *Big Cities, Big Water, Big Challenges: Water in an Urbanizing World.* World Wildlife Fund, 2011.

Gumprecht, B. *The Los Angeles River: Its Life, Death and Possible Rebirth.* Baltimore: The Johns Hopkins University Press, 2001.

Jones, J. A. A. *Water Sustainability: A Global Perspective.* London: Hodder Education, 2010.

Karvonen, A. *Politics of Urban Runoff: Nature, Technology, and the Sustainable City.* Cambridge, MA: MIT Press, 2011.

Lewin, T. *Sacred River: The Ganges of India.* Boston, MA: Houghton Mifflin/ Clarion Books, 2003.

Melosi, M. V. *Precious Commodity: Providing Water for America's Cities.* Pittsburgh: University of Pittsburgh Press, 2011.

Solomon, S. *Water.* New York: Harper Perennial, 2010.

Swyngedouw, E. *Social Power and the Urbanization of Water: Flows of Power.* Oxford: Oxford University Press, 2004.

Uitto, J. and Biswas, A., eds. *Water for Urban Areas: Challenges and Perspectives.* Tokyo and New York: United Nations University Press, 2000.

SUGGESTED READINGS ON GREEN SPACE

Austin, G. *Green Infrastructure for Landscape Planning: Integrating Human and Natural Systems*, First Edition. New York: Routledge, 2014.

Brears, R. *Blue and Green Cities: The Role of Blue-Green Infrastructure in Managing Urban Water Resources*, First Edition. London, UK: Palgrave Macmillan, 2018.

Benedict, M. and McMahon, E. *Green Infrastructure: Linking Landscapes and Communities*. San Francisco: Island Press, 2006.

Dover, J. *Green Infrastructure: Incorporating Plants and Enhancing Biodiversity in Buildings and Urban Environments (Routledge Studies in Urban Ecology)*, First Edition. Routledge Studies in Urban Ecology. Routledge, 2015.

Gandy, M. *Concrete and Clay: Reworking Nature in New York City*. Cambridge MA: MIT Press, 2002.

Ladner, P. *The Urban Food Revolution: Changing the Way We Feed Cities*. Gabriola Island, BC, Canada: New Society Publishers, 2011.

McHarg, I. *Design with Nature*, First Edition. New York: Wiley, 1995.

Reynolds, K. and Cohen, N. *Beyond the Kale: Urban Agriculture and Social Justice Activism in New York City*. Athens, GA: University of Georgia Press, 2016.

SUGGESTED READINGS ON WASTE AND RECYCLING

Engler, M. *Designing America's Waste Landscape*. Baltimore and London: The Johns Hopkins University Press, 2004.

Gandy, M. *Recycling and the Politics of Urban Waste*. New York: St. Martin's Press, 1994.

Hawkins, G. *The Ethics of Waste: How We Relate to Rubbish*. Lanham, MD: Rowman and Littlefield, 2005.

Ludiwig, C, Hellweg, S. and Stucki, S. *Municipal Solid Waste Management: Strategies for Sustainable Solutions*. Berlin: Springer, 2003.

Mancini, C. *Garbage and Recycling*. Farmington Hills, MI: Greenhaven Press, 2010.

Rogers, H. *Gone Tomorrow: The Hidden Life of Garbage*. New York: The New Press, 2006.

Royte, E. *Garbage Land: On the Secret Trail of Trash*. New York: Little Brown, 2005.

Strasser, S. *Waste and Want: A Social History of Trash*. New York: Owl Books, 2000.

Vaughn, J. *Waste Management: A Reference Handbook*. Santa Barbara, CA: ABC-CLIO, Inc., 2008.

Williams, P. T. *Waste Treatment and Disposal*, Second Edition. Chichester: John Wiley & Sons Ltd., 2005.

SUGGESTED READINGS ON SMART CITIES

Glaeser, E. *Triumph of the City: How Our Greatest Invention Makes Us Richer, Smarter, Greener, Healthier, and Happier.* New York: Penguin Books, 2012.

Goldsmith, S. and Crawford, S. *Responsive City: Engaging Communities Through Data-Smart Governance.* San Francisco, CA: Jossey-Bass/Wiley, 2014.

Greenfield, A. *Against the Smart City.* New York, NY: Do Projects, 2013.

Song, H., Srinivasan, R., Sookoor, T. and Jeschke, S. *Smart Cities: Foundations, Principles, and Applications.* Hoboken, NJ: Wiley, 2017.

Townsend, A. *Smart Cities: Big Data, Civic Hackers, and the Quest for a New Utopia.* New York, NY: W. W. Norton & Company, 2014.

Appendix A: List of Cities Used in This Research Project

Ann Arbor, Michigan
Aspen, Colorado
Atlanta, Georgia
Austin, Texas
Baltimore, Maryland
Bend, Oregon
Birmingham, Alabama
Boston, Massachusetts
Boulder, Colorado
Burlington, Vermont
Charleston, South Carolina
Charlotte, North Carolina
Chattanooga, Tennessee
Chicago, Illinois
Cincinnati, Ohio
Cleveland, Ohio
Dallas, Texas
Denver, Colorado
Detroit, Michigan
Flint, Michigan
Grand Rapids, Michigan
Houston, Texas
Irvine, California
Juneau, Alaska
Kansas City, Kansas
Kodiak Island, Alaska

(continued)

© The Author(s) 2019

M. Keeley, L. Benton-Short, *Urban Sustainability in the US*,
https://doi.org/10.1007/978-3-319-93296-5

(continued)

Las Vegas, Nevada
Lackawanna, New York
Los Angeles, California
Louisville, Kentucky
Madison, Wisconsin
Memphis, Tennessee
Miami, Florida
Miami Beach, Florida
Milwaukee, Wisconsin
Minneapolis, Minnesota
New Haven, Connecticut
New Orleans, Louisiana
New York City, New York
Newark, New Jersey
Newport News, Virginia
Palm Springs, California
Philadelphia, Pennsylvania
Phoenix, Arizona
Pittsburgh, Pennsylvania
Portland, Maine
Portland, Oregon
Providence, Rhode Island
Richmond, California
Sacramento, California
Salt Lake City, Utah
San Diego, California
San Francisco, California
San Jose, California
Santa Cruz, California
Santa Fe, New Mexico
Seattle, Washington
Shoreline, Washington
St. Louis, Missouri
St. Petersburg, Florida
Tulsa, Oklahoma
Washington, District of Columbia
West Palm Beach, Florida

Index[1]

[1] Note: Page numbers followed by 'n' refer to notes.

GPSR Compliance
The European Union's (EU) General Product Safety Regulation (GPSR) is a set
of rules that requires consumer products to be safe and our obligations to
ensure this.

If you have any concerns about our products, you can contact us on

ProductSafety@springernature.com

In case Publisher is established outside the EU, the EU authorized
representative is:

Springer Nature Customer Service Center GmbH
Europaplatz 3
69115 Heidelberg, Germany